LEBANON 1860–1960

Claude Boueiz Kanaan

LEBANON 1860–1960

A Century of Myth and Politics

SAQI

British Library Cataloguing-in-Publication Data
A catalogue record for this book is available from the British Library

ISBN 0 86356 539 5
EAN 9-780863-565397

This edition first published 2005

SAQI
26 Westbourne Grove
London W2 5RH
www.saqibooks.com

To my husband Emile Kanaan
without whom no research could have been done

Contents

Maps, Illustrations and Tables

Maps

Illustrations

Tables

Acknowledgments

This book developed from a thesis guided by Dr. Malcolm Yapp, for whose initial interest and guidance I am grateful, and by Dr. Ulrike Freitag and Prof. Ralph Smith, who subsequently directed my studies and helped me develop the material and shape the final product.

I would also like to thank Dr Judith Rowbotham, who first introduced me to SOAS. I owe a debt of gratitude also to Dr Kamal Salibi and to Talal Abu Hussein, for reading my first chapter, on the pre-Mandate history of Lebanon. Dr Sofia Saadeh also discussed many of the issues with me, and I am grateful for her insights.

Sincere thanks are also due to the people who granted me access to essential source material; without their generosity, this book would have been impossible. His Beatitude, the Maronite Patriarch Boulos Sfeir, most kindly allowed me access to the Patriarchal Archives of the Maronite Church – making me privy to some of the material relevant to his predecessor, His Beatitude Paul Meouchi – even though the Patriarchal Archives are currently closed.

I would like to thank General Emile Bustani, who loaned me the typed manuscript of his unpublished memoirs, and Samir Moubarak, Lebanese Ambassador to the United Nations, who gave me access to some of his father's papers – notably the correspondence between his father Moussa Moubarak and Pierre Bart, the French ambassador to Lebanon.

The staff of *al-Hayat* newspaper and especially the director, Mr Jihad al-

Khazin, have given me invaluable help, including access to the newspaper's archives. Shaykh Clovis al-Khazin gave me access to his family's papers, which provided valuable additional material. Dr Raghid al-Solh allowed me to view the papers of Khazem al-Solh, including the text of an unpublished manuscript. Mr Yussuf al-Achkar, the PPS president in 1994–5, and Mr César Rizkallah kindly gave me access to some papers from the PPS archives, notably the party president's speech of 1958. Access to the archives of *an-Nahar* has also been crucial, and again, my thanks are due to the staff there and to Mr Ghassan Tueni in particular.

Several people were kind enough to assist my research by granting me personal interviews. Mr Raymond Eddé, the president of the Bloc National, has been an invaluable source of reference. President Amine Gemayel, Mr Saeb Salam (the opposition spokesman in 1958 and several times the prime minister of Lebanon), Mr Ghassan Tueni, Dr Albert Moukheiber, Mr Joseph Freiha, Mr Salim Nassar, Mr Ahmad al-Hajj and Mrs Pierre Gemayel have all given me the benefit of their comments on the subject of this book.

In addition to discussing key issues, Dr Sofia Saadeh, daughter of Antun Saadeh of the PPS, also permitted me to interview her. Many other people in the Arab community in London have kindly discussed the subject of this book and its themes with me over the years; for the most part their names are too numerous to mention individually, but my gratitude to them is still enormous. They have sharpened my perceptions and understanding of this period of Lebanese history and its wider connections and implications as well as giving me moral support. I must, however, mention the particular support given to me by Susan Hamza, Maha Sukarieh, Latifa Osta and Mary Abouchalache.

Also, this book could not have been completed without practical help in its production. Thanks are due to the whole Medawar family, Georges, Rima, Laya and Ghassan, for their aid in printing out chapters of my thesis at various stages, as well as giving me other help in meeting the deadline for the thesis. The staff at *al-Hayat*, again, provided me with help and support in this respect. In addition, I would like to thank the library staff at SOAS and at the Centre for Lebanese Studies in Oxford; thanks also to the staff at the American University of Beirut and St Esprit University in Kaslik, as well as the staff at the Public Records Office, Kew, and the Quai d'Orsay in Paris and Nantes. My thanks also to Mr George Achkar who is and will always be an invaluable source of information for all Lebanese historians. Many of the photographs in this book appear courtesy of Mr Carlos Eddé, who kindly allowed me access to his personal archives. They were all unvaryingly courteous and helpful to me in tracking down and accessing materials of all kinds.

It is the memory of my mother, Jacqueline Boueiz, that has inspired me to undertake research work. In the Middle East of the 1940s and 1950s, when women had little official status, she was a firm believer in the importance of the woman's role and in women's capacities, and so in their ability to contribute to the societies in which they lived, and I learned much from her. Last, but by no means least of all, I owe a great debt to my husband, Emile Kanaan, and to my children, Lynn and Georges. They have had much to bear from me over the years of study that have resulted in this thesis and have made many sacrifices to give me the time and space to complete this work, especially over this past summer. My husband has also been a frequent source of information and perceptive comments. I cannot thank them adequately, but it is to them that I dedicate this book, with love and with gratitude.

A Note on Transliteration and Abbreviations

I have used familiar forms of Lebanese/Arabic names for individuals or places that were, or still are, in common usage in Europeanised form, such as 'Camille Chamoun', 'General Shihab', 'Nasser' or 'Beirut'. Otherwise I have used a transliteration convention based on the *International Journal of Middle East Studies (IJMES)*.

Abbreviations Used

AUB	American University of Beirut
CLS	Centre for Lebanese Studies (Oxford)
FO	Foreign Office
PPS	Parti Populaire Syrien
UAR	United Arab Republic
UN	United Nations
UNOGIL	United Nations Observer Group in Lebanon

Introduction

During the 1950s tremendous socio-political upheavals occurred throughout the Arab world, as Nasser rose to power in Egypt and Nasserism drove a resurgent pan-Arab nationalism. The 1958 crisis in Lebanon has often been interpreted in the context of those broader upheavals and/or the Cold War, because the United States intervened in that crisis. Considerable evidence justifies such a perspective. This was the period during which Western hegemony in the Middle East was threatened by pressures from within the region itself and by the growing power of the USSR. At one level, this struggle over the political leadership of the Arab world resulted in the polarisation of Arab politics into two hostile camps, with one eventually led by anti-Western Egypt and the other by pro-Western Iraq. The struggle was apparently, if temporarily, resolved in 1958 when the coup in Iraq brought down the pro-Western government and replaced it with one identified as having an anti-Western stance, like that taken by Egypt.[1] Thus, when a crisis occurred the same year in Lebanon, another state identified as having a pro-Western stance, many historians saw it as clearly linked to this broader struggle.

In this book I make a different argument: I believe that the 1958 crisis in Lebanon originated mainly as a failure of consensus over the nation's identity, a failure linked to differing perceptions of community identity. These perceptions were based on profoundly different interpretations of Lebanon's past, and coherent community identities depended on these interpretations. Because the different communal groupings in Lebanon interpreted current

15

regional developments in ways that fit these interpretations, they invoked the broader issues affecting the Arab world and its relations with the West in the 1950s to justify and explain their actions, in the interests of sustaining their specific community identities.

Important observers outside of Lebanon, including Americans and President Nasser of Egypt, interpreted the Lebanese crisis as part of the upheaval in the Arab world, in terms of both its origins and resolution. Historians later agreed with them. But most of these observers have misunderstood or underestimated the Lebanese contribution to the crisis, and the longer-term effect of that contribution. An interpretation based primarily on short-term, regional factors, however tidy, ignores a major factor in Lebanese life: a significant part of the Lebanese population in the 1950s did not accept that Lebanon was part of the Arab world and used versions of 'Lebanese' history to 'prove' their contentions. The resultant creation of community mythologies played a crucial role in moulding and sustaining popular attitudes, especially at times of crisis.

The Christian Maronite community saw itself, and Lebanon, as part of the world of Western civilisation; thus they acted like honorary Europeans. The existence of this separate Lebanese entity was crucial in sustaining this perspective, with all its implications for community identity. Kamal Salibi believes that from 1920, when Lebanon emerged as a state, 'the Christian and Muslim Lebanese have been in fundamental disagreement over the historicity of their country.'[2] In contrast to the Maronite belief that this Lebanese entity was 'natural', the Muslim populations in Lebanon have generally seen the Lebanese state as an artificial creation, dependent largely on the actions of Western – French – imperialism, similar to other states in the Arab world like Syria or Iraq. Thus, Muslim communities have created a different popular mythology for themselves, seeing the state's political boundaries as matters of political convenience (or inconvenience) that do not detract from the cultural unity of the Arab world.

By contrast the Maronite perspective sees Lebanon's state boundaries as reflecting a non-Arab cultural integrity. As Camille Chamoun insisted in his retrospective on the 1958 crisis:

> *Les frontières du Liban ont été relevées en 1862 par le contingent français envoyé par l'Europe à la suite des massacres du Liban … On voit ainsi que ce n'est pas la France qui a créé le Liban ou en a fixé les frontières qui existaient avant le Mandat Français.*[3]

[The Lebanese borders were drawn in 1862 by the French contingent sent from Europe following the massacres in Lebanon ... We can see, therefore, that the French neither 'created' Lebanon, nor fixed its borders, which already existed before the French Mandate.]

These views, however, do not divide neatly according to Christian and Muslim demographics. One Muslim community, the Druze, tends to sympathise with aspects of the Maronite perspective, because it shares some history. For example, the memorial to the Druze 'martyrs' of 1958 at Mukhtara refers to their brave defence of '*la liberté, l'indépendence*' and also '*pour sauvegarder la souveraineté nationale* (*al-siyadat al-wataniyyah*) ... *pour renforcer l'unité nationale* (*al-wahdat al-wataniyyah*)'. Since this is also seen as a defence of 'l'arabisme', however, this tendency cannot be taken too far. Also, it was more consciously supported at elite levels of society, amongst the traditional land-owning class, whose interests were best served by maintaining a discrete entity.[4]

Thus, if we interpret the crisis through a primarily regional or international perspective, we cannot entirely explain the Lebanese dimensions of the crisis, including its causation. In the Lebanese context the crisis was a case of history repeating itself: one more in a sustained pattern of internally generated crises that provoked external intervention. Within this pattern the communities, particularly the Maronites, had habitually tried to involve external forces during times of crisis rather than relying on internal mediation and compromise to resolve tension. So, traditionally, the various communities in Lebanon have demonstrated little will to resolve crises through internally generated compromises. This fact makes it important to examine the crisis from the Lebanese perspective rather than the international one, looking especially at external intervention in the 1958 crisis.

That is my aim in this book: to examine the crisis primarily within the context of tensions between the Lebanese communities, and their conscious and unconscious contributions to the escalation of tension to crisis point in the summer of 1958.

To do that, it is first necessary to understand the composition of Lebanon, since the state includes several different communities which had, by the 1950s, developed self-conscious, distinct, and discrete community identities. Of the several Christian communities, the Maronites were the largest; of the several Muslim communities, the Sunnis were – at the time – the largest. I will focus primarily on the Maronite community and its relationship with other communities in Lebanon, notably the Sunnis and Druze. I do so partly because an identifiably Maronite community has been a continuing factor in the intercommunal equation throughout Lebanon's history. Compared to other communities, it developed its own agenda relatively early. This Maronite agenda had a significant impact in 1958.

I focus on the Maronite community for another reason: despite this continuity, its role in the 1958 crisis has received comparatively little attention. Several historians, including Najla Attiyah,[5] have studied the Sunnis in particular in the 1950s. Without a comparable study of the Maronite community, we cannot fully comprehend how both the Maronite and Sunni communities contributed, both consciously and unconsciously, to the escalation of tension in 1958.

As Maronite historians have written most of Lebanon's history, we would expect that Maronite communal identity has received a considerable amount of critical analysis. But this has not happened, and particularly not in relation to 1958. Thus I focus on 1958, examining the creation of community identity amongst the Maronites and the role of clashes between such feelings of communal identity at times of crisis.

This approach requires us to assess how much the seeds of conflict in 1958 lie within Lebanon's history rather than being simply a matter of factors arising after 1943, when the independent Lebanese state emerged. E. H. Carr has commented that history is 'a dialogue … between the society of today and the society of yesterday'; but in the Lebanese context history plays a more powerful role, as a crucial factor unifying the Maronite community in particular through its 'awareness of a common history'.[6] For instance, the period of co-habitation between the Maronite and Druze communities between the late sixteenth and early nineteenth centuries has been crucially important in the evolution of Maronite identity in relation to 'their' territory of 'Lebanon'. To understand this history I have synthesised Lebanese history based on existing secondary sources and some primary source material, such as that of Henri Lammens.[7]

To illuminate the internal cultural dimensions of the crisis, we must begin with the history of Lebanon's communities and intercommunal relationships and the history of the Lebanese entity, as well as the links between this entity and its communities. One reason to take a long-term historical perspective on the 1958 crisis is the political rhetoric of Lebanese politicians, particularly Maronites, within independent Lebanon. Maronite speakers have consistently stressed Lebanon's evolution from an ancient historical past and the effects of its unique geography on the Maronite character. They used both factors to interpret and justify more predictable themes such as the importance of the Maronite religion and kinship ties, the nature of Lebanese nationalism and issues of external relations. In other words, the Maronite communal identity stresses its historical dimension, relying on scholars like Lammens to provide intellectual defences for this perspective.

I will also show that this emphasis moves beyond the usual rhetoric about the historical nature of national identities. Consider this line from a 1982 speech to the United Nations by Amine Gemayel: 'My country ... is one of rugged mountainous terrain. The people are hardy and proud, like their mountains.'[8] Other communities have recognised, if not welcomed, this Maronite perspective. The Sunni opposition figure Saeb Salam, comparing the 1975 and 1958 crises, commented critically that their origins lay in history and its interpretation, implicitly laying blame on the Maronites.[9] More recently, in June 1995, a comment by Walid Jumblat showed how Maronite identity depends on interpretations of history: 'Life is a continuous battle with the inner self and with history'. He urged the Maronites to move away from this dependence for the sake of Lebanese unity.[10]

For both the Maronites and the Druze, the traditions derived from Mount Lebanon continue to have an impact on socio-political attitudes. While much of the Maronite community is still located in urban settings, as it was in the 1950s, it has maintained strong connections to the concept of the village and village cultures, traditions and loyalties. Kinship ties have remained powerful. The majority of Maronites, even those born in cities, feels ties to a village where relatives congregate on weekends and on holidays. Lebanon's political system sustains this phenomenon by requiring voters to go to the villages to vote.[11] Even communities that have traditionally been more urbanised, such as the Sunnis, retain a dimension of this tradition. Given this context, traditional patterns and loyalties naturally have a powerful effect on voting behaviour and popular beliefs and agendas.

An Introduction to Co-habitation

The communal mix in Lebanon has ensured a long tradition of co-habitation;

different social groups have lived side by side with other social groups they regard as significantly different. But no spirit of mutual trust and harmony has resulted between these groups; no consensus has developed between their perspectives. Instead, their perspectives have tended to compete, ensuring that tension and suspicion will continue. I define co-habitation as the relationship of communities occupying a shared territory which all participants see as 'theirs'. But they are 'theirs' for different reasons, and their competing agendas tend to assign one particular community superiority over another, or even to deny another community the ability to claim any intrinsic 'right' in the territory at all. This individual sense of possession can co-exist with others, but equally it contains an element of perpetual tension and stress. At times, the tension and suspicion have escalated to crisis point. At other times, consensus has apparently developed, at least at elite levels.

What Is Consensus?

I define consensus as individuals and communities sharing territory and laying claim to it, but doing so on the basis of a mutually developed compromise between the communities' agendas. This kind of consensus, of course, depended on a self-interest that was usually short-lived. The 1943 attempt to establish an independent Lebanon, governed by the terms of the National Pact, was undoubtedly a genuine attempt to achieve a durable intercommunal consensus. Virtually every Lebanese political leader since 1943 has praised the consensus enshrined in the pact.[12] But I believe the basis for that consensus was not wide enough to allow the communities to overcome their long-established reactions based on co-habitation, even amongst figures who praised the concept of consensus. All too frequently, for what they identified as reasons of individual and communal self-interest, both sides abandoned the consensus. This occurred even more often at mass levels of society, especially when grievances and suspicions between communities reached critical levels of tension and they could not so clearly see the benefits of consensus that their leaders advertised. Moreover, the community that most frequently acted as one element in the equation (either alone or with other communities such as the Greek Orthodox) was the Maronite community.

Thus the communal perspective is crucial to understanding the 1958 crisis. As Amine Gemayel has commented, 'The Lebanese are first and foremost members of their community, not citizens of their state'.[13] This community perspective has had a considerable impact on the question of what constitutes the Lebanese national identity. In the political dimension, it has enshrined a fundamental difference between the Maronites (and other Christians) and the Muslim communities. The Maronites, in particular, require a sectarian-based political system at the heart of the political system, to serve as an insurance policy for the various religious interests. Muslim politicians see such sectarianism as unnecessary and even divisive.[14]

Any useful analysis of the impact of historical patterns and interpretations on Lebanon's communal history requires an effective marriage between the theoretical and the empirical perspectives. Details will be important in assessing an individual case study, like the events of the 1950s that I address in later chapters. But the longer-term factors, in the shape of recurring attitudes and behaviour expressed differently in different eras, are also critical.

Thus, in this book I emphasise the role that ordinary people play in political history, especially in the mass democracy that Lebanon enjoyed in 1958. By looking at this mass of people, we begin to understand how political orientations and feelings of national identity evolve at the popular level, along with communal and individual behaviour. Such behaviour was frequently dictated by cultural considerations and constraints at the popular level, which in turn had an impact on policy. Thus the historian interested in this perspective must focus on the popular level and the operation of community identities and cultural mythologies. This approach is commonplace in the social sciences but less so in history. It is not always easy to combine these with the demands of a historical perspective that that includes a firm chronology. In the case of the 1958 crisis, it is important to assess the interrelationships between social structure and culture on the one hand, and popular behaviour in terms of identifiable events on the other.

The cultural approach can help explain the patterns of identified political behaviour that were most significant as the crisis evolved. Thus this approach provides a conceptual tool for assessing political culture, at popular as well as elite levels. In this approach the attempt to identify community psychology is as significant as the analysis of the actual events and the actions the communities undertook, because the attitudes that result from that community psychology are key triggers to action. Important elements in this might include, if available, mass surveys of public opinion and attitudes, or equivalent attempts to assess opinions and attitudes. Also crucial is a close study of the roles of key individuals and their opinions and attitudes, drawing on private sources and comparing and contrasting them with their public statements and speeches. These tools enable us to assess the public and popular gloss that such individuals felt they needed to place on their opinions and policies at particular times and in particular contexts. The survival and significance of popular myths and legends in the various communities can also be useful when they play a role in the development of key episodes such as those leading to the 1958 crisis.

The Role of Memory

An equally important theme is how people remember events. As Eric Hobsbawm has commented, 'the past is … an inevitable component of the institutions, values and other patterns of human society,' but it depends on selections from a range of information and ideas that individuals and groups 'remember' on the basis of their own interests.[15] In any political system, remembering will affect the evolution and practice of policy: 'our political judgements are permeated by a sense of the past' because 'our sense of personal identity demands roots in the past'. Essentially, groups of people, such as the communities in Lebanon, 'assimilate and interpret their own experience' in ways that place 'history' at the 'heart of political culture'.[16] Benedict Anderson has pointed out the result in states such as Lebanon: 'imagined' communities have assumed a real solidity because there is a powerful will to believe that they are real.[17]

I draw on the attempts by several participants in the 1958 crisis to understand and interpret the past. It as a way to understand the cultural dimensions in the history of Lebanon and its communities. But any historian will encounter problems in trying to involve such factors in an analysis. First, the significance of these dimensions can be difficult if not impossible to quantify, so we must rely on a range of judgments relating to a series of subjectivities. But we cannot ignore these subjectivities; mythologies rooted in the past, justifying community identity, have had an impact on institutional as well as cultural and social contexts, as Raphael Samuel and Paul Thompson have argued.[18]

An example of such a mythology is the way that the office or institution of the presidency in Lebanon had acquired a quasi-mystical significance relating to the survival of group identity for the Maronite community by

22

the mid-1950s, as I will show later on. Equally, as I will show, 'the ruling groups' in a society will have what John Tosh calls 'an interest' in creating an imagery that promotes 'mythical pasts' where that imagery serves to sustain or 'legitimise' the power base of such groups. In particular, such imagery is often invoked to create or sustain 'popular' support within electoral constituencies for potentially contentious policies, through propaganda linking the survival of community identity to the success of particular policies.

The Role of Myth

Events in the 1950s certainly demonstrated that cultural myths relating to community identity influenced people's perceptions and actions in relation to clearly identified policies.[19] Arguably, such behavioural patterns were strongest in communities that had been excluded from power in the past, or felt they had been. This made the collective 'memory' or myth about such exclusion more relevant to both community action and community perceptions, because the myths were presumably linked with the community's survival as an identifiable, discrete entity. Thus, the perception of persecution was frequently crucial; it could create a powerful bond within a sizeable community by providing elements of a common history based on endurance in the face of considerable difficulties. It also made it more difficult either to criticise or to modify elements of the community identity.[20]

The Roots of the Crisis

The 1958 crisis is officially seen as beginning with the murder of Nassib al-Matni, a journalist, on 8 May of that year, and lasting until 8 August. But no historian conscious of the factors above will be misled into seeing the crisis purely in terms of those dates. Instead, for Lebanon, the roots of the crisis lie in an earlier period, regardless of the factors apparently involved in the broader Middle Eastern context. Thus we must study the social structure of Lebanese society and its historical evolution to explain how the 1958 crisis developed. My analysis shows that conflicts within Lebanese society were part of a long-established pattern of social dynamics, rather than relating predominantly to the events of the 1950s in the region.

Social Structure: Community and Class

It is common to see the social structure of Lebanon, or at least some of its communities, as being 'feudal'. Some commentators have used this term for the Druze, and for rural Maronites in the early 1800s.[21] But this term does not apply to all of Lebanon, as that structure was never universal. When 'feudal' characteristics did develop, they did so within the Mount Lebanon region, but not in the peripheries that would later be included in the independent Lebanese state. Moreover, even around Mount Lebanon, Koranic law hampered the development of feudalism. For example, these laws decreed that any inheritance, including land, would be divided among the children of the deceased, making it harder for a succession of single heirs to acquire large tracts of land.

The involvement of the Ottoman empire further complicated the development of feudalism as key factor in social organisation. Ottoman officials sometimes benefited personally or conferred benefits on favourites through *iqta'*, a system of land endowment; these benefits, however, were neither permanent nor hereditary. Land grants under this system reverted back to Ottoman control on the death of the beneficiary. Only in the middle 1800s did Ottoman reforms lead to private hereditary ownership in Lebanon on a significant scale. Since we cannot easily describe the system that had prevailed earlier, we cannot make straightforward assumptions about the ways that communities evolved from such bases.[22]

A related issue is the hierarchical patterns within social groupings in Lebanon. Philip Khoury says classes 'undoubtedly existed before this time but they were much more difficult to identify and their lifespans much shorter', due mostly to their much less stable relations 'to the means of production and especially property'.[23] Equally, a class structure did not easily cross confessional boundaries in Lebanon. The possible exception is the elite levels where the Maronite, Druze and Sunni communities may have had enough common economic interests to begin believing they were sharing the same social level. Although the *zu'ama* or land-owning elites in these communities apparently shared common interests, they also saw the need to identify themselves with their own confessional grouping and its policy stance (especially in terms of foreign policy).

Thus, any class feeling at this level was generally tenuous and short-lived, as the dominant social hierarchies tended to be specific to communities.

Looking at the state's overall social hierarchy, it is difficult to argue that certain confessional groupings occupied higher or lower socio-economic positions. The range of exceptions is so wide that any coherent case collapses. Given all these facts, I believe that no modern class structure evolved in Lebanon during the historical period, and it is difficult to interpret the groups in Lebanon even as late as the1950s in classical class terms.

Some sociologists use the 'community approach' to interpret communal structures like those found in Lebanon; they enquire whether the different communities were homogeneous or heterogeneous.[24] Allied with the sectarian approach, this seems to fit the Lebanese setting well. F. Tonnies, the German sociologist, describes the *Gemeinschaft* or community as revolving around three intertwined elements. The first was the 'element of descent', in which the focus is on blood and kinship ties and 'family' life provides the basis of social organisation.[25] The second was provided by location, the actual territory linked to a particular 'village community'.[26] The final element was provided by employment or occupation, expressing itself through trade or craft guilds, corporations and offices.[27]

Unlike feudalism or tribalism, these three elements can be clearly identified within the Lebanese social system regardless of sectarian community. In general, family life has served as the centre of social organisation, and village territoriality and (predominantly male) occupation have also been key characteristics in all the communal sub-groups found in Lebanon. This pattern holds true to this day, and even in urban areas. For instance, the majority of the population of Ashrafiyyah, in eastern Beirut, identifies itself primarily as village emigrants rather than urban dwellers. In other words, its links to non-urban locations continue to be a strong factor in its sense of individual and group identity.

Linked to this, geographical factors can be said to provide another key to Lebanon's communal patterns. The very terrain promoted geographical isolation, between villages and between communities. In addition, communications between villages were so difficult that regular and positive social intercourse was more the exception than the rule. As a result, villages, each usually identifiable as belonging to a particular sectarian community, regarded other villages linked to different communal affiliations with fear and suspicion. The more communities isolate themselves, the more they distrust each other, and the more society becomes fragmented. This certainly has held true historically in Lebanon, and it has left a significant legacy in the modern period.[28]

In the modern period, the majority of Lebanon's population has lived in cities. Suddenly the Maronite and Sunni communities found themselves in close proximity, although they tended to live in particular districts identified as 'belonging' to their particular confessional grouping.[29] With the urban population in the majority by the 1940s at the latest, it becomes possible to talk of 'masses' in relation to particular communities but not in relation to the Lebanese population as a whole. A working class or proletariat or 'lower' class that crossed confessional boundaries simply did not emerge within Lebanon, partly because each community engaged in quite different economic activities, but competed for the few available jobs.[30] The Maronites, for example, dominated the profitable trade with Europe and tried to keep its significant benefits within their own community.

If it is not possible to talk of a Lebanese working class, it is possible to identify 'masses' within the Maronite and Sunni communities. This term implies the bulk, quantitatively speaking, of the members within a particular community, people who belong to the middle and lower strata in each community's individual social hierarchy. Thus, in class terms, the masses might be said to include the petty bourgeoisie, the proletariat or working class, and the sub-classes of a community as well as, where appropriate, the rural working or peasant classes. In other words, the masses are the people who depend economically on the commercial, administrative or landowning elites, but – especially in the cities where they live and work in constant contact – develop a sense of shared interests against these elites that is likely to come into play at times of crisis.

In this book, then, the term 'masses' refers to a very substantial number of people within a community who are willing and able to act together to communicate a particular perspective. This would be one they evolved among themselves, not one handed down by an elite, or adopted from an element within the community elites and modified to make it populist. Under 'normal' conditions, the masses would usually be prepared to let themselves be led, or 'manipulated', by their community elites. But when the masses felt their own interests were threatened, they would seek to pressure their elites to bring about a change in policy, for instance. At such times it was common for the masses to describe their own interests as those of the community as a whole.[31] In the case of the Maronite and Sunni communities, this expression of mass community interest generally justified itself by reference to community mythology – perceptions of past events – which they could use to interpret the more immediate causes of a crisis.

Thus, if we are to examine community identity in the modern period, we must first examine a variety of contemporary perceptions of the past, rather than merely the events of the twentieth century. In particular, the period of Ottoman control over the region has left a crucial series of consequences for mass and elite agendas in the various communities. One of the most significant of these is the differential impact on the communities of corruption in government and administration. The Ottomans offered, or forced, different treatment on the communities, often injuring the Maronites. The habits and customs of administration established under the Ottomans continued during the modern period, as an independent Lebanon sought to be 'democratic' along Western lines. The problems involved in continuing these Ottoman habits, including the opportunities to form an opposition around the issue of corruption, were particularly well-displayed during the regime of Bishara al-Khoury.

The confessional structure of Lebanese society also led to social stratification. The Ottomans had operated from an Islamic perspective in structuring the societies under their control, based on function, but also on the overall status awarded to the different religious communities. With a few rare exceptions, lasting group mobility, either upward or downward, was difficult.

Stratification on the basis of religious affiliation was already an established Muslim practice.[32] At one level, Islam organised Muslims as a *Jama'ah* or community and thereby excluded the non-Muslim social groups who were either polytheists or People of the Scriptures or the Book (Christians and Jews). The status of Christians and Jews came to be regulated by a *dhimmah* or contract. Thus at its simplest, society came to be divided simply into Muslims and *dhimmis*. Following this principle from the seventh century on, Muslim rulers established Christian groups as inferior in social ranking to Muslims because of their faith. Reflecting this inferior status, *dhimmis* had to pay the *Jizyah* or poll tax and the *Kharaj* or land tax; they also faced a range of other restrictions on movement and opportunities.[33]

But this was not the only type of social division operating under the Ottomans. Muslim groups were also distinguished on the basis of sectarian allegiance. In the predominantly Sunni Ottoman empire, 'nonconformist' Muslim sects such as the Druze and the Shi'ite were differentiated and granted a lower social status. Although that status might be higher than non-Muslims were granted, it created a distinct and lasting social gulf between the various Muslim sects. Moreover, these social rankings were not a matter of simple acceptance: in their ongoing relationships the communities developed various amounts of resentment, mistrust and even outright hostility and fear. For instance, the *dhimmah* could protect the Christian groups somewhat while leaving other Muslim sects such as the Druze and Shi'ite open to persecution by their fellow Muslims, authorised by the Ottomans. At other times Christian groups were persecuted by all the Muslim groups, including the 'nonconformist' ones, again with Ottoman endorsement. Thus, in practice, this social ranking kept all the communities in the region from developing a sense of stable social relations.

Another factor was the involvement of external forces – notably Europe – in the region, especially from the nineteenth century on. From the 1700s, as Europe became more secular in its attitudes, religious divisions in European society became less significant. Instead, the various European states were moving towards the idea that an individual state could exist by right for reasons that had little to do with the religion of its elite or with mere hereditary loyalty towards that elite. At all levels, as the concept of the 'citizen' evolved, individuals theoretically – if not always practically – gained certain fundamental rights regardless of social status or religious affiliation. This development had little impact on the Ottoman empire as a whole. Within that empire the idea of communities distinguished on confessional grounds continued to have legal force, thus continuing the linkage between temporal and religious power structures.

However, in areas like Lebanon – where at least some of the communities had access to European ideas – members of non-Muslim communities learned about the different path that Europe was taking. They saw that, at least in theory, Western ideas of secular democracy enabled individuals and groups to initiate desired changes in society without fearing reprisals for their confessional allegiance. Moreover, they saw that under secular democracy, a long-standing presence in a particular location could give communal groups the right to make their voices heard. And they saw that in the West an established territorial identity conferred upon groups and individuals a national identity that superseded any confessional differences. Thus they saw that change was possible without losing individual or group identity.

Within the Ottoman empire, however, a change in confessional allegiance was the only permanent way a group or individual could make changes or have grievances addressed. Sofia Saadeh has pointed out that historically in the Lebanon region, 'where identity is not based on residence and land, but on religious communal ties', change threatened 'the very existence of the community'. Thus all communities, especially the minority ones, developed a deep conservatism as the best way to avoid being 'eradicated' in a particular location.[34] Because anything that might prompt the central authority to reassess the community's identity might endanger its very survival, any change that did occur was made to look like it conformed strongly to established practice, rather than challenging established practice – as was happening in the West. This conservatism also meant that communities rarely relied on themselves to bring about useful and positive change, even when they saw the need to do so. Instead, they increasingly took on passive roles as a matter of self-defence, and relied on outside forces to intervene to effect needed change.[35] Especially for the lower-ranking Christian communities, this attitude helped to set the agenda for their relations with and expectations of the Western powers.

In effect, then, because the Ottomans classified communities on religious grounds, individuals absorbed a sense of identity that was essentially religious. In turn, whether they were in dominant or inferior positions, they classified others around them in the same or in different communities using precisely the same religious terms. For members of all communities, this habit of classification became the basis for interpreting the identity of other forces that became involved in the region. When the West began to dominate the Arab countries, the religious dimensions and differences became identified as the most 'obvious' features of Western identity. Through this process religion became the element that was most likely to raise antagonisms in Muslim Arab society, rather than reactions to more Western concepts like colonialism or economic domination.[36] This long-standing perspective remained powerful in 1958, as certain Muslim groups in Lebanon interpreted the West as a Christian bloc that was intent upon undermining their identity. Given that the Maronite Christians tended to see the West as their natural protector, clashes over the role of the West could potentially affect the sense of identity of some communal groups within Lebanese society.

The Role of History

The ways that the various Lebanese communities interpret their historical context also has the potential to produce radically different understandings of historical narratives of the region. There is a powerful belief that each community has its own particular history and its own background. Controversies about the history of Lebanon tend to arise on a communal basis, rather than on a class or national basis as is more common in the West. Since the nineteenth century, various communities have grappled with the question of how to write the history of Lebanon, including even its starting date. Several have tried to impose their own interpretation as the standard, and to establish that standard as a keystone in constructing a 'Lebanese' identity. Thus the Maronites wish to begin with the Phoenician period, while the Sunnis focus on the Islamic period, underlining the state's Arab identity. This leads to a very fundamental fragmentation of opinion about what constitutes a 'Lebanese' identity.[37]

Nor is it just a matter of invoking the historical past in order to define a 'Lebanese' identity in the image of a particular communal identity. The very definition of 'modernism' is also controversial. At one level it is related to support for or antipathy towards the West and the nature of the Western impact on Lebanon in terms of social values and lifestyles. As modernisation is also associated with change, frequently imparted through an educational system, it invokes another set of complexities relating to communal identity beyond the merely confessional dimension. Modernisation as change, spread through education, helped an identifiable educated urban middle class to evolve in Lebanon in the 1950s. Yet that predominantly Maronite middle class found itself excluded from any real exercise of power, particularly political power. For the Maronites and other communities, the power remained in the hands of the traditional, predominantly rural elites. It is a measure of the continuing significance of original village locations that even for most Maronites, this educated class did not have a widespread appeal. At the same time, however, the traditional elites were finding it harder to maintain the same level of popular appeal they had enjoyed in the past.

The role of traditional leaders or 'notables' had shifted slightly over time, particularly while Lebanon evolved as a distinct entity. The traditional, quasi-feudal nature of some of this leadership had modified into what Arnold Hottinger calls the *Za'im* concept.[38] As confessionally identified social groupings began to evolve, a social hierarchy dominated by a land-based aristocracy began to develop, with each community's aristocracy evoking loyalty predominantly from its own confessional members. Within this hierarchy, the notables generally set the agenda in terms of values and beliefs; few had the freedom to express ideas and thoughts outside the ideas passed down by their own community notables. Such social hierarchies were under threat in all of Lebanon's communities by the early twentieth century. This process was undoubtedly aided by French rule over Lebanon through the mandate system.

Economic power was shifting away from these land-based aristocracies, and becoming more concentrated in the hands of urban commercial elites. Yet the political power structure set up during the Mandate, and modified for the independent Lebanese state, relied heavily upon the traditional elites. Thus political arrangements essentially depended on intercommunal relations through a network of relations set up between the traditional elites of these various communities. In turn, these relations relied on the elites' ability to command loyalty within their communities – which they could no longer take for granted. Compounding the problem, some of the traditional elites were slow to recognise the change themselves. In making policy decisions, they assumed they could call on the loyal backing of their own communities – only to find it was not automatically forthcoming. Such developments tended to produce tensions both within and between communities.

This dynamic is particularly well-demonstrated in the workings and breakdowns of the so-called National Pact, which I describe in chapters three and four. This agreement between two traditional notables, Bishara al-Khoury and Riyadh al-Solh, was intended to provide the basis for political compromise between the various communities in Lebanon, especially the two identified as 'dominant' by the 1940s: the Maronites and the Sunnis.[39] Far from being a recipe for stability, the National Pact not only allowed successive crises to occur, but may have even encouraged them. In the rest of this book I focus on how communal consensus broke down in 1958 and people returned to patterns of co-habitation. I aim to show that while external factors undoubtedly contributed, it was internal dynamics within the Lebanese state that allowed the events of the 1950s to produce a major crisis that shook the state to its foundations. Classifying political systems, Gabriel Almond argues that a culturally fragmented system is liable to be static, even to produce dictatorships.[40] He also argues that such a system 'resists' social change because changes must be agreed upon by all the constituent elements in the state. But each social element keeps seeking to gain more for itself, and refuses to yield any of whatever it already has. Thus compromise and collaboration become virtually impossible. The question is: how far does this analysis reflect the realities of the independent Lebanese state during the 1950s?

Michael Hudson addresses this question, commenting that in 1958 'consociationalism' caused 'breakdown and chaos' because it 'led to a degree of immobilism that prevented government from dealing with socio-economic and ideological challenges'.[41] He argues that by the 1950s, Lebanese society was shifting away from the confessional sects that had held power in the past, and was now organising itself behind a range of essentially secular political identities and ideologies. Sofia Saadeh expands on the concept of consociation, calling it 'a system that contradicts the rules of Western democracy because it does not treat equally all citizens in a country'.[42]

These two commentators, like others who evoke the concept of consociational democracy in the modern period, downplay the confessional element. In doing so they point to six interlocking factors: 1) distinct lines of cleavage; 2) a multiple balance of power; 3) the existence of popular attitudes favourably disposed to a coalition between the various elements; 4) the existence of an external threat; 5) levels of national feeling that do not outweigh other potentially divisive factors; and 6) a 'relatively low total load on the system'.[43]

R. H. Dekmejian, for instance, evokes the consociational approach in analysing the segmented political cultures in Lebanon, arguing that Lebanon fits the consociational model in some important ways and departs from it in others. He suggests that these 'deviations' contributed to that model breaking down in Lebanon.[44] For example, he says, the Maronites refused to compromise with the Muslim sects because they were unwilling to give up any of their power base. Dekmejian points to the state's lack of coercive control, and Lebanon's traditionally unsettled regional context. These factors, he argues, could have been significant in addition to a breakdown in the consociational formula in the 1950s, because 'refusal to change can generate dissatisfaction with the system and when the situation is under stress or in a conflictual state because of different perceptions of events there are no chances to change it for better; this degenerates into a crisis'.[45]

These points are all valuable, but because they do not sufficiently stress the long-standing confessional element in community identity, they assume that communal identities can be modified, a claim that becomes harder to justify on closer examination. Dekmejian himself uses a confessional case to support his argument without identifying its potential to undermine his more secular interpretation.

Here is where the role of perception becomes key. As A. N. Oppenheim points out, perception is 'not a passive process but a dynamic one'. Perceptions evolve not just in relation to external factors, but also within 'the perceiver's culture, attitudes, expectations, needs, experience and many other aspects'.[46] Of course, the process of building a national identity need not become increasingly secularised, contrary to what many commentators imply on the basis of the Western experience. In any community, individual and group perceptions affect communications with other groups, especially those in the same or closely linked locations, through a complex process. In Lebanon, the potential for division and agreement is contained within language and linguistic values, social and cultural values, the visual expectations of others and, of course, the historical past as it affects the present.

Throughout this book I argue that, rather than adopting consociationalism, what the Lebanese have actually continued into the modern period are their habits based on co-habitation. Social groups that see themselves as having different cultures (even if 'outsiders' perceive considerable similarities) will often be prepared to underline differences rather than seek similarities. When decision-makers lose their claim on automatic group loyalty, but stilll want the groups' support, they find it necessary to stress such differences themselves, making compromise and collaboration more difficult. I argue that this situation was evolving in Lebanon in the 1950s; I would also argue that the basis on which the communities distinguished themselves from other groups was still predominantly confessional, at least regarding their attitudes to other groups. Even if some of the individuals and social strata within these groups had personally become somewhat more secular in their own personal beliefs, they still did not see the other groups in equally secular terms. Thus the tensions between groups could still be shaped by such secular perceptions.

Confessional allegiances also influenced Lebanese perceptions of the regional context of the 1958 crisis, and of Lebanon's foreign policy; they also continued to influence the powers then involved in Lebanon, however unconsciously. These external powers used the information they received from the social groups in the region to help define and identify those groups, especially in confessional terms. This was not surprising, given that the identities of the various external powers often related directly to those confessional elements. Modern France, with its history of Roman Catholic Christianity, related readily to the Christian communities in Lebanon and was prepared to be convinced that the Muslim communities were 'different'. Thus, in understanding both the internal and external dimensions of the

1958 crisis it is important to remember that throughout Lebanon's history, external powers had used coercive control and control by consensus. But how does that relate to the more widely accepted definitions of the crisis and its evolution – and particularly to these external dimensions?

In terms of the wider regional and international dimension, the most important short-term factors date from 1955, although 1952 saw the beginning of tremendous socio-political upheavals in the Arab world which clearly had implications for Lebanon. During this period Western hegemony in the Middle East was threatened by the growing power of the USSR and also by pressures from within the region itself. At one level a struggle over the political leadership of the Arab world led Arab politics to polarise into two hostile camps, with Egypt leading one and Iraq the other. Yet, as F. Qubain makes plain, these upheavals went much further.[47] Diametrically divergent concepts such as revolutionary republicanism versus monarchical gradualism; aristocratic conservative government versus socialist or semi-socialist states; and co-operation with the West versus development of independence from the West all began to play major roles in the thinking of the Arab world.[48] This polarisation split the Arab world on two levels, governmental and popular, and it included Lebanon, where 'the cleavage on the popular level took an acute character and because of the structure of the country carried with it confessional overtones.'[49]

Sources of Information

In addition to choosing a different focus from previous authors, I also use different sources. None of the authors above made consistent use of newspapers, or of private papers such as those of Ambassador Moussa Moubarak or General Emile Bustani. These are my major sources, along with American, British and French official sources. I also interviewed several individuals. The value of private papers needs no discussion. In a book that seeks to illuminate popular attitudes, however, oral sources are especially valuable in complementing other sources such as newspaper reports. As Tosh has pointed out, oral traditions are an important element of popular culture, especially in communities without high literacy levels.[50] In contrast, the politicians' papers relating to 1958 tend to concentrate on immediate issues, and on self-justification.

Newspaper evidence, along with oral traditions relating to the crisis, can indicate how much non-politicians interpreted the crisis as part of an established tradition. Thus newspaper editors like Ghassan Tueni and Salim Nassar provide important insights into the attitudes of certain sections of the masses in each confessional community. They emphasised their interest in understanding the popular mood, at least amongst their readership, and in identifying it amongst other communal groups. They tried to reflect that understanding in their papers as they chose what 'news' to report and which editorials and articles to carry. This reflection was crucial to continued sales of their papers, and as the crisis escalated, both commented that they felt increased pressure to reflect a 'popular' mood 'in tune' with their readership.[51] They emphasised that other editors and journalists held the same attitude. Thus newspapers are a valuable and credible source of information on popular attitudes.

I also used many other private papers. Some were already in the public domain, such as those of Saeb Salam and Kamal Jumblat, though no one had used them to analyse the 1958 crisis in any sustained way. Other, largely untapped, sources also proved fruitful. I gained some access to the Patriarchal Archives at Bkirki, allowing me to assess the role of the Maronite church at all levels, from the Patriarch to the ordinary clergy and even the relations of the ordinary clergy with their congregations, a key to popular attitudes. I also drew on the papers of Pierre Bart, Lebanon's ambassador to France, and the unpublished memoirs of General Emile Bustani in the 1950s, as well as the uncatalogued al-Khazin family papers.

Unfortunately, the private papers of several significant individuals are not available. Those of Charles Malik are currently in the US, in his son's possession. Others have not survived. Dory Chamoun, son of Camille Chamoun, has claimed that his father's papers – certainly those relating to this period – were destroyed by shelling during the civil war. The papers of Bishara al-Khoury met the same fate, and, according to Amine Gemayel, so did the papers of Pierre Gemayel. The wife of General Fouad Shihab deliberately destroyed his papers.

In addition to reading many documents, I interviewed several individuals who could provide useful perspectives, including Raymond Eddé, Amine Gemayel, Saeb Salam and Dr Albert Moukheiber. In particular, they could describe popular perceptions of Chamoun's intentions and aspects of the relationship between the elites and the masses within the Maronite and Sunni communities relating to events in 1957 and 1958. I also interviewed

Salim Nassar, a leading figure in Lebanese journalism in 1958. In addition to providing insights into newspaper policy, he commented on several issues and episodes that were not fully reported in 1958, because of censorship or other factors. This interview was especially significant because in 1958 Nassar was writing for *al-Sayyad*, a journal with pro-Egyptian leanings.

Oral evidence became necessary in my research because a variety of factors, including the recent civil war, have destroyed or rendered inaccessible the private papers of several individuals who played significant roles in 1958. Also, I was able to check oral evidence from one person against that from others and compare it to information from other sources, especially the official archives and newspapers.

In addition, as Catherine Hall has commented, oral evidence involves a process of selectivity that also provides important clues for the historian: what is remembered and what is forgotten? It helped me assess the different communal perspectives and the persistence of important mythologies related to community identity. Examples are the Phoenician origin of the Maronites and the Maronite conviction that a significant threat to Lebanese independence existed in 1958 and that only they could thwart it.[52]

A third argument for the value of oral evidence in this research is the fact that despite increasing literacy levels, the Lebanese people – especially the Muslims – still maintain significant elements of an oral culture.[53] While it was easier to arrange access to Christian, especially Maronite, interviewees than to Muslim interviewees, I remained conscious of the need to maintain a balance. Thus it was important to interview Saeb Salam, a leading spokesman for the Sunni opposition in 1958, and neutralist/opposition figure Raymond Eddé. I also interviewed Mrs Geneviève Gemayel, Pierre Gemayel's widow, and his son Amine Gemayel, who led the populist Maronite Kata'ib party. These interviews provided insights into a party that had a mass following in the Maronite community. Unfortunately, however, I was unable to gain access to figures representing the Sunni activist stance at a more populist level than that provided by Saeb Salam.

For the nineteenth century, however, to trace the evolution of a conscious Maronite identity, I have treated the work of Henri Lammens as a primary source. Although his works have been criticised as inaccurate, they do reveal how historians used the earlier period of Lebanese history in creating community identities, particularly the Maronite. In the 1940s and 1950s, for instance, Maronites used his work to provide a quasi-intellectual justification for their central myth: that their community is of Phoenician origin. They then used this myth to justify their claims for primacy within the Lebanese state and the popular perspective that their community was Lebanon.

For the period of the Mandate, and for the 1940s and 1950s, I drew on British, French and American official archives. The American archives were copies of State Department archives held at the Centre for Lebanese Studies at Oxford University. These archives were not fully organised; some boxes had references, while other useful documents were unclassified.[54] Thus I am unable to provide specific box locations for all the documents I refer to from this source. I also used some recently published, and properly referenced, collections of key documents for the Middle East between 1955 and 1960. For British archives, I reviewed Foreign Office papers at the Public Records Office, Kew, concentrating on the comments of those who observed the crisis at the British embassy in Beirut.

To understand the French perspective, I used the Quai d'Orsay archives in Paris and Nantes, again concentrating on reports from the French embassy for 1957 and 1958 in the *Documents Diplomatiques*, volumes of selected papers. Although other archives at the Quai d'Orsay are closed for this sensitive period, this is not a particular problem because, during that period, France was less of a key player than the US or Britain. In any case, such sources provide only an onlooker's perspective on the development of inter- and intra-community tensions.

The source materials I used most intensively are the archives of the Lebanese press, which can best illuminate popular attitudes within each community. In the 1950s, relatively speaking, the Lebanese press was a free press. Brief periods of press censorship – for example, of the opposition press in 1958 – were seen as unusual and unjustified, and therefore were rarely effective.[55] Thus I argue that the Lebanese press reflected people's ideas without much filtering through direct censorship.

In addition, the Lebanese press was prolific, with a wide range of daily newspapers and weekly and monthly periodicals. Most of these targeted specific audiences, carrying information that was relevant in terms of community allegiances, political perspectives and social position within a community. In the 1950s, the press disseminated most information, and most widely amongst the Maronite and other Christian communities, which had the highest literacy levels. However, the Sunnis and other Muslim communities had acquired at least basic levels of literacy, enabling them to read aloud, and ensuring that newspapers had an important role to play there too.[56]

Throughout the twentieth century, the press played an important part in Lebanon's political life. According to one survey undertaken within a decade of 1958, 74% of the population over 16 read a newspaper; 56% of those readers were Beirut-based.[57] While we must obviously allow for an upward trend in such figures it seems likely, given the numbers of titles aimed at all shades of opinion within Lebanon, that the figures for the 1950s were not significantly lower. Amongst the Maronite community, the wide variety of newspapers and periodicals indicates how widely political views within that community diverged. The newspaper archives make it possible to critically reassess the cliché of a united Maronite community and show that in 1958, for instance, intra-communal unity rarely lasted long. Usually it was manufactured out of fear of a common threat or enemy like the Nasserist-inspired Arab intervention in Lebanon and the negative reaction to the United Nations observers' report on their plight.

This reveals another way the Lebanese press archives are useful: they facilitate insights into the opinions and ideas of various factions and communities, allowing us to trace both modifications over time, and the arguments used to justify and explain those modifications. Some question how much the press in any society creates opinion, claiming it simply reports or mirrors opinion already in existence.[58] Certainly individual newspapers and newspaper editors claim either to create or to mould the opinion of their readership, and such claims are hardly new.[59] But expecting that the readership is ready to be guided assumes a level of passivity for which we have little evidence in Lebanon, where the tensions of competing community agendas and other aspects of co-habitation have ensured a very conscious sense of identity. According to Anis Moussallem, the stances that individual newspapers and periodicals took within the Lebanese press are the result of popular opinion within the communities.

Given such clearly defined political positions and opinions, any newspaper editor who wanted his paper to sell consistently and thus survive had to reflect the perspective of a particular community, or part of one. Thus the Lebanese press 'is the voice of all the political factions, as well as read by these factions, their leaders and the government to the extent that it diminishes the role of parliament as the representative voice of public opinion, as well as being a link between the government and the citizen'.[60] Or, in the words of Bernard Voyenne,

Qu'elle parle ou qu'elle se taise, la presse Libanaise reflète dans la société Libanaise les échos des événements selon les convictions et les intérêts de chaque journal, ou au contraire, leur interdit cette consécration, elle authentifie ou elle étouffe.[61]

[Whether reporting or keeping silent, the Lebanese press reflects events in society according to the convictions and interests of each periodical or – on the contrary – it prohibits such sanction; it authenticates, or it stifles.]

Certainly American observers at the time believed that the Lebanese press provided a useful insight into popular opinion because it was largely uncensored. Writing to the State Department, an embassy employee reported that the 'press generally reflects public reaction accurately' and continued, 'Newspaper comments [are] perhaps more important as mirrors than as influence on opinion … Press mirrors official opinion only somewhat murkily'.[62]

Apparently, then, the press in Lebanon provided a channel through which religious and ethnic pressure groups placed their opinions in the public domain, seeking popular support for their perspectives and in turn pressuring the government to respond.[63] Within the Maronite community, the church used the press in this way, as did others including the populist Kata'ib Party. Indeed, the editorial section was the most important section in any particular paper; attending to the attitudes of the readership, it provided commentary on the information contained elsewhere in the paper.[64]

I draw largely on those papers that Moussallem identified as reflecting significant or influential bodies of opinion within Lebanon: *al-Hayat, an-Nahar, L'Orient,* and *Le Jour.*[65] They were all published throughout the 1950s, and, of course, in 1957 and 1958; several also provided valuable information on Lebanon's history earlier in the century. Judging by the comments in these papers as well as in the archives, private papers and interviews mentioned above, two editors were most influential: Kamal Mroueh (*al-Hayat*) and Ghassan Tueni (*an-Nahar*).[66] Thus, I have quoted heavily from them. Other newspapers, including *Beirut al-Massa, Beirut,* and *al-Siyassa* have been less accessible, given the disruption caused by the civil war and its aftermath. I did consult some copies of these papers, especially for 1957 and 1958, either outside Beirut or in the library at the American University of Beirut.

An-Nahar has been by far the most useful single source. It sought to provide its readership with 'authentic' information on government affairs, reporting the speeches of ministers and deputies of all shades of political opinion and community allegiance. Where possible, it also reported on the 'secret' affairs of government. As a highly respected figure who remained neutral, especially on foreign policy, Ghassan Tueni had access to information not readily available to other journalists. In the spirit of the National Pact, the compromise that was to govern Lebanon's political life, Tueni and *an-Nahar* sought to maintain a stance that was identifiably neither pro- nor anti-Western, and neither for nor against an Arab world context for Lebanon. In practice this meant that while the paper aimed primarily at an opposition Christian readership, and contained ideas and opinions that would appeal to its various elements, it was not overtly hostile to the government. In addition, because it carried high-quality information, it attracted many readers outside its target readership – even members of the Sunni political and commercial elites. This fact validated its claim of neutrality.[67]

In the 1950s, *al-Hayat* was the most widely read newspaper in the Arab world; while it was produced in Lebanon its non-Lebanese readership was also reflected in its attitude, particularly on foreign policy. This wider audience makes it a particularly useful source of information on foreign policy, including the reporting of Nasser's speeches and actions within Lebanon. In terms of foreign policy, however, it maintained a pro-Western stance and advocated right-wing ideas and policies; thus it opposed Nasser and his agenda for the Arab world.[68]

Also important is *Beirut al-Massa*, a Muslim opposition newspaper with a consciously sectarian stance.[69] From 1957 it played an important role in mobilising Sunni opinion, and had some effect on the other Muslim communities. It sought to identify Sunni grievances and suggest remedies for them; these remedies were often clearly derived from the Nasserist agenda for Egypt and, after February 1958, the United Arab Republic. It also encouraged its predominantly populist Sunni readership to more vocally express resentment about its position and demand its 'rights'; it supported the Muslim move to direct action on the streets in 1958.[70]

Some less important and less accessible newspapers and periodicals provided insights into particular episodes and community perspectives. Among these are *al-Amal*, the newspaper for the activist Maronite grouping, the Kata'ib Party. Most of this paper's readers were party members; as the 1958 crisis escalated, the party's membership grew and so did the paper's readership according to its own circulation figures.[71] *Al-Bina* reflected the perspective of the Parti Populaire Syrien, a political grouping with a complex stance in 1958, which I discuss in chapters four, five and six.

Nida' al-Watan was an unofficial channel through which the Maronite Church, at least at elite levels, put across its views, especially those of the Patriarch, Boulos Boutros Meouchi. This is significant because in 1957 and 1958, the ordinary clergy was distancing itself from Meouchi's stance, and was more regularly expressing its views through newspapers such as *al-Hayat* and *al-Amal*. Thus, by examining these sources at a time when the Patriarch was actively involving himself in the evolution of the 1958 crisis, we can see the opinions of those at other levels of the church hierarchy and the ways the ordinary clergy sought to identify itself with the congregations.[72] Finally, I consulted two French-language newspapers whose readership was essentially Maronite, and certainly Christian and bourgeois. To provide some balance, I also consulted *al-Siyassa*, a pro-Egyptian opposition newspaper with a predominantly Sunni readership.[73]

While I focus primarily on the Maronite community and its role in 1958, this focus also requires a survey of Lebanese history and of the attitudes and roles of other communities – notably the Druze in the historical context and the Sunni in the contemporary one – in order to determine how much the Maronite community evolved its identity and its agendas in direct relation to events and ideas involving these other communities. The other communities in Lebanon, notably the Greek Orthodox and the Shi'ite, had roles to play in 1958 as in previous episodes of intercommunal crisis. However, the principal protagonists in the history of intercommunity co-habitation in Lebanon have been the Maronites and the Druze and, in the context of 1958, the Maronites and the Sunni.

Chapter Outline

In chapter one I focus on how the Maronites developed mythologies that gave them a sense of distinct community identity by the end of the nineteenth century. They developed this sense by interpreting their history in a way that distinguished them from the Druze community in particular. In my analysis I touch on the mythological Phoenician roots of the Maronite community, but I focus on the Ottoman period. Thus I concentrate on Mount Lebanon, the geographical area that both Maronites and Druze identify as their heartland, and the area where a distinctive sense of territorially-linked community identity emerged, first amongst the Maronites and later amongst the Druze. I make no attempt to narrate events. Instead, I highlight certain episodes in the history of the Maronites and Druze co-habiting Mount Lebanon that were key to the evolution of these mythologies, especially those that raised the level of competition between the communities for power, both political and economic.

I argue that these episodes enabled both communities, especially the Maronites, to develop a sense of difference based on concrete examples and events, and not just on such intangible emotions and claims as the Maronites' Phoenician heritage. In addition, episodes like the *Imarah* fuelled the process of the Maronites coming to identify the boundaries of 'Lebanon' for themselves. A series of confrontations escalating to crisis point between the Maronite and Druze communities was also the background for the evolution of a distinctively Maronite interpretation of the history of 'Lebanon', providing the basis for claims that Maronite community identity was a 'national' feeling.

In chapter two I examine another force that contributed to the development of community identity: external powers that were willing to be drawn into the intercommunal confrontations and crises. They did so via patron-client relationships that identified particular powers or groups of powers with particular communities but, at least from the European perspective, they did so in reaction to community mythologies. Thus, in several crises, external agency had a significant impact on the development of distinct community identity because it helped strengthen patterns of co-habitation by externally endorsing aspects of community mythology. When external forces were involved, the communities saw less need to move from co-habitation towards compromise and consensus.

For a variety of reasons including the church's role in the community, the Maronites instituted the pattern of involving outside intervention at times of crisis; they also defined the nature of that intervention from their own perspective. The Maronite church's links with the Roman Catholic Church ensured that the outside intervention in their interest was both Christian and European. In the nineteenth century, however, the Druze imitated the Maronites' pattern of seeking external – European – support in intercommunal crises. For most of the key periods in Lebanon's history the Ottoman empire was the most powerful agency regulating affairs in Lebanon.

When the Ottoman empire collapsed in the twentieth century, however, Lebanon entered a new phase in its history. Now the Maronites played a key role in ensuring that Europe – notably France – remained a key player in Lebanon's affairs.

In chapter three I address the next phase in Lebanon's history: the French mandate over Lebanon. Established as a discrete entity, partly as a result of pressure from the Maronite community, it included a wider territory than the Mount Lebanon heartland. This expansion had a significant consequence for intercommunal relations, as it emphasised Maronite-Sunni relations rather than the historical Maronite-Druze relationship. By the early twentieth century, enough Maronites had emigrated from Mount Lebanon to ensure a sizeable Maronite population in urban centres such as Beirut, where they became major participants in commercial activity. Along with other Christian communities, they could take better advantage of trade with Europe than could the Sunnis. Migrating both inside and outside Lebanon, they brought along their community mythology as the basis on which they could maintain an identity separate from other communities in Lebanon.

Once the Mandate was established, the Sunnis became the major competitor with the Maronites, in co-habitational terms. Against the background of the collapsing Ottoman empire and the establishment of the mandated Lebanese state, a Sunni community identity emerged. But it was not confined, locationally, to Lebanon. Indeed, opposition to the creation of Lebanon was one distinguishing element in the identity of the Sunni community, as it linked its dreams of fulfilling its community agenda to the setting up of a larger and distinctively Arab and/or Islamic state. This agenda acquired its own mythological status.

These divergent perspectives on Lebanon made it difficult for these two communities to move beyond co-habitation. As mutual hostility developed to the French administration of the Mandate, however, at least at elite levels, a collaboration based on expediency emerged at a time of crisis instead of confrontational behaviour. Both communities believed they could move away from habits of depending on outside intervention to solve the problems between them. Indeed, all the communities in Lebanon shared this belief in the possibility of present and future co-operation. The political aspect of this collaboration, termed the National Pact, made it possible to move to a fully independent Lebanon with a wide base of support. When France was no longer a direct factor, however, the temporary nature of that expediency began to become apparent, and the communities returned to the patterns of co-habitation, confrontation and crisis.

In chapter four I examine how collaboration, or consensus, broke down within the Lebanese administration, culminating in the crisis of 1958; I then locate that crisis within the patterns of intercommunal confrontation already identified. The basis of this collaboration was the National Pact, and the interpretation of that pact and its scope acquired its own mythological dimension, differing in each community according to its own agendas. In the years before 1958, an administrative system that, at least in theory, would permanently end intercommunal confrontation was demonstrated to have significant weaknesses. This was particularly so in the area of foreign policy, as the leaders of each community increasingly linked the orientation of that policy with their own agendas. No one had anticipated such a development within the National Pact, as in 1943 few foresaw significant anti-Western feeling in the Arab world, or the Cold War. Thus the pact contained no mechanism to organise compromise, and, even amongst Lebanon's elite, no one was willing to seek consensus without invoking outside agency to strengthen its own case.

As an international crisis in the Middle East coincided with an essentially internal Lebanese crisis caused by a classic scenario of a president wishing to renew his mandate, tension within Lebanon escalated to levels that apparently threatened the very existence of the Lebanese state. Now the flaws of the consensus encapsulated in the National Pact became obvious; ultimately its provisions, and equilibrium, were restored partly through external intervention that defused the crisis. But the 1950s atmosphere of growing intercommunal confrontation, and the eventual crisis of 1958, affected more than just the elites who were directly involved in managing the Lebanese state. Pressures from their own communities, rather than from outside, explain why these Maronite and Sunni elites could not, or would not, prevent the crisis from escalating. Any analysis of the crisis must therefore move beyond high-level politics and consider the popular interpretation of the past, which was a major factor in maintaining separate community identities.

In chapter five I focus on the attitudes, agenda and role in the crisis of Lebanon's Sunni masses. Whatever the claims of the Sunni leadership, we cannot assume that the opinions and beliefs of the masses were the same as those of the elite. These masses had not been consulted on the terms of the National Pact and its broader implications. The pact had a socio-economic impact on the community that made it more willing to develop a relationship with the Maronite community based on consensus. In practice, the patterns of co-habitation seemed increasingly attractive; though the Sunnis had come to accept the existence of a separate Lebanese entity they were increasingly unhappy with the way it operated and the way it conflicted with the mythology associated with their own sense of community identity and destiny.

Thus it had implications for their future roles in Lebanon, both socio-economic and political. For instance, the Sunni masses were conscious that they had different socio-economic benefits than the Maronite masses; they began to resent not only the Maronites but also their own leaders for endorsing the status quo. In this context, the rise of Nasser was to have a crucial impact. As the Sunnis and other Muslims lacked a charismatic popular leader within Lebanon itself, Nasser provided an ideal model. The agenda he promised for Egypt, and later the United Arab Republic, seemed to sum up what ordinary Sunnis wanted for themselves in Lebanon. Thus, without necessarily wishing to see Lebanon absorbed into the United Arab Republic, significant numbers of ordinary Sunnis were willing to use Nasser as a hero in a quasi-mythical sense, as part of a strategy to persuade their own leaders to develop an agenda more in the interests of ordinary Lebanese Sunnis, laying the ground for competition with the Maronite community.

Starting in the mid-1950s, the Chamoun government began to take a foreign policy stance that these ordinary Sunnis saw as hostile to Nasser and aiming to detach Lebanon from the Arab world. They clearly needed to persuade their leadership to distance itself from the current political status quo, which seemed to be based on an intercommunal consensus that privileged the Maronites. Aware of this acute need, the masses were increasingly willing to safeguard the Arab nature of Lebanon by taking direct action. Meanwhile Nasser encouraged their behaviour, even providing arms and funds in the so-called Arab intervention. As the crisis escalated in 1958, the masses and the leadership did draw closer together – but only to oppose the policy of the Chamoun government and to counteract the effects of Maronite behaviour. Ultimately, the leadership acquiesced in the American-brokered solution. The masses, however, saw this settlement as really offering only a return to the status quo before 1958. In this situation, we can find interesting parallels and contrasts with the Maronite community and its attitude towards intercommunal consensus at popular levels.

In chapter six, then, I explore the Maronite community's attitudes, agenda and consequent role in the 1958 crisis, but focusing on the masses. As with the Sunni community, we cannot assume that the opinions and beliefs of the masses automatically coincided with those of the leadership; an added complication was the intra-communal tension that arose because of Chamoun's personal political agenda. Many in the Maronite community believed they had the 'right' to primacy in setting Lebanon's political agenda, a right conferred by their 'history' or, rather, mythology. But this agenda was usually invoked during periods of insecurity.

Historically, the Maronites had been a minority community, even if they were now theoretically presumed to be part of a Christian majority in independent Lebanon. Thus they saw external support as essential to fulfilling their agenda. While the Sunni community wanted to see Lebanon move away from links with Europe and the West, towards a closer relationship with the Arab world, the Maronites saw this desire as a threat to their community and consequently to Lebanese independence. Overall, they reacted by returning to patterns of co-habitation because they now linked intercommunal consensus with a threat to their discrete Maronite identity and thus their security. As the political rhetoric surrounding developments in 1957 and 1958 grew more alarmist, the Maronite community began to see itself as threatened by the Sunni community; with the Sunnis and other Muslims apparently willing to take direct action to support their goals, the Maronites responded with their own direct action. In an interesting parallel with 1943, only direct intervention by American troops could persuade key elements in the Maronite community to return to a position where consensus was again possible, and assurances of Lebanese independence and of Maronite security within Lebanon could be accepted. Using this approach I examine the pivotal role the Maronites and their persistent mythologies played in the 1958 crisis at all levels, thus emphasising the internal dimensions to the crisis.

Notes

1.   For a more detailed discussion of these events in the Middle East see Malcolm Yapp, *The Near East Since the First World War*, Longman, London, 1991, chapters 9, 10, 11.
2.   K. S. Salibi, *House of Many Mansions. The History of Lebanon Reconsidered*, I.B. Tauris, London, 1988, p. 3.
3.   Camille Chamoun, *Crise au Moyen Orient*, Gallimard, Paris, 1963, p. 118.
4.   Kamal Jumblat, Inscription at Mukhtara, quoted in Dominique Chevallier, *La Société du Mont Liban à l'Epoque de la Révolution*, Librarie Orientaliste Paul Geuthner, Paris, 1971, p. 22.

5. Najla Attiyah, 'The Attitude of the Lebanese Sunni towards the State of Lebanon', unpublished PhD thesis, University of London, 1973.

6. E. H. Carr, *What is History*, Penguin Books Ltd, Handsworth, 1964, p. 55; John Tosh, *The Pursuit of History*, Longman, New York, 1984, p. 3.

7. Lammens' work forms an important part of Maronite historiography.

8. Amine Gemayel, *Peace and Unity*, Colin Smythe, London, 1984, p. 19.

9. Saeb Salam, *Masirat al-Salam*, Markaz Saeb Salam, Beirut, n.d., p, 21.

10. Walid Jumblat, *al-Hayat*, 13 June 1995.

11. David McDowall, *Lebanon: A Conflict of Minority*, Report no. 61, Minority Rights Group, London, 1983, p. 9.

12. See, for example, the words of two leaders from opposing traditions: Saeb Salam, *Masirat al-Salam*, p. 21; and Amine Gemayel, *Peace and Unity*, p. 5; and also a 'neutral' figure, Raymond Eddé, *Raymond Eddé and Raymond Helmick, Correspondance: La Question Libanaise selon Raymond Eddé expliquée aux Américains par Raymond G. Helmick*, Libanica II, Cariscript, Paris, 1990, p. 46.

13. Amine Gemayel, *Rebuilding Lebanon*, University Press of America, Boston, 1992, p. 14.

14. See *ibid.*, pp. 14; 17, for example. Note that in these comments, the Maronite Gemayel clearly views the Muslim political perspective as linked to that of the *'ulamas*, so emphasising the theoretical unity of politics and religion in Islam. This underlines the attitude of Maronite suspicion of 'real' Muslim motivation.

15. Jan Vansina, *Oral Tradition as History*, James Currey, London, 1985, p. 119; Eric Hobsbawm, 'The Social Function of the Past', *Past and Present*, 55, 1975, p. 3.

16. Tosh, p. 1.

17. Benedict Anderson, *Imagined Communities. Reflections on the Origin and Spread of Nationalism*, Verso, London, 1983.

18. Tosh, p. 224; Raphael Samuel and Paul Thompson, *The Myths We Live By*, Routledge, London, 1990, p. 52.

19. *Ibid.*, pp. 20; 60.

20. Samuel and Thompson, pp. 14–15; 19; 60; Tosh, p. 3.

21. In 1858, for example, there was a revolt in Kisrawan which is best classified as a revolt of Maronite peasants against their feudal lords, yet even so the issue is complicated by the fact that the peasants were backed by the Maronite order.

22. Philip Khoury, *Urban, Notables and Arab Nationalism: The Politics of Damascus, 1860–1920*, Cambridge University Press, Cambridge, 1983, p. 4.

23. *Ibid.*

24. Samir Khalaf, *Lebanon's Predicament*, Columbia University Press, New York, 1987.

25. G. P. Murdock, *Social Structure*, Macmillan, London, 1949, p. 82.

26. J. Coleman, 'Community Disorganisation and Conflict', in R. Merton, ed., *Contemporary Social Problems*, Harcourt, New York, 1971, p. 658.

27. F. Tonnies, *Community and Association [Gemeinschaft and Gesellschaft]*, Routledge and Kegan Paul Ltd, London, 1955, p. 69.

28. See M. Hudson, 'The Problem of Authoritative Power in Lebanese Politics: Why Consociationalism Failed', in Nadim Shehadi and Dana Haffar Mills (eds), *Lebanon: A History of Conflict and Consensus*, I.B. Tauris, London, 1988, p. 225.

29. This was also true for other communities, meaning that maps of urban areas would display a patchwork of districts monopolised by particular communities.

30. Michael Johnson, *Class and Client in Beirut: The Sunni Muslim Community and the Lebanese State, 1840–1985*, Ithaca Press, London, 1986, p. 4 also makes this point.

31. See *ibid.*, pp. 4–8 for a discussion of the social composition of the Sunni community in Beirut.

32. B. Turner, *Weber and Islam, a Critical Study*, Routledge, London, 1974, p. 97.

33. Antoine Fattal, *Le Statut Légal des Non-Musulmans en Pays d'Islam,* Imprimérie Catholique, Beirut, 1958, pp. 81–2.

34. Sofia Saadeh, *The Social Structure of Lebanon: Democracy or Servitude?*, Dar an-Nahar, Beirut, 1993, p. 41.

35. Marwan Buheiry, 'External Intervention and Internal Wars in Lebanon: 1770–1928', in Laurence Conrand, ed., *The Formation and Perception of the Modern Arab World*, Darwin Press Inc., Princeton, 1989, p. 137.

36. Hisham Sharabi, *Arab Intellectuals and the West: The Formative Years, 1875–1914,* Johns Hopkins Press, Baltimore, 1970; Albert Hourani, *Arab Thought in the Liberal Age 1798–1939*, Oxford University Press, Oxford, 1962.

37. Salibi, chapter 11, especially pp. 201–3, points out the 'war' over Lebanese history in recent years; he also points out that as early as 1935, Nakkash and Farrukh produced a text in which 'Lebanon was denuded of all special historicity outside the Syrian Arab context'. The Maronite response was a work published in 1937 which 'emphasised the special historical character of Lebanon'.

38. Arnold Hottinger. 'Zu'ama in Historical Perspective', in L. Binder (ed.), *Politics in Lebanon,* John Wiley and Sons, New York, 1966, pp. 85–105.

39. For comment on the National Pact, see Raghid al-Solh, 'Lebanese and Arab Nationalism, 1936–1945', unpublished PhD thesis, St Anthony's College, Oxford, 1986.

40. Gabriel Almond and James Coleman, *The Politics of Developing Areas*, Princeton University Press, New Jersey, 1960.

41. Michael Hudson, *The Precarious Republic*, Boulder, New York, 1985, pp. 87–105; 325–30.

42. Saadeh, p. 122.

43. A. Lijphart, 'Typologies of Democratic Systems', *Comparative Political Studies*, I.I, 1969, pp. 3–44.

44. R. H. Dekmejian, 'Consociational Democracy in Crisis: The Case of Lebanon', *Comparative Politics,* 10.2,1978, pp. 251–66.

45. A. N Oppenheim, 'Psychological Aspects', in Margot Light and A. J. R. Groom (eds), *International Relations: A Handbook of Current Theory*, Pinter, London, 1994, p. 208.

46. *Ibid.*, p. 203.

47. F. Qubain, *Crisis in Lebanon*, The Middle East Institute, Washington DC, 1961, p. 38.

48. *Ibid.*, pp. 38–9.

49. *Ibid.*, p. 39.

50. Tosh, pp. 30; 206.

51. Ghassan Tueni, interview, Beirut, 30 July 1992 ; Selim Nassar, interview, London, 20 May 1995.

52. Catherine Hall, 'Rethinking Imperial Histories', unpublished conference plenary paper, Women's History Network Conference, 16 September 1995.

53. For comments on communities in transition between the reliance on oral culture and on a literate culture, see Vansina, and John Tosh, *The Pursuit of History: Aims, Methods and New Directions in the Study of Modern History*, 2nd edition, Longman, London, 1991.

54. A proper classification is now being undertaken of some items, but too late for the purposes of this book.

55. Nassar, interview.
56. For comments on the importance of newspapers to communities with only basic literacy see David Vincent, *Literacy and Popular Culture*, Cambridge University Press, Cambridge, 1989, pp. 175–6, 230; 241–58.
57. Bernard Voyenne, *La Presse dans la Société Contemporaine*, Armand Colin, Paris, 1969, p. 194.
58. Voyenne, p. 194; Stephen Koss, *The Rise and Fall of the Political Press in Britain*, 2 vols, Hamilton, London, 1984.
59. See, for instance, the claims of editors of nineteenth-century British newspapers such as *The Times*, which Koss as discusses in his vol. 1.
60. Anis Moussallem, *La Presse Libanaise*, pp. 20–22; Nassar, interview.
61. Voyenne, p. 191.
62. *Foreign Relations of the US, 1958–1960*, vol. XI, Lebanon and Jordan, Department of State Publication 9932, Washington DC, 1992, pp. 196–7, reporting American Embassy, Beirut to Department of State, 13 January 1957.
63. Moussallem, pp. 20–1.
64. *Ibid.*, p. 73.
65. *Ibid.*, p. 92.
66. Nassar, interview. In 1958, Nassar was working for *al-Sayyad,* a weekly periodical with pro-Egyptian leanings; since 1966 he has been writing for *al-Hayat.*
67. Moussallem's survey of the Lebanese press endorses my own conclusions based on research into the Lebanese press in the 1950s. See Moussallem, p. 202.
68. *Al-Hayat* maintained this stance and this wide readership until the assassination of its founder and editor, Kamel Mroueh, in 1967. See also Moussallem, p. 210 for her comments, which again support my own investigations. In my research, I benefited from being allowed to use the *al-Hayat* archives in London and to discuss the past history of the newspaper with its present staff and ownership.
69. Only since 1990 has travel between (Christian) East and (Muslim) West Beirut been practical or safe. Even now, however, the war damage to Beirut has ensured that those archives that have survived have been moved to locations that are not always easy to identify. In addition, without accurate maps of Beirut as it is now, drivers are unfamiliar with the layout of the city outside their own confessional localities.
70. *Beirut al-Massa* ceased publication in 1960. As before, my own research and opinion on the value of this source are endorsed by the conclusions of Moussallem, p. 85.
71. This information came through Gemayel. See also Moussallem, p. 87.
72. See also Moussallem, p. 84 for some further comment on this newspaper and its orientation.
73. See also *ibid.*, p. 101.

CHAPTER ONE

Community Relations in Lebanese History: The Long-term Internal Perspective

In this chapter I examine how Lebanese communities, especially the Maronites, created mythological traditions over a sustained period. I emphasise the process rather than simply narrating how the communities evolved, because 'the historical consciousness expressed in a body of tradition' links not just to the concerns of the time when they were first recorded, but also to those of the later periods when they were repeated, elaborated and re-interpreted.[1] Raphael Samuel and Paul Thompson have argued that 'powerful myths influence what people think and do' and I aim to illuminate how the communities developed their mythologies about community identity over a long period and endowed them with power that remains strong in modern times.

At one level, such mythologies were part of a tradition passed on to 'children and kin, their neighbours, workmates and colleagues as part of the personal stories which are the currency of such relationships'. At another level, these stories acquired a broader cultural and social context that affected popular understanding of institutions including the Lebanese state itself.[2] The Maronites' mythology had a powerful impact on other communities such as the Druze and Sunni who, in response, created their own mythologies interpreting the past, in ways that would sustain their communities against the pressure of the Maronite agenda. These reactive processes were particularly noticeable at times of crisis, when the Maronites were also particularly eager to publicise their mythology. Thus the roots of many of the political perspectives of the 1958 crisis can be linked to different communal myths.

One of the most significant elements in the Maronites' mythology is the 'genesis' myth which distances them from the other Lebanese communities. According to Jan Vansina, every community in the world has a way of representing 'the appearance of their own particular society and community'.[3] But the Maronites' origins mythology aims to differentiate them racially and culturally from Lebanon's other communities, and to establish the primacy of their position in the region. The Maronite community seeks to relate itself to a Phoenician or Aramaic ethnic identity, claiming the right to an essentially Western cultural identity for Lebanon. By contrast, the Muslim communities in Lebanon relate to an Arab ethnic identity and its associated genesis, stressing the Arab cultural dimension of Lebanon. This, as Selim Abou points out, makes for a 'soul-searching' difference in perspective.[4]

The positions that the Maronite and Muslim communities took before and during the 1958 crisis reveal the workings of this phenomenon. The Maronites in particular interpreted incidents from the past to justify their different agendas in ways that went beyond rhetoric. I argue that their sense of identity depended on establishing the veracity of their version of Lebanon's history and their own role in that history. So while short-term factors were crucial in causing the crisis, we must also assess the longer-term historical dimensions in order to deeply understand the Maronite agenda. Thus mythology played a crucial role in the political behaviour of the communities during the 1958 crisis.[5]

Most of the key incidents in this mythology occurred before the Mandate, when the major players in the various clashes were the Maronites and the Druze. In this chapter, therefore, I focus on Maronite-Druze relations. Each community created a distinct identity in that context, defining itself as much in terms of difference from the other as in terms of an internal agenda, using myth as a major tool in that process. My geographical focus is Mount Lebanon, which the Maronites consistently evoke as the birthplace of their identity. Many accept that its inaccessible terrain has allowed it to retain a population that, at least in part, can justifiably claim an ancient pedigree, undoubtedly the oldest in Lebanon. The crucial question, however, is how ancient that pedigree really is. Mount Lebanon's ruggedness played another role in the evolution of a Maronite mythology: many modern historians discuss how the difficult geography has favoured the evolution of communities with distinct, self-sufficient identities insulated from contact with the outside world. This has supposedly enabled both the Maronites and the Druze to keep their special characteristics.[6]

Since at least the 1800s, Maronites have believed that they evolved directly from the Phoenicians, who had moved inland after the collapse of 'Phoenicia' or 'Ancient Lebanon'. This myth undoubtedly had its origins in the increasing Maronite desire to distinguish themselves from an Arab and Muslim heritage. They could do this most effectively by claiming a heritage that predated any meaningful Arab or Islamic heritage in the area. Nineteenth-century Western archaeologists and scholars provided evidence of Phoenician remains in the area, enabling nineteenth-century Maronite historians like Henri Lammens to produce scholarly works based on this idea.[7] His ideas were so powerful in his time that modern Maronite historians cannot entirely ignore them.

Nor can modern historians entirely disprove Lammens's work. K. S. Salibi shows that in antiquity, the Phoenicians – a maritime people – did develop a city-state system along part of the seaboard between modern Lataquia and Acre.[8] But no academically credible evidence shows that the Phoenician city-state system ever coalesced into 'Phoenicia', a single entity, let alone one that could be identified with Lebanon. If anything the evidence seems to indicate the that these city-states were separate.[9] Thus, as Salibi indicates, there is no evidence of a sense of unity during the Phoenician period which the Maronite community could have been maintained over a long historical descent. Thus we have no academic proof of a proto-Lebanon, despite the popular Maronite mythology looking to such a Phoenician past.

Such scholarship, however, has had little impact on popular Maronite belief, because the claim to a Phoenician heritage is key to Maronite perceptions of their difference from other communities in Lebanon. This claim rests on the belief that the Phoenicians originated crucial aspects of Western civilisation, notably the alphabet, which the Greeks then adopted.[10] Laying claim to this heritage allows the Maronites to place themselves as part of Western civilisation since classical antiquity, sharing key elements of that civilisation with Western Europe.[11] Because this attractive idea is so central to Maronite ideology, it has continued to be widely popular and has resisted re-interpretation, even after credible research by historians like Salibi. For example, Phillippe Hitti, writing a history of Lebanon in 1957, included the Phoenician period and thus implied a link, but was careful not to say he believed in the Maronites' Phoenician heritage.[12]

Lammens was particularly important in articulating this belief; though serious academics have revised his thesis, Maronites have consistently referred to his work over the last half-century.[13] By the 1950s his ideas had been incorporated into the Maronite school curriculum as 'history', and they remain there today.[14] In the past decade, the Maronite press has reported on the discovery of the walls and other parts of the Phoenician predecessor of Beirut.[15] And Maronite political figures have consistently drawn on this heritage. For example, Amine Gemayel called the Maronites 'the heirs to a great – indeed unique – cultural heritage', and continued, 'Ancient Lebanon sent out her ships not to conquer the world, but to disseminate learning and the use of the alphabet.'[16] Arguably, one factor that has helped the Maronites survive as a discrete community is their tradition that, as a minority community they are consistently out of step with official authority in the region and thus subject to persecution for their beliefs, which they are determined to maintain.

The mythology of the Phoenician period gives few individual accounts of past events, relying more on general cultural statements such as those on the alphabet. But the Maronites also draw on other historical periods. For instance, historiographers do say the Maronite community was identifiable quite early, due to its distinctive religious profile, as a distinct grouping in the Mount Lebanon area. Certainly that was the area where the Maronite Church, with its separate theology originally based on monotheism, evolved in the period after 685, when the Muslims conquered the region.[17]

Equally certainly, the church provided a coherence that enabled the Maronites to begin developing community feeling in a religious sense. As Benedict Anderson comments, a distinctive religious community is one of the most important elements in a sustained community cultural system; such communities develop a 'confidence in the unique sacredness of their languages and thus their ideas about admission to membership'. This confidence undermines secular impulses toward assimilating with other communities who have common interests.[18]

This Maronite self-identity, especially its religious dimension, also evolved in relation to the Druze – another minority community out of step with official authority in the region and also located in Mount Lebanon. The distinctive religious profiles of both communities acted as an effective barrier to assimilation between them. The Druze are an Islamic group but – in an interesting parallel with the Maronites – not an orthodox sect. The Druze movement derived from the Ismaili strand of the Shi'ite element in Islam, becoming an identifiable factor in the communal map of Mount Lebanon by the end of the eleventh century.[19] Like the Maronites, the Druze were conscious of the special nature of their religion and culture and determined to resist efforts either to eradicate or to assimilate them.[20]

While never entirely confined within the Mount Lebanon region, especially in the Ottoman period, both communities identified with it closely. The result was co-habitation rather than collaboration: a degree of co-existence and compromise, sometimes breaking down into outright hostility. Each group defined the region, or parts of it, as peculiarly their own, and in some areas where the population was mixed Maronite-Druze, claims to identical territory led to particular tensions with implications for the rest of the area. As I will now show through a series of case studies, long-term competition for land, power and privileges within the region has helped to shape not just these two groups' self-perceptions of communal identity, but also the habits or 'rules' for co-habitation. These rules evolved in relation to the clashes which gradually highlighted and hardened the traditions of 'difference' between the communities.

The history of the region reveals the extent of past co-habitation and the ways it was sustained, establishing patterns that continue in modern Lebanon, in particular the Maronite tendency to invoke mythology relating to their own sense of identity. Various theories seek to explain how such mixed societies evolve and co-exist, and how they can even form a unified entity that can be termed a nation-state with clear elements of internal cohesion and a shared sense of tradition in a cultural sense. But others recognise that such a process is not inevitable and that the 'imagined communities' that evolve in a political state may not be coherent. This is the case of Lebanon.[21]

Until the twentieth century, except for the Maronites, 'Lebanon' was simply a geographical term for a region that was part of a variety of eastern Mediterranean empires; it was not equivalent to the modern state. From 685 to 1918, the region was controlled by successive Muslim empires, culminating with the Ottoman empire; thus it was subject to a process of attempted Islamicisation.[22] But Christian communities, including the Maronites, survived throughout the period of Islamic rule despite periodic persecutions.[23]

From 1516 to 1918, when Ottoman sovereignty over the region was officially unbroken, the Maronites' individual communal identity began to coalesce, and they determined the basis on which they were prepared to co-habit, peacefully or not, with other communities, most of which had also become well-entrenched in the region.[24] Thus, during this period the Maronite community felt a need to begin evolving myths that supported their right to existence. During the Ottoman period the other communities also evolved many of their prejudices and assumptions about co-existence and co-operation.

Until 1918, few such assumptions coalesced into major coherent traditions or mythology of self-identity in direct reaction to Maronite beliefs (except for the Druze). But these traditional assumptions about the nature of the Maronites were to affect non-Maronite mythologies after 1918. Thus the 'history' of relations with the Maronites is important to most of the region's other communities.[25] In an important cultural fracture the Muslim communities, even the Druze, were seen, and saw themselves, as integral parts of the Ottoman empire. By contrast the Christian communities were seen as outsiders and not truly part of the Islamic world; if tolerated to some extent, they still experienced an implicit pressure to conform and assimilate. But as part of their strategy to survive as a discrete entity, the Maronites continued to insist on their 'right' to territory, and to the status this conferred.[26] This tension between perspectives was a consistent undercurrent no matter how much either group may have been in or out of favour with official authority at various times.[27]

By the late 1400s, Sunnism had become established as the majority system of belief in the Ottoman empire.[28] The Maronite and Druze communities of Mount Lebanon both experienced discrimination by Sunni authority; their defence strategies invoked mythology relating to community identity.[29] In an interesting parallel with the Maronites, Abdul Rahim Abu Hussein argues that the sense of discrimination the Druze experienced was a key factor in turning this community of mountain peasants into a quasi-feudal society by the sixteenth century. They became a society culturally conditioned by and for war; their social hierarchy centred on military service, with consequent implications for the community's modern self-image.[30]

Abu Hussein also argues that this mixed relationship with the Sunnis had a significant impact on the Druze: it helped sustain the quasi-feudal system into the modern period, and thus to concentrate power in the hands of the Druze chiefs who provided community leadership and were generally prepared to collaborate with Ottoman authority.[31] While such claims are notoriously difficult for scholars to prove, this belief remained part of the Druze communal tradition even after the Ottoman empire fell in 1918. It was thus significant in shaping Druze participation in communal politics leading up to the crisis of 1958.

The Maronite community had a different social organisation because it was led by the Maronite Church and secular elites. It did not use its military skills or reputation, as the Druze did, though the Maronites were equally determined to fight if necessary to prevent themselves being overrun. Certainly no one saw the Maronites as potential Ottoman mercenaries. They did, however, show a capacity to co-operate with local Ottoman authority in non-military ways when that seemed to their advantage.[32]

Thus Maronite social evolution took a different path from that of the Druze, both in Ottoman times and more recently. For example, early in the Ottoman period the Maronites developed a social system that some Maronite historians have claimed paralleled European feudalism. This system of land-holding used a complex range of taxes and requirements for service, with Maronite 'lords' passing on to the Ottoman state some or all of the taxes they extracted from their 'tenants'.[33] This system lasted into the nineteenth century in rural areas, and created a land-owning Maronite elite that remained important into the twentieth century if only because it provided many political leaders.[34] While I hesitate to overstate the parallels between European and Maronite 'feudalisms', a particularly tight social structure did exist, especially in the Kisrawan district. It gave considerable power to the landed elite, to whom the peasants owed a form of labour service that kept them tied to the land.[35]

The rise of a more urban-based Maronite commercial elite spreading outside Mount Lebanon itself eventually challenged the power of traditional land-owning Maronite leaders. As the twentieth century progressed, the majority of the Maronite population was also to be found outside Mount Lebanon, taking advantage of the economic opportunities offered by the commercial elite. The result was the evolution of a slightly modified, nostalgic, Maronite mythology that saw the 'old' values as being essentially rooted in the peasant society of Mount Lebanon, rather than in the region's land-owning elite. But this mythology still emphasised the territorial roots of the community's identity.[36] These two traditions existed side by side over a sustained period, but Albert Hourani has argued that by the Mandate period, 'influences radiating from Beirut' were dominant, even within the Mount Lebanon region itself.[37] A commercial elite begin to evolve in the 1500s as a result of trade with Europe, particularly the silk trade, and began to locate itself in urban areas. Only in the nineteenth century, however, and mostly outside Mount Lebanon, did this elite acquire significant influence over the Maronite masses.[38] However, certainly in the period up to 1958, the land-owning elite retained a powerful influence over the masses, if only because of the linkage with events seen as contributing to Maronite community identity.

Under the Ottoman empire central authority was generally administered through local functionaries, but a vast range of different practices and effects obtained locally.[39] Thus in considering Ottoman authority over modern Lebanon we must ask how much and in what ways that central authority made itself felt. Moreover, what impact did this have at varying periods on the various communities of Mount Lebanon and their relationships with each other and with Ottoman authority, both local and central? The Ottoman state officials with most direct contact and influence over local districts and their peoples were the *amirs* or the governors of sub-provinces or *sanjaks*; the region contained several such units. The *amirs* commonly competed amongst themselves for favour and power from the centre – with serious implications for their districts. But when implementing policy and making practical decisions, local Ottoman officials were also likely to find themselves responding to forces from below just as much, if not more, than to pressures and instructions from above. This was a common experience in empires.[40]

The Imarah

An example of this provides the first case study. Lebanese historians have traditionally considered that the *Imarah* provides a prototype for a separate Lebanon, something that could be termed a truly 'Lebanese' and local administrative entity. Certainly the Maronites referred to it that way into the 1950s, and used it to justify the creation of an independent Lebanon within its modern boundaries. Recently historians like Abu Hussein, drawing on Ottoman sources, have forced a reassessment of what Salibi now refers to as the 'imagined principality'.[41] But this does not alter the importance of the traditions surrounding the *Imarah* in Maronite mythology, including the belief that it was the precursor of the *Mutassarifiyyah*, and thus of an independent Lebanon.

The *Imarah* emerged within the context of Ottoman rule as early as the seventeenth century, and lasted into the nineteenth century.[42] During that era it had no fixed boundaries; the territory included in the administrative scope of the *Imarah* expanded and contracted, based on the various *amirs'* differing relations with the Ottoman state. *Amirs* on good terms with the state were likely to find their administration expanding to cover larger areas and vice versa.[43] Mount Lebanon was always part of the *Imarah*, but at its widest extent, such as in 1861, the *Imarah*'s boundaries more or less paralleled those of Mandate and independent Lebanon. Conscious of this fact, members of the Maronite community invoked the *Imarah* as justification for the shape of modern Lebanon. But the *Imarah* is also important to the Maronites for its 'Lebanese' nature; they came to see themselves having a unique role and importance within it, and believed it conferred pre-eminent status on them in comparison to the other communities included within its boundaries. Thus the history of the *Imarah* illuminates the developing community consciousness of both the Maronites and the Druze, though it also affected other local communities such as the Sunni and the Shi'ite.

Most Maronite historians see the *Imarah*'s initial evolution as largely Druze, resulting from the efforts of Fakhr al-Din II, *amir* between 1590 and 1633.[44] A considerable amount of mythology – predominantly Maronite – has surrounded Fakhr al-Din; non-Maronite communities resent this 'misrepresentation'. Since the 1920s, Lebanese history texts have taught children to regard him as the first ruler or *amir* of 'Lebanon' and thus the historical founder of the Lebanese state.[45] Although I believe the scholarly realities are less significant than the established mythologies, a review of the history is in order.

An indigenous Druze chief, Fakhr al-Din was first appointed *amir* of the *sanjak* of Sidon-Beirut, which included the Druze heartland in Mount Lebanon; from this base, he sought to increase his local power.[46] At that period, in the early 1600s, central authority in the Ottoman empire was weak,[47] and Fakhr al-Din took full advantage of this weakness. Another factor working to his advantage was European intervention in Ottoman affairs in the area.[48] The European interest apparently led Fakhr al-Din to believe that the Europeans would support his attempts to carve out more power for himself at Ottoman expense. This was to prove a miscalculation.

Fakhr al-Din's efforts had a positive by-product, however: the Druze and Maronites in Mount Lebanon entered a period of positive co-habitation, based on some real co-operation between elements in both communities. The genuinely collaborative and local administrative system that evolved had considerable autonomy within the Ottoman empire and functioned for much of this period, creating an entity that began to make Lebanon more than a mere geographical term. This in turn had an effect on Maronite mythology, giving it focus and substance.

Lebanese historians have generally accepted that even after the central Ottoman authority removed Fakhr al-Din in 1633, the concept of the *Imarah* survived.[49] Because it seemed to provide more effective control over the area the Ottoman authorities endorsed its continuation, initially under another Druze chief, Ahmad Ma'n. When he died in the late 1600s, however, the Ottomans imported a Sunni Muslim dynasty, the Shihabi, from the southeastern Biqa' region.[50] By this time, successive *amirs* had seen clearly that the *Imarah* worked on the basis of a continuing overall co-operation between leading elements in the Druze and Maronite communities based on a degree of resistance to central Ottoman authority.[51] It was the one point of agreement for leaders in both communities, although the Druze were undoubtedly dominant.

The Shihabis realized they had to cope with, if not endorse, this Mount Lebanon 'tradition' of some resistance to central authority, though they naturally attempted to modify it. Thus, despite the Ottomans' expectations, the *Imarah* actually did little to make the area more amenable to central control. Moreover, the continuing European interest in the region generally restrained central Ottoman intervention, because the Christian West and the Ottoman empire maintained a relative power balance in the eighteenth century.[52]

The result in practical terms, at least within the *Imarah,* was that the elites of both communities had a degree of freedom unknown elsewhere in the Ottoman empire. For instance, Ottoman authorities rarely had sustained direct control in the region: they depended on the local elites to co-operate with their fiscal, military and political policies. While they could remove *amirs* who seemed to be growing too powerful – like al-Din – the Ottomans realised that on a daily basis, they had to work through the *amirs*, as they could not directly impose a long-term coherent central authority. This meant that the *Imarah* became 'a political institution that became a quasi-autonomous hereditary principality'.[53]

This can be seen as the first step in developing a self-conscious, separate and culturally-based sense of community identity, at least at elite and educated levels, one that trickled down the social hierarchy as the mythology was repeated. This sense of community was strongest and most widely felt amongst the Maronites, largely because they assumed an increasingly important administrative role within the *Imarah*. Initially, Druze interests dominated the *Imarah*'s affairs and thus its administrative policy. Given the social structure of the Druze community, Druze interests essentially meant those of the chiefs, the landowning class.[54]

Although Druze interests were primary, the Ottoman central authority generally tolerated the *Imarah*, believing it could rely on the *amir* to prevent the local authority from gaining excessive power and engaging in the kind of outright rebellion that had occurred under al-Din. At this stage the personal co-operation at elite levels in the communities had promoted the quasi-feudal landowning elite amongst the Maronites, mirroring the authority the Ottomans gave to the land-based Druze chiefs. In some senses, it can be argued, this situation brought the communities closer together. Undoubtedly in the first century-and-a-half of the *Imarah*'s existence, this Maronite elite identified its interests firmly with those of the Druze, despite their religious differences.[55]

But this apparent intercommunal collaboration did not survive, and it never extended beyond the elite. At first, the Maronite elite was in no position to do more than accept Druze leadership; it apparently recognised this and acted accordingly, to protect its interests. At lower levels of the hierarchy, however, relations were less cordial. Capable Shihabi *amirs* such as Bashir I (1691–1707), along with influential community leaders, prevented active hostility; but given differences in religious cultural backgrounds, the mass of Druze and the mass of Maronites never felt particularly close to one another. Unlike the landowning elites of the two communities, they had no real shared interests to move them beyond a periodically uneasy co-habitation.

Beginning in 1711, however, the Druze community at all levels gradually began to feel at a disadvantage *vis-à-vis* the Maronites within the *Imarah*. This situation would eventually undermine the potential for the elites to co-operate successfully and would bring down the *Imarah* itself. By around 1750 the feeling became palpable, and the Druze indeed had grounds to fear oppression and unequal treatment by the *amirs* and the *Imarah* bureaucracy. The result was a gradual breakdown of the earlier co-operation and a return to co-habitation at all levels, marked by increasing Druze resentment of the Maronites. In addition, the Sunni Shihabi *amirs* of the eighteenth century were not able or ready, for a variety of reasons, to cultivate close links with the Druze.[56] The Battle of Ayn Dara in 1711, between warring Druze factions, weakened the Druze community as a whole; in addition to those who died in battle, those in the defeated faction were largely slaughtered or exiled.[57] This conflict was particularly unfortunate for the Druze elite, making it harder to sustain a high-profile administrative role within the *Imarah*.

The Maronites had seen the potential for such a situation to develop, and took advantage of it to consolidate a position of power within the *Imarah*. After 1711 they took over more and more of the administrative posts available within the *Imarah* and thus could control access to the *amirs*: a lever of influence they had never before experienced. Their community mythology reflects a lasting interest in this history and a sense that it is beneficial to seek co-habitation rather than consensus. Equally, this development gave the Druze a new sense of oppression.[58]

By the early 1800s, valuing their long-established traditions and culture and empowered by their recent experiences within the *Imarah,* the Maronites were becoming an increasingly cohesive community; all social levels shared a sense of special identity that derived from their collective mythology. Capable of sufficient internal discipline, they could be said to be acting as a community on certain key issues. Certainly they shared aspirations about exercising some degree of autonomy in their own affairs, and achieved it through the *Imarah*. The quasi-feudal social structure described above was undoubtedly one cohesive factor. But others also promoted this sense of shared identity.

As I have already suggested, the church was a very significant factor. It not only provided internal coherence for the Maronite community by demonstrating religious distinctiveness, but also promoted external links that sustained the community's 'Western' orientation. By the early 1800s it could look back at a longstanding relationship with the Roman Catholic Church, having started with informal contacts during the eleventh century which became more formal in 1584. By the late 1500s the Papacy granted the Maronite Church status and acceptance[59] that allowed Maronite priests to go to Rome for training. When they returned they retained their Maronite identity, and sought to define it in ways acceptable both to their fellow Maronites and to the essentially Western Roman Catholic tradition.[60] This relationship had another implication: the leaders of the Maronite community (including religious leaders) could use their Roman Catholic connections to secure and maintain political support from the West. They saw such support as helping protect them from any serious acts of central Ottoman hostility.[61]

The priests performed another function of major cultural importance to the Maronite community by simply being present amongst them. For the bulk of the Maronite population, contact with Maronite clergy was a major factor in sustaining their social solidarity as a community. This bulk must be classed as peasants or sharecroppers, working for landowners, both Maronite and Druze, whose interests were generally removed from those of the peasants. Alhough many of the clergy came from the landowning class up to the nineteenth century, they still provided the regular daily leadership for the Maronite community and thus served as a major channel for interpreting the mythology relating to community identity.

They were particularly able to do this as they founded and ran village schools to spread literacy in both French and Arabic; these schools also provided a version of information about the community that promoted both the Maronite Church and its Western orientation, and the distinctiveness and superiority of the Maronite community.[62] Some of these schools even developed into more sophisticated and important educational centres. The church's motivation was plain: the policy helped to perpetuate their role and power within the community. A second result was that, by the nineteenth century, the Maronite community was a much more educated social group than the Druze. This relatively literate community then read and heard their history as written by Maronite historians who were also clerics, and whose aim in writing it was 'not so much to establish its history as to vindicate its claims' in the contemporary period to a special identity produced and justified by this past: to develop a mythology that was accepted as 'valid' historically.[63]

This work by the church had another effect: it helped to modernise the internal social and class structures of the community, especially since it was associated with Maronite involvement in trade with Europe. Here, the increasingly literate and Western-oriented Maronites had an advantage over Lebanon's other communities. As Maronite links with the West, especially France, flourished, the silk trade had a considerable socio-economic impact on the Maronite community as a whole, especially in Mount Lebanon.[64] Silk from Mount Lebanon was of high quality; it stimulated the economy both there and in Beirut, through which most of it was exported, as people realised its potential to bring profits.

In addition, silk provided the community with an economic base on which to build an educated class, as more families found themselves both able to pay to educate their children, and aware that education would let them participate in the trade on a more equal basis with their Western partners.[65] The sustained existence of a Maronite educated class, able and willing to take on positions of authority in the public affairs of the *Imarah,* also meant that in government the Maronites had become more prominent as early as the seventeenth century. Educated Maronites found work with the Shihabi *amirs* and even with local Druze chieftains. As a result Maronites were in a position to determine or at least significantly influence both the policy of the *amirs* and local intercommunal politics, a situation that continued for some time within the *Imarah.*[66]

In time, the Maronites so thoroughly replaced the Druze as the politically dominant community that by the reign of Bashir II (1788–1840) the *Imarah* had acquired a Christian character, which had a profound impact on the region's communal balance. This Christian character was the more apparent because Bashir II was a convert to Maronite Christianity, and the remaining Shihabi *amirs* were also Maronite.[67] Thus, for both practical and ideological reasons, Maronite officials became still more plentiful and powerful in the administration, as the wealthy and well-organised Maronite Church grew in power.[68] However, the next stage in the region's communal history was to be less happy for the Maronites. As the case studies of events in 1820, 1840–2 and 1858–60 demonstrate, however, this unhappiness would also promote Maronite communal identity.

In the mid-nineteenth century, Ottoman central authority saw an opportunity to restrict what it saw, with some justification, as the growing autonomy of the *Imarah* region. A complex scenario arose. The battle lines were eventually drawn up in 1840 between three parties: the central Ottoman authority; the Christian *amir*, Bashir II and his largely Maronite supporters; and leaders of the Druze community, predominantly from the Jumblat family. The scenario was complicated, as external European powers tried to intervene on one side or another.[69] The Maronites, and other Christians under his rule, interpreted Bashir II as a 'reigning prince and the scion of a dynasty of reigning princes'. This was in direct contrast to the Ottoman interpretation, and the perspective on Bashir II that entered Druze and Sunni mythology. In this interpretation Bashir II was 'a mere fiscal functionary of the Ottoman state'. The issue at stake was the legitimacy accorded to any independent rule or policy made by Bashir II.[70]

In 1841, this issue led to a civil war, the first that can with any veracity be termed a Lebanese civil war. The origins of this war and its aftermath to 1860 are worth examining in some detail, given their long term impact on Maronite-Druze mythologies in relation to each other and to 'Lebanon'. The political mythology for the area that developed during this period, based on assertions of the primacy of religious and communal identity, has proved remarkably durable, as the events of 1958 demonstrate.

The background to this conflict was a clash between Bashir II and his superior in the Ottoman administration, Abdallah Pasha, the governor of Acre, that dated back to 1819. Both as an Ottoman official and on his own account, Abdallah sought to reduce the autonomy of the *Imarah*. Abdallah was determined to bring Bashir II to his knees. As soon as he took up his appointment in 1819, Abdallah demanded from Bashir II an exorbitant tribute, hoping to cause a conflict. Bashir II was forced to obey, but when his agents tried to collect the tax it provoked the population of the Matn and the Kisrawan, two regions in Mount Lebanon, to outright rebellion.

This rebellion, known as the '*ammiyyah* or commoners' rising, was important for being an essentially and consciously Maronite rebellion, involving all levels of the Maronite community in the region and also the Maronite Church, and justified by reference to community mythology.[71] The Maronite nature of the resistance is underscored by the fact that although the Druze also had to pay the hated taxes, they did not rise to active dissent.[72] As the Druze were generally a bit less wealthy than the Maronites, the Maronites probably did not revolt because of economic overburdening. Instead, the *ammiyyah* reflects the development of a mythologically-based community social culture among the Maronites, drawing on both a religious and secular base.

With its sophisticated institutional organisation, the Maronite Church promoted this sense of shared identity amongst the congregations by evoking mythical 'rights' of exemption from Ottoman control. Through its priests, the church spread information and ideas to the Maronite community, and it used its spiritual authority to increase popular resentments to the point of physical resistance. The church had accumulated both land and cash over the previous three centuries. It had relied on the landed elite for protection up to the late 1700s; by the 1800s, however, it was becoming independently powerful within the community. It even drew its personnel from all levels of the Maronite social strata and not just from the elite.[73]

Now it was prepared to use that power against what it interpreted as an Ottoman attempt at intervention. This attitude reveals how powerful a force it was in creating and maintaining a self-conscious, mythologically and ethnically-based Maronite communal identity; this would have profound implications for events in the twentieth century. For example, a letter in 1818 from the Maronite Patriarch Joseph Tyan to Pius VII referred to the Maronite 'nation', a term which is best understood in the context of the time as 'people', or 'ethnic group'.[74]

While it would be hard to sustain a case that in 1820, this closed communal identity amounted to 'nationalism' in a Western sense, the *ammiyyah* is important because it indicates how strong a separate identity the Maronites now had bound up with a sense of location. This identity was both widespread and coherent in its beliefs and aims. Those aims extended far beyond resistance to paying taxes; the demand was presented to the Maronites in the region, and accepted, as part of a resistance to Ottoman authority that the community needed in order to maintain itself and its separate traditions. Traditional hierarchical bonds remained important and powerful within the community. They simply combined with what Samir Khalaf has termed 'a more communal form of social cohesion where the sources of political legitimacy were defined in terms of ethnicity and confessional allegiance'.[75] In a sense, though, as events in Kisrawan were to show, the peasantry and the church were ahead of the landed and commercial elites in their position on community autonomy; when their interests coincided, the elites still found reasons to co-operate with both Ottoman authority in the form of the *amir*, and with leaders of other Muslim communities.

Given that the Ottoman authority in the region could neither control the rebellion nor collect the required revenue, the *ammiyyah* clearly had an impact. In fact, in 1820, Bashir II abandoned the emirate and went into voluntary exile in the Hawran. But Abdallah could not cope with the situation in Lebanon either; it deteriorated so badly that he was forced to call Bashir II back to office in 1821. Because of other factors, Bashir remained only a few months before going into exile again.[76] This time, he went to Egypt, where he was welcomed by Muhammad Ali Pasha (1805–49), a strong figure who effectively ruled Egypt as an independent entity within the Ottoman empire. Muhammad Ali was interested in extending his power base, and particularly coveted Syria.[77] In 1822, as a result of Muhammad Ali's intervention with Ottoman central authority, Abdallah and Bashir II were both returned to their old positions.[78]

Bashir II apparently believed that the Ottoman officials above him in the hierarchy would not challenge this third round of governing his emirate, and that he could therefore afford to reassert his authority within the Mount Lebanon region. Over the next eighteen years he did so, successfully alienating virtually all his subjects. His policies also increased intercommunal hostility, leading to a crisis, considerable intercommunal violence and the end of the *Imarah*, since its vital elements had split too acutely for it to continue.

Shortly after he returned in 1822, Bashir II turned the Druze community even more strongly against him. He realized that some had actively opposed his return, notably Bashir Jumblat, a leading Druze and former ally. Once back in power, Bashir II imposed a crippling fine on Jumblat for plotting against him. Jumblat refused to pay, and tried to raise the Hawran district against Bashir II, providing Bashir with an excuse to destroy him militarily. By January 1825, Jumblat headed a coalition of Druze leaders in open revolt. But Bashir II won, and established a position of political dominance in Lebanon supported by the Maronite community.[79] Salibi points out why these events were important: the Druze were convinced that Jumblat was crushed because he was a Druze, rather than because he was a dangerous 'political rival'.[80]

In the power vacuum that followed, Maronites increasingly dominated the administration of Mount Lebanon, ensuring their support for Bashir II in the period to 1831, while the Druze seethed in practically powerless resentment. Beginning in 1831, however, events proceeded differently, as the region effectively came under Egyptian control. For the rest of that decade, the Druze had another cause for dissatisfaction with Bashir II and an opportunity to demonstrate it by openly supporting the Ottoman central authority. When Bashir II had returned to power in 1822, his protectors were Egyptians, not the central Ottoman authority. Thus he required continued Egyptian support to remain in power. Muhammad Ali intended to establish control over Syria, including the *Imarah*, and expected to use Bashir II in achieving his goal. In 1831 Muhammad Ali dispatched his son, Ibrahim Pasha, to establish control over Syria; he also planned to use Lebanon as a base and a source of goods and manpower. Keenly aware that the central Ottoman authority was willing to depose him whenever an opportunity arose, Bashir II had little choice but to become involved with the Egyptian plans.

Within the *Imarah*, the Druze discovered a new loyalty to the Ottoman state, and took up arms on its behalf after 1831, leading to immediate clashes with the Maronites within the *Imarah*. Initially the Maronites accepted Bashir II's alliance with the Egyptians, who were prepared to establish a state of genuine religious toleration and equality including them and the Muslim communities. The Maronites hoped this would further strengthen their position within the *Imarah*.[81]

Relationships between the communities, however, quickly became even more complex. Elements in the Maronite community, especially at the lower levels, resented the Egyptian involvement. Ibrahim Pasha remained in charge in Syria for nine years, with Bashir II acting as his vassal or agent in the *Imarah*. In order to run Syria effectively and to build a strong Egypt, Ibrahim had to impose burdensome taxes, and to establish an administrative system within the *Imarah* that would allow him to collect those taxes effectively.[82] He also had to conscript local men into the Egyptian army. If the Maronites had originally welcomed Ibrahim's arrival, both ordinary Maronites and their church soon grew to resent the taxation and the conscriptions, which involved them in fighting for a Muslim state.

During the 1830s the Druze were even more hostile to these developments. The Egyptians forced Bashir II to help suppress a Druze revolt – and to use Maronite conscripts in doing so. The suppression succeeded, and Bashir II tried to restore peace between the Druze and his administration and between the two communities, under the most generous peace terms he could arrange. But he still had to levy fines and impositions, and exile some Druze leaders, so it hardly had a conciliatory effect.[83] The Druze could neither forget nor forgive the fact that the *amir* had used the Maronites to suppress them. This had considerable implications for the future of co-operation between the communities, at least in the *Imarah*.

But the Maronite leaders were soon seeking ways to collaborate with other opponents of Bashir II's rule, within the *Imarah* and outside it, including the Druze. The Maronites were driven by the fear that more men would be conscripted from their community to fight for the Egyptians in Syria; the resulting revolt helped to bring down both Bashir and Ibrahim. Ibrahim was evicted from Syria, primarily because Britain, France and Russia intervened to settle 'The Eastern Question'; the action also brought down his ally, Bashir II.[84] When the *Imarah* finally collapsed, the cause was primarily local, although European powers remained involved to arrange the region's post-*Imarah* administration.

In May 1840, Bashir discovered that the Maronites and Druze had united in their hostility to him, as the majority of leaders from both communities in Mount Lebanon led their followers in an uprising against him. With help from Ibrahim Pasha, he was initially able to suppress it. However, once the Egyptian army had begun to collapse, during September and October of 1840, he also lost his ability to contain the uprising. Two days after Ibrahim was finally defeated on 10 October 1840, Bashir II fled Lebanon for the last time.[85]

The events of 1840 do not deserve a full review here, but a few points are key. First, as in 1819–20, the Maronite initiative against Bashir II was taken by the peasants, backed by the church. Second, the events of 1840 made it plain that co-operation between the Druze and Maronites during the *Imarah* had not developed beyond narrow self-interest: neither side attempted to reconcile their differences. This situation is highlighted by the reasons that the summer phase of the 1840 rebellion failed. In addition to getting support from the Egyptians, Bashir II succeeded in splitting the Maronite-Druze alliance against him and turning their attention back to intercommunal hostilities by promising Druze leaders that he would 'make them masters of the Maronite district of Kisrawan'.[86] In the event, Bashir II never had the chance to live up to his promises, and despite this initial success neither he nor the *Imarah* were to survive the continuing tensions in the region.

With Bashir II in exile, the interested European powers arranged to replace Bashir II with Bashir III, another member of the Shihabi family. Bashir III turned out to be particularly incompetent – and short-lived.[87] But even a competent *amir* might not have been able to avoid the intercommunal unrest between 1840 and 1860, including the 1841 civil war. The violence of 1841 started with a small-scale quarrel in the spring between Maronites and Druze in the Dayr al-Qamar region. But the quarrel tapped a deeper issue – the respective property rights of members of both communities – and led to more hostilities during the summer of 1841.

In October 1841, the quarrel escalated significantly, with many casualties on both sides. Central Ottoman authorities intervened in November, tipping the scale against the Maronites, especially as Bashir III was now in Druze hands.[88] In January 1842, Bashir III left Lebanon for Istanbul, ending the period of Shihabi rule in the *Imarah*, and effectively, if not yet officially, the *Imarah* itself. The small but solid consensus between the Maronite and Druze elites when the *Imarah* began had slowly eroded, but now its last remnants had disappeared, since neither side had any reason to sustain it. Under the administration of 'Umar Pasha, appointed by the Ottoman state to restore order in the Mount Lebanon region, anti-Maronite violence lessened, but his policy in the region had a clear anti-Maronite bias.

The violence of 1841 can be directly attributed to the legacy of intercommunal suspicion and resentment created by Bashir II's policies and the consequent mythology surrounding him.[89] The Druze resented the administrative set-up and regional officials that his regime left behind, and the clear benefits to the Maronites of his activities against the Druze. He had ordered confiscated Druze property to be given to Maronites, and the Druze had had to watch the Maronites enjoying and displaying their newly-acquired wealth and property. Even if the Maronites turned against Bashir II in the end, they also benefited from his rule for years. Their improved status and power within the administrative system, displayed in a spirit of political confidence, deeply irritated the Druze at every level.[90] If Bashir II had succeeded in largely destroying the political power of the Druze feudal lords, however, he had not undermined the community's feudal social organisation. The loyalties of the Druze masses, mainly rural peasants, remained firmly with their lords. So they were not happy to see these lords reduced in power and status.[91]

The relationship between the two communities and between the Druze and the regional administration had never been very stable. On coming to power, Bashir III had swiftly managed to make things worse by continuing to oppress and try to crush any remaining Druze power.[92] The attitude of the central Ottoman authority provided a further complication. The Ottomans saw the deteriorating regional situation as potentially useful; they hoped it would make the area ultimately more amenable to direct rule from Istanbul. So they were prepared to encourage dissent between the communities and to discourage co-operation between residents and Bashir III.[93] Of course they would be discreet, to avoid upsetting the interested European powers. But the suspicions and resentments were also part of longer-term intercommunal resentments stemming from each community's beliefs that they had developed 'rights' to pre-eminence in the Mount Lebanon region. In this context, the civil war of 1841 and 1842 was predictable, and nasty.

That situation, and later troubles into the 1860s, were complicated by the intervention of Europeans, especially those concerned about the shedding of Christian blood. By this time, with their state considerably weakened, the Ottoman authorities could not afford to simply ignore such intervention, especially the European protests about events in the Lebanon region and the Ottoman failure to control the violence in 1841.[94] The development of the

Tanzimat throughout the Ottoman empire is a good example of this dynamic.[95] Overall, during the *Tanzimat* period (1839–76), the Ottomans made sincere efforts, if only because of European pressure and observation, to include more non-Muslim subjects in their administration.

For the Ottomans, however, the *Tanzimat* provided an advantage: under this policy, the European powers could hardly complain if Lebanese autonomy ended, as long as it apparently aimed to improve administrative efficiency and democratic participation for both Muslims and non-Muslims. As far as Mount Lebanon was concerned, however, the Ottomans' real priority was to bring the region under direct control from Istanbul. Thus they continued, despite assurances to the contrary, to prevent the restoration of stable, if not friendly, co-habitation; they saw continued instability as the only effective way to end Lebanese autonomy without provoking a hostile European intervention.[96] Thus they did little initially to halt the bloodshed in 1841, and they may have even encouraged and armed the Druze. Certainly Ottoman troops joined in against the Maronites on occasion. At other times, they merely stood by and watched the conflict, intervening to protect the Maronites only after damage was done.[97]

The Ottomans, however, were not alone in intriguing to prevent a return to stable co-habitation in 1840–2. In 1841 the Maronite Patriarch wanted to see Bashir II restored. He hoped to create such instability that both communities would be prepared to forget the past and demand his return, and the Ottomans would be forced to endorse it, to the long-term advantage of the Maronite community and church.[98] In intercommunal terms this intriguing destroyed any possibility of peaceful relations, although the communities desperately needed consensus if they were to resist Ottoman efforts at centralisation. When Druze lords sought to reclaim former property, the ensuing series of disputes with the current owners – mainly Maronites – stirred resentments into clashes and a series of massacres of Maronites by Druze, and Druze by Maronites.[99]

Eventually, in late 1841, interested Western powers – notably France and Britain – forced the Ottoman authorities to try harder to settle the dispute.[100] In fact, they took advantage of the clear collapse of Maronite-Druze collaboration, announcing in January 1842 that it was no longer possible to sustain a Lebanese autonomy based on that assumption. The time had come, they said, for a new arrangement, in effect direct Ottoman rule.

The new governor of Mount Lebanon, 'Umar Pasha, appointed in January

1842 after the fall of Bashir III, had no connections with the area. His main objective quickly became clear: to consolidate direct rule by destroying any remnants of the *Imarah* and past autonomy and any hope of a Shihabi restoration. His initial policy was, as far as possible, to gain the support and loyalty of those elements that had opposed the Shihabis. In the Mount Lebanon area this essentially meant the Druze, though he saw some potential for favours among the Maronite lords who had opposed both Bashir II and Bashir III. But despite 'Umar's efforts, Mount Lebanon did not become easier to govern, nor did intercommunal relations improve. Maronite-Druze hostility remained high in the aftermath of the bloodshed. Without incentives to resolve these issues, which would have compromised Ottoman control and risked further European intervention, neither side was willing to co-operate with 'Umar in administering the area.[101]

Intercommunal relations actually disintegrated further as 'Umar Pasha ordered some Druze lands returned to their former owners, and made other concessions to try to reconcile the Druze to his rule. Though he failed, his efforts gave the Druze a renewed sense of superiority over the Maronites in the region, thus increasing Maronite resentment.[102] Despite the great hostility both communities felt towards the imposition of direct Ottoman governmental control, the elites could not bring the communities together. Druze and Maronite leaders met in Mukhtara on 19 November 1843 to discuss a Druze-Maronite pact, but the intercommunal hostility prevented any action, though leaders from both communities did try to rebel against 'Umar Pasha. The elites from both communities, however, continue to refer to the Mukhtara meeting; as Tosh points out, such groups will always seek to promote 'mythical pasts which serve to legitimise their power or win support for particular policies'.[103]

European involvement in the area during the 1840s and 1850s caused further problems, as European governments and missionaries, bringing their own rivalries to the area, were willing to endorse indigenous rival mythologies to boost their standing with different communities.[104] The Maronite Church added another dimension. As the Maronite community became modernised during the nineteenth century, and gradually developed a class system, the traditional Maronite landowning elite lost power, especially outside Mount Lebanon. The church filled the power vacuum, increasingly sustaining and passing on the community's values and traditional culture.

In addition, Maronite clergy such as Bishop Nicola Murad continued to develop a 'Lebanese' historiography, based on the Maronite view of the area's history. This added an academic gloss to long-standing beliefs like the Maronites' direct descent from pre-Arab inhabitants of the Mount Lebanon area.[105] Thus the church had been responsible for collecting many of the community's traditional beliefs and presenting them coherently and authoritatively, and so justifying the development of an exclusive Maronite identity separate from that of the Arab Muslims in the region and throughout the Ottoman empire.[106]

Given its links with Rome, the Maronite Church was naturally hostile to British Protestant missionaries on purely religious grounds, forcing them to turn their attentions to the Druze. But following the church's lead, many Maronites also became hostile on cultural grounds. The religious dimension established in Maronite cultural thinking ensured that in general they saw the British as heretics. Thus they were a threat to the Roman Catholic, and thus the Maronite, Churches, and in turn to Maronite cultural identity. France, by contrast, was a faithful daughter of the Roman Catholic Church, and thus could be seen as a protector of Maronite religious and cultural interests. And established trade links favoured France and linked Maronite economic prosperity to contact with France. The Maronite Church certainly benefited from the community's general prosperity.

By the 1840s, both the Druze and the Maronites were aware that they could use European interest in Lebanon to reduce the impact of Ottoman rule there. In addition, both communities aimed to take advantage of any European intervention. To counteract the positive impact for the Maronites of links with France and the Roman Catholic Church, the Druze sought to use British interest in the region. The British demonstrated their interest through various channels, including the state and Protestant missionaries, who met little success given Druze disregard for their 'civilising' conversion message.

The Druze were mostly interested in the British because they could counterbalance the French and Roman Catholic interest in the Maronites. Support from Britain was also critical to their own resistance to Ottoman direct rule, and to containing Maronite ambitions within Mount Lebanon.[107] From 1841 to 1860, relations between the communities and with Ottoman authority were marked by frequent clashes, which kept the European powers concerned and thus susceptible to appeals from the communities in which they had an interest.

In 1843, the *Imarah* was replaced by a new administrative system proposed

by the European powers and accepted, with some modifications, by the
Ottoman state. The Europeans aimed to restore intercommunal stability;
the Ottomans wanted to increase their central authority.[108] In fact, the new
system served to entrench and formalise the patterns of intercommunal
hostility in the period up to 1860 and gave the Ottomans only a temporary
increase in power. This system involved the division of Mount Lebanon into
two *qa'immaqamiyyah* or administrative districts; the division was theoretically
based on separating the two main religious communities under the direct rule
of an official of their own religion, answerable to the *amir* appointed by the
Ottomans.[109] In practice, the European powers demonstrated how well they
understood the communities involved on the basis of the mythologies they put
forward, with the Maronites in particular claiming primacy in certain locations
rather than seeking a more practically-based division. The area covered by
these *qa'immaqamiyyah* more or less paralleled the area of modern Lebanon:
under Bashir II the area of the *Imarah* had expanded, and the arrangements
of 1843 reflected that expansion.

Whatever the plan, in practice it was impossible to separate two
communities, and the civil war continued under the *qa'immaqamiyyah*. A sizeable
Druze population lived in the official Maronite district, and the majority of
those in the official Druze district were Maronites. This situation ensured that
intercommunal strife would continue, especially since some Druze peasants
had Maronite landlords and vice versa. The peasants were quick to interpret
any harsh policies by landlords as having a confessional dimension, rather
than being simple economic oppression.[110]

Despite various attempts to make the system work effectively, the continuing
intercommunal tension almost guaranteed failure. In some years, such as
1845, the tensions flared into bloody conflict. At other times an apparent
calm reigned, but easily degenerated into hostile incidents. The continuing
Anglo-French involvement clearly sustained the hostility and made it even
more complex.[111] Leading Maronites, including the al-Khazin family, were
increasingly willing to invoke French support against both Ottoman authority
and the Druze.[112] In addition, in the districts the Maronites administered,
divisions also developed within the community. The Maronite administrators
were drawn from the traditional landowning elite, but many ordinary Maronites
and even ordinary clergy opposed their policy of co-operating with Ottoman
authority and Druze elites. Many of the clergy were now drawn from the
people because of the continuing intercommunal violence and resistance to
Islamic rule.[113]

In 1858 the tensions burst out again into full-scale violence, both inter- and intra-communal. The Maronites suffered most; they both felt, and were, at a disadvantage. One reason was their lack of outstanding leaders who could command mass loyalty. This was one consequence of the tensions between the ordinary Maronites and the feudal landowning elites. In the eyes of the masses, the elites who were involved in administering the new system had proved themselves to be untrustworthy and incompetent; hence the revolt of Maronite peasants against their Maronite landlords in Kisrawan.[114] But this was not the only problem. Maronites throughout Lebanon were aware that the anti-Christian feeling was no longer simply local; it was to be felt everywhere in the Ottoman empire since the *Tanzimat* was implemented – with the involvement of Christian Europeans.[115]

Maronites learned about anti-Christian incidents that Ottoman authorities, including the military, had encouraged or at least ignored; these included the massacres of Christians in Damascus, Aleppo and Jerusalem.[116] One key area of tension in Lebanon itself was Kisrawan; the unrest that began there spread to neighbouring areas where it acquired an inter-communal aspect, involving Druze and Maronites.[117] According to Khalaf, Druze leaders in Mount Lebanon generally succeeded in deflecting the grievances of their own Druze peasantry by provoking sectarian rivalry. Mixed areas such as the Shuf and the Matn were particularly vulnerable to this between 1858 and 1860.[118]

Thus the pattern of events in 1859 and 1860 seemed to bear out the worst Maronite fears that the Ottomans were conniving in the massacres. Certainly the Ottoman authorities made no effective attempts to halt the intercommunal violence, which reached a peak between May and August of 1860. Because intracommunal tensions had kept them from banding together to fight the Druze, the Maronites were badly defeated. Then, according to Meir Zamir, 'Within few weeks over 10,000 Christians in Lebanon were massacred and another 100,000 made homeless.'[119]

The events of 1860 have had a lasting effect. Not only were they evoked during 1958, but as recently as 1981, Bashir Gemayel explicitly linked the events of 1975 and the massacres: 'The immediate cause of this war was the threat addressed to the Maronite community by the Druze leader Kamal Jumblat, a threat that could not but awake in our Christian subconscious the memory of the 1845 and 1860 massacres'.[120]

The peace settlement arranged in 1860 made no serious attempt to punish the Druze for their excesses; this further exacerbated the long-term hostility between the communities, and Maronite resentment of Ottoman rule. It did, however, unify the Maronite community.[121] For practical reasons they could do little, given the large numbers involved and their reluctance to stand up and testify against their attackers – which they feared could lead to unchecked reprisals.[122] The ultimate importance of 1860 to Maronite communal mythology was that it provided Maronite martyrs, who could become a focus for shared grief and pride.[123] It also helped to coalesce political feelings in the Maronite community and to further a common Maronite agenda. As Zamir has commented, from their perspective the tragedy 'proved' the need for an autonomous entity.[124]

During this period Europeans were developing concepts of national identity that justified the existence of independent states. Some Maronites, aware of these developments, began to express their ambitions in nationalist terms – including references to a specifically-defined 'national' territory as the rightful location for the Maronite 'nation'.[125] On this basis they began to develop a political agenda including the dream of a 'Lebanese' independence. It found its first expression in 1861, after both Ottomans and Europeans reacted to the events of 1860 and tried to restore stability to Lebanon.

. *The Mutassarifiyyah*

In late 1860 to 1861, another new administrative entity was set up to replace the *qa'immaqamiyyah*. Both Ottomans and Europeans believed that one reason the *qa'immaqamiyyah* had failed was the territory included in the districts; the settlement of 1861 aimed to do better. A *Mutassarifiyyah*, or autonomous province within the empire, was set up to replace the *qa'immaqamiyyah*, regulated by the 1861 *Règlement Organique* and its later modification, the *Protocole* of 1864. The terms of the settlement were worked out in order to modify the impact of central Ottoman control over the area.[126] The Ottomans naturally did their best to restrict this return to autonomy, decreeing that though the governor was to be Christian, he was also to be non-Lebanese or, in other words, not a Maronite.

In practice, however, the arrangement actually involved a series of compromises between the Ottomans and the European powers: first between Druze and Maronite interests; then between the local wish to return to complete autonomy and the Ottoman desire to restrict it; and finally, between

Map of Lebanon in 1862 (from Raymond Eddé's archives).

the Ottomans who wanted to retain full sovereignty over the area and the interested European powers who sought to ensure a role for themselves. The *Règlement Organique* thus represented an official Ottoman recognition of Mount Lebanon's unique autonomous status at a time when they were otherwise trying to centralise the entire empire. For the first time 'Lebanese' identity had acquired a legal definition and was associated with a 'modern' system of administration.[127] Moreover, this new entity was essentially Christian in character, with the Maronites as the dominant element.[128]

While the Maronites welcomed this dimension, territory became a crucial issue for them. The *Mutassarifiyyah* was much smaller than the *Imarah* in 1841–2 and the *qa'immaqamiyyah*; it covered only Mount Lebanon itself and omitted the Beirut, Biqa', Tripoli and Sidon regions. The international commission working out the settlement had intentionally included in the *Mutassarifiyyah* only those regions that had an identifiable 'Christian' (i.e. Maronite) majority, in order to reduce the risk of interconfessional conflicts.[129] For the Maronites, however, Mount Lebanon was not enough: they now knew that in order to claim to be a national group, they had to link that claim to a larger territory, one that could reasonably be described as more than a mere region, and with some natural defining boundaries.

Although the Maronites were given concessions in terms of internal autonomy within the *Mutassarifiyyah*, they were not at all satisfied with the arrangement. In response, they drew on their mythology to develop an argument that 'natural' geographical boundaries to the area 'proved' a Maronite 'historical' claim to predominance within a wider territory. They defined the geographical limits of the 'country' as Nahr al-Kabir in the north, the crest of the Anti-Lebanon in the east, and the Litani River in the south. In geographical terms the quoted lines were not boundaries that defined a discrete territorial unit, but they ignored this fact, relying on myth rather than cold reality.[130]

The Maronites also used myth to make another argument: that their historical claim to the areas was validated by the contemporary fact that most of the Christians (mainly Maronites) in these areas favoured annexation to Mount Lebanon to create a wider entity. This was undoubtedly the case. But it ignored the claims of the Druze and Muslim populations of these areas, who were in the majority. That was the reason they had been excluded from the *Mutassarifiyyah* in the first place.[131] But national cultural feelings were not the only factor behind the Maronite determination to claim these four areas. Also important was a practical consideration: the reduction in area was seriously detrimental to the economy of the *Mutassarifiyyah*. The Maronites realised that Mount Lebanon alone could never be completely autonomous within the Ottoman empire, let alone independent outside it, without an expansion in territory.

The economic problems were complex and varied. Mount Lebanon had little arable land, and no high-grade pasture or open plains for cultivating cereals. It was also cut off from the coast, and thus from access to port facilities and to the external contacts and trade so vital to Maronite prosperity. In addition, the inhabitants of Mount Lebanon had come to rely on imported foodstuffs because their own crops were largely cash crops: silk and tobacco. Without port facilities of their own, they would have to pay heavy tariffs to the Ottoman empire.[132]

Starting in 1861, and continuing until the *Mutassarifiyyah* finally collapsed in 1920, the Maronites repeatedly called for the 'return' of four regions they regarded as integral to their idea of 'Lebanon'. They repeatedly quoted their 'historical', 'geographical' and even economic arguments to justify their claims over these areas, arguing that the *Imarah* had had clear boundaries, which should be restored to their fullest extent. If it was a specious claim, given the fluctuating size of the *Imarah* in historical reality, it was also a necessary one if Maronite 'national' ambitions were to be realized, politically or economically. The Maronite reasoning to this effect reveals how sophisticated their political mythology – and its expression – had become.[133]

In their restricted territory under the *Mutassarifiyyah*, the Maronites continued to feel vulnerable both to Ottoman attempts to restrict their autonomy and to Druze hostility. Almost immediately, they began to express their dissatisfaction with the new arrangements, both administrative and territorial. They developed a political agenda, supported by the Patriarch, as the terms of the *Règlement Organique* became clear in 1861; to best safeguard current Maronite autonomy they sought the return of a Shihabi Maronite as governor instead of a Christian Ottoman representative.[134] This agenda provided an opportunity. The group, which I believe can be called a nationalist Maronite movement, seized this opportunity to further the cause of Maronite autonomy.

Its leader was Yussuf Karam, a Maronite from the North. Its supporters were generally influenced by the Western ideas on nationalism described above, including the territorial definition of 'Lebanon'; they were also inspired by the patriotic 'Lebanese' history portrayed by writers like Nicola Murad. Convinced by Western-inspired ideas to express their patriotic feelings through a political agenda demanding independent national status within a defined territory, the movement rebelled openly in 1861 against Ottoman authority and the administrative system in Mount Lebanon. When their 1861 uprising was defeated, Karam went into temporary exile. But the grievances that had inspired the movement – and had gained it wide support – remained. Karam tried a second rebellion in 1866, but that, too, was defeated.

Though Karam went into permanent exile in 1867, his actions gave the Maronites a popular hero with whom to identify their national feelings and their resistance to the *Mutassarifiyyah*'s limits. Though it would not endorse open rebellion, the Maronite Church also supported him and his ideas, thus helping to solidify his profile as hero.[135] Another piece of the Maronite myth was born. As Zamir has pointed out, 'The strong support [Karam] continued to receive even after his expulsion proved how deeply nationalist ideas were already rooted in the Maronite community.'[136]

Once these two rebellions failed, however, the Maronites had little hope of expanding the *Mutassarifiyyah*. The European powers approved the administration of the entity as successive governors set up measures to ensure administrative honesty and efficiency and developed public works programmes to build a sound infrastructure for Mount Lebanon. But despite these efforts, between 1861 and 1914 many Maronites emigrated from the *Mutassarifiyyah* to Beirut and overseas to places like the US, Egypt, and West Africa.[137] This exodus, however, hardly eroded Maronite communal feeling, and in fact deepened it amongst both those who went and those who stayed. France played a significant role in this development, endorsing Maronite national claims in its political and intellectual rhetoric, though not in terms of active interference.[138] As a community and a culture, the Maronites flourished between 1861 and 1914.

By contrast, the various Muslim communities in the area of modern Lebanon, whether inside or outside the *Mutassarifiyyah*, were far less satisfied. They all resented the new concessions granted to the Maronites and other Christians. The Druze were especially resentful, as so many lived within the *Mutassarifiyyah*. As effective cultural and economic contacts between the Maronites and the West increased, and as the Maronites became more prosperous and vocal in their demands, these communities had to watch the Ottoman empire decline ever more rapidly, culturally, politically and economically.

If the Maronites feared the long-term consequences of not having their own coastal access, Muslims increasingly feared what they saw as unofficial Christian expansionism and domination. After 1861, Salibi says, the Druze were 'reconciled … to their status as a minority'.[139] But acceptance, *faute de mieux,* is hardly the same as being permanently reconciled and renouncing past hostilities. Rather, they continued co-habitation, realising they had little other option. The other Muslim communities found similar ways to cope with this increased practical and cultural Maronite self-confidence.

As the Maronites grew confident in their increasingly coherent 'national' culture, the Muslim communities had little to compare to it, and certainly nothing that could be termed a national feeling. But missionaries working amongst the Druze and the Sunnis did have an impact, as they taught literacy and set up an Arabic press.[140] By around 1900 the Druze and Sunnis had become far more literate than before. This equipped the intellectuals among them to explore Western ideas, extracting those concepts that did not directly conflict with Islam, and using them to create coherent and widely acceptable cultural concepts. In contrast, as Maronites developed their own cultural ideas, they cherished the Western contact for its own sake. But as they did among the Maronites, such skills promoted the spread of more uniform versions of Druze and Sunni myth-based community identity.

In addition, an Arabic literary revival developed in the Islamic world in the late 1800s. Centred in Beirut, it sought to draw on an indigenous cultural tradition in the area, not a Western one, in evolving a mythology. While this movement involved both Christians and Muslims, its most important effect was to encourage a wider cultural reawakening amongst Muslims generally, and the Lebanese Muslims saw this clearly. Drawing on ideas initially put forward by Christian Arabs, they evolved a concept of 'nationalism' that drew essentially on the idea of Arabia rather than being pan-Islamic.

The leaders of this movement looked back to a pre-Islamic origin and then to a golden age in the early days of Islam, and went on to argue that the days of Arab glory had been stolen by the Persians and the Turks. Now, they argued, Arabs had the opportunity to rediscover Arab history and make it the basis of a great new cultural and national movement that was essentially secular.[141] Interestingly, as Muslim historiography developed and raised interest in a past golden age, the Muslim element in the region began to see the period of the Crusades as significant to their myths, especially those characterising the Maronites.

For example, during the period of the Crusader kingdoms (1098–1291), part of the region of Lebanon had been under Christian rule, and the first real links between the Roman Catholic and Maronite Churches had developed. Moreover, while some Maronites did clash with the Crusaders, many others supported them, either actively or passively.[142] Muslim historians began to research this period from their own perspective and, ignoring the evidence of earlier Muslim co-operation, began to argue that Muslims had long-standing reasons, as well as the more recent ones, to resent the Maronite population in Lebanon.[143]

Such ideas made a certain amount of progress in Lebanon, as elsewhere, in the years around 1900. They helped restore some pride among the Lebanese Muslim communities, and a sense that theirs was a worthwhile culture with long historical roots to give it global credibility. Still, it was not nationalist in the way that the Maronite cultural feeling had become. Rather, they sensed themselves as part of a greater Arab entity, one that included Lebanon within 'Syria', Iraq and Arabia.

The Early 1900s

In the final case study of this chapter I focus on the period 1908–9, when a series of events accelerated cultural and national developments, and differences between the Maronite and Muslim communities of Lebanon, and further coalesced their different communal agendas and perceptions of one another. In Turkey, the decline of the Ottoman empire had encouraged the development of an essentially secular Turkish nationalism, encapsulated in the so-called Young Turk movement. It aimed to restore the central authority of the Ottomans in an essentially modern and secular way, and required eradicating any separatist feeling within the Ottoman empire, whether Christian or Arabist.[144] The army's involvement in the Young Turk revolt was particularly ominous for the non-Turkish parts of the empire, as it gave the Young Turks a way to enforce their policies of Turkification.[145]

Until this time the Muslim Arabs of Lebanon had been willing to accept the Turks as brothers in Islam, even if they did blame them for denigrating Arab culture by wresting control of the Islamic world from them. But the activities of the Young Turk regime left them feeling alienated and resentful.[146] In response, popular Arab feeling developed more quickly in areas like Lebanon, where Arab elites were beginning to protest the Young Turk policies, demanding that specifically Arab entities be recognised and protected in special administrative entities.

At the same time the Maronites and other Christians in the region of Lebanon were distinctly alarmed by the Young Turks. While they still expected European protection of their special status, they were alarmed to see Europeans apparently approving the developments the Young Turks initiated.[147] Hence Abbé Louis al-Khazin appealed to Pius X, begging the Pope to assure '*la sécurité de la nation Maronite au Liban et a préserver sa foi dans des situations critiques*'.[148] Even if the Young Turks' plans did not mean an automatic end to the *Mutassarifiyyah*, the Maronites feared they would interfere with their continuing plans for independent status and demands to expand their territory.

After the Young Turks set up their regime in 1908, the Arabic cultural reawakening in Lebanon had one obvious result. A group of Christians – some of them Maronites – who supported the concept of Arab nationalism, came together with members of the Muslim elite to develop and promote an essentially 'Arab' mythology. The collaboration was limited by its small membership and its lack of a practical agenda. Some historians, however, have identified this as the start of modern Arab nationalism, with real implications for separating Lebanon from the Ottoman empire and instituting a nation-state of Lebanon based on a compromise between Christian and Muslim elements.[149]

Such interpretations, however, gloss over the very different agendas. The Maronites, in particular, sought full independence from Ottoman rule, while the Muslims would have been content with an arrangement guaranteeing special status to an Arab homeland within the empire. The Muslims in Syria and Lebanon hoped to invoke British support for this arrangement, basing their claim on their interpretation of a great Arabic historical and cultural heritage and a shared language.[150] By 1912 these demands were alarming the Maronites; they feared that an Arab empire would still be essentially Islamic in character and that Western forces – especially the British – might support the Arab case over theirs. Were such an empire set up, they feared they would lose even the autonomy they had under the *Mutassarifiyyah*.[151] The Maronites were undoubtedly more frightened by Muslim attitudes towards them in both Lebanon and the region, in the years 1911–14, when popular pan-Islamic feelings were sparked by fears of foreign invasion, by resentment of the

Turkish programme of intervention and, above all, by the humiliation of Turkish armies in the Balkan wars.[152]

With the Ottoman empire clearly on the brink of collapse, the Lebanese Muslims had corresponding fears for their future. They viewed the active French involvement in the region as a sign of imminent occupation. They were convinced that occupation would lead to the creation of a Maronite Lebanese state with a Muslim minority at the mercy of the Maronites, including areas of real importance to the Sunnis, Druze and Shi'ites. To forestall such developments, Muslim leaders sought to reform the area's overall administration, including all the areas the Maronites coveted.

In this context Muslim leaders sought to enlist Maronite acceptance of continued existence within the Ottoman empire in an autonomous, essentially Arab entity covering the area of Lebanon. They offered to share representation equally in any future administration, even though the Christians would, numerically, be a minority in any such province.[153] Some Christians, even some Maronites, liked the idea, though it won little widespread Christian support.[154] With the Turks increasingly crushing both Arab and Maronite separatist efforts in 1913, a genuine degree of co-operation did begin to emerge, even without a concrete agenda for any joint future. But it was still more like co-habitation, based as it was on mutual hostility to the current Turkish regime rather than on cultural unity based on shared local feelings and ambitions. The Maronites still sought independence, and most Muslims still sought autonomy within the empire.

It was in this atmosphere, then, that in the two years before World War I the Maronites developed various societies and communities as centres for political activity to achieve the goal of an independent political state. Despite their small memberships, these groups had a great influence on the expression of Maronite Christian aspirations in national terms.[155] In addition, they presided over an expansion of the secular element in Maronite communal feeling, as many were Western-educated lawyers and journalists, less susceptible to the control of the Maronite Church.[156] These groups sustained the links with France, through secret contacts with French representatives, laying the ground for Maronite involvement in setting up the Mandate. Their objective was an independent Lebanon with extended boundaries, but as an entity under French protection. Such developments could not improve co-operation between Maronites and Muslims,[157] especially as World War I began. They were to have a crucial impact on community relations in Lebanon.

The Turkish regime, allied with Germany, installed in Lebanon a Muslim Ottoman governor – Ahmed Jamal Pasha – who was especially harsh on anyone with separatist aspirations. Thus Maronites and Muslim Arab nationalists became particular targets, especially because of their links with the Allies.[158] A number were executed, adding to the list of Maronite 'nationalist' martyrs and creating 'Arab nationalist' ones. But 1916 saw the beginnings of dramatic change for the Ottoman empire and thus for Lebanon. Encouraged by the British, Arabs revolted throughout the Ottoman empire in the Middle East.

In Lebanon, the resulting collapse of Ottoman authority left an Arab administration in charge, under the leadership of 'Umar al-Da'uq, a local Sunni Muslim leader. In 1918 Faisal, the son of Sharif Hussein, arrived in Lebanon with a token force to signify endorsement of this development, as part of his claim to setting up an Arab kingdom including all of Syria and Lebanon. The Maronites were dismayed, and the Muslim communities delighted, but these feelings were swiftly reversed as the victorious European powers intervened. Their role in the region is my focus in the next chapter. They were also affected by the myths, and often considered them when they formulated policy, rather than basing policy on a dispassionate assessment of the situation.

Notes

1. Jan Vansina, *Oral Tradition as History*, James Currey, London, 1985, p. 120. Throughout this chapter, much of my interpretation relates to 'the community's present-day self-image put into time perspective', rather than being a dispassionate account of the region's history. But it is precisely this contemporary perspective on the past that is crucial to this book. John Tosh, *The Pursuit of History*, Longman, London, 1984, p. 224.

2. Raphael Samuel and Paul Thompson, *The Myths We Live By*, Routledge, London, 1990, pp. 14–15, 25.

3. Vansina, pp. 21–2.

4. Selim Abou, *L'Identité Culturelle, Relations Inter-ethniques et Problèmes d'Acculturation*, Editions Anthropos, Paris, 1981, p. 42.

5. J. E. McGratto, *Social and Psychological Factors in Stress*, Rinehart and Winston, New York, 1970, chapters 9, 10, 11, 14; N.J. Demereth III and Richard A. Peterson, *System, Change and Conflict*, The Free Press, New York, 1976.

6. See, for example, K. S. Salibi, *A House of Many Mansions. The History of Lebanon Reconsidered*, I.B. Tauris, London, 1988, p. 58; Engin Akarli, *The Long Peace. Ottoman Lebanon 1861–1920*, University of California Press, Berkeley, 1993, p. 6; Antoine Nasri Messara, *Théorie Générale du Système Politique Libanais*, Cariscript, Paris, 1994; Phillippe Hitti, *Lebanon in History. From the Earliest Times to the Present*, Macmillan, London, 1957.

7. See, for example, Henri Lammens, 'Inventaire des Richesses Archeologiques du Liban', *al-Machriq*, Beirut, vol, 1. 1898, and also the 1914 edition of this work.

8. Salibi, pp. 4, 12.

9. For instance, see Dominique Chevallier, *La Société du Mont-Liban à l'Epoque de la Révolution Industrielle en Europe*, Librairie Orientaliste, Paul Geuthner, Paris, 1971, p. 21; Salibi, p. 27.

10. An important element in Maronite craftwork offered for sale today in Artisanats remains pieces of embroidery featuring the letters of the Phoenician alphabet. See also Phillippe Hitti, *History of the Arabs: From the Earliest Times to the Present*, Macmillan Education, Basingstoke, 10th edn, 1970 (1st edn 1937), p. 71.

11. Salibi points out the 'basically polemical nature of Maronite historiography' as well as the origins of that historiography in the West, among Rome-trained clerics, K.S. Salibi, 'The Traditional Historiography of the Maronites' in B. Lewis and P. Holt, eds, *Historians of the Middle East*, Oxford University Press, Oxford, 1962, pp. 212–16.

12. Or at least he found it politic not to indicate his disagreement in any way. Hitti, *Lebanon in History*; see also Salibi, *House of Many Mansions*, p. 173.

13. For indications of the implicit use that Maronite academics, other than Phillippe Hitti, make of this issue, see Jawad Boulos, who has argued, for instance, that Mount Lebanon has been densely populated ever since the Phoenician period; Jawad Boulos, *Tarikh Lubnan* [History of Lebanon], Dar an-Nahar lil Nashr, Beirut, 1972, p. 53; see also Henri Seyrig, 'Statuettes Trouvées dans les Montagnes du Liban', in Dominique Chevallier, ed., *La Société du Mont-Liban à L'Epoque de la Révolution Industrielle en Europe*, Syria, 1953, pp. 5, 39, 47. The popular affection for this myth is illustrated by the attention given to the discovery of the Phoenician walls in the centre of Beirut. See *an-Nahar*, 5 June 1995. The most famous contemporary Lebanese poet, Said Akl, is the symbol of this school of thought; and one book of his verse is even titled 'Phoenicianism'. Boutros Khawand devoted a whole chapter to the Phoenicians in his study of the Katai'b Party; see Khawand, *al-Quwat al-Nizamiat al-Kata'ibiat* [The Kata'ib Organised Forces], Habib Eid Publishing, Beirut, 1986.

14. For example, Jean Hayek, *al-Tarikh al-Ilmi* [The Scientific History], al-Jizq al-Awal Maktabith Habib, Beirut, 1994, aimed at 12- to 13-year-olds, traces Lebanon's history from Phoenician times. Walid Jumblat, current leader of the largest Druze faction, made links between the events of 1958 and incidents in more recent Lebanese history, especially the fact that the Maronites have 'always denied our Arab origin in favour of claiming the Phoenicians as their ancestors just to refute this Arab origin', thus underlining the continuing impact of this myth.

15. For instance, see *an-Nahar*, 5 June 1995.

16. Amine Gemayel, *Peace and Unity: Major Speeches 1982–1984*, Colin Smythe, London, 1984, p. 120.

17. Monothelitism, in theological terms, represents 'an attempt at compromise' between the doctrinal positions taken by the Western (or Roman) church and the Eastern church, and groups such as the Nestorians: 'the Monotheletes ... held that Christ had two natures but one will', according to Hourani's brief summary. Albert Hourani, *A History of the Arab Peoples*, Faber and Faber, London, 1991, pp. 8–9.

18. Benedict Anderson, *Imagined Communities*, Verso, London, 1991, pp. 12–13.

19. Salibi argues that the Druze actually became Druze in a religiously identifiable sense in Mount Lebanon, as had the Maronites. See Salibi, *House of Many Mansions*, p. 12.

20. Karam Rizk, *Le Mont Liban au XIXe Siècle de L'Emirat au Mutasarrifiyyah*, Publication de l'Université St Esprit, Kaslik, Lebanon, 1994, pp. 43–5; Sami Makarem Nasib, *The*

Druze Faith, Caravan Books, New York, 1974, p. 28; Robert Brenton Betts, *The Druze,* Yale University Press, 1988; Toufic Touma, *Paysans et Institutions Féodale chez les Druze et les Maronites du Liban du 18e Siècle à 1914*, publications de l'Université Libanaise, Beirut, 1971, p. 22.

21.   Charles H. Codey, *Social Organisation*, Harper and Row, New York, 1962, pp. 23–31; Kenneth P. Laughton, *Political Socialisation*, Oxford University Press, Oxford, 1969, pp. 3–20, 140–179; Gabriel Almond and B. Powell, *Comparative Politics. A Developmental Approach*, Little Brown and Co., Boston, 1966, pp. 64–72; Edward Shils, 'The Prospect of Lebanese Civility', in L. Binder, ed., 1966; *Politics in Lebanon,* John Wiley, New York, 1966, p. 966; Kenneth Laughton, *Political Socialisation*, Oxford University Press, Oxford, 1969, pp. 3–20, 140–179; Anderson, p. 6.

22.   With the exception of the period 1098 to 1291 when the coastal and northern areas were part of the Christian crusader kingdoms.

23.   Generally, the Islamic empires showed greater tolerance for the Christian communities in their jurisdictions than the Byzantine empire had usually shown towards religious minorities; such tolerance was usually part of the ruling policy of the Islamic empires. See N. A. Faris and M. T. Husayn, *The Crescent in Crisis*, University of Kansas Press, Lawrence, 1955, p. 108.

24.   The majority elements in the intercommunal mix had been settled in the region of modern Lebanon by the end of the eleventh century. They included a variety of Christian communities, notably the Greek Orthodox and Greek Catholics; a sizeable Shi'ite community was settled mainly in parts of the Biqa' Valley, and the Sunni population was in the coastal areas of modern Lebanon, especially in the developing towns there.

25.   See Churchill's comments on this in the nineteenth century. Charles H. Churchill, *The Druze and the Maronites under Turkish Rule from 1840 to 1860*, first published London, 1862, republished Garnet Publications, London, 1994.

26.   Samuel and Thompson, pp. 18–19. They point out that such a reaction is common for excluded groups, as well as the invocation of 'collective memory and myth'.

27.   Periodically, the Druze were severely persecuted by Ottoman authorities, especially near the beginning of the Ottoman period, during the sixteenth century. Despite this, even European powers in the region, such as the French, saw the Druze as an integral part of the Ottoman empire. See Salibi, *House of Many Mansions*. For the Ottoman persecution of the Druze see Abdul Rahim Abu Hussein, 'The Korkmaz Question: A Maronite Historian's Plea for Ma'nid Legitimacy', *al-Abhath*, XXXIV, 1986, pp. 7–8; Rahim Hussein, 'The Ottoman Invasion of the Shuf in 1585: A Reconsideration', *al-Abhath*, XXXIII, pp. 13–21.

28.   Hourani, p. 221.

29.   *Ibid.*, p. 240.

30.   Abdul Rahim Abu Hussein, 'Problems in the Ottoman Administration during the 16th and 17th Centuries: the Case of the Sanjak of Sidon-Beirut', *International Journal of Middle East Studies*, 24, 1992, pp. 666–70; Chevallier, p. 9; See also Betts, p. 54.

31.   Abdul Rahim Abu Hussein, 'The Feudal System of Mount Lebanon as Depicted by Nasif al-Yaziji', in S. Seikaly, R. Baalbaki, P. Dodd (eds), *Quest for Understanding: Arabic and Islamic Studies in Memory of Malcolm H. Kerr,* American University of Beirut, Beirut, 1991, pp. 36–40. He argues that certainly in the period up to the mid-nineteenth century, the social organisation of the Druze community was more 'tribal' than feudal. Salibi, however, considered the organisation of the Druze as essentially feudal, at least by the end of the nineteenth century. See Salibi, *The Modern History*

of Lebanon, Caravan Books, New York, 1990, p. xxi. Perhaps we can reconcile these two perspectives by seeing the last half of the nineteenth century as the period of transformation from tribal to feudal for the Druze.

32. Abdul Rahim Abu Hussein, 'The Korkmaz Question', pp. 3–5; Salibi, *House of Many Mansions*.

33. Abdul Rahim Abu Hussein, 'The Feudal System of Mount Lebanon', pp. 33, 37–8.

34. Families such as the Shihab, the Eddé, the al-Khazin and the Gemayel families, for instance.

35. There is some debate over the parallels that can be drawn. Chevallier argues for important distinctions while Harik draws clear parallels between Lebanese feudalism in this period and that of the European Middle Ages; see Chevallier, p. 85; Iliya Harik, *Politics and Change in a Traditional Society; Lebanon 1711–1845*, Princeton University Press, New Jersey, 1968, pp. 37–8; Abdul Rahim Abu Hussein, *Provincial Leaderships in Syria, 1575–1650*, American University of Beirut, Beirut, 1985, pp. 70–81.

36. Samuel and Thompson, pp. 140–1.

37. Quoted in Salibi, *House of Many Mansions*, p. 163.

38. Lewis points out that the Crusaders had first 'opened the way' to closer commercial relations between the Muslim world of the Middle East and the Christian West, and that these became more regular and sustained from the sixteenth century. In the region of Lebanon the Maronites took most advantage of this. See Bernard Lewis, 'The Use by Muslim Historians of Non-Muslim Sources', in Lewis and Holt, eds, *Historians of the Middle East*, p. 182. See also Maurice Shihab, *Le Rôle du Liban dans l'Histoire de la Soie*, University of Lebanon Press, Beirut, 1968 and Rizk, pp. 198–215, for details of the silk trade in Lebanon.

39. Claude Dubar and Salim Nasr, *Les Classes Sociales au Liban*, Presse de la Fondation Nationale des Sciences Politiques, Paris, 1976, pp. 13–14.

40. See, for instance, Edward Said, *Culture and Imperialism*, Chatto and Windus, London, 1993, pp. 230–1.

41. Salibi, *House of Many Mansions*, p. 117.

42. Historians use the term *Imarah*, but it was not used by the Ottomans at the time. They referred to it as an *Iltizam*, a term used for the farming out of taxes.

43. The favoured *amirs* were effectively rewarded by being given extra administrative districts removed from less successful *amirs*.

44. Fakhr al-Din died in 1635. See Salibi, *The Modern History of Lebanon*, Caravan Books, New York, 1977, p. 3. Abu Hussein provides an alternative interpretation of the origins of the *Imarah*; he argues that in fact, the historical validity of seeing Fakhr al-Din as the founder of the *Imarah* is dubious, though most modern Lebanese historians support this view. He argues that the *Imarah* had 'no real existence before 1667, when Ahmad Ma'n' came to power. See Abu Hussein, 'The Korkmaz Question', pp. 3–4. In this book, however, the importance of popular communal belief justifies my presenting the established arguments, rather than considering such an alternative in depth.

45. Underlining the importance of this, Walid Jumblat has argued that a rewriting of such texts to eradicate 'Christian-fabricated myths' would be essential to any 'lasting political settlement in Lebanon'. Salibi, *House of Many Mansions*, pp. 200–202.

46. A modern view might see Fakhr al-Din as a Syrian strongman given an opportunity by the Ottoman state to subdue and destroy local leaderships in Mount Lebanon on their behalf who actually succeeded in achieving a 'symbiosis' between the Maronites of Kisrawan and the Druze of the Shuf. Salibi, *ibid*. For an older view, see Michel

Chebli, *Une Histoire du Liban a L'Epoque des Emirs*, Librairie Orientale, Beirut, 1955; Adel Ismail, *Histoire du Liban du 17ème Siècle à nos Jours. Le Liban au Temps de Fakhr al-Din II (1590–1633)*, Maisonneuve, Paris, 1959, Vol I, p. 11; Chebli argues that 'l'Histoire des Shihabs est l'histoire d'une résistance. C'est l'histoire d'une communauté Nationale, faite de commun autés confessionelles établies sur une montagne maritime qui leur sert d'inviolable réfuge et unis pour la défense et la preservation de leurs libertés spirituelles et temporelles'.

47. On this point, see, for instance, M. S. Anderson, *The Eastern Question 1774–1928: A Study in International Relations*, Macmillan, London, 1966.

48. See Chapter Two for more detailed discussion of the European intervention and perspective on events in this area.

49. Hussein, 'The Korkmaz Question', pp. 3–4; Akarli, p. 17; K. S. Salibi, *Histoire du Liban du 18ème Siècle à nos Jours*, Nawfal Publishers, Beirut, 1988, pp. 38–114. Fakhr al-Din was 'sent in chains to Istanbul where he was put to death by strangling in 1635', Salibi, *Modern History of Lebanon*, p. 3.

50. Hussein, 'The Korkmaz Question', p. 3, points out that the Shihabs were related through the female line to the Ma'ns, giving the Shihabs a certain legitimacy in the eyes of local elites.

51. At first, these leading elements were essentially the landed elites of both communities. Over the period of the *Imarah* these leading elements expanded, especially amongst the Maronite community, to include the educated classes, often with a strong clerical element, and the commercial/mercantile classes. This co-operative spirit had little impact on the lower orders of society in each community, as is indicated by the constant danger of small-scale intercommunal violence, which was mostly kept in check by local leaders.

52. See Frank Bailey, *British Policy and the Turkish Reform Movement: A Study in Anglo-Turkish Relations, 1826–1835*, Harvard University Press, Cambridge, Mass., p. 42; Matti Moosa, *The Maronites in Modern Times*, p. 281; Touma, p. 66.

53. Abu Hussein, 'Problems in the Ottoman Administration', pp. 671–3; K. S. Salibi, 'The Lebanese Emirate, 1667–1841', *al-Abhath*, XX, 3, 1967

54. Touma, pp. 23–4.

55. Albert Hourani, 'Lebanon: The Development of a Political Society' in L. Binder, ed., *Politics in Lebanon*, p. 15.

56. For further details of the relations between the Shihabi *amirs* and the Druze, see Salibi, *Modern History of Lebanon*, pp. 6–12.

57. Historians are currently debating which Druze factions were involved. Relying on the work of a nineteenth-century historian, Nasif al-Yaziji, they have traditionally seen this battle as taking place between the Qaysi and the Yemeni. Abu Hussein argues that it was, in fact, between the Yazbaki and the Jumblats. See Abu Hussein, 'The Feudal System of Mount Lebanon', pp. 39–41; Salibi, *Histoire du Liban*, pp. 50–3.

58. Salibi, *Histoire du Liban*, pp. 52–3.

59. Matti Moosa, *The Maronites in History*, Syracuse University Press, 1986, pp. 220–21; 280; K. S. Salibi, 'The Maronite Church in the Middle Ages and its Union with Rome', *Orients Christianne*, XLII, 1958, pp. 92–104; Nasser Gemayel, *Les changes Culturels entre les Maronites et l'Europe du Collège Maronite de Rome (1584) au Collège de Ayn Warqa (1789)*, no publisher, Beirut, 1984, 2 vols.

60. Nasser Gemayel; Harik, p. 130. Harik gives the examples of Ibn Quilan, the earliest Maronite writer, and of Istfan al-Duwayhi (1629–1704) Maronite Patriarch, as stressing the 'unbroken orthodoxy' of the Maronite faith. Many Maronite historians

were priests, and they have effectively glossed over the earlier monothelistic heresy of the Maronite Church, while stressing the Western origins and orientation of the community as a whole, something they argued was 'proved' by the closeness of the Maronite and Roman Catholic Churches. Salibi, 'The Traditional Historiography of the Maronites', pp. 213–4.

61. Salibi points out that though in fact the Maronites 'remained comparatively free from Muslim tutelage', they were a people 'on the defensive as a community and as a Church'. Salibi, *ibid.*, pp. 215–6.

62. Anderson, pp. 12–13; Salibi, *House of Many Mansions*, p. 113.

63. *Ibid.*, p. 216.

64. This is not to say that only the Maronite community benefitted economically from the silk trade; it did, however, benefit the most. See Chevallier, p. 137.

65. The presence of disease in the mulberry trees of Italy and France and the demand for silk from centres such as Lyons ensured that the French merchants who were particularly involved in the trade were very eager to foster the trade and see that all sides benefited financially. See Shihab; Rizk, pp. 200–201; Chevallier, p. 201.

66. Harik, p. 170; Moosa, *The Maronites in History*, p. 284.

67. Salibi, *Histoire du Liban*, p. 53.

68. Of course, other Christian communities such as the Greek Orthodox also benefited from these developments. In this chapter, however, I focus on the Maronites.

69. Salibi, *Histoire du Liban*, p. 74.

70. Salibi, *House of Many Mansions*, pp. 109–10.

71. Samir Khalaf, *Lebanon's Predicament*, Columbia University Press, New York, 1987, pp. 32–3. Members of the landed elite were involved only in a limited way and around particular agendas. Among those involved were two of Bashir's own cousins who wanted the emirate for themselves, along with their immediate supporters. So while it was largely a rebellion of the lower orders it did have a wider constituency. This rebellion even included some of the personnel of the Maronite Church, which was now recruiting from the lower orders, something the educational system it had instituted made possible.

72. Maronite leaders of the uprising tried, but failed, to involve the Druze. See Khalaf, p. 35.

73. *Ibid.*, pp. 32–35.

74. Joseph Tyan, 'Patriarch of the Maronite Church, to Pope Pius VII', 24 October 1818, in the unpublished al-Khazin family papers.

75. *Ibid.*, p. 35. Khalaf argues also that the rising 'embodied a nationalist fervor and a desire to seek independence from Ottoman control'. However, this is taking matters to an unsustainable extreme: a continuance of autonomy, yes; outright independence was not yet an issue.

76. For details of the dispute involving Abdallah Pasha of Acre, Muhammad Darwish of Damascus and Bashir himself, leading to the exiles of both Abdallah Pasha and Bashir and the installation of Muhammad Darwish in Acre as well as Damascus; see Salibi, *Modern History of Lebanon*, pp. 25–6.

77. Akarli, pp. 22–3.

78. Salibi, *Modern History of Lebanon*, p. 26.

79. Because Bashir was determined to make his victory complete, he arranged for Jumblat to be returned from Damascus, where he had taken refuge, to Acre, where he was conveniently strangled, thus robbing the Druze of their most prominent leader at the time. Bashir also had other Druze leaders arrested and confiscated Druze

property on a widespread basis. Though Druze leaders then appealed to Ottoman central authority, and were indeed granted decrees for the return of their property, etc, neither that authority nor the Druze were, in the aftermath of this defeat, able to enforce the *firmans* (written orders or decrees) granted against Bashir. See Salibi, *Modern History of Lebanon*, pp. 26–7.

80. *Ibid.*, p. 27.

81. *Ibid.*, p. 28.

82. Khalaf, p. 35–6. Khalaf points out that the period of Egyptian control led to an expansion in foreign trade, and not just with Europe, as well as to other administrative developments.

83. Salibi, *Modern History of Lebanon,* pp. 34–6; p. 40; Touma, p. 145.

84. The European powers were prepared to support Ottoman authority at least partly because the Ottoman empire had begun a programme of administrative reforms, encouraging centralisation and collectively known as the *Tanzimat*, which seemed to be in line with European developments at this time. For a Lebanese perspective on this, see Salibi, *Modern History of Lebanon*, p. 40.

85. The British took him into exile in Malta.

86. Khalaf, p. 37.

87. Salibi, *Modern History of Lebanon*, pp. 40–4.

88. *Ibid.*, pp. 49–52.

89. Salibi, *House of Many Mansions*, pp. 109–10, points out that Maronites in the twentieth century still viewed Bashir II as an essentially benevolent despot, while the Druze in particular typecast him as a malign figure in history.

90. Harik, pp. 225–7; Leila Fawaz, *An Occasion for War*, I.B. Tauris, London, 1994, pp. 21–3.

91. Touma, p. 136–47.

92. Salibi, *Modern History of Lebanon*, p. 45.

93. *Ibid.*, p. 46.

94. Akarli, p. 27.

95. See note 84 above and H. Lammens, *La Syrie Précis Historique*, Dar Lahad Khater, Beirut, 1994, p. 303.

96. Rizk, pp. 170–1.

97. Churchill, pp. 52–6; Salibi, *Modern History of Lebanon*; Rizk, p. 239; Akarli, p. 30; Joseph Abou Nohra, 'L'Evolution du Système Politique Libanais dans le Contexte des Conflits Régionaux et Locaux, 1840–1864', in Shehadi and Mills, *eds*, *Lebanon: A History of Conflict and Consensus*, I.B. Tauris, London, 1988, p. 42.

98. In contemporary perspective, this was perhaps less unlikely as it might appear now. After all, Bashir II had returned before from exile, and he was a son of the Maronite church, which had also benefited from his emirate. The Patriarch's efforts to restore the Shihabis ended in 1845 when Bashir II's son, Amine, became a Sunni Muslim.

99. See Salibi, *Modern History of Lebanon*, pp. 49–52, for some discussion of events in this period.

100. Akarli, p. 31; Churchill, p. 132; Hitti, p. 438.

101. Abou Nohra, pp. 42–3.

102. The level of Maronite fears about Ottoman policy at this point, and the fact that the Ottoman authorities made no real attempt to relieve those fears, is indicated by a letter of 1847: '*Il est possible que les habitants de la Montagne en voyant enlever leurs armes croient que quelques anciens privilèges que la Sublime Porte leur a accordé relativement à l'administration arrêtée ici, de concert avec les représentants des 5 grandes puissances, et que votre*

excellence est chargée d'établir seront modifiés et changés, et que cette idée inspire de la frayeur. Ou la Sublime Porte n'a aucune pensée à pareille chose'. Letter extract from a *Vizir* (unidentified) to *Amir* Chekib Effendi, 12 November 1847, in the unpublished al-Khazin family papers.

103. Tosh, p. 20; Salibi, *House of Many Mansions*, p. 203.

104. Akarli, Chapters 2 and 3; Rizk, p. 226.

105. Salibi argues that Maronite historians have never clearly understood 'the relationship of Maronite and Lebanese history to the history of Muslim Syria and Islam'; also that 'historiographical isolation led Maronite historians to depend only on predecessors and so repeat them'. In other words, they had little will to understand the broader context of this history. Salibi, 'The Traditional Historiography of the Maronites', pp. 216–7. See also Harik, pp.126, 140.

106. Harik, pp. 128, 142.

107. Akarli, p. 27.

108. In other words, it imposed another layer of administration between the *amir* and the population of the old *Imarah*. See John Spagnolo, *France and Ottoman Lebanon*, St Anthony's College, Oxford, 1977, p. 38.

109. The line of division ran roughly along the Beirut-Damascus highway with the Maronites to the north and the Druze to the south, with the northern district administered by a Maronite official and the southern one by a Druze official.

110. Salibi, The *Modern History of Lebanon*, p. 63.

111. Yussuf Karam to Patriarch Boulos Massad, extract from letter quoted in Salibi, *Modern History of Lebanon*, p. 79.

112. See, for instance, French Consul in Beirut to Shaykh Wadih; Shaykh Elias and Shaykh Wablin al-Khazin, 4 September 1845, responding to Maronite pleas for intervention. For discussion of the European perspective on such pleas, see Chapter Two.

113. Salibi, *Modern History of Lebanon*, pp. 18–19, comments on the international implications of this; also Rizk, p. 153.

114. Another complication was the gap between the secular Maronite landed elite and the Maronite Church leadership at this point. In November 1854, Bishop Boulos Massad was elected patriarch. Unlike his predecessors he was not from the landed elite and was noted for marked dislike of this feudal class, which had important implications for the unity of the community as a whole at this point. After his election the church was never to return to its former degree of support for the landed element, but had a wider popularity as it took a more broad-based perspective towards the Maronite social hierarchies. See Malcolm Kerr (ed.), *Lebanon in the Last Years of Feudalism, 1840–1868. A Contemporary Account by Antun Dahir al-Aqiqi and Other Documents*, American University of Beirut, Beirut, 1959, pp. 12–13, 95–150. This is a contemporary manuscript history first published only in 1938, and describing 'the disintegration of political and social authority in the northern half of Lebanon', especially in the Kisrawan, according to Kerr in his preface, p. x. See also Salibi, *Modern History of Lebanon*, pp. 93–4 for a more detailed discussion of the events in Kisrawan in 1858; also Khalaf, p. 39.

115. FO 787/1383, Mr Finn, Vice Consul of Sidon to Mr. Malmesbury, 22 July 1858, Beirut.

116. Rizk mentions the anti-Christian graffiti painted on the walls of the churches of Acre and Aleppo, as well as referring to meetings between elements from the Sunni, Shi'ite and Druze communities, plotting a general massacre of Christians in the region. See Rizk, p. 184; Salibi, *Modern History of Lebanon*, pp. 93–4. During the Damascus

massacres, for instance, the *pasha* there had refused to use his troops against the Muslim agitators. See Rizk, pp. 184; 224.

117. Kerr, pp. 55, 94–150; Rizk, pp. 151–231.

118. Samir Khalaf, *Persistence and Change in Nineteenth Century Lebanon*, American University of Beirut, Beirut, 1979, p. 87.

119. Meir Zamir, *The Formation of Modern Lebanon*, p. 8. The massacres particularly affected the Kisrawan district, indicating Muslim incursions. See also Churchill, Chapter 6 for some contemporary comments; and Fawaz, pp. 47–77. This latter book is primarily an account of the massacres.

120. *Al-Hayat*, 14 June 1985; Bashir Gemayel, *L'Orient-Le Jour*, 23 June 1981.

121. Several prominent Druze chiefs, including Said Jumblat, were arrested and tried, but except for Said Jumblat, who died from natural causes in prison, the sentences against them were allowed to lapse. Nothing was done to punish the lesser Druze chiefs involved, along with those Sunnis and Shi'ites who had joined in.

122. Salibi, *Modern History of Lebanon*, p. 109.

123. Again, Bashir Gemayel in 1981 referred to the fact that he 'never felt an inferiority complex' as a result of his minority background, because of his heritage and links to these martyrs. *L'Orient-Le Jour*, 23 June 1981.

124. Zamir, p. 8.

125. The traditional sense of community and place, and a shared history and religion all fitted in with the European agenda of the time for identifying a national people, and for accepting that such a national people should express that national feeling through a state coinciding with 'national' territory. This encouraged the Maronites, who had long referred to themselves in the old sense as a 'nation', to develop an essentially Christian sense of nationalism in the context of the Ottoman empire. It should be stressed, however, that if the Maronites used European terminology as it developed to express that feeling, the feeling was locally originated, and not 'created' by European intervention. Anthony Smith, for example, provides a definition that includes the Lebanese or Maronite national movement as fitting his definition of a national movement. See Anthony Smith, *The Ethnic Revival in the Modern World*, Cambridge University Press, Cambridge 1981, pp. 3–4.

126. The *Règlement Organique* gave the interested European powers a voice in nominating the *mutessarif* or governor, who was now to be a Christian, for instance. As a further indication of the erosion of Ottoman authority, only a small Ottoman garrison could now be stationed in the Mount Lebanon area. The *Sanjak* now had its own council and administration and drew up its own budget. Its inhabitants enjoyed tax privileges and exemption from Ottoman military service, a privilege arranged by European intervention. See Akarli, pp. 82–3; 103–4; 133–47.

127. Modern, at least in the European sense of the time, which was one valued by the Maronites themselves, and certainly a contrast to the rest of Syria.

128. Moosa, *The Maronites in Modern Times*, p. 287; Youssef M. Choueiry, 'Ottoman Reform and Lebanese Patriotism', in Nadim Shehadi and Dana Haffar Mills (eds), *Lebanon: A History of Conflict and Consensus*, I.B. Tauris, London, 1988, p. 70.

129. The Ottoman government supported this element of European policy, because it sought to limit the area within which its sovereignty would be restricted and to reduce the revenue loss that would ensue from the economic privileges granted to the residents of the area.

130. Moosa, *The Maronites in Modern Times*, p. 287; Ahmad Beydoun, *Identité Confessionnelle et Temps Social chez les Historiens Libanais Contemporains*, Publications de l'Université

Libanaise, Beirut, 1977, chapter 1; M Jouplain, *La Question du Liban: Etude d'Histoire Diplomatique et de Droit International (1908)*, Fouad Bitan and Cie, Jounieh, 1961.

131. Necessarily so, given that consideration of their perspective would destroy the Maronite claim. As Tosh points out, part of the problem with mythology is how much it supports the focus on one's own community at the expense of knowledge or understanding of the perspectives of other peoples. Tosh, p. 22.

132. Marwan Buheiry, 'The Rise of the City of Beirut', in Lawrence I. Conrand, ed., *The Formation and Perception of the Modern Arab World*, Darwin Press, Princeton, 1989, pp. 483–97.

133. Fouad L. Bustani, *Introduction à l'Histoire Politique du Liban Moderne*, FMA, Beirut, 1993, p. 126; Yussuf Saouda, *Fi Sabil al-Istiklal* [For Independence], Dar al-Rihani, Beirut, 1967.

134. Akarli, p. 37.

135. Zamir, pp. 10–1.

136. *Ibid.*, p. 11.

137. Albert Hourani and Nadim Shehadi, eds, *The Lebanese in the World: A Century of Emigration,* I.B. Tauris, London, 1992, pp. 4, 21–2. See also Zamir, p. 15, who argues that approximately one quarter of the population of the *Mutassarifiyyah* emigrated.

138. Salibi, *Modern History of Lebanon*, p. 114; Zamir, pp. 16–7.

139. Salibi, *Modern History of Lebanon*, p. 118.

140. *Ibid.*, pp. 113–5.

141. Beydoun, pp. 25–33; Stephen Hemsley Longrigg, *Syria and Lebanon under French Mandate,* Oxford University Press, Oxford, 1958, p. 52.

142. To be very historically accurate, some Muslim leaders also had co-operated with the Crusaders, such as Bani Ammar in Tripoli. However, this element in the history of the period was largely ignored.

143. Salibi, The *Modern History of Lebanon*, pp. 157–158; see also Michael Johnson, *Class and Client in Beirut*, Ithaca Press, London, 1986, p. 16, for comments on the development of Arab nationalist ideas as well as 'Lebanese ones relating to this concept.'

144. Akarli, pp. 71–3.

145. Salibi, *Modern History of Lebanon*, p. 157.

146. *Ibid.*

147. Akarli, p. 75.

148. Abbé Louis al-Khazin to Pope Pius X, undated but from the letter's internal evidence from the period 1909–14, in the unpublished al-Khazin Family Papers. The letter seeks particular assurances that the Young Turks will not be allowed to secularise the educational system – by now a critical element in the power of the Maronite Church itself – and that the Pope will maintain and develop Maronite communal or 'national' feeling. It is worth noting the reference here to the Maronite 'nation'; by this time it is clearly meant in the modern 'nationalist' sense.

149. Georges Antonius, *The Arab Awakening: The Story of the Arab National Movement*, first published 1939, reprinted Librairie du Liban, Beirut, 1959, chapter 5.

150. Zein N. Zein, *The Emergence of Arab Nationalism, with a Background Study of Arab-Turkish Relations in the Near East*, first printed 1958, reprinted Caravan books, New York, 1973, pp. 54–9.

151. Youssef M. Choueiri, 'Ottoman Reform and Lebanese Patriotism', in Nadim Shehadi and Dana Haffar Mills (eds), *Lebanon: A History of Conflict and Consensus,* I.B. Tauris, London, 1988, p. 75; Akarli, p. 78.

152. *Ibid.*

153. Such an offer can be seen as the precursor to the National Pact of 1943; see chapter three.
154. Akarli, p. 100.
155. Salibi, *Modern History of Lebanon*, p. 159.
156. One of the first such societies was *al-nahda al-Lubnaniyyah* (the Lebanese revival).
157. See Claude Dubar and Salim Nasr, *Les Classes Sociales au Liban*, p. 322; Johnson, pp. 16, 22; 25. Johnson argues that the Muslims resented Christian economic dominance, but that the commercial links did create some sort of link between elements within the communities, essentially the commercial/mercantile classes and the elites or notables. Certainly these elements shared a common wariness of the impact of a popular radical movement that might endanger their political and economic dominance. Yet equally, Maronite leaders started using rhetoric of various kinds, including an appeal to religious values, to sustain their power, thereby raising confessional tensions. This tactic was also adopted by Sunni leaders; and the tendency of leaders of both communities to use these tactics continued, as subsequent chapters will show.
158. Salibi, *Modern History of Lebanon*, pp. 159–61.

CHAPTER TWO

External Perspectives in the Historical Setting

As a constant in twentieth-century Lebanese politics, each major community has held to myths involving an external power it identifies as a 'protector' of its particular interests. The Maronites have held to these myths especially hard, making them part of their unconscious collective tradition; although they rarely examine them deeply, they are always willing to rework them to suit a particular situation or crisis. These perspectives have also been sustained because external powers collaborate in them, for a range of reasons, and because indigenous communities present a community profile likely to evoke sympathy.

This dynamic, in turn, has resulted in external powers creating their own mythologies about the Lebanese communities, and indeed about the Middle East as a whole. As I will show in this chapter, a series of myths about 'Lebanon', particularly Western ones, were based on superficialities rather than on a genuine, historically-based understanding of the region.[1] These shared myths relating to community identity became very important at times of crisis like 1958, because indigenous communities had the habit of invoking 'protection' from outside forces to defend their interests, and because the external powers were willing to be drawn in.

Marwan Buheiry comments that Lebanon has never had internal conflict without external intervention; he sees this as 'constituting perhaps a law of Lebanese history'.[2] Both territorially and culturally, he says, Lebanon's strategic position has 'provided a fertile ground for the patron-client game in international relations'; the different Lebanese communities have seen themselves as possessing 'one or more traditional sponsors' from outside Lebanon and have involved these sponsors in Lebanese affairs from time to time. This perspective is a useful one through which to consider external involvement.[3] It is also useful for understanding the dimension external perspectives have added to the evolution of both community mythologies and identities over time, both in terms of experience and the rhetoric used to define such identities.[4]

One of the most significant external contacts throughout Lebanon's history has traditionally been with Western Europe, including the papacy, starting with the Crusades at the end of the eleventh century.[5] The Crusader period had lasting effects, if only because Western powers became involved in the region after an appeal from there; it was not a question of 'unprovoked' Western interference.[6] During this period external Western European powers, especially France and the Vatican, began to evolve many of their crucial assumptions about the region of Lebanon and its inhabitants.[7] In the eleventh century Western Europe – Latin Christendom – was emerging from the chaos of the previous century and beginning to regain confidence in itself and its wider destiny as the only true guardian of the Christian message. The Crusades were in many ways a manifestation of these feelings, particularly the superiority that Western or Latin Christianity felt towards other versions of Christianity – notably those prevalent in the Middle East. They also involved a mixture of religious and materialistic fervour.[8]

The Crusaders further justified their enterprise by noting that 'corrupt' Christian communities such as the Maronites existed in the area.[9] If the Franks were the natural leaders of Christians everywhere, then it was their duty to liberate the Holy Land and recover Jerusalem. At the same time, they claimed, their willingness to undertake the task was tangible proof that they had been granted the leading role and had the right to judge their fellow Christians! Thus they could also argue that they were coming to rescue these other Christian communities from their own heresy, which Byzantium had failed to do, and also rescuing the entire region from Islam, for which God would duly reward them.[10]

The Crusaders could see their own motivation quite clearly, but the 'infidel barbarians' of the region were puzzled by Western Christian motivation and horrified by the 'barbarism' of the Crusaders.[11] Faced with an invading army, Islam mobilised to defend its territory and its faith. Meanwhile, the inhabitants of the Lebanon region split, thus beginning the process of creating Western stereotypes, and thus perceptions, of the region's peoples: stereotypes based mostly on confessional assumptions. Some Maronites sided with the Christian West, thus earning themselves a special status in the eyes of the West.[12] Even those Maronites who did not openly or actually side with Latin Christendom were seen by the Crusaders as doing so, earning them the status of 'natural allies' of Christendom. In Western eyes this had the effect of creating an enduring myth about their 'right' to interfere in the region, a myth they could invoke when needed, whether or not they regularly valued their relations with Middle East Christian communities. Equally important over the long term, Muslims increasingly saw the Maronites as natural allies of Christendom, a perception that may have driven them towards the West in the conflict between Christendom and Islam.[13]

By contrast, within the Islamic context, we would expect the Druze to have taken the side of Islam in the conflict. Their actual position during this period was much more complex, however, and their motivation much more ambiguous to outsiders. The Druze were motivated by their perceptions of their own localised self-interest, rather than any sense of loyalty to the Islamic world. Thus the majority of the Druze were perfectly prepared to take the side of the Crusaders rather than that of Islam if it seemed to suit their agenda at the time.[14] Over time, this willingness to collaborate had little impact on Islamic perceptions of the Druze.[15] It did have some effect on Western perceptions, but the Druze were rarely important to the West until Western expansionism reoccurred in the nineteenth century. The same was not true of the links between the West and the Maronites – especially in the period from the fourteenth to the nineteenth centuries.

Those involved in sustaining such links saw clearly that they were not merely informal. Nor were they simply religious. With the failure of the crusading movement, secular Western interest in the region of Lebanon was primarily economic until the late eighteenth century, when it again acquired a strategic dimension. France was the one Western power to sustain its links throughout this period, though other powers periodically sought economic benefits through this means. In the fifteenth and sixteenth centuries, for example, the Italian Medici family attempted to create a sphere of influence in Lebanon. Venice was involved in trade with other parts of the Ottoman empire, and sought to take over from France in Lebanon. But both efforts failed.[16]

By the early modern period, France had established the basis for lasting and sustained contact – very largely on its own terms – by establishing a presumption, both ideological and practical, that acknowledged them as the superior element in the link. This link originated in the efforts of the French monarchy to assert its power in Christendom. Using the Crusades as part of these efforts, in 1259 Louis IX promised the Maronites his special protection.[17] Successive kings of France would sustain and formalise the assumption of French 'special protection' because of the tangible benefits it brought to France. Letters to this effect exist from kings of France from the sixteenth to the nineteenth centuries, including Henry IV, Louis XIV, Louis XV and Louis Phillippe.[18]

Indeed, even the Islamic authorities sometimes acknowledged French influence. For example, in 1535 Francis I of France and Sulayman the Magnificent signed a treaty giving France certain privileges, and tacitly acknowledging the French role in protecting the Maronite community.[19] French involvement in the region's trade focused on silk, and thus on the Maronites who dominated that trade; the French took advantage of their 'traditional links' with the Maronites.[20] Though the context for this France-to-Lebanon link changed, as well as French motivations for sustaining it, the presumption of French cultural superiority did not disappear. Indeed, it grew stronger.

Nor was France alone in developing a 'special relationship' based on an exchange of presumptions rather than realities with the Maronite community in the crusading period – and then sustaining it. The spiritually and temporally ambitious Latin or Roman Catholic Church also became directly involved through the channel of the Maronite Church.[21] Serious missionary efforts brought the Maronite Church into a form of union with Rome in 1180. Rome forgot the 'heresy' of the original Maronite Church and worked hard to improve on and expand its links with the existing Maronite Church, with considerable success.[22] For instance, the papacy established the concept that it had to 'approve' the appointment of a Maronite Patriarch; as a result the Patriarch was given a special ambassadorial status. Many Maronite clerics trained or studied in Italy starting around 1500, and a Maronite college was established in Rome in 1584.[23]

But the Vatican did not rely only on the presence of Maronites in Rome to sustain its influence in the Maronite Church and through that, on the community as a whole. Roman Catholic missionaries (mostly Franciscans, Jesuits, Capucins and Lazarists) were active in Lebanon itself, working hard to further develop the links between the papacy and the Maronite Church. From about 1600 on, these missionaries materially increased the local importance of the Maronite Patriarch and the church, but also strengthened the confessional base of Maronite community identity by emphasising the links with Rome.[24]

From the late eighteenth century, as the Ottoman empire weakened in comparison to the European states, several of those states became more interested in the Middle East, including Lebanon. The so-called Eastern Question in this period can be summed up as the clashes and tensions surrounding relations between the Ottoman empire and the Christian West, focusing on the relations between Ottoman authority and minority communities, especially Christians in that empire.[25] These minority communities increasingly sought protection and support from the West and used Western rhetoric to express their ambitions for autonomy, or even independence, within that empire.

This development had an important impact on intercommunal relations in Lebanon, especially for co-habitation with Muslim communities, and those communities' reactions to the Maronite agenda. The West understood these expectations and reactions in relation to the background of myths it had already established about the region. During this period, only France had a serious economic interest in the region, through its involvement in the silk trade. For other European powers, interest in the region combined strategic interests and cultural imperialism, including a renewed missionary fervour, but this time focusing on a largely Protestant evangelism, which in itself led to myth-creation.[26]

In addition, during the Enlightenment, European cultural attitudes had hardened towards non-Europeans, because Enlightenment thought encouraged a habit of 'classifying' and 'listing' the objects of the natural world, both animate and inanimate. Long before Darwin published his ideas, Europeans had become accustomed to ranking items and people according to ideas of 'superiority' and 'inferiority'. This ranking tended to be based on physical appearance and the resemblance of cultures to European cultures: the greater the resemblance, the more 'civilised' the people and thus the higher they ranked. Such exercises also included the potential for people to move up the rank order by improving their civilisation, and thus refining their physical appearance. One key to moving up was possessing, or accepting, Christianity. A comment in one nineteenth-century children's text indicates the kinds of stereotyping established:

> We will not say that the Turks cannot mend, but ... they are trying for the externals of our civilisation without the Christian faith ... Before any great improvement can take place in their condition, they must ... renounce almost every quality which we in Western Europe have hitherto considered to be synonymous with the name of a Turk.[27]

As Darwin's ideas spread, and then the ideas of social Darwinism, they simply provided scientific reinforcement to already-established myths. Thus Lebanon could be valued because it had a well-established 'civilised' Christian community which led Europeans to see a duty to protect it. This enabled the West, or at least its Roman Catholic element, to endorse unequivocally its preference for the Maronites. The Western Protestant perspective saw the Maronites as Christian but in need of help to see the light, and identified the Druze as a backward group, greatly in need of Western help if they were to be 'improved' and converted. This thinking helps to explain the nineteenth-century British and American interest in the area, and provides some context for Anglo-French rivalry.[28]

European imperialism in the nineteenth century drew on these ideas. As Edward Said argues, 'In the expansion of the great Western Empires, profit and hope of further profit were obviously tremendously important, but there is more than that to imperialism and colonialism'. He adds:

> Neither imperialism nor colonialism is a simple act of accumulation and acquisition. Both are supported and even impelled by impressive ideological formations that include notions that certain territories and people require and beseech domination as well as forms of knowledge affiliated with domination.[29]

This perspective was not new in Lebanon's experience with the West: French missionaries had long had a 'civilising' mission there.[30] What was new was its expression in the shape of paternalism, in the context of Europe's global dominance in the nineteenth century.[31] Confessionally-based stereotypes were still powerful as Europeans developed their attitudes towards the Lebanese communities, such as this example of the Protestant British attitude towards the Maronites and the Druze in Mount Lebanon:

> Taken by themselves, [the Druze] are a race with many good qualities – bold, active and industrious, but their sense of religious animosity once roused, they are most ferocious, and while they retain their peculiar tenets, there is no hope of their ever becoming a really civilised people.[32]

The Protestants saw the Maronites, whom they identified as 'members of the Church of Rome', as an improvement on the Druze. For one thing, they were physically cleaner. But implicit in Protestant descriptions of the Maronites and their dispute with their Druze neighbours was the idea that though they were Christian, they were not really civilised because their Roman Catholicism was an inferior or debased form of Christianity compared to Protestantism.[33]

Popular British mythology about the region was affected by the writings of Charles Churchill, who settled in Lebanon around 1850 and envisioned a future for the region independent of Ottoman rule. Such a country, he said, could only 'become English or else form part of a new independent state' which he envisaged as pro-British. He attempted to develop British links with the area by writing about the Druze and Maronite communities in Mount Lebanon. Introducing one such work, he wrote that 'The time is fast approaching when the imperative claims of Christianity and humanity must and ought to absorb all others in the much vexed Eastern Question.' He hoped his work would 'induce some to take [that] point of view when contemplating England's present or anticipated action in the political affairs of the Ottoman empire'.[34]

Considering the long-established French links in the area, and the strong French belief in their superior civilisation, such British attitudes laid the foundation for an Anglo-French rivalry in the area.[35] Aware that the Ottoman empire was crumbling, and ever more convinced of European superiority in all matters, both Britain and France believed that they had a duty – even a right – to oversee the affairs of the Ottoman empire. In describing this duty they referred to their established mythologies about communities in regions like Lebanon. The result was a new phase in European-Ottoman relations.

In addition to this belief in their own superiority, the European powers had another reason to support the Ottoman empire: to protect their complex variety of political, religious and cultural strategic interests in the region the Ottomans governed. Thus they also felt a right and a duty to intervene in aspects of internal Ottoman policy that they saw as impinging on their interests or those of their 'clients'. It was in defence of their own wider interests, for example, that Britain and Austria had intervened in Ottoman affairs to expel the Egyptians from Syria in 1840.[36]

Between 1836 and 1876 European pressure on the Ottomans produced the *Tanzimat*, a programme intended to 'civilise' the empire in a European sense through a process of 'democratisation'.[37] Though the Ottomans were able to use the programme for their own ends, it also produced considerable resentment – often directed against the minority communities the Europeans favoured. This in turn created practical dilemmas for the European powers that claimed to support and protect these communities' interests.[38]

The confessional dimensions of the Lebanese problem, including the Catholic-Protestant tensions of the European powers, ensured that nineteenth-century Europe would not be able to produce a solution acceptable to all the European powers, let alone the confessional communities in Lebanon.[39] In escalating the tension between Maronites and Druze, the *Tanzimat* thus ensured that the interested European powers would act to sustain Ottoman rule in the region; expectations of European intervention may well have lowered the chance of any compromise of interests between the communities.[40]

Yet the series of nineteenth-century crises in Lebanon did confirm both Britain and France in their belief that they, rather than the Ottomans, should be managing the region including Lebanon, and that Anglo-French relations, rather than local agendas, would determine the level of European intervention.[41] Since all parties in Lebanon could see that any autonomy – let alone independence – from the Ottoman empire would depend on European support, the Maronites in particular expressed their agenda increasingly in terms acceptable to European powers, rather than addressing the other communities and seeking to evolve joint agendas. Thus they deepened their patron-client relationship with the French and saw co-habitation rather than co-operation as being in their best interest.

The French focused their regional policy on influencing the management of the Eastern Question as a whole by retaining influence in Lebanon. Economic interests mattered too, given the many French banks, commercial houses and other firms involved in textile – mainly silk – production in Lebanon. This industry was important to the Lebanese, especially around Mount Lebanon.[42] But these French firms made an important contribution to the French economy, and relied heavily on the supply of cheap silk from Lebanon. Just before World War I, France was absorbing 93% of Lebanon's silk.[43] Given these facts, the French were interested in fostering the concept that they were the Maronites' natural ally in hard times.[44] France thus emphasised its 'time-honoured' role as protector of Catholics and Catholic-related Christians.[45]

France recognised that the Maronite agenda included at least virtual independence from the Ottoman empire – to be achieved with French support.[46] By this time, however, the Europeans had established a set of reasonably coherent criteria for establishing an independent state, and there was considerable debate over whether those criteria were fulfilled in Lebanon. From a European perspective, the only 'genuine' basis for creating an independent state was the existence of national feelings and aspirations.[47] French political and intellectual circles became receptive to the idea of a national feeling developing in Lebanon, under French tutelage.

The emergence of Yusuf Karam was greeted in French political and intellectual circles with enthusiasm and encouragement, but without much surprise.[48] In exile in France, Karam became a heroic figure.[49] The French could now claim that Lebanon had a 'nationalist leader' with popular support. They could then construct a theory of an emerging national feeling in Lebanon which was essentially Christian and dependent on French support. This was an interesting development of the myths about Lebanon in the patron-client context.[50]

The situation was more complicated, however, as the Maronites were not alone in thinking about nationalism. Protestantism, both European and American, had encouraged the development of the 'Arabic scholarly and literary revival of the nineteenth century',[51] because it saw Lebanon as part of an essentially secular Arab world, not as some outpost of Western Catholic civilisation. Initially, this perspective posed no threat to the Maronites' ideas, since the Arabs also wanted to end Ottoman dominance. European reactions, however, were far from neutral, with serious implications for Lebanon. For instance, this Arab nationalism implied the creation of an independent Syria including Lebanon, a concept the British favoured because of the opportunities it offered. But the French vehemently opposed the idea of a secular Arab Syria because it appeared contrary to their interests.[52] Equally, British 'support' for the Arab cause would have a impact on the level and seriousness of Arab nationalist expectations of that support, especially after 1914, in ways that related less to concrete expectations of economic or other benefits, and more to established ideological patterns.[53]

A completely separate factor brought Britain and France together in the early years of the twentieth century: their perception of a growing German threat, in the Middle East as elsewhere.[54] The 1905 Entente Cordiale contained the first tentative defensive arrangements, which would dictate the post-1918 pattern of European involvement in the Middle East.[55] This spirit of general Anglo-French co-operation in the Middle East continued until World War I broke out in 1914. Ottoman involvement in the region only increased this co-operation, since both sides tacitly acknowledged that after any victory they could divide the spoils; in fact, they began planning for the time when they would be major beneficiaries of the Ottomans' imperial possessions.[56] This planning had implications for Lebanon's future, as the Maronites were quick to realise. Along with their counterparts in France, they undertook a publicity campaign, including speeches and articles on the disposal of the post-war Ottoman empire, to convince the French public that French influence must be maintained in the region.[57] This was particularly crucial for Lebanon, since it was, in the words of the British, not a 'purely Arab' area. In the brief time it had to consider the issue, the French public agreed that the French 'civilising mission' should continue and prevail in Syria and Lebanon, because France had 'rights' there. This emotional dimension had implications for French domestic politics, making it a sensitive national issue.[58]

By now, Britain had also become quite involved in the Middle East equation, and in a more complicated way. The French stance was relatively straightforward: they wanted to preserve their influence in Syria and Lebanon. The British position was complicated by their military campaign against Germany in the region, by their imperial responsibilities including India and Egypt and by Arab nationalists and Zionist activists competing for British support.[59]

The British needed an Arab revolt. Consider the correspondence between Sir Henry MacMahon, Britain's high commissioner in Egypt, and the Arab leader Sharif Hussein in 1915 and early 1916. In July 1915 Hussein indicated to MacMahon that, in return for a series of 'basic provisions' – the creation of an Arab nation that would include Syria and Lebanon – Britain would be granted preferential status, and the Arabs would undertake a revolt.[60] MacMahon's response can certainly be read as promising British support for the creation of an Arab state at least partially covering Syria and Lebanon, although, as the Arabs were to find, it was open to other interpretations.[61] After all, in addition to its interests in Palestine and Mesopotamia, Britain had wider imperial responsibilities; it also needed to generate support at home for a post-war settlement that included these areas as part of the British sphere. These factors help explain why the British failed to support the Arabs at the Peace Conference.[62]

In 1916, these considerations lay behind the British negotiations with France over disposing of the former Ottoman empire. The British informed the French of the content of the McMahon letters, and made it plain that they need not affect the progress of negotiations.[63] In the spring of 1916, François Georges-Picot and Sir Mark Sykes drew up an agreement for France and Britain to share the spoils in a post-Ottoman Middle East.[64] The Sykes-Picot Agreement underlined and incorporated the perception that Lebanon was a part of Syria, rather than a separate entity. The French government considered Lebanon a geographical region within Syria, although some groups – even within France – favoured a separate existence for Lebanon, whatever its form. The French Foreign Ministry was aware of some complexities: the Maronites would not easily be absorbed into a wider Syria, but perhaps they would realise that they could no longer demand their privileges after their 'liberation' from Ottoman dominance, since the motivation for those privileges would no longer exist.[65] But the post-war settlement set up separate mandates for Syria and Lebanon. What led to this change of emphasis?[66] Both Britain and France saw the need to reconcile conflicting perspectives, and for a time, to relegate the mythologies to a supporting position.

In September 1919, the British announced that they were withdrawing from Syria and handing over military control to France; General Henri Gouraud, commander-in-chief of the French troops there, became the French high commissioner for the region, in charge of setting up the post-war civilian administration.[67] During the November 1918 post-war peace negotiations, the negotiators realised that, despite the Sykes-Picot Agreement and the claims of Arab nationalists, the French had seriously inflated their ambitions in the Middle East. They now demanded that other parties acknowledge their control over all of 'Syria', which now included not only Palestine but also northern Iraq, Cilicia and a large area of Asia Minor.

France now stressed its 'traditional rights' in the region so outlined, based, as Longrigg put it, 'on her ancient Capitulations; her protectorate of Catholics, her educational and philanthropic work, her economic effort in the territory'. As was true of other French imperial interests, significant elements of French intellectual thought and certainly a large section of French popular thinking included Syria as a part of France '*outre mer*'.[68] But as the victorious Allies thought about all these issues, France believed its trump card in claiming this entire region was the 'affection' of the 'Syrian' people; it expected that affection to counter any talk of national feeling in the peace negotiations.[69]

We must remember that the French had long resisted any idea of a pan-Arab national feeling; before the war, for instance, they had firmly rejected any talk of a pan-Arab Syrian unity as being contrary to their interests. As early as 1913, the English had commented on French sympathies for Christian minorities in the Ottoman empire and the resulting disregard for any incipient Arab national feeling.[70] Thus, when the French negotiators first encountered the concepts of Maronite and Arab national feeling, they refused to take them seriously. They argued that Arab nationalism was the work of the British, who had deliberately created an anti-French feeling, rather than genuine nationalism, amongst the Arabs.[71] They also argued that a 'Bedouin', Sharif Hussein, was not capable of inspiring or leading any genuine mass national feeling in the region. Never mind that he ruled Mecca and was a member of the Prophet's own tribe. Such leadership capacity could be found only amongst the more Westernised, or 'Catholic' communities of the region. Thus they went into the negotiations convinced that the Arabs favoured French control.[72]

In these arguments, the French ignored recent evidence.[73] They argued that any form of self-government such as the Arabs were proposing was not suitable for such a primitive group; experience of benevolent French policy would show them their folly.[74] Working from this attitude, the French began to talk to Arab leaders even before the peace negotiations began formally; this position helps explain the emphasis on a Syrian entity and not a separate Syria and Lebanon. In this way, the French hoped to portray themselves as the protectors of Muslim as well as Christian interests; thus it would be in everyone's best interests if the French secured a mandate over the whole region.[75] Picot attempted to persuade Faisal that only through a French mandate over the region could he achieve a future pan-Arab entity which included Lebanon, since only France could unify the region securely and peacefully in the short term.[76] In a meeting on 13 April 1919, the French believed they achieved a basis for co-operation: Faisal would gain popular Arab approval for a French mandate over a Syria that would take the form of a 'federation of local communities'.[77]

Things were not as easy as the French hoped. Faisal was also exploring the extent of British and American support for the Arab nationalist cause. He proposed, for instance, that the Peace Conference base a settlement on the wishes of the population in the Middle East, and that they set about finding out those wishes – a move calculated to win American involvement in the settlement of Syrian affairs. Faisal clearly believed that any such enquiry would endorse Arab claims – a belief that worried the French and the Maronites,[78] and led the French to seriously consider the claims for a separate Lebanon.

French and Maronite Policies Converge

When Faisal's plan was mentioned at the conference, the 'Lebanese' delegation responded that 'Lebanon' would not consent to integration with Syria: 'Lebanon' was not Arab, though the Arabic language had infiltrated during Ottoman rule, and it needed French protection to maintain its distinctive non-Arab personality.[79] This interchange indicates how much the French government, led by Clemenceau, was also exploring alternatives to his agreement with Faisal, particularly with this evidence that Faisal was not prepared to stand by the April 1919 agreement.

What most concerned the French was President Woodrow Wilson's advocacy of the principle of self-determination for formerly subject peoples. The claims of various groups – including Arab and Maronite nationalists – convinced Wilson that it was crucial to investigate the situation in the Middle East. Wilson's attitude towards Lebanon was informed by the opinions of Howard Bliss, the principal of the Syrian Protestant College of Beirut (later the American University of Beirut).[80] In the summer of 1919, the King-Crane Commission was set up to enquire into the feelings and aspirations of the peoples of the Middle East, with a brief to visit Syria, Lebanon and Palestine.[81]

Aware that the commission might not endorse their aspirations, and equally aware of the impact of Arab nationalism, the French were forced to abandon their grand dreams for the Middle East, and, falling back on the Sykes-Picot Agreement, to make the most of their traditional influence. They proceeded to capitalise on their old links with the Maronite community in Lebanon, promising to support the establishment of a French mandate there. The French now had to move to a position in which a separate Lebanese entity was part of French policy. So, rather than ignoring the Maronite nationalists, it became important to convince them that a period of French rule was 'perhaps the best guarantee for a separate and independent Lebanon' – eventually.[82] Thus, to quote Salibi, 'French and Maronite interests clearly converged' from the later months of 1919.[83]

The King-Crane Commission visited Lebanon in the summer of 1919. However, as their 1922 report indicated, they found that only the Maronite and Greek Catholic communities wholeheartedly favoured a French mandate, and the commission questioned their dominance in the area. They also saw no real unity amongst the other confessional communities in the region. The Sunnis, for instance, generally supported incorporation into an Arab state, but the Druze generally supported a British mandate over the region. The commission's conclusions effectively negated the French claim to a mandate in Lebanon, but by the time its report was published, in 1922, the region's affairs had already been settled essentially on the basis of the Sykes-Picot Agreement.[84] With British backing, the French were able to convince the Allied Supreme Council of their case, and on 28 April 1920 France was offered the right to set up mandates in Syria and Lebanon.[85] The Peace Conference even left it up to France to decide on the extent of a separate Lebanon, despite furious protests from Damascus.[86] The French moved swiftly to set up their mandate administration. Given a 'free hand', France was eventually to decide that its best interests lay in the creation of a Greater Lebanon.

French-Maronite relations deserve some analysis at this point. Historians, including Gerard Khoury, have described the complex process that led the French to this position. The most consistent element in French policy between 1916 and 1920 was a willingness to use the Maronite agenda when, but only if, it suited their broader strategy. This interpretation helps to explain both intercommunal relations in Lebanon just after the war, and French-Maronite relations in the mandate period. A key factor altered the emphasis of French policy in relation to Syria and Lebanon: during the summer of 1919 Faisal refused to accept the persuasions of men like Clemenceau and Picot, and decided to rely instead on the international commission of enquiry to settle matters in the region and give due weight to Arab claims.

Sunni Hostility towards Maronite 'Myths'

Faisal's attitude led to a rift between the continuing and expanding Arab and Lebanese nationalist movements; within Lebanon, it directly influenced the thinking of the Sunnis and thus their relations with the Maronite community.[87] The Sunnis, used to being part of a greater entity, were less attracted by the concept of an independent Lebanon. Also, well aware of Western attitudes towards them, they saw no personal, political or economic advantages to any future that drew Lebanon further into contact with a Western power. In this sense, the Sunni community was more clearly opposed to the policy of the Maronites than were the Druze. It was, after all, at this point that French policy provided a Greater Lebanese entity which would involve a larger Sunni element because it included some parts of the former Ottoman Syria. At this point, and in reaction to this external dimension, the internal power struggle over the future of Lebanon switched from being primarily between the Maronites and the Druze to being primarily between the Maronites and the Sunnis. That power struggle would be increasingly expressed in terms of Sunni hostility to Maronite myths about Lebanon, and the apparent French endorsement of those myths.

Once the plans for creating a unified Syria under a French mandate in co-operation with the Arabs had finally collapsed, the French became more susceptible to pressures from the Maronites inside and outside Lebanon – including the pro-Maronite lobby in France itself.[88] Moreover, in late 1919 and early 1920, the French were growing concerned that pro-French feeling was declining amongst the Maronite community within Lebanon itself, if not amongst emigrant circles. Maronites had become suspicious about the negotiations with Faisal and had feared a sell-out. These fears became more concrete when a Maronite deputation reported hearing Picot say that 'France would have the mandate over all of Syria, which would safeguard the interests of Lebanese Christians.' Thus, he said, Lebanon would not have to be separated from the rest of Syria.'[89]

With such reports circulating in Lebanon, Maronites began to speak out against the French, and large demonstrations indicated that the entire Maronite community opposed French policy. Bkirki, the seat of the Maronite patriarchate, was the focal point for this Maronite opposition to French policy. Patriarch Howayek's fears of Muslim domination in a greater Syrian entity, and thus his sense of French betrayal, led him into taking a crucial step, breaking a long tradition of Maronite loyalties: he approached General Allenby to request British protection within a British mandate over the area.[90]

These developments did not please the French authorities: Picot complained to the Quai d'Orsay that the Maronites, and the Patriarch in particular, were acting in a selfish and short-sighted way. They were creating an anti-French agitation 'inspired only by the concern to protect the privileged status which circumstances had granted to them in former Lebanon'.[91] Despite their outrage, however, the French realised that it was in their own interests to restore good relations and dispel Maronite resentments.[92] After all, if Syria ever became difficult to control, France could fall back on Lebanon. Thus the French began to mark out a Lebanese entity that, apart from anything else, included the best part of the region's coastline.[93]

Although they were still unhappy with the French government, the Maronites had concluded that the only way to counter the Arabs' claims – to which both the British and Americans were sympathetic – was to rely on the French. Consequently the Maronite delegation to the Peace Conference was encouraged to ask for a French mandate.[94] This pleased France's foreign minister, Stephen Pichon.[95] The delegation consisted mainly of Maronite emigrants settled in France, who had begun to coalesce into coherent groups early in the century. For example, the Comité Central Syrien, or CCS, was founded in June 1912 by a group of Paris-based Syro-Lebanese, headed by Chekri Ganem, with Dr George Samne as the secretary general. It had close ties with the Comité de l'Orient and generally to imperial interests in France. Drawing on French foreign ministry archives, historians believe that the Quai d'Orsay found it in its interest to fund such groups occasionally. Then, in times of need, such as the settlement of the old Ottoman territories, the ministry could make use of them.[96]

It would be a mistake, however, to say that these Maronite pressures on the French government led directly to France's establishing a separate Lebanese entity based on the concept of a Greater Lebanon. The French had no objections to the Maronite demand for expanded borders for Lebanon – what harm would it be if France were to seize as much territory as possible, and leave the British with little? They could do so by capitalising on the terms of the Sykes-Picot Agreement, thus blocking Arab aspirations in the region.[97] By 1920, the only way to do this effectively was to respond positively to the demands of the Maronite community, effectively endorsing their mythology of a separate Lebanon. The confusion and conflicting claims surrounding the peace process in the Middle East, however, along with the report of the King-Crane Commission when it emerged, served to exacerbate tensions between the communities in Lebanon itself.[98]

The Maronites may well have had a strong effect on the shape of a Greater Lebanon, but in deciding to endorse that solution the French had primarily considered their own interests, not Lebanese ones. Indeed, Maronite thinking on the shape of Greater Lebanon arguably had more impact because the 'man on the spot' to shape the borders happened to be General Gouraud, commander-in-chief of the French forces in the region. Many sources on both sides, including Faisal as well as Robert de Caix, Gouraud's own secretary, indicate that for personal reasons Gouraud was very susceptible to pressure and suggestion from the Lebanese Christians.[99] For example, de Caix warned against creating a Greater Lebanon that took in too much of the territory where Muslims constituted an overwhelming and undoubted majority of the population. But inspired by the concept of France's 'grandeur' in the region, and his own religious fervour, Gouraud ignored such warnings. Personally sure that 'the real Syria desired and awaited France', he acted accordingly.[100] His policy was to lay a fresh emphasis on the links between the Christian (and especially the Maronite) communities and France. This added to Muslim hostility towards France – not the best basis for administering the new entity, as the French were to find out.

Complicating the situation was some Maronite disappointment with France, especially since the French troops under Gouraud's control had not managed to prevent Muslims killing a number of Christians in Lebanon in 1919 and 1920. France itself – or at least some of its important political and intellectual elements – was disappointed to be awarded only a mandate, and had already begun to identify the task as a thankless one. The terms of the mandate would restrict French freedom to govern as it saw best, and would thus reduce the impact of the French civilising mission. So the Mandate period started with no great feelings of optimism on any side.[101]

Still, the mandate was set up quickly, and with ceremony, once France had dealt with the problem of Faisal. On 1 September 1920, General Gouraud formally announced the institution of a self-contained Greater Lebanon.[102] It was the result, he said, of France's aim to help the populations of Syria and Lebanon achieve their aspirations of freedom within the context of autonomous entities, and France intended to help the new state achieve its dreams by overseeing its early stages. In reality, of course, it fulfilled the ambitions of the Christian population – except those who supported nationalism – but definitely not the desires of the vast majority of the Muslim population.

It has been argued that a nation exists 'when a significant number in a community consider themselves to form a nation or behave as if they formed one'.[103] Anthony Smith states that 'nations' are formed 'on the basis of pre-existing ethnie and ethnic ties', in a process where 'ethnic' ties were transformed into 'national ties and sentiments through processes of mobilisation, territorialisation and politicisation'.[104] In Lebanon, an identifiable national feeling coalesced in the nineteenth century, but in relation only to one single, and self-consciously well-defined ethnie: the Maronites. It was a vision based on what Salibi describes as the core of any politically conscious community: 'a common vision of their past'.[105] The other communities in the Mandate territory, however, did not share that common Maronite vision.

Notes

1. See John Tosh, *The Pursuit of History*, Longman, London, 1984, p. 3, for some historiographical commentary on such processes.
2. Marwan Buheiry 'External intervention and internal wars in Lebanon: 1770–1938', in Laurence I. Conrand, ed., *The Formation and Perception of the Modern Arab World*, Darwin Press Inc., Princeton, 1989, p. 137. Buheiry also commented on a series of further external interventions in Lebanon without the excuse of internal conflict to justify intervention, but that concept does not seem to be borne out by case studies of external interventions. Certainly it was not a factor in those interventions highlighted in Chapter 1, and was not a factor in 1958.
3. *Ibid.*, p. 138.
4. This rhetoric has increasingly related to the European concepts of nationalism; see chapter one.
5. The First Crusade started in 1096–7. For comments on the European background at the time of the crusades, see David Nicholas, *The Evolution of the Medieval World, Society, Government and Thought in Europe 1312–1500*, Longman Group Ltd, London, 1992, pp. 264–5 in particular.
6. The Byzantine emperor, Alexius I Comnenus, appealed to Pope Urban II (1088–99) for aid against Turkish invaders which he saw as threatening Byzantium. However, the emperor had expected cash aid and a few reinforcements, rather than the crusading army which actually turned up, especially since that army turned its attention against the Muslim ruler of the Holy Land rather than helping Byzantium to repel the Turkish invaders from Central Asia. See Nicholas, pp. 262–6; Jonathan Riley-Smith, *The Crusades*, Athlone Press, London, 1987, pp.1–2; Maurice Keen, *Medieval Europe*, Penguin Books, London, 1968, p. 124.
7. See, for example, Edward S. Creasy, *History of the Ottoman Turks from the Beginning of their Empire to the Present Time*, London, 1878, reprinted Khayat, Beirut, 1961, p. 64;

also J. A. R. Marriott, *The Eastern Question*, Oxford University Press, Oxford, 1951, p. 66. Marriott explicitly sees the Eastern Question, from the European perspective, as dating back to the crusading period.

8. I do not intend here to go into great detail about the Crusades. But a few points are important. By 1096 Western Europe had an established tendency to see the heresies that afflicted it as coming from the East, leaving it with the impression that only Western Christianity preserved the 'true' faith in unadulterated form. This resulted in hostility not just towards Islam but also towards Byzantium. Both states and individuals hoped both to gain financially and to demonstrate moral superiority from these adventures. See Keen, p. 123; Riley-Smith, pp. 4, 5–7,14–15; Norman Daniel, *The Arabs and Medieval Europe*, Longman Group Ltd, 1979, p. 127.

9. The conviction of moral superiority comes out clearly from the messages of Pope Urban to his flock, rallying support for the Crusades, where he talks of the Franks as the natural leaders of Christianity. See J. R. S. Phillips, *The Medieval Expansion of Europe*, p. 117; Keen, pp. 123–5.

10. Such a reward was to be both earthly and heavenly, communal and individual. See Daniel, p. 117; Keen, pp. 123–5.

11. This horror was not just religious. Some also expressed distaste at the 'barbarity' of the personal hygiene and medical knowledge of the crusading invaders. See Nicholas, p. 266.

12. *Ibid.*, p. 263. This was increasingly invoked by the Maronites as well, especially from the nineteenth century on. See, for example, Henri Lammens, *La Syrie: Précis Historique*, first printed 1921, reprinted Dar Lahad Khater, Beirut, 1994, pp. 146–7. While Lammens may be a problematic historical source, he is useful because he indicates later European traditions and perceptions, as well as Maronite ones, of the crusading period. See K. S. Salibi, 'Islam and Syria in the Writings of Henri Lammens', in P. Lewis and B. Holt (eds), *Historians of the Middle East*, Oxford University Press, Oxford, 1962, p. 342. See also chapter one for comments on Maronite and Muslim perspectives on this period.

13. The evidence would seem to indicate that the crusaders almost took it for granted that the Maronites would look to Christendom and that they treated the Maronite community in the light of that expectation. See M. Jouplain, *La Question du Liban: Etude d'Histoire Diplomatique et de Droit International*, first published 1908, reprinted Fouad Biban and Co, Jounieh, Lebanon, 1961, p. 61.

14. This was particularly so for the period 1100–1125, when the Crusaders were occupying the area of the modern Lebanese coast, more or less, and the Druze community felt it necessary to collaborate with them. However, later in the crusading period, at least, both the Franks and the Muslims were to take harsh measures against them.

15. Because the crusading period has traditionally been of much less significance to the Islamic world than the Western world, the participation by a group like the Druze who were apostate anyway was of less long-term significance than their general apostasy. This is an interesting contrast to the emphasis laid on Maronite participation by the West. As Bernard Lewis points out, at the time and subsequently, the crusades were 'not regarded by Muslims as something separate and distinctive'. Bernard Lewis, 'The Use by Muslim Historians of Non-Muslim Sources', in Lewis and Holt (eds), *Historians of the Middle East*, p. 181. Also see Lammens, pp. 195–6.

16. Lammens, pp. 242–5; M. Jouplain, pp. 104–6; 111.

17. Later canonised – undoubtedly adding to the status of the French monarchy – Louis IX (reigned 1226–70) was seeking in this instance to gain an advantage over Henry III of England, his rival both in Europe and in the Holy Land.

18. See Albert Hourani, *A History of the Arab Peoples*, Faber and Faber, London, 1991, pp. 258–9, for instance.

19. At this time France was seeking to develop economic links with the Ottoman empire as a whole, though it was not a major part of its trading policy. See Lammens, p. 242.

20. *Ibid.*, pp. 242–5.

21. Indeed, Rome was able to view its efforts with the Maronite Church as one of its few, as well as one of its lasting, successes stemming from the crusading movement.

22. Jouplain, p. 38.

23. K. S. Salibi, *The Modern History of Lebanon,* Caravan Books, New York, 1977, pp. 12; 122.

24. In the context of the *Imarah*, the Roman Catholic Church ensured that its missionaries used their influence with Fakhr al-Din II, for instance, and with subsequent *amirs*, to advance Maronite interests – and they made sure that the Maronites were aware of this. The Capuchins were particularly important during the time of Fakhr al-Din II, when they played on his ambition to develop an independent power base in Lebanon. See Lammens, pp. 244–5.

25. See M. S. Anderson, *The Eastern Question, 1774–1923*, Macmillan, London 1966 and William Doyle, *The Old European Order*, Oxford University Press, Oxford, 1992, pp. 288–9. For a non-European perspective see Salibi, *Modern History of Lebanon*, pp. 16–17; Malcolm Yapp, *The Making of the Modern Middle East, 1792–1923*, Longman, London, 1987, pp. 59; 114.

26. Salibi, *Modern History of Lebanon*, pp. 56–7; D Chevallier, *La Société du Mont-Liban à l'Epoque de la Révolution Industrielle en Europe*, Librarie Orientaliste Paul Geuthner, Paris, 1971, pp. 202–208, p. 293.

27. Mrs Bessie Parkes-Belloc, *Peoples of the World,* Cassell, Petter and Gilpin, London 1867, p. 158.

28. John Spagnolo, 'Franco-British Rivalry in the Middle East', in Nadim Shehadi and Dana Haffar Mills, eds, *Lebanon, History of Conflict and Consensus*, I.B. Tauris, London 1988, p. 107.

29. Edward Said, *Culture and Imperialism*, Chatto and Windus, 1993, pp. 8–9. Said also refers to 'An almost metaphysical obligation to rule subordinate, inferior or less advanced people', *ibid.*, p. 9. The various communities of Lebanon, Christian or not, certainly fell into this subordinate category.

30. Henri Laurens, *Le Royaume Impossible*, Armand Colin, Paris, 1990, p. 118.

31. See, for example, Kathryn Tidrick, *Empire and the English Character*, I.B. Tauris, London, 1990, p. 3 for some comments on paternalism in operation.

32. Parkes-Belloc, p. 219.

33. *Ibid.*, pp. 216; 217–218. Another British observer, Charles Henry Churchill, accused the Maronites of 'persistent jealousy' which led to outbreaks of violence in the area, such as the events of 1860. See Charles Henry Churchill, *The Druze and the Maronites Under Turkish Rule, from 1840–60*, Bernard Quaritch, London, 1862, pp. 1–3. The British focus on the Druze in this period was first established by Lady Hester Stanhope. Her own colourful memoirs first aroused British consciousness of the region at the level of popular literacy. Churchill was another British eccentric

and refugee from disapproval at home. See Robin Bidwell, Introduction, reprint of Charles Churchill, *The Druze and the Maronites*, Garnet Publishing, London, 1994, p. x.

34. Churchill, Preface, p. v.

35. See, for instance, Colin Mooers, *The Making of Bourgeois Europe*, Verso, London 1991, pp. 44–6.

36. See chapter one; see Chevallier, p. 37.

37. In chapter one I discussed this programme in terms of its impact on Lebanon; for a more general survey and for the European dimension, see Yapp, p. 111; also see Albert Hourani, Philip S. Khoury and Mary Wilson, eds, *The Modern Middle East*, I.B. Tauris, London, 1993.

38. In terms of Lebanon, of course, this was brought home to the European powers with the events of 1858–60, when they had to face the fact – as did the Ottoman government – that the *Tanzimat* was not well-received by those it was intended to benefit. See Yapp, pp. 59, 114.

39. In this context, it is interesting to compare the cases of Lebanon and Montenegro within the Ottoman empire. They had in common the geographical setting of remote mountains and a past of virtual autonomy for Montenegro and periods of practical autonomy for Lebanon, for example during the emirate period. But Montenegro became secularised from the mid-nineteenth century. Thus when the inhabitants of the region united to fight for independence from the Ottomans in 1878 they won general European aid and approval. European intervention advanced Montenegro's claims for independence essentially because it did not directly impinge on existing European rivalries. See Yapp, p. 60.

40. The British primarily supported the Druze while the French maintained their long-standing support of the Maronites. Ottoman officials could, and did, take advantage of this to neutralise European support for any further autonomy in the region by setting one European power against the other. In an age of rivalry between the European powers, especially Britain and France, in the imperial arena this had the effect of increasing the tensions between these powers in areas outside the Middle East as well as within it. As a result, the European perspective on the Middle East problem became so involved that any incident taking place in Lebanon had its echoes in Europe and political relationships there. See Yapp, p. 136; Salibi, *Modern History of Lebanon*, p. 3; John Spagnolo, 'Franco-British Rivalry in Lebanon', Nadim Shehadi and Dana Haffar Mills, eds, *Lebanon. A History of Conflict and Consensus*, I.B. Taurus and Co Ltd, London, 1988, pp. 109–10.

41. French willingness to co-operate with the British in the region varied according to a variety of factors. After 1870, France was in direct competition with the British in areas like Africa, and was seeking to assuage her humiliation in the Franco-Prussian War of 1870–1. Therefore, in the period 1870–1905, French co-operation with Britain in Lebanon was minimal. The renewal of good relations between the powers, in the 1905 *Entente Cordiale*, also signalled a new willingness to seek solutions to rivalries in this area, as elsewhere, on a basis of compromise. However, it would always be a mistake in this period, as later, to ignore the continual strand of French suspicion of British motives and actions in Lebanon and elsewhere. See Spagnolo, *Franco-British Rivalry*. See also John Spagnolo, *France and Ottoman Lebanon*, St Anthony's College, Oxford, 1977; Gerard Khoury, *La France et l'Orient Arabe*, Armand Colin, Paris, 1993, pp. 30, 65. For the wider perspective see Bernard Porter, *The Lion's Share: A Short History of British Imperialism 1850–1983*, Longman, London, 1984; Chevallier, pp. 162, 167.

42. It is estimated that between 1911 and 1912, for instance, 50% of the population of Mount Lebanon was dependent on the trade for its living. See Boutros Labaki, *Introduction à l'Histoire Economique du Liban, Soie et Commerce Extérieur en Fin de Période Ottomane*, publication de l'Université Libanaise, Section des Etudes Economiques, IV, Beirut, 1984, pp. 147–9.

43. The indigenous production of raw silk in France was badly affected by disease; Lebanon's low taxes and cheap labour, relative to levels in France, ensured a cheap supply of silk, making French silk cloth a profitable commodity to all concerned. *Ibid.*

44. This was not difficult in the period up to 1914. The Maronites accepted the French advertisement that they had intervened on behalf of the Maronites in 1860, for instance, convinced by the rhetoric that France was committed to furthering Maronite interests but failing to comprehend the wider agenda from the French perspective.

45. It must be remembered that other Catholic powers, notably the Austrians and Italians, were also interested in increasing their power in the region by persuading the Maronites to look to them, but the Maronites did not reciprocate their interest.

46. In fact, French willingness to commit to the Maronite cause was limited, especially since the French did not feel that the British threatened their hold over the community. In 1860, for instance, it was not until after Christians were massacred in Damascus that the French government despatched troops to intervene. The instructions to the 7,000 troops sent to Beirut were that they were to help the Ottomans re-establish order in Lebanon, as well as to guard the Christians there. Equally, the compromise that settled the 1860 crisis consisted of a formula that supported Ottoman power rather than supporting the Maronites or any other local community such as the Druze. See Salibi, *Modern History of Lebanon*, p. 109; Leila Fawaz, *An Occasion for War*, I.B.Tauris, London, pp. 192–228.

47. This had 'justified' the creation as nation-states of Italy and Germany, for example. Greece was an example of a nation-state created in a former area of the Ottoman empire, in 1830. But all these examples had, in European eyes, the gloss of nationalism according to European definitions. Khoury, pp. 20, 30; E Gellner, *Nations and Nationalism*, Basil Blackwell, Oxford, 1983; E. Hobsbawm, *Nations and Nationalism since 1780*, Cambridge University Press, Cambridge, 1990; Elie Kedourie, *Nationalism*, Praeger, London, 1960.

48. Karam was a Maronite leader from Ihdin in the north who first came to prominence in the *Tanzimat* period, co-operating with the Ottoman authorities, notably in subduing the Kisrawan peasant revolt. He had expected to be rewarded with high office aftr the 1860 settlement. Disappointed, he turned to rebellion against the Ottoman state. On his defeat in 1866, Karam had been sent into exile in Europe. See Salibi, *Modern History of Lebanon*, pp. 113–14; Spagnolo, *France and Ottoman Lebanon*, pp. 151–5; Meir Zamir, *The Formation of Modern Lebanon*, Croom Helm, Beckenham, 1985, p. 17; Khoury, p. 30.

49. Spagnolo, *France and Ottoman Lebanon*, pp. 151–5, 201.

50. In fact, the support even among the Maronite community in Lebanon was by no means universal, but by this time, the established Maronite emigrant community in France could ensure Karam certain publicity. See L. Baudicour, *La France au Liban*, Dentu, Paris, 1879, Chapter 6.

51. A leading 'Lebanese' figure in this was Butrus al-Bustani, an American-educated scholar who drew on the techniques of European scholarship to fuel the discovery of a notable and noble Arab culture in the past. There was a European perspective on

Arab history which pointed to past influence of Arab culture on European thought. This movement was not just confined to Lebanon, but Lebanon played an important part in this movement. See Salibi, *Modern History of Lebanon*, pp. 147; 154–6; Albert Hourani, *Arabic Thought in the Liberal Age, 1798–1939*, Cambridge University Press, Cambridge, 1983, pp. 100–1, 132–45.

52. France felt the need to demonstrate the linkage between French and Maronite interests explicitly, to counter British support for Arab nationalism in the period to 1914, See Adel Ismail, *Documents Diplomatiques et Consulaires Relatifs à l'Histoire du Liban et des Pays du Proche Orient du XVIIe siècle à nos Jours*, Editions des Œuvres Politiques et Historiques 1975–1978, vol. 20, no. 69, pp. 214–6.

53. See Elizabeth Monroe, *Britain's Moment in the Middle East 1914–1917*, Chatto and Windus, London, 1918, p. 19.

54. The 'Arab Question' was assuming greater importance in the early years of the century, as the Ottoman empire became ever more unsettled as a result of internal unrest. In 1905 Young Turk activity in the heartland of the Ottoman empire became significant, and they addressed a manifesto on the Arab dream to the Great Powers. In 1908 the Young Turk movement came to power. In the period 1908–14, this had a considerable impact on Lebanon, leading the Maronites to appeal to the European powers involved in the 1860 settlement. But the new *rapprochement* between Britain and France cannot be seen as a direct response to this local unrest; it was part of wider considerations. See chapter one for the Maronite position; Zeine N. Zeine, *The Emergence of Arab Nationalism, 1973, With a Background Study of Arab-Turkish Relations in the Near East*, Caravan Books, New York, 1973, pp. 66–72, 86–91.

55. For instance, German plans for a Berlin-to-Baghdad railway set alarm bells ringing in London and Paris as part of a German global strategy. As part of the *Entente Cordiale*, Britain and France agreed on a series of imperial rivalries in areas where their interests had clashed during the nineteenth century. Thus Britain was to have a free hand in Egypt in return for France having similar freedom in dealing with Morocco. Equally, spheres of hegemony in the Levant were agreed, with France looking to Lebanon and Syria and Britain to Palestine and Iraq. Monroe, p. 79; Zeine, pp. 102–3. See also J. A. S. Grenville, *A World History of the Twentieth Century*, Vol 1, 'Western Dominance, 1900–45', Fontana Press, London 1987, pp. 50–60, for a brief summary of diplomatic patterns in this period.

56. Grenville, p. 54; Zeine, pp. 100–6.

57. We must not forget the economic dimension; the war seriously affected the silk trade, for instance, as French firms were expelled from Lebanon in 1914, and the banks, commercial houses and firms involved in the trade wished to see it restored with greater guarantees of its continuance. This would be best achieved by a formal acknowledgment of French involvement in the area in some form or other. See Labaki, IV, pp. 147–9; Michel Seurat, *L'Etat de Barbarie*, Editions du Seuil, 1977, pp. 173–220.

58. Stephen Longrigg, *Syria and Lebanon Under the French Mandate*, Oxford University Press, Oxford, 1968 edition, pp. 44; 81.

59. See Zeine, pp. 103–4, 106–8, 115–23; George Antonius *The Arab Awakening*, first published in 1939 by J. B. Lippencott Co., New York, reprinted by Hamish Hamilton Ltd, London, 1969, pp. 127–36, 258–70.

60. Sharif Hussein to Sir Henry McMahon, 14 July 1915, given in full in Antonius, Appendix A, pp. 414–15.

61. Sir Henry McMahon to Sharif Hussein, 30 August 1915; Sharif Hussein to Sir

Henry McMahon, 9 September 1915; Sir Henry McMahon to Sharif Hussein, 24 October 1915; Sharif Hussein to Sir Henry McMahon, 5 November 1915; Sir Henry McMahon to Sharif Hussein, 13 December 1915; Sharif Hussein to Sir Henry McMahon, 1 January 1916; Sir Henry McMahon to Sharif Hussein, 30 January 1916, all given in full in Antonius, Appendix A, pp. 415–27. Antonius argued that 'The area of the Turk's defeat was precisely the area of Arab aspirations. … The leaders felt that they had amply fulfilled their share of the bargain concluded between Sir Henry McMahon and the Sharif Hussein, and they confidentially looked to Great Britain to fulfil hers. But when it came to a reckoning at the Peace Conference, there was a wide divergence between what the Arabs claimed and what Great Britain was willing to recognise as her share of the bargain'. See Antonius, pp. 276–7.

62. The Balfour Declaration had been made in 1917, establishing the principle that Britain was favourably disposed to a 'Jewish national home in Palestine, provided this did not prejudice the civil and religious rights of the other inhabitants of the country', a position which established a basic contradiction. Hourani, *A History of the Arab Peoples*, pp. 318–9; Antonius, p. 261.

63. Archives of the French Foreign Ministry, Paris A-Paix, vol. 178, folios 1–3, Paul Cambon, French Ambassador to London to Aristide Briand, 11 November 1915. The French were not happy, and were not fully informed of the extent of McMahon's rhetoric, but in the short term, the letters had little effect on the progress of Anglo-French negotiations in 1916. See Khoury, p. 88; Longrigg, p. 73.

64. In broad terms, this agreement effectively agreed to French control over Syria and Lebanon, and British control over Palestine and Iraq. For a more detailed outline, see Salibi, *The Modern History of Lebanon*, pp. 159–60. See also Antoine Hokayem and Marie Claude Bitar, *L'Empire Ottoman, Les Arabes et Les Grandes Puissances, 1914–1920*, les Editions Universitaires du Liban, Beirut, 1981.

65. Hokayem and Bitar; Archives of the French Foreign Ministry, Paris, A-Paix, vol. 178, folios 1–3, Paul Cambon, French Ambassador to London to Aristide Briande, 21 December 1915.

66. Archives of the French Foreign Ministry, Nantes, Canton 2364, Telegram, François Georges-Picot to Mustapha Cherchali, Jeddah, 23 May 1917, from the Papers of François Georges-Picot.

67. After the success of the Arab revolt, the British had established military control in Syria and Lebanon as well as Palestine, from October 1918. See Salibi, *The Modern History of Lebanon*, pp. 160–2; Zeine, pp. 122–3.

68. Longrigg, p. 73; Salibi, *The Modern History of Lebanon*, p. 160; Yapp, p. 277. See Archives of the French Foreign Ministry, Paris, A-Paix, vol. 178, folios 1–3, Paul Cambon, French Ambassador to London to Aristide Briand, 11 November 1915, for some hint that the French might move to such a position; Seurat, pp. 177–204.

69. This, of course, underlines the extent to which the French were in the immediate aftermath of peace, ignoring the existence of indigenous agendas in the area, including the Maronite agenda. See Longrigg, p. 73; Zamir, p. 70.

70. Le Caire, *Documents Diplomatiques et Consulaires,* Adel Ismail, 19 June 1913, vol. 20, no. 69, pp. 214–16.

71. They also accused Britain of being motivated by a spirit of anti-Catholicism, which blinded them to the 'real' interests and desires of the inhabitants of the region, as well as to French disinterest in seeking to pursue her '*mission civilatrice*' there. In their pro-Protestant bitterness at having failed to establish themselves as a major force in the area, they argued, the British were using 'a Bedouin and his horde of bandits' to

create a false impression of Arab popular nationalism, because they had bribed the 'Bedouin' into a pro-British stance. Longrigg, pp. 74–81; *Lyon Republicain*, 4 August 1920.

72. *Ibid.*; Lammens, pp. 329–40.

73. For instance, they ignored the 1912 incident of the Syrian Martyrs and the impact it had had on Arab feelings in arguing that Arab nationalism was a purely British creation which would disappear once France embarked upon their great and historic task of civilising the Middle East. See Lammens, pp. 335–40; Longrigg, pp. 73–4; Zamir, p. 59.

74. Lammens, pp. 335–40; Longrigg, pp. 73–4; Zamir, p. 59.

75. Indeed, it was Picot who was entrusted with the task of negotiating with Faisal. He certainly had no wish to see a separate Lebanon, which he saw as 'incompatible' with the good administration of a French mandate over the whole of Syria. Zamir, p. 56.

76. *Ibid.*, pp. 56–64.

77. *Ibid.*, pp. 60–1.

78. Khoury, p. 174.

79. Archives of the French Foreign Ministry, Paris, Arabie vol. 5, fol. 69/70/r/v; Khoury, p. 187.

80. Bliss had Wilson's ear because his father-in-law, Cleveland Dodge, was a close friend of Wilson's.

81. It was initially intended to be a four-man commission, consisting of representatives from France, Britain, Italy and the US. However, European opposition to it meant that it was in fact a two-man commission, conducted by two American delegates who gave their name to the commission: Dr Harold King and Charles Crane. See Khoury, pp. 171, 190; Monroe, p. 63.

82. Salibi, *The Modern History of Lebanon*, p. 164.

83. *Ibid.*, p. 163.

84. It was soon clear that the commission would be irrelevant to the settlement of the region and that even leaders like Faisal realised this. Khoury quotes an accord of 6 January 1920 between Clemenceau and Faisal in which Faisal agreed to recognise a separate Lebanese entity under a French mandate, but would leave it to the Peace Conference to decide the limits of the entity. Khoury, pp. 243–4, 311.

85. Salibi, *The Modern History of Lebanon*, pp. 162–4.

86. Faisal had, by this time, declared independence and been 'crowned' king of Syria in March 1920. In the summer of 1920, he led his troops in an attempted invasion of Lebanon. General Gouraud defeated Faisal's army with relative ease, and proceeded to evict the Arab nationalists from Damascus also, as a prelude to the setting up of French administrations in both Syria and Lebanon. See Salibi, *The Modern History of Lebanon*, p. 164; Zamir, pp. 77, 88–93; Khoury, pp. 307; 336.

87. Khoury, pp. 307, 336; Zamir, pp. 79–80; Longrigg, pp. 106–7.

88. The possibilities for a separate Lebanon, and for its being a significant size, had always been part of French rhetoric. At the same time he was negotiating with Faisal, Clemenceau had taken care to make noises of support for the Maronite agenda. See, for example, Archives of the French Foreign Ministry, Paris, E. Levant, 1918–1929, Syrie, Liban, vol. 19, folio 40, Clemenceau to Howayek, Maronite Patriarch, 10 November 1919.

89. Zamir, p. 62.

90. In fact, the British stayed loyal to the spirit of the Sykes-Picot Agreement, if only to protect their own plans from French interference, and responded with advice to

the Patriarch to appeal directly to the King-Crane Commission. See FO 371/4181 105815/2117, GHQ, Cairo to Foreign Office, 8 July 1919.

91. Archives of the French Foreign Ministry, Paris, E Levant, vol. 13, no. 724, Beirut, François Georges-Picot to Stephen Pichon, 23 May 1919; 3 June 1919.

92. Clemenceau wrote to the Patriarch, promising to help the Lebanese maintain an autonomous form of government and an independent national status, in the expectation that this would provide a basis for Maronite acquiescence in the French takeover. Clemenceau hinted that this entity would take account of Maronite territorial claims, giving the 'Mountain' access to the coast and the territorial plains since these were 'necessary to its prosperity', and argued that French sympathy with the aspirations of the 'people' of Lebanon had led him to these conclusions. In this light, he was sure that the Lebanese 'people' would welcome a French mandate over them, saying that 'I want to hope that the definitive solution to the Syrian question … will allow the French government to advance the wish of these people'. Archives of the French Foreign Ministry, Paris, E. Levant, 1918–1929, Syrie, Liban, vol. 19, folio 40, Clemenceau to Howayek, 10 November 1919.

93. Longrigg, p. 117.

94. Khoury, p. 187.

95. Khoury, p. 176, quoting Archives of the French Foreign Ministry, Nantes, fonds Beirut, carton 2208, Telegram, Stephen Pichon to François Georges-Picot, E. Levant 1918–1929, Vol 57, Syrie, Liban folios 25–52; B. Oudet, 'Le Rôle du Comité Central Syrien dans la Politique Syrienne de la France, 16 June 1917–24 July 1920', unpublished MA thesis, Sorbonne, Paris, 1986, p. 41.

96. Zamir, p. 48; Khoury, pp. 172, 181.

97. Longrigg, pp. 87–8.

98. For instance, there was a breakdown in co-habitation and intercommunal violence, with killings on all sides, in the early months of the Mandate. *Ibid.*, pp. 87–93; Zamir, pp. 56–8;80–7.

99. Longrigg, pp. 100–7; Zamir, pp. 74–5, 93–4.

100. *Ibid.*

101. Zamir, pp. 89–90, 100–2.

102. For details of the constitution and the decrees setting up Greater Lebanon, as well as its territorial extent, see Nicola Ziadeh, *Syria and Lebanon*, Ernest Benn Ltd, London, 1957, pp. 49–51.

103. Benedict Anderson, *Imagined Communities,* p. 6.

104. Anthony Smith, *Theories of Nationalism*, Camelot Press Ltd, London, 1971, p. 22.

105. K. S. Salibi, *House of Many Mansions: The History of Lebanon Reconsidered*, I.B. Tauris, London, 1988, p. 216.

CHAPTER THREE

The Creation of Independent Lebanon, 1920–1943

The proclamation that established Greater Lebanon under a French mandate set up a scenario that theoretically also confirmed a state based on Christian-Muslim co-operation. In reality, it merely continued the established co-habitational patterns that made use of differing reactions to the myths surrounding that scenario. But eventually, towards the end of the period 1920–43, Lebanese from widely different confessional and other outlooks did manage to balance the tensions over such myths. The pressure of mutual hostility to the French agenda led them to create something new: a consensus that was to be a basis for setting up an independent Lebanon.

In this chapter I examine the evolution and basis of the consensus in this period, to show how deeply it was based on compromises relating primarily to particular issues current in those years, rather than being a genuine compromise based on a settling of those tensions and resentments that the various communities, especially Maronite and Sunni, expressed in their mythologies. This occurred because the 'consensus' was primarily an arrangement based on short-term expediency; in the long term, it was satisfactory only to the political elites of these two groups. Thus it did not really represent a move

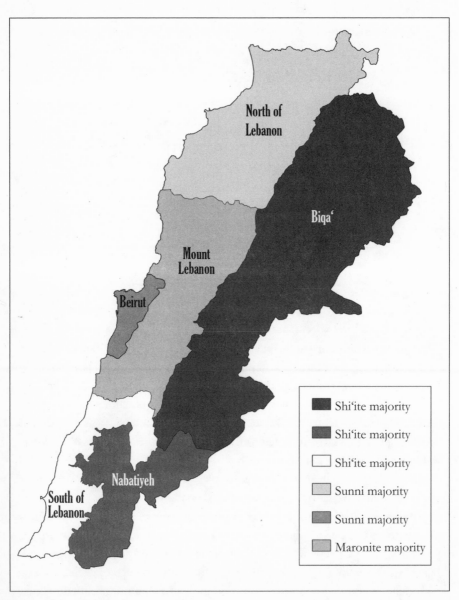

Regions of confessional predominance.

away from co-habitation to real consensus, as I will show in later chapters where I describe how conflicting community mythologies continued. Here we must also remember that if the 1920 proclamation did set up the concept of Christian-Muslim co-operation, it also encapsulated the potential for very divisive and contradictory future ambitions within that state.

Between 1920 and 1943, few new dimensions developed within the long-standing intercommunal patterns. Intercommunal tension did expand significantly to areas outside the Mount Lebanon area itself.[1] In addition, from 1920 onwards, in the context of Greater Lebanon, the focus of this tension shifted to the relationship between the Sunni community and the Maronites, rather than between the Druze and the Maronites. The tension expressed itself in concern about the balance of power between those communities in a separate Lebanese entity, with each side seeking to protect its own position and mythology.

Thus, in this chapter and the rest of the book, I focus on how the relations between Sunnis and Maronites were based on their differing perceptions of themselves and the 'other', and how they translated these understandings into action and policy. Quantitatively, the Sunnis were the majority Muslim group within the new Mandate and, in 1920, also identifiably the most significant group whose agenda and hopes for the future (as part of an Arab entity) were widely divergent from those of the Maronites. In the Ottoman empire, the Sunnis had developed a tradition of dominance, as they had been in the majority throughout its existence.

In confessional terms, the Ottoman empire had been essentially a Sunni entity. As it began to collapse, many leading figures within the empire had hoped to maintain that historical dominance within an Arab context. Now they were forced to define themselves in a context that was neither Muslim nor Arab. The other Muslim groups in Lebanon, the Druze and the Shi'ites, were not unsympathetic to the Sunni vision of the ideal future of Lebanon, but it was less crucial to them for a variety of reasons linked to their history as minority groups within the Ottoman empire and their resultant community mythologies.

Thus, compared to the Sunnis, neither community felt as strong a sense of defeat at the creation of the Mandate, even if they resented the French intrusion and feared that the Maronites would be overly favoured. Individual elements in the Druze community, notably the Arslan family, did take up an actively anti-French and pro-Arab stance, but most sought compromises with the French, if not the Maronites. The Shi'ites quickly recognised that they were better off as a sizeable minority in a Greater Lebanon than as a minority in an overwhelmingly Sunni Arab entity or French-administered Syria. In both communities, the traditional social structure ensured that the population generally adopted the position of the leaders.[2]

Like the Sunnis, the Maronites in the Greater Lebanon of 1920 also felt themselves to be dealing with a new situation. Not only did they now see the Sunnis as the major protagonists in any future struggles over Lebanon's evolution as a separate state; they also feared that the West no longer automatically saw them as an unquestioned majority community. They had been a powerful force in Mount Lebanon, but not in many of the other areas of Greater Lebanon. Practically, many feared their heartland would be submerged in a Muslim sea, forcing them to seek increased protection from traditional European allies. Thus their desires for a separate Lebanese future were mixed with doubts about its potential to survive on its own terms.[3]

There were other Christian communities in areas outside Mount Lebanon; but these did not automatically fall in line with the pro-Western stance of the Maronites. This was true of the Greek Orthodox community which formed a significant presence in the coastal towns and ports, and which had no particular commitment to a separate Lebanese entity. The wealthy Greek Orthodox merchants, particularly in Beirut and Tripoli, relied on trade with the Syrian interior and wished to remain on good terms with the Sunni community in general. Concepts of Arab nationalism had attractions for some Greek Orthodox elements also. Thus they took up a consciously neutral stance in relation to the internal tensions of Greater Lebanon and the differing communal agendas, seeking to hold themselves aloof from any potentially clashing community visions.[4] Practically, many Maronites were fearful of finding their heartland submerged in a Muslim sea, making them more in need of protection from traditional European allies, rather than less.

These differing perceptions became fundamental to the relationship between these two 'new' protagonists even before the Mandate was set up, as they disagreed on the geographical outlines of Greater Lebanon. A major issue was the fate of the coastal area and the four *qada's* that the Maronites claimed were part of 'Lebanon'. Most Maronites believed that a separate Lebanon could not exist without them, and they began to describe them as 'disputed territories'. But the predominantly Sunni population of the territories considered them to be part of 'Syria'.[5] Particular acrimony surrounded the inclusion of Tripoli in Greater Lebanon, and its role within that entity, as it was then an important port and a political centre.[6] Tripoli's inclusion in a Greater Lebanon would significantly boost that entity and be a real loss for Syria. Ultimately, the Maronites succeeded in persuading the French to choose Beirut over Tripoli as their headquarters, because of its proximity to Mount Lebanon. A by-product was enduring Sunni resentment.[7]

To some extent, the official presentation of the new Mandate in 1920 disguised the French endorsement of the Maronite vision of Greater Lebanon. Both the mufti and the Maronite Patriarch attended the ceremony, giving the appearance that both communities supported the Mandate.[8] But General Henri Gourard's actual words indicate how strongly the French had rejected the Muslim position. He stressed the role of the French soldiers in freeing 'the Lebanese' of what he described as 'the evil power that wanted to dominate them'.[9] Rubbing salt in the wounds of those who resented the French role, he informed 'the Lebanese' that they owed France a debt of gratitude for the French blood so generously 'donated' to safeguard them from this 'evil power', with the implication that that they should demonstrate this gratitude through their docility within the Mandate and its policies:

> *C'est en partageant votre joie et votre fierté que je proclame solenellement le Grand-Liban et qu'au nom du gouvernement de la république Française je le salue dans sa grandeur et dans sa force, du Nahr-El-Kebir aux portes de la Palestine et aux crêtes de l'anti-Liban … Il y a cinq semaines, les petits soldats de France … donnaient l'essor à tous vos espoirs, en faisant s'évanouir en une matinée de combat, la puissance néfaste qui prétendait vous asservir.*[10]

[It is while partaking in your joy and your pride that I solemnly proclaim the country of Great Lebanon, and in the name of the government of the French republic I salute it in its magnificence and strength, from Nahr El-Kebir to the gates of Palestine and the crests of the Anti-Lebanon … It has been five weeks that the soldiers of France … have given wings to all your hopes, and banished, in one morning of combat, the ill-omened powers that had intentions to enslave you.]

The Sunnis showed no such spirit of gratitude; for them, the proclamation simply emphasised the extent of their defeat.[11] From the start, they were willing to co-operate with any groups in Lebanon that opposed French policy. Thus their reaction was more emotional than considered and rational in 1920 when the overwhelming majority of Muslims rejected the Mandate by refusing to participate in its political mechanisms.[12] In fact, the few Sunni figures who did co-operate with the Mandate in the early years by taking on political positions could pull no personal followers into the Mandate system and instead faced hostility from their own community. Men like Shaykh Muhammad al-Jisr, speaker of the Chamber of Deputies from its institution in 1926 until 1932 and a presidential candidate in 1932, represented only their own personal opinions.[13]

Emotion was equally important to the Maronite community as it first reacted to the Mandate.[14] Preaching the need for a separate Lebanon in which the Maronites would have primacy, the church had taken a leading role in setting up the Mandate and expected that to continue.[15] Zamir describes the Maronites' 'almost mystical belief' in the validity of a Greater Lebanon as the natural 'homeland' of their 'people'; the church played a key role in sustaining that very strong belief.[16] A key point here is the firm conviction about the church's role.[17] This 'crucial' Maronite role in creating a separate Lebanon, by ensuring the creation of the Mandate, became part of Maronite tradition. Thus it gave popular justification to the view that Salibi describes:

> In the story of modern Lebanon the principal line of historical continuity between the Mount Lebanon of the nineteenth century and the Greater Lebanon of the twentieth, certainly at the internal political level, was the Maronite connection. Their destiny is linked with the survival of the Lebanon.[18]

In particular the Maronites believed that where their own visions of a Greater Lebanon conflicted with French policy, it was the French policy that changed, not their own visions. This belief helped establish their claims of a 'right' to dominance in Lebanon as a matter beyond question. In other words, 'Lebanese nationalism' was essentially based on Maronite communal mythology.

Nationalism has been described as the myth of historical renovation. In Lebanon, during the Mandate period, that process primarily involved myths of origin that could specifically promote Maronite traditions. The myths I described in chapter one, of a Phoenician and Mardaite ancestry for Lebanon, were central to the nationalism that both Maronites and French supported; to 'prove' their validity Maronite leaders such as Emile Eddé cited such nineteenth-century Maronite scholars and clerics as Henri Lammens.[19] In addition, several Maronite societies that had developed before 1914, including *al-Nahda al-Lubnaniyyah* (the Lebanese Revival), despite their small memberships, had a significant impact on the political expression of Maronite 'nationalism'.[20]

The diaspora of Maronites identified in chapter one also played a role, as groups of emigrants in France, Egypt, South America and the United States established societies supporting the concept of an 'independent' Greater Lebanon and used the mythology to 'prove' that Lebanon's origins were Western rather than Arab, effectively distancing the Maronites from other communities in Lebanon that claimed an Arab origin.[21] Thus the Maronites sought to develop a Lebanese nationalism that did not include non-Maronite traditions.

Equally, those elements of the population conscious of their Arab descent, mainly the Sunnis, Shi'ites and Druze, reacted angrily to a scenario that rejected that Arab heritage. In particular, they completely rejected the myths of Phoenician and Mardaite descent – for themselves as well as for the Maronites. Thus, in 1920, no obvious common ground existed on which to create a discrete national feeling among the communities in Lebanon through reference to a shared past, mythical or otherwise.

In understanding how the Mandate operated, we must consider how the various communities reacted to French perceptions of the Mandate itself and of the Greater Lebanon that it created.[22] First, the men entrusted with setting up the Mandate's administrative systems consciously set about establishing a meticulous, perfectionist structure that would be a contrast to the less rigid structures of the Ottoman empire.[23] This approach, probably more than any resentment amongst the communities, initiated the endless series of troubles and crises that eventually alienated both the Sunnis and the Maronites from the French administration. Given the lack of effective control at the centre, Ottoman administration had been quite parochial; local leaders in Lebanon had become accustomed to brokering much of the region's daily administration for themselves. In addition, bribery had been used to establish a range of privileges and powers at all levels of local society. Thus the region's inhabitants were unprepared for a system that would apply laws strictly and expect people to defer to a strong central authority. But this was precisely the system that the French were determined to set up in Lebanon.

In setting up their administrative structures and policies, French officials were aware that they would have to cope with confessional complications, to create a balance between Christians and Muslims. At first, Gouraud had high hopes of achieving a suitable formula.[24] On 22 November 1919, before the Mandate was officially set up, he expressed these hopes :

Mais si nous sommes les descendants des Croisés, nous sommes les fils de la Révolution, épris de liberté et de progrès, respectueux de toutes les religions et fermement résolus à assurer une justice égale aux adeptes de chacune.[25]

[But if we are the descendants of the Crusaders, we are also sons of the Revolution, enamoured of liberty and progress, respectful of all religions, firmly resolved to ensure equal justice to the believers of each.]

He returned to this theme on 6 December 1919, speaking at the Omari Mosque:

Représentant de la France dans ce pays aux religions si nombreuses et si diverses, j'entends les faire respecter toutes en me plaçant au-dessus de toutes les confessions et je fais appel en retour au plus large esprit de tolérance de tous.[26]

[Representing France in this country of religions so numerous and diverse, I strive to respect them all, submitting myself to every denomination, and I appeal to all for the broadest spirit of tolerance in return.]

His early confidence, however, was soon replaced by exasperation at the attitudes of the local population.

The French were very conscious that they were setting up a Mandate, while they were used to administering a colony.[27] Even so, they were determined to set up a system that they believed was sound – and involved all elements of Lebanon's communal mix in a balanced way. But they could not order such a system; they could only persuade. Thus they faced an uphill task with the Sunni community, which clearly resisted participating.[28] They faced an equal but opposite problem with the Maronites who were too enthusiastic about participating. Believing that they were responsible for creating a separate entity in the first place, they also believed they had a right to be centrally involved in evolving policy for and actively administering Greater Lebanon.[29]

Yet even the Maronite willingness to participate developed into a complex issue for the French. The gratitude that the French had expected did not materialise in the shape of a co-operative attitude towards the administration of the Mandate. The Maronites had expected to take a dominant role in the Mandate, given how often the French had endorsed their mythology and the 'rights' it conferred. Complicating the issue, some feared that France would abandon both the Mandate and the Maronite cause. According to persistent rumours between 1918 and 1920, the French planned to evacuate both Syria and Lebanon; those who were insecure about the level of French commitment to the Maronite cause pointed to the French insistence on involving all the communities in administering the Mandate. The Maronite nightmare was that the French would succeed so well in establishing better relations with the Muslim communities that the Maronites would lose their prime position in the French order of priorities.[30]

If the Maronites generally supported Greater Lebanon, they did not generally agree on the exact methods and policies that would let the entity continue and prosper. Indeed, from the start, the Maronite community was politically divided and prepared to be critical of the French. For example, some quickly began to press for a French policy in the Mandate that would lead to rapid independence, while others sought a practical autonomy that would leave the French in the Mandate as mere figureheads. To further these separate agendas by pressuring the French, individual Maronite leaders soon showed themselves willing to co-operate with politically conscious leaders from other communities in Lebanon.[31]

As a result of all this confusion, co-habitation continued in patterns based on mutual suspicion and mistrust. Maronite-Sunni relations, for example, were so dominated by these patterns that, as Zamir put it, 'To every action taken by one community there is a counteraction from the other'; these actions and counteractions had little to do with the new practicalities the French were attempting to institute and much to do with established mythology and the expectations they raised.[32] French administrators found all this exasperating and incomprehensible; Gouraud, for example, described the Maronites as 'difficult, spoilt and greedy'.[33] But it was within this communal complexity that they sought to make the Mandate work.

Some have argued that the very establishment of the Mandate harmed the communal relations in Lebanon; it certainly deepened the divisions in Maronite-Sunni relations. At the same time, however, the French presence during the Mandate period was key to the process by which Greater Lebanon became more than an artificial entity sustained only by an external power.[34] It was only the French presence, and the actively interventionist stance of French Mandate officials, that suppressed effective Muslim opposition to the concept of a separate Lebanese entity for long enough to enable an independent Lebanon to survive in the post-Mandate period.

As the Mandate survived, it forced sufficient numbers of Muslims into a position of collaboration, if not always directly with the French then at least with elements in the Maronite community. And the Maronites were even more committed than the French to seeing a separate Lebanon continue.[35] Thus the positions of the relevant players did not remain fixed throughout this period. The factors leading to shifts and developments in Maronite-Sunni communal relations will provide the focus for the rest of this chapter.[36]

A Constitution

Under the terms of the Mandate, Lebanon was to be given a constitution, which would inaugurate a period of indigenous administration under French tutelage. This was to be in place before the end of September 1926.[37] An insurrection in Syria in 1925 had spread to Lebanon by 1926, but it had not created a major crisis. It was to avoid further conflict, according to Philip Khoury, that the constitution was set up; simultaneously, the French army contained agitation among the Muslim elements in Lebanon.[38] The French hoped that promulgating a constitution would defuse Muslim agitation, but the Muslims held a different perspective: accepting the constitution would mean accepting Greater Lebanon within its current boundaries. This line of thinking was made plain at a meeting on 5 January 1926, when thirty-seven of the most important Sunni leaders and notables of Beirut voiced their refusal to participate in drafting the constitution.[39]

Despite Sunni hostility, a Lebanese republic with a parliamentary system was installed under French guardianship in 1926.[40] This relationship limited the new republic's freedom of action: according to the constitution, France still controlled its political and legal system as the mandatory power.[41] The 1926 constitution recognised Lebanon as an entity distinct from Syria, in the shape of a constitutional republic with some freedom to act independently. But the constitution also required its inhabitants to accept French power, under the terms of the original Mandate.[42] These provisions would remain at the heart of Lebanese political life as long as the Mandate lasted, because they set the agenda for both opposition to and support for Lebanon as a separate entity.

In Sunni eyes, the constitution formally endorsed an entity and a mythology that they profoundly opposed.[43] It also introduced an element of populism into the management of affairs within Lebanon, unlike the traditional hierarchies of power in the Sunni community.[44] The elected assembly had a democratic base, which threatened the traditional elites, making them more hostile to the Lebanon that this constitution encapsulated.[45] By contrast, for the Maronite population it meant a permanent settlement of the Lebanese question in a way that they had long desired.[46] Once again the majority of Maronites could look to France uncritically, accepting France as their traditional saviour as well as the guarantor of their safety.[47]

One goal of the constitution was to set up a political system that would provide for the equitable representation of the various communities. To allow Lebanon to react to a changing communal balance, the constitution did not include a specific formula for proportional representation, nor did it reserve specific government positions for each community. According to Salibi, 'the constitution did not lay down hard and fast principles for co-operation between the various confessions' because the French believed that the system would work best if it was not too prescriptive but left room for a spontaneous 'process of give-and-take'.[48]

In practice the system slowly brought the Maronite and Sunni communities closer, but not as the French had hoped. This closer relationship grew from shared resentment of the French based, for example, on expectations that ended in disappointment and frustration when they could not be fulfilled. According to Fadia Kiwan, the series of crises during the 1926–34 period was caused not so much by the French as by the attempts of various Maronite leaders to exercise their 'right' to a powerful role.[49] In the first few years after 1926, as the Sunni community refused to participate, a French-educated Maronite intelligentsia in fact exercised much of the power that was in Lebanese rather than French hands. Prominent figures included men who had participated in the peace conference in Paris: Habib Pasha El-Saad, Daoud Ammoun, Emile Eddé and Bishara al-Khoury. The Maronite Patriarch,

Elias Howayek, was also influential. Sunni leaders in Lebanon particularly resented these men and their high profile under the Mandate.[50] But when this resentment led Muslim leaders to express their opposition, they did so outside the Mandate structure. The French were disappointed to see that even this level of opposition could not persuade these Muslim leaders to participate in administering the Mandate.[51]

Until 1932, not one Sunni political notable with a significant following showed any sign of cooperating with the mandated Lebanese republic. The only Sunni figure of any note who was prepared to work with the republic was Shaykh Muhammad al-Jisr, and even he had few followers.[52] Al-Jisr had been a politician under the Ottomans; between 1926 and 1932 he was effectively the sole representative of the Sunni community in the republic's administration.[53] When the French sought Sunni involvement, al-Jisr became speaker of the new chamber virtually unopposed. His involvement in mandate affairs provided an excuse that eventually drew various Muslim political leaders into some degree of involvement. Though he was criticised for co-operating, in 1932 he stood in the presidential election.

By the early 1930s, Sunni leaders were seeing that Lebanon as a whole was flourishing economically under the Mandate and that standards of living were rising.[54] Shrewd leaders amongst the various communities could not ignore this fact as they evolved their strategies towards the Mandate. By 1932, local political groupings were evolving amongst the Sunni community in Lebanon. But leaders in these groupings, like Salim Salam, Abd al-Hamid Karami and Riyadh al-Solh were still calling for union with Syria.[55] They found it difficult to reconcile their desire to be involved in local Lebanese politics with their refusal to follow any policy that might seem to endorse the existence of Greater Lebanon. Their reaction to al-Jisr's candidacy in 1932 reveals the depth of this dilemma.

As al-Jisr participated in the administration of the new republic he naturally co-operated with Christian leaders, especially Maronites. But in 1932, the likely alternatives to al-Jisr were not only Christians but Maronites, and most had been involved in persuading the French to create Greater Lebanon. Al-Jisr was the only figure likely to be able to contest the presidency against men like Bishara al-Khoury or Emile Eddé, both of whom planned to stand in 1932. Not only would al-Jisr collect Muslim votes; he could also hope to secure some Christian backing.[56] But men like al-Solh continued to stand aloof; they could not bring themselves to endorse al-Jisr's candidacy because of the perception that in so doing they would 'recognise' the existence of Greater Lebanon.

At the same time, some of the Sunni mercantile elite in Beirut began to see the value in accepting the reality of Lebanon, rather than continuing to dream of being part of Syria.[57] Thus, by the mid-1930s, that elite began making tentative moves towards co-operation; since this mercantile elite was one source of Sunni political elites, it made some Sunni leaders more willing to move towards political involvement.[58]

Ironically, by this time the French Mandate officials had undertaken a policy that was discouraging the Maronites from cooperating wholeheartedly with the French. As the 1932 presidential election drew near, the French were extremely concerned that Muslim leaders – especially Sunnis – were still not collaborating. Feeling that the state was insecure as long as this continued, they sought ways to end the stalemate. But they tended to blame Sunni-Maronite hostility rather than any failure in their own policy. Hoping to lure the Sunnis into supporting the Mandate to some degree, they used the occasion of the election to distance themselves somewhat from the Maronites.

Within the Maronite community, the two leading political leaders were Bishara al-Khoury and Emile Eddé, both well-respected and successful lawyers with considerable political ambitions. Both intended to stand for president in 1932.[59] Eddé was more French in his cultural orientation than al-Khoury, and a strong supporter of anti-Arab views. He also endorsed aspects of popular Maronite mythology. For instance, he supported the idea of a Phoenician origin for the Maronites and was close to the poet Charles Corm, one of the most vocal proponents of this concept, as the following lines indicate:

> *Si je rappelle aux miens nos aïeux Phéniciens*
> *C'est qu'alors nous n'étions au fronton de l'histoire*
> *Avant de devenir musulmans ou chrétiens*
> *Qu'un même peuple uni dans une même gloire*
> *Et qu'en évoluant nous devrions au moins*
> *Par le fait d'une foi encore plus méritoire*
> *Nous aimer comme au temps ou nous étions païens! ...*
> *Mon frère musulman, comprenez ma franchise;*
> *Je suis le vrai Liban, sincère et pratiquant.*[60]

[If I recall our Phoenician forebears
For then we were at the gables of history

Before becoming Muslims or Christians
One people, united in the same glory
And that in moving on we would become at least
By the fact of a faith even more worthy
To love us like the time we were pagans!
My Muslim brother, understand my candour;
I am the true Lebanon, sincere, observant.]

If Eddé did not go to the same extremes as Corm, he certainly liked to think of Lebanon as Christian and part of a Western Mediterranean world; according to Salibi, he associated the Arab world 'with the desert'.[61] This position was popular among the Maronites.

By contrast, al-Khoury was less openly and vocally devoted to the concept of Lebanon as part of a Mediterranean world. Though he personally endorsed the concept, and firmly supported a separate Lebanese entity, he was also a pragmatist. To secure this entity in the long term, he believed, would require co-operating with the Arabs, so he took positions that would further Muslim-Christian co-operation. However, he was less popular with the French officials since his strategy was to develop links with Muslims by opposing the Mandate, arguing instead for full Lebanese independence.[62] Both set up political parties with predominantly Maronite followings: al-Khoury led the Bloc Constitutionel and Eddé, the Bloc National.[63]

The French officials were determined to find a compromise position between the communities in the political arena. In 1926, the Greek Orthodox Charles Dabbas had been appointed to the presidency, rather than elected.[64] He had held office from 1926 to 1929, and seemed so successful that he was reappointed for the period 1929–32.[65] The officials had hoped that by 1932 the Mandate would be sufficiently well-established to allow the president to be selected through an electoral system, as envisaged in the 1926 constitution. However, as the election approached and the three candidates manoeuvred for position, few saw much chance that the Lebanese would elect a compromise candidate supported by significant elements from all the communities.[66] A fresh cause of tension was added to the scenario when a census, demanded by the Muslim Congress, found that the territory included in the Mandate did not have a Muslim majority, as Table 1 shows.[67]

Table 1: Results of the 1932 Census in Lebanon[68]

Community	Population	Percentage (approx.)
Maronites	226,378	29%
Greek Orthodox	76,552	10%
Greek Catholic	45,999	6%
Armenians	31,156	4%
Other Christian groupings	22,308	3%
Total Christian Population		52%
Sunni Muslims	175,925	22%
Shi'ite Muslims	154,208	19%
Druze	53,047	7%
Total Muslim Population		48%

The French arrived at a short-term solution: they suspended the constitution and re-appointed Charles Dabbas as president for another term. In 1933 they replaced him with Habib El-Saad, a seventy-five-year-old politician whom they hoped would not be strong enough to cause trouble.[69] They also dissolved the Chamber of Deputies, and promised new elections in 1934. Thus French officials delayed moves towards a directly elected administration and continued to hold effective administrative power. They simply continued appointing local figures to the Chamber of Deputies, men like Dabbas whom they expected would be co-operative. Initially, this move increased tensions between the communities, but the French attempt at even-handedness and compromise was to be a significant factor in changing the nature of French-Maronite relations and Maronite attitudes towards the Mandate.[70]

As the years passed, doubt about the Maronite role under the Mandate spread beyond the disappointed Maronite leaders.[71] By 1936, when the French summoned the Chamber of Deputies to elect a successor to El-Saad, a considerable legacy of mistrust had built up.[72] Emile Eddé was elected – by a majority of one vote. But many Maronites believed the French had tried to prevent this outcome, because they wanted a president dependent on them rather than a powerful figure with a strong following in the Maronite community. This opinion indicates how much the Maronites had lost respect for the Mandate.[73]

Another indication of deteriorating French-Maronite relations occurred in 1935, when the Maronite Patriarch, Antoun Arida, began a dispute with the high commissioner over the future status of the tobacco monopoly in

Lebanon. The French controlled this extremely lucrative monopoly under the terms of the *Régie des Tabacs et Tombacs*, but the Patriarch wanted to see it opened up for Lebanese (essentially Maronite) participation. In the face of French resistance, he began to take a very critical position towards the French administration of the Mandate.[74] His demands for significant Lebanese control over its own economic – and political – affairs caught the notice of the Syrians. Syrian leaders actually began to come to Bkirki to talk to the Patriarch, and they began to develop a working relationship.[75] The Patriarch's statement in 1935 indicates how much the Patriarchate had changed its attitude:

> *J'ai montré que je m'occupais avec intérêt de la question syrienne. Le Liban et la Syrie sont liés par la communauté de langue, des mœurs, des traditions, d'intérêts économiques. C'est pourquoi il est difficile d'établir entre eux une séparation absolue.*[76]

> [I have shown that I was seriously following the Syrian question. Lebanon and Syria are connected by a commonality of language, custom, tradition, economic interest. That is why it is difficult to separate them unequivocally.]

This was an enormous change, and coming from this source, had a real impact. Bkirki was now established as a channel for discussions between Muslims and Maronites. Though these were not always fruitful, they helped to create an illusion, at least, of consensus between the communities.[77]

This development was crucial, as it helped create an atmosphere in which the leadership of the Lebanese Muslim and Christian communities, especially the Sunnis and Maronites, could begin to cooperate during the final years of the Mandate. In 1936, however, trouble flared again in Syria, and again found an echo in Lebanon; these troubles intensified intercommunal hostility among some Maronites and Sunnis.

In this context two new parties emerged. The Kata'ib Party, a group of Maronite phalangists who called themselves 'Lebanese', were primarily urban-based young radicals who aimed to defend, by militant means if necessary, the Maronite community and its mythology of a separate Lebanon. A group of Sunnis formed the Muslim equivalent, the Najjadah Party.[78] In reaction to the apparent potential for violent unrest, the French sought to re-negotiate the terms of both the Syrian and Lebanese mandates; they aimed to establish a basis on which both could be recognised as sovereign states, eligible to join the League of Nations.

Though the French hoped this process would defuse tensions in Syria and Lebanon, they still intended to maintain considerable control over both states. For instance, the armies were to remain under French supervision, and the French ambassadors were 'to take precedence over all others'.[79] On 13 November 1936, the Lebanese Chamber of Deputies ratified the proposed treaty, on the grounds that it would lead to the end of the Mandate and still guarantee that a separate Lebanon would continue. In addition, the treaty guaranteed a 'just' representation of all of Lebanon's communities in government and administration to the highest levels.[80]

But the Franco-Syrian treaty of the same year had an even greater impact on Lebanese Muslim opposition groupings than did the Franco-Lebanese treaty and its promises. Under the Franco-Syrian treaty, Syria was to accept the existence of Greater Lebanon as a legitimate entity in its own right. This development left Lebanon's pro-Syrian elements isolated. While some individuals and groups held on to their dream of union with Syria, the majority at this point saw the way forward as lying 'in the creation of an internal unity within the various states of the Arab world'.[81] This development brought to

Emile Eddé signing the Franco-Lebanese treaty of 1936, with Damien de Martel at his side and Khaled Chehab on the left. (Emile Eddé archives)

prominence one particular Sunni politician, Kazem al-Solh. He was the first major Sunni politician to argue that the way forward for both Muslims and Christians in Lebanon was to accept an independent Lebanon in which the communities could seek common ground.[82]

Sensibly, al-Solh was vague about the nature of any future relationship between Lebanon and the wider Arab world. For him the key to the current situation was demographics: if his fellow Sunnis succeeded in having Lebanon absorbed into Syria, they would alienate half the population, according to the 1932 census. Yet if Mount Lebanon were to be excluded from a Greater Syria to avoid this situation, the Maronites would inevitably seek continuing French protection, and that colonial presence would continue in the region. Potentially, Mount Lebanon could effectively become a 'French province', and a centre of subversion against the Arab nation[83]. Al-Solh saw no reason why an independent Lebanon should automatically be left out of any larger Arab entity created in the future. An independent Lebanon need be no more of an issue than a separate and independent Syria and Iraq, for example, assuming the Arab entity were a decentralised one.[84]

Thus, instead of displaying hostility towards the Maronites, Kazem al-Solh wanted Sunni leaders to become missionaries for Arab nationalism among the Christian Lebanese. He pointed to the positive attitude the Maronite Patriarch was taking towards Syria and his open criticism of the French; this demonstrated the potential for even the Maronites to change their attitudes. Al-Solh's strategy would require the Maronites to reject the Mandate, but in return, Muslims would accept an independent Greater Lebanon with a strong Christian element. Al-Solh's argument had an influence on some other Sunni politicians, especially those from Beirut; among them was Riyadh al-Solh, the future architect of the National Pact.

In the late 1930s, however, neither Sunni nor Maronite politicians were prepared for more than tentative collaboration. Though some Maronites were not content with the French, their position was not yet extreme enough for a majority of leaders to seek an end to the Mandate. Equally, liberal-minded Christian intellectuals were growing interested in Arab nationalism, but their programme was more theoretical than practical. At the same time, however, a mutual acceptance of a separate Lebanon was evolving during the last half of the 1930s, allowing Muslims and Christians to collaborate closely at elite levels. Helping this collaboration, the constitution was restored in January 1937. This led to a period of indigenous constitutional government which for the first time included Sunni politicians who were accepted by the mainstream of Sunni opinion.[85] It was during this period that a pattern was established where a Maronite president had a Sunni prime minister.[86]

The Second World War, starting in 1939, finally pushed both sides – at least the elites – to begin working together towards an independent Lebanon. The war confirmed the belief of even most Maronite elites that direct French rule was not in their interest. The way forward lay with an independent Lebanon. The various communities still had differing hopes for an independent Lebanon: the Maronites looked to the Western world, and to close (but not colonial) links with France, while the Sunnis and other Muslims looked to the Arab world. But at last they considered it less important to resolve this potential conflict than to end the Mandate. As the war proceeded, events only heightened the traditional elites' willingness to work together in an atmosphere of agreement about where the greatest evil lay for all of them.

The first such event came with the very outbreak of war, as Gabriel Puaux, then high commissioner, swiftly suspended the constitution, dissolved the Chamber of Deputies and appointed Emile Eddé as president and head of state. Puaux believed this was necessary to keep control over the situation in the Lebanese Mandate (a similar pattern was followed for Syria) because France could not risk having its efficient wartime administration disrupted by petty local politics. This was an interesting indication of how the French viewed the intercommunal relationship at elite levels, at least in Lebanon. In the best interests of both France and Lebanon was 'a good prefect and an obedient general council'.[87] Resenting the way the Mandate was actually undermining, and not promoting, their freedom of action, the community elites preferred to collaborate with each other than to continue the Mandate.

Resentment, at least at elite levels, deepened as the war progressed.[88] The fall of France and the setting up of the Vichy regime complicated the situation considerably, especially for the Maronites. Which side – Vichy or the Free French – would best serve their agenda? As the Middle East became strategically important to all sides in the conflict, Lebanon's internal situation became significant far beyond its borders, especially to those interested in the allegiance of internal factions. Initially, Vichy France officially carried on the administration of the Lebanese Mandate, and suspended any promise of independence. This move did not make the administration popular, and provided an opening to the other side: the British-backed Free French government-in-exile.

As part of the arrangements between the British government and the Free French government-in-exile, Britain initially promised to respect France's privileged position in Syria and Lebanon. Winston Churchill sought a compromise that would enable the Free French to act to undermine the Vichy-run administration in Lebanon, so it could be replaced with something more sympathetic to the Allied position. Foreign Office officials informed the Free French leaders that Britain would recognise them as exercising 'the rights which France derives from the Mandate' in the Levant, agreeing that the Mandate system could be terminated only if it was replaced with a treaty along the lines of the intended 1936 treaties, thus binding Lebanon to France.[89]

But this spirit of co-operation was not to last. As the British became more aware of the actual situation inside Lebanon, and considered their own strategy, they saw that they could hardly continue endorsing a position that delayed any announcement of Lebanese independence. Thus, on 6 June 1941, they announced their support for Lebanese and Syrian independence.[90] The Free French reacted with a counter-proclamation, continuing the Mandate – and creating great hostility. A public meeting at Bkirki on 25 December 1941 drew representatives of nearly all the communities within Lebanon, including some dissident Eddéists. Those present, including the Maronite Patriarch and other leaders, publicly rejected a continuation of the Mandate.

It was this joint rejection of the Mandate, setting the tone for relations with France over the following period, that can first be termed genuinely 'Lebanese'. But it would be a mistake to take this spirit of collaboration between the communities as also expressing a genuine resolution of the areas of conflict between them – though few of the leaders realised this at the time. For instance, the Maronites would never have been prepared to accept a Lebanon that was simply a prelude to the creation of a future unified Arab state, though the potential for this was still part of the Sunni agenda and thus implicit in their insistence in the National Pact on locating Lebanon as part of the Arab world. Equally, the Sunnis would not accept a long-term future for Lebanon that sustained a perception of Lebanon as part of the Western world – though this was still central to Maronite thinking and also implicit in the National Pact.[91] But in 1941, seeing their situation as an emergency, they did not consider such conflicts to be serious obstacles.[92] Searching for common denominators, the leaders were ignoring any need to clearly define their different positions for the future.[93] It was in this spirit that the National Pact itself evolved in 1943.

Demonstrations held in front of Spears' residence in 1943. The confrontations left many wounded.

British support for Lebanese independence was a crucial factor in 1943.[94] Between 1941 and 1943, Sir Edward Spears, the British ambassador in Lebanon, deliberately used his position to undermine the French position there by promoting collaboration between the communities on the basis of shared anti-French feeling.[95] Spears became increasingly influential.[96] Against this background, the French took a serious risk in trying to regain control over Lebanon in 1943. The French administrators in Lebanon arrested the independent administration of Lebanon and imprisoned its leaders, including Bishara al-Khoury. Emile Eddé agreed (out of a sense of duty, he claimed) to lead an administration under French Mandate rules.[97] This precipitated a crisis, with demonstrators in the streets demanding that the French release the prisoners and restore a free administration. When the British unequivocally backed the demonstrators, the French could only back down.

This was the beginning of Lebanese independence *de facto*. It was in this context of crisis that the National Pact emerged, and it must be understood as a response to crisis rather than a carefully calculated plan based on long-term aspirations. It was, in Michael Johnson's words, 'an unwritten gentlemen's agreement' between Riyadh al-Solh and Bishara al-Khoury to run the state, drawn up as the need for it became apparent.[98] It drew on the experience of the landed and commercial elites across confessional boundaries, working together under the Mandate, and against the French administrators.

It also drew on a point reached in the abortive 1936 Franco-Lebanese treaty: that the basic principle for a political compromise in Lebanon was 'the fair representation of all the country's sections in the government and high administration'.[99] This meant a division of responsibilities in governing Lebanon – on a confessional basis. Almost certainly it was the Maronites' commercial significance that enshrined a Maronite and Christian 'majority' in the government.[100] In other words, the non-Maronite elites accepted the need to safeguard the Maronite role in the economy by guaranteeing their political voice. Thus the majority of deputies in the Chamber of Deputies were to be Christians, and the president was to be a Maronite. However, the prime minister was to be a Sunni, enshrining that community's influence relative to the growing Shi'ite community.[101]

This pact was intentionally vague in its numbers of deputies and the relative powers of the various state offices, in order to permit future flexibility and modifications of the constitution within the broad outlines of the pact. Accepted by the elites, it was to become the basis of the permanent political arrangement for an independent Lebanon.[102] The political elites, both Maronite and Sunni, saw the pact as representing a genuine intercommunal consensus; they say it moved the communities beyond co-habitation to co-operation based on mutual conciliation.[103] But in 1943, as Farid al-Khazin points out, for those leaders the pact was merely an expression of the 'lowest common denominators' rather than a carefully developed agreement that provided a genuine basis for the communities to collaborate in the long-term.[104]

In other words, this informal agreement was not in fact a 'national' pact. It was born out of particular conditions – including the intervention of external forces. It materialised only when the Syrian and British interests, as well as internal Lebanese interests, all converged in a desire to defeat the French, who wanted to maintain the Mandate. This pact did not provide any new basis for dealing with the confessional problem in Lebanon; instead, it provided a basis for the communities to work together against a greater enemy. But when the crises had passed and reasons for co-operation were less apparent, it perpetuated the likelihood of co-habitation rather than consensus, because it institutionalised, rather than modified, existing confessional divisions – and thus different conceptions of a 'Lebanese' national identity.

The Western powers, especially the French and British, utilised the established myths as it best suited them – but this also ensured that they tended to see the Maronites in particular as the Maronites defined themselves, in terms of that mythology. This was to have profound implications for the relations between an independent Lebanon and external powers at times of crisis. Required to react under pressure, Western powers were likely to resort to the resultant stereotypes in order to interpret what was going on instead of making more dispassionate assessments.

Notes

1. Though the Maronite community had spread outside the Mount Lebanon area, tensions between Maronites and other communities in places like Beirut did not reach the levels as within Mount Lebanon, where the communities were competing over the same territory.

2. This was particularly true for those in Jabal Amil, though the Shi'ites of the Biqa' were less content. See K. S. Salibi, *A House of Many Mansions: The History of Lebanon Reconsidered*, I.B. Tauris, London, 1988, p. 169; Meir Zamir, *The Formation of Modern Lebanon*, first published 1958, reprinted Croom Helm, Beckenham, 1985, p. 136.

3. Fadia Kiwan, 'La Perception du Grand-Liban chez les Maronites dans la Période du Mandat', in Nadim Shehadi and Dana Haffar Mills, eds, *Lebanon, A History of Conflict and Consensus*, I.B. Tauris, London, 1988, pp. 127–9.

4. See Zamir, p. 133; Rashid Khalidi, Lisa Anderson, Muhammad Muslih, and Reeva S. Simon, eds, *The Origins of Arab Nationalism*, Columbia Press, New York, 1991, pp. 3–23; Zeine N. Zeine, *The Emergence of Arab Nationalism*, Caravan Books, New York, 1973.

5. They invoked the past Ottoman government of the areas to support their claims that the idea of a Greater Lebanon involved the 'dismemberment' of traditionally Arab land, and called on support from the population of the proposed Syrian Mandate to prevent the disputed territories being incorporated into what they saw as a predominantly Christian entity. Maronite assumptions were based on the fact that many of these territories had been part of the *Imarah* at some period in the past. See chapter one.

6. Buheiry argues that up to the nineteenth century 'in terms of population size, construction activity, artisanal production and trade', Tripoli was the leading city in the region. Though Beirut's importance developed during the nineteenth century, Tripoli remained important. Marwan Buheiry, 'Beirut's Role in the Political Economy of the French Mandate 1919–39', in Laurence I. Conrand, ed., *The Formation and Perception of the Modern Arab World*, Darwin Press Inc, Princeton, 1989, p. 538; Michael Johnson, *Class and Client in Beirut: The Sunni Muslim Community and the Lebanese State 1840–1985*, Ithaca Press, London, 1986, pp. 11–12.

7. From the perception of French administrators of the Mandate it possibly made most sense to include Tripoli in Greater Lebanon because several experts liked the idea of having the Mandate's administrative quarters there. Arguably this might have

compensated the inhabitants of Tripoli for their official detachment from Syria. But Emile Eddé and the Patriarch, Howayek, seem to have played pivotal roles in switching attention to Beirut. Their perception, and that of the Maronite mercantile elite which was predominantly Beirut-based, was that Tripoli needed to be in Lebanon but subordinate to Beirut, promoting chances of Maronite economic dominance at the same time as allowing an exploitation of the trade that traditionally passed through Tripoli. According to Salibi and Salam, the inhabitants of Tripoli recognised this agenda, which helps to account for the enduring resentment Tripoli displayed at being included in the Lebanese entity. This demonstrated itself in rhetoric that was both anti-Maronite and anti-French into the period of independence. See Buheiry, p. 538; Zamir, p. 118; K. S. Salibi, *The Modern History of Lebanon*, Caravan Books, New York, 1965, p. 169; Saeb Salam, oral interview, Geneva, 4 January 1991.

8. Kiwan, p. 128.
9. In other words, the Syrian kingdom Faisal had briefly set up in 1918.
10. No mention was made of an Arab connection for Lebanon; instead, mention was made of the area's Phoenician as well as Greek and Roman heritage. See the report in *Le Réveil*, 2 September 1920. See also Edmond Rabbath, *La Formation Historique du Liban Politique et Constitutionnel*, Publication de l'Université Libanaise, Beirut, 1986, p. 372.
11. The timing of the proclamation also hurt; it came just after French troops entered Damascus to forcibly put down protests against French rule in Syria. Given these circumstances the Muslim population of Greater Lebanon, and particularly the Sunni element, regarded the French as an occupying force and the existence of a separate Lebanon as a demonstration of French power. See Elizabeth Monroe, *Britain's Moment in the Middle East, 1914–17*, Chatto and Windus, London, 1981, p. 80.
12. I do not claim the Muslims had no such rational grounds for hostility, but simply emphasise the emotional nature of this initial reaction. See Rabbath, p. 381.
13. Salibi, *Modern History of Lebanon*, p. 174.
14. Nor was this emotion confined to the Maronite community in Lebanon itself; it was also a powerful force in the various emigrant communities, such as those located in France.
15. Elias Howayek, the Patriarch, seems genuinely to have played a key role in convincing Gouraud that Greater Lebanon was the 'right' path to follow, for instance. See chapter two.
16. As a result of the experiences of wartime starvation in Mount Lebanon, the Maronite Church had been very insistent that Greater Lebanon include the ports, for instance. See Zamir, pp. 117–9.
17. Elias Howayek, 'Revendication du Liban: Mémoire de la Délégation Libanaise à la Conference de la Paix', 25 October 1919, Paris, in *Documents of the Maronite Patriarch*, Maronite Church, Bkirki, 23 February 1936.
18. Salibi, *The Modern History of Lebanon*, p. 1.
19. This was a very public exercise in the Mandate period, not something confined to scholarly circles. See, for example, the comments of Emile Eddé reported in *an-Nahar*, 28 August 1937.
20. Zamir, p. 23.
21. Historians, including Edmond Rabbath, have even suggested that 'Lebanese nationalism' arose amongst such emigrant Maronite communities rather than in Lebanon. See Rabbath, pp. 360–8. However, this ignores the emotions within

Lebanon itself. Undoubtedly ideas were interchanged, and these undoubtedly served to reinforce the development of a 'nationalist' agenda for Lebanon. Equally, the French certainly used such societies to demonstrate support for the Mandate. See Zamir, pp. 70–8.

22. The creation of the Lebanese and Syrian Mandates was a complex issue in France itself. For example, some in France were hostile to the Mandate, either because they were anti-colonial, or because they wanted a colony and not a Mandate. For further details of the creation of the Mandate, and for further details of French expectations, see Briand's addresses to the Senate, 5 April 1921 and 12 July 1921, as recorded in *Asie Française*, no. 192, 1921, pp. 205–8; 378–80; Poincare, address to the Chamber of Deputies, 1 June 1921, as recorded in *Asie Francaise*, no. 192, 1921, p. 268. See also Stephen Hemsley Longrigg, *Syria and Lebanon under French Mandate*, Oxford University Press, Oxford, 1968; and Philippe Gouraud, *Le Général Henri Gouraud au Liban et en Syrie, 1919–1923*, L'Harmattan, Paris, 1993.

23. Monroe, *The Mediterranean in Politics*, London, 1939, p. 76.

24. Longrigg, p. 114.

25. Longrigg, p. 118; Henri Gouraud, speech given at a reception, 22 November 1919. See Philippe Gouraud, p. 39.

26. *Ibid.*

27. The French public servants entrusted with this task were accustomed to having total power in this respect, and found it difficult to adapt to a situation where they were expected to act only as advisers, rather than giving orders. See Longrigg, p. 114.

28. From the French perspective, the Sunni position was contradictory and thus profoundly irritating. On the one hand, accustomed to participating in the Ottoman administration, they complained of being under-represented in the new state and resented their 'omission'. On the other hand, they refused to endorse the legitimacy of the Mandate by agreeing to participate in its mechanisms. For instance, in 1922, they refused to participate in the elections to set up a Chamber of Representatives. See Zamir, p. 127; Johnson, pp. 23–4.

29. See the comments in Bishara al-Khoury, *Haqa'iq Lubnaniyyah* [Facts About Lebanon], Maktabit Basil, Harissa, 1960, vol. 1, pp. 124–6.

30. The case of Cilicia seemed ominous, since France had evacuated Cilicia despite previous declarations that this would not happen. French sensitivity to their position and international links was far from welcome to the Maronites, who saw it as something of a betrayal. See Yussuf al-Sawda, personal papers, unpublished and unclassified, Université du St Esprit, Kaslik.

31. Even some small Maronite elements were so opposed to the Mandate that they were prepared to forge alliances with Muslim opinion. However, this did not signify a willingness to endorse an Arab nationalist position; rather they tried to recruit politically conscious leaders from the Muslim elements to the cause of a separate and independent Lebanon. See Kiwan, p. 124; Zamir, p. 124; Farid al-Khazin, 'The Communal Pact of Identities', Papers on Lebanon, Centre for Lebanese Studies, Oxford, October 1991, p. 8.

32. Zamir, p. 117.

33. At least during the early years of the Mandate, the French saw this Maronite attitude as unnecessary, if only because the Sunni's continued attitude of minimal co-operation with the Mandate created practical constraints. Effectively, the French had to continue to involve the Maronites! *Ibid.*, pp. 121–3.

34. Longrigg, pp. 114–18.

35. Zamir, p. 91; Gouraud, pp. 77, 128.

36. The various other communities in Lebanon also had a mixture of reactions to involvement in the Mandate, but it was the Maronite-Sunni axis that has been most significant. For the attitudes and reactions of the Greek Orthodox community, see Joseph Abou Jaoude, *Les Partis Politiques au Liban*, Université St Esprit, Kaslik, 1985, pp. 170–1; Zamir, p. 102. For those of the Shi'ites, see Zamir, p. 68. For those of the Druze, who continued to focus on preventing Maronite dominance in Mount Lebanon, see *ibid.* and Longrigg, pp. 148–52.

37. This promise was endorsed by the Representative Council for Greater Lebanon, set up in 1922, as the first attempt by the French to create an administrative system. For further details see Rabbath, p. 379.

38. The spread of trouble to Lebanon was a cause of very real concern to the French authorities there because it was not just confined to one social level or Muslim community. It involved the masses and the intelligentsia, for example, and can be taken as indicating very widespread discontent with the Mandate. Philip S. Khoury, *Syria and the French Mandate: The Politics of Arab Nationalism, 1920–1945*, Princeton University Press, Princeton, 1987, pp. 151–204. For further details on the Syrian insurrection and its impact on Lebanon, see Longrigg, pp. 148–52; Rabbath, pp. 379, 401–2.

39. Zamir, p. 210; Rabbath, pp. 378–9.

40. Though this hostility did not, from 1926, lead the Sunni to continue their 1922 boycott of elections. Instead, they used 'parliamentary democracy' as 'an expression of protest rather than a means to government'. In other words, they participated to disrupt the process, rather than to further it. See Johnson, pp. 23–4. See also Rabbath, p. 399.

41. Fouad L. Bustani, *Introduction à l'Histoire Politique du Liban Moderne*, FMA, Beirut, 1993, pp. 150–1 for the text of the Constitution.

42. The new republic was limited in its freedom of action: as the mandatory power, France essentially controlled the political and legal systems, and this was actually enshrined in the constitution. In addition, the governor inherited the wide range of prerogatives that the high commissioner had held, and the French had an enormous amount of control over the local bureaucracy. The Mandate administrative system came to include services dealing with nearly all the functions of a modern state, and these services were expected to operate according to standards and agendas laid down by the French and not by the indigenous communities. For the text of the constitution see Bustani, pp. 150–238. For more on the constitution and administrative system see Rabbath, pp. 370–9, 399; Salibi, *Modern History of Lebanon*, pp. 165–7.

43. For instance, the 1926 constitution declared that the boundaries of Lebanon established in 1920 were permanent and unchangeable, and required an elected president of the republic to swear loyalty to a Lebanese nation as it existed within these boundaries. See the text of the constitution in Bustani, pp. 229–38.

44. This, of course, was also true for other Muslim communities.

45. Salibi, *Modern History of Lebanon*, p. 167.

46. There were 'Kiyanists' who were ready to accept and endorse Greater Lebanon or *al-Kiyan* (the Entity) regardless of their religion; even in 1926 the group did include a small number of Muslim leaders who were ready, for economic political or personal reasons, to endorse the idea of *al-Kiyan*. But the majority were from the Christian communities.

47. The setting up of the constitution did lessen the sense of insecurity about French

146

intentions that had existed at the start of the Mandate. See Rabbath, p. 379.

48. Salibi, *Modern History of Lebanon*, p. 167. It was also seen in Lebanon as being partly a continuation of the 'divide and rule' approach the French had used in their colonial past, as well as a genuine attempt to take account of the internal map of Lebanon, as the work of Zamir, first published in 1958, makes plain. See Zamir, pp. 203–15.

49. Kiwan, p. 124. As Salibi has pointed out, however, any Maronite resentment of the French was initially restricted to the political elites, and did not represent the attitude of the masses, for whom the period was one of 'consolidation and achievement'. Salibi, *Modern History of Lebanon*, p. 177. If this disappointment was most acutely felt by the ambitious amongst the Maronite community, both Sunnis and Maronites (and leaders from the other communities) shared in the dislike of a number of French officials such as General Sarrail, High Commissioner of Lebanon, who, ignorant of the Levant, made unnecessary errors of judgment in dealing with leaders from the various communities. See Longrigg, pp. 148–54.

50. They were seen as having played a significant role in the creation of a separate Lebanon. Howayek's words in 1919, that '*Rien n'unit ces deux pays (le Liban et la Syrie)*' [Nothing unites these two countries (Lebanon and Syria)] were not lightly forgotten or forgiven. See *Le Réveil*, 23 November 1977, which reprinted Howayek's words, thus providing a useful indication of the enduring effect of this text. See also Salibi, *Modern History of Lebanon*, pp. 169–77.

51. Perhaps inevitably, those who had been Arab nationalists before the Mandate took the lead here. See Rashid Khalidi, 'Ottomanism and Arabism', in Rashid Khalidi et al. (eds), *The Origins of Arab Nationalism*, Columbia Press, New York, 1991, p. 55. They sought inspiration and tactics from Syrian opposition groups. For instance, the General Syrian Congress met once in 1928 and twice in 1933 to voice their opinion about the existence of Lebanon in its present boundaries. It was argued that the 'disputed territories' should be returned to Syria, but that Mount Lebanon should be independent. However, after the insurrection of 1925–7 was suppressed, this opinion stayed largely at the level of rhetoric. See Edmond Rabbath, *Unité Syrienne et Devenir Arabe*, Librairie Marcel, Paris, 1937, pp. 166–7; Amine Naji (ed.), 'Minutes of the Congress', *al-Amal*, no. 7, 1977, pp. 119–55.

52. Salibi, *Modern History of Lebanon*, p. 174.

53. Al-Jisr was prepared to become involved because he held no personal ideology that led him into conflict with the aims of the Mandate, while he did have personal ambition and a dislike of being out of power.

54. As Longrigg points out, Lebanon (and Syria) were even less affected by the depression of 1928–35 than France itself, for example, to say nothing of other states in the Middle East. Longrigg, pp. 271–83.

55. This, of course, ensured that the French Mandate authorities were at best cautious in their attempts to involve them until they had demonstrated that they had abandoned this position.

56. Salibi, *Modern History of Lebanon*, pp. 175–6.

57. As Johnson points out, only through cooperation with the Mandate could the mercantile elite make the most of their key economic position. See Johnson, p. 25.

58. Marwan Buheiry, 'Beirut and the Political Economy of the Mandate' in Laurence Conrand, ed., *The Formation and Perception of the Modern Arab World*, Darwin Press, Princeton, 1988, p. 558.

59. Camille Chamoun, *Mudhakkarati* [My Memoirs], Beirut, 1969, p. 8, logged at the headquarters of the Bloc National.

60. This poem has remained important to those Maronites who endorse the Phoenician concept. See Charles Corm, 'La Montagne Inspirée', republished in *La Revue Phenicienne*, Beirut, 1964, pp. 53–61.

61. Salibi, *Modern History of Lebanon*, pp. 172–3.

62. He was deeply influenced by the ideas of his brother-in-law, Michel Chiha. As a banker, Chiha was an important figure in the commercial world, but he was also a figure in the intellectual world. A far-sighted pragmatist, Chiha argued that a genuine nation-state of Lebanon could only come about if all the communities were able to feel their perspectives were valued. Chiha had been an important influence in ensuring that the constitution did in theory permit such a state to evolve. Still, in his writings on Lebanon, Chiha referred frequently to the Phoenicians. Salibi, *Modern History of Lebanon*, pp. 167; 173–4. See Michel Chiha, *Politique Interieur*, Editions du Trident, Beirut, 1964 for a further discussion of his ideas.

63. These parties were to represent the two key positions around which Maronite alliances were formed, whether in opposition of some kind or support for the Mandate. Thus these two determined much of the nature of Maronite political life during the Mandate. But for all their differences, both shared a fundamental support for the idea of a distinct, separate Lebanon. Even al-Khoury did not take his support for collaboration with the Arab position to the extent of endorsing ambitions to restore all or part of Greater Lebanon to 'Syria'. Michael W. Suleiman, *Political Parties in Lebanon*, Cornell University Press, New York, 1967, pp. 251–60; W. Awwad, *Ashab al-Fakhama Ru'assa Lubnan*, [Their Excellencies, the Presidents of Lebanon], Dar al-Ahliyyah, Beirut, 1977, pp. 112, 131, 157.

64. His main qualifications in French eyes were that, in the atmosphere of tension in 1926, he was sympathetic to pan-Arab ideas, and so might hope to conciliate the Muslim communities. However, his commitment to a separate Lebanon had been demonstrated by his membership in the 1919 delegation to the Peace Conference.

65. He had shown himself to be a capable administrator, and made few mistakes. He did make one significant mistake: endorsing moves to increase the role of Roman Catholic missions in the country, which effectively meant an increase of foreign influence. Still, the evidence indicates he was a popular figure across confessional boundaries. See Salibi, *Modern History of Lebanon*, pp. 170–1.

66. Though some deputies saw al-Jisr as best option, the Maronite Patriarch vehemently opposed his candidacy. But Eddé decided to endorse al-Jisr's candidacy to block al-Khoury's chances. See Kiwan, p. 124.

67. The Congress, held in Beirut in January 1932, had demanded that the constitution be amended to make it mandatory that the president be a Muslim, since the delegates (including al-Jisr) believed that there was a Muslim majority in Lebanon. See Johnson, p. 24; Kiwan, p. 146.

68. David McDowall, *Lebanon: A Conflict of Minorities*, Minority Rights Group, London, Report No. 61, p. 11.

69. For more on Habib al-Saad, see Salibi, *Modern History of Lebanon*, pp. 165, 170–1, 177.

70. Kiwan, p. 146.

71. Al-Khoury's followers, for instance, began to talk of French despotism as al-Khoury, on personally bad terms with Henri Ponsot, made it plain that he thought he had no future politically under a French-run Mandate. See *ibid*.

72. Ponsot's successor as High Commissioner, Count Damien de Martel, was prepared to take a more pro-Maronite stance.

73. Salibi, *Modern History of Lebanon*, p. 179; Raymond Eddé, interview, Paris, 19 July 1994; Dr Albert Moukheiber, interview, Bayt Meiri, 15 April 1995.

74. Longrigg, pp. 205–7.

75. Philip Khoury, p. 454.

76. *Le Jour*, 11 September 1935.

77. Said Murad, *al-Haraka al-Wahdawiyyah fi Lubnan Bayn al-Harbayn al-Alamiyatayn 1914–1964* [The Unionist Movement in Lebanon Between 1914 and 1964], Maahad al-Inma al-Arabi, Beirut, 1968, pp. 264–5.

78. While these groups caused concern to both community leaders and French Mandate officials in the late 1930s, they were still relatively small; the Kata'ib Party was also capable of more pragmatic politics. See Itamar Rabinovich, 'Arab Political Parties: Ideology and Ethnicity', in Milton J. Esman and Itamar Rabinovich, eds, *Ethnicity, Pluralism and the State in the Middle East*, Cornell University Press, Ithaca, 1988, p. 163; Johnson, p. 24; Suleiman, p. 114; Rabiha Abou Fadel and Antun Saadeh, *al-Naqidwaal Adib al-Mahjari* [The Critics and the Writers of Emigré Literature], Maktab al-Dirasat al-Kimat, al-Matn, 1992; Longrigg, pp. 225–6. For a more detailed discussion of the events of 1936, including the riots of November 1936, see Salibi, *Modern History of Lebanon*, pp. 179–81; Farid al-Khazin, 'The Communal Pact of National Identities', *Papers on Lebanon*, Centre for Lebanese Studies, Oxford, October 1991, especially p. 12.

79. Salibi, *Modern History of Lebanon*, p. 181. Salibi also provides a useful discussion of the further details of the treaties, *ibid.*, pp. 181–2.

80. In the end, the French ratified neither the Franco-Lebanese treaty nor the Franco-Syrian treaty. Albert Hourani, *Syria and Lebanon: A Political Essay*, Oxford University Press, London, 1946, pp. 202, 314, 337. Also see Salibi, *Modern History of Lebanon*, pp. 181–3.

81. Najla Attiyah, 'The Attitude of the Lebanese Sunni towards the State of Lebanon', unpublished PhD thesis, University of London, 1973, p. 131. See also Raghid al-Solh, 'The Attitude of the Arab Nationalists towards Greater Lebanon During the 1930s', in Shehadi and Mills, eds, *Lebanon*, I.B. Tauris, London, 1988, pp. 157–61.

82. Kazem al-Solh papers, unpublished, held by Raghid al-Solh, Oxford.

83. 'Mu'tamar al-Sahil' [Conference of the Coast], unpublished manuscript in Kazem al-Solh papers. See also al-Khazin, p. 14.

84. *Ibid.*

85. In 1937, for example, a Sunni deputy, Khayr al-Din al-Ahdab, formed a government under Eddé's presidency. For a previously fervent Arab nationalist, this was a significant move. His actions were to set an important precedent for the involvement of Muslim leaders in a Lebanese government.

86. In March 1938 Khayr al-Din al-Ahdab was succeeded by Khalid Shihab, a Sunni Shihabi emir, and he in turn was succeeded by Abdallah Yafi, a Sunni lawyer.

87. Gabriel Puaux, *Deux Années au Levant*, Hachette, Paris, 1952, pp. 56, 60–5, 225–6.

88. Emile Eddé was prepared to work with the French in the Mandate, but that should not be taken as an indication that he was opposed to Lebanese independence. After all he had signed the Franco-Lebanese treaty of 1936. But he did feel in 1939 that Lebanese, and Maronite, interests were best served by a continuation of French interests and protection. Raymond Eddé, interview, 19 July 1994.

89. Charles de Gaulle, *War Memoirs: The Call to Honour. 1940–42 Documents*, London, 1955, pp. 312–13; Elizabeth Monroe, *Britain's Moment in the Middle East*, p. 80; Salwa Mardam Bey, *Awraq Jamil Mardam Bey Istiklal Suria 1939–45*, Shirkat al-Matbu'at lil

al-Tawzi'wa al-Nashr, Beirut, p. 154.

90. *An-Nahar*, 27 November 1941. See also Raghid al-Solh, 'Lebanon and Arab Nationalism 1936–45', unpublished PhD thesis, St Anthony's College, Oxford, 1986, pp. 202–4.

91. See al-Khazin, pp. 13–18.

92. *Ibid.*

93. Seen from a wider perspective, Syrian leaders accepted a separate Lebanon as long as Syria itself was independent from France. See al-Solh, p. 216.

94. The regional balance of power was drifting in Britain's favour, and Arab leaders in Syria were generally more pro-British than pro-French. Equally, the realities of the situation meant that the Free French regimes in Syria and Lebanon depended on British support, and this was widely apparent to the populations in the Mandates. See Mardam Bey, pp. 188–91.

95. Spears realised that this was one thing that, in the context of events in 1943 at least, would hold the communities together; it could also earn Britain some long-term goodwill, at least from the pro-Arab elements (more important than the Maronites, given Britain's wider responsibilities in the Middle East), and it would give him a chance to work out a personal grudge against de Gaulle. See al-Solh, p. 185; A. B. Ganson, *The Anglo-French Clash in Lebanon and Syria, 1940–45*, Macmillan, London, 1987, pp. 146–51; al-Khazin, p. 34.

96. He used this to promote the concept of future Lebanese co-operation with other Arab states, though leading figures such as Bishara al-Khoury and Riyadh al-Solh. See Mardam Bey, p. 189; al-Khazin, p. 18.

97. Nicola Ziadeh, *Syria and Lebanon*, Ernest Benn Ltd, London, 1957, p. 76; Raymond Eddé, interview, 19 July 1994.

98. Johnson, p. 26. The pact was an agreement worked out in private between these two men, broadly to preserve the interests of the elites in their communities. It was never formally recorded in writing. Insofar as it does exist in any written form it is to be found referred to in Riyadh al-Solh, Speech, 7 October 1943 in *Cabinet Papers 1926–1948*, Muassassat al-Dirasat al-Lubnaniyyah, Beirut, 1986, vol. I, p. 126; in Bishara al-Khoury, Vol. I, p. 264; Vol. II, pp. 15–21. See also Bassem al-Jisr, *Mithaq 1943: Limaza Kan wa Limaza Saqat* [The National Pact, 1943, with Reasons for its Existence and Failure], Dar an-Nahar lil Nashr, Beirut, 1978, pp. 142–60; al-Solh, pp. 274–8.

99. Salibi, *Modern History of Lebanon*, pp. 181–2; Johnson.

100. As Michael Johnson points out, the Muslim commercial sector had no wish to upset the Christian commercial sector, and could see advantages for themselves in such an arrangement. See Johnson, pp. 117–8.

101. Shi'ite numbers were growing, but the community was little regarded by either the Sunni or the Maronites within the terms of the National Pact. Most members of the community were poor, and consequently relatively powerless in this period. *ibid.*, p. 118.

102. Al-Khazin, p. 34.

103. Raghid al-Solh argues, for example that the main significance of the pact was its 'contribution to the emergence of a democracy by conciliation', arguing that for men like al-Jisr, it 'came to symbolise national integration and confessional unity'. Al-Solh, pp. 274–8.

104. *Ibid.*, p. 23.

CHAPTER FOUR

The Crisis Develops, 1943–1958

The National Pact of 1943 has been described as 'a compromise formulation on the identity of the country and on power-sharing between the religious communities', because it involved 'a number of mutual renunciations and guarantees'.[1] If this interpretation of the unwritten 'gentleman's agreement' fairly sums up the pact, in both origin and practice, then explaining the pact's collapse in 1958 requires more than simply saying the Lebanese returned to earlier habits of co-habitation. Other factors are also needed to account for the breakdown of the new 'Lebanese' consensus.

Indeed, many explanations of the 1958 crisis have highlighted external intervention, especially by Nasser and the United States, as the major causatory factors. Salibi, for example, comments that 'It was largely events external to the Lebanese domestic scene which caused the last years of Chamoun's Presidency to be marred by violence and crises'.[2] In this chapter I focus again on the internal dynamics of Lebanese intercommunal relations. I argue that those dynamics ensured that the events of the 1950s resulted in a major crisis and that the undoubted involvement of external powers must be seen in the context of a continuation of Buheiry's patron-client game.[3]

I also reassess the National Pact, seeing it essentially as an attempt by elites to reconcile the various community mythologies relating to self-identity and a 'naturally' separate Lebanon, and to the role that the various communities (or their elites) would play in any future state. The elites involved in its evolution saw that attempt as necessary because of the 'crisis' of 1943, and they accepted it as being in their interests. But it took little practical account of any other interests within the community, being made in haste and under pressure. In association with the National Pact, those elites created a new mythology, establishing it in political rhetoric as central to the existence and survival of an independent Lebanon. Even here, however, it was presented differently to the various communities.

Moreover, the attempts to 'sell' the National Pact and an independent Lebanon to the masses of the various communities did not tackle basic underlying disagreements and differences at the lower levels of society. This was particularly true for the Sunni masses, both urban and rural. They were less influenced by the supposed material opportunities for the Lebanese state and in general, as Najla Attiyah has pointed out, were still emotionally disposed to favour a link with Syria, as being in the best interests of their religion and traditions.[4] On the Maronite side, many – especially followers of the Eddés – were not favourably inclined towards the National Pact and immediate Lebanese independence, preferring either a continuation of the Mandate, or even a future as a *'territoire d'outre-mer'*.[5]

Explanations of the crisis must evaluate the assumptions the National Pact contained about the state and nature of intercommunal relations, especially those between the Maronites and the Sunnis. The crisis allowed no time for those assumptions to be tested before being put into practice as the basis for a long-term consensus. But in 1943 the various elites – political, land-owning, and commercial – certainly saw it as in their interests to assume both that the consensus contained in the pact was workable, and that they either represented, or could dictate, the opinions and loyalties of their followers, thus giving the appearance of universal support for the pact. They tacitly accepted an important assumption: that the intercommunal balance of power within Lebanon was stable and that the balance of power within the region as a whole would remain the same for the foreseeable future.

Michael Johnson points out that 'such a vaguely defined Pact' allowed the Christian and Muslim elites to agree that 'their economic links with Europe and the West were essential'; furthermore, what he calls 'their moderate Arabism' would preserve those links, ensuring that 'they maintained their market in Syria and extended their access to the wider Arab market beyond'.[6] In other words, this arrangement was supposedly based on mutual self-interest at elite levels, and they expected it to work flexibly enough to ensure that benefits would be appropriately distributed at these levels. It was the gradual discovery that these assumptions were flawed in the context of developments in Lebanon itself, and the Middle East, in the years after 1947 in particular, that brought about the events culminating in the American landings of 1958.

The limitations of the pact quickly became clear. Even as the administration of an independent Lebanon got underway, the communal leaders, especially Maronite and Sunni, began to have identifiably mixed feelings. Maronite leaders remained somewhat nervous about the prospects of working with the various Muslim communities without the direct involvement of a Western imperial power to protect their interests.[7] Sunni leaders were happy about the apparent Maronite willingness to stop running to France at every point of difficulty, but still unsure how much the Maronites saw Lebanon as primarily an Arab entity.[8]

The Pact Collapses: Three Reasons Why

Shortly after World War II ended, the inherent contradictions contained in the pact began to create practical difficulties for those running the state. I argue that three factors led to the pact's gradual collapse. The first was simple government corruption. Second, to promote their own agendas, some individuals with political power sought to change the way Lebanon was governed. Third, some Lebanese politicians and political parties used traditional contacts with both Western and Arab states to bolster the positions and ambitions of individuals and groupings at elite levels.

Corruption is crucial in understanding why the pact collapsed, because it was one of the earliest issues to become apparent, and remained a matter of concern. The al-Khoury regime, in power from 1943 to 1952, swiftly acquired a reputation for corruption, favouritism and nepotism. Gebran Tueni and Kamel Mroueh, two leading journalists, highlighted the issue in a series of editorials in early 1946. On 12 January, Tueni attacked the 'favouritism, clientelism and nepotism' of the regime, asking in March, 'How much longer can the government continue with this profiteering mentality?'[9] On 24 April, Mroueh wrote: 'Silence is not golden. We need to tell the thieves that they are thieves'.[10] Embodying the regime's corruption, the president's brother,

25 May 1947. President Emile Eddé with Druze notables. From second left: Salah Labaki, Nohad Arslan and Nohad Boueiz.

sometimes called 'Sultan Selim', was known to exercise great influence behind the scene. Gebran Tueni, for instance, condemned the 'use of power by the relatives of the President for his own purposes.'[11]

The corruption issue caused significant tensions in 1947 when elections for a new legislature were held. These were the first since independence, and would be a preliminary to a presidential elections in 1949. It also became clear that self-interested members of the political elite were trying to modify Lebanon's government – the second theme I mentioned above. Under the terms of the constitution, the composition of the Chamber was of crucial importance in deciding the presidency. A president could not stand for a second consecutive term, but in 1947 Bishara al-Khoury wanted one. To make this possible, he needed a Chamber that was so favourably disposed towards him that it would amend the constitution to permit his candidacy as an emergency expediency.

On 13 May 1947, Kamel Mroueh indicated his fear that the elections would be corrupt: 'We are behaving morally and politically like a people who have become decrepit; we are reaching the period of collapse.' On 24 May, the day before the elections, he warned that 'the whole country is being used

154

for the benefit of some families'.[12] The election result, and the reactions to it, certainly seemed to indicate fraud. Serious accusations came from several prominent figures, notably Antun Boutros, the Maronite Patriarch, and two prominent and respected archbishops, Augustus Moubarak and Boulos Akl.[13] Moubarak's stance is especially important here, as he was related to al-Khoury and they had been friends for over forty-five years. Now he was referring to the al-Khoury regime as 'a despotic government' and the new Chamber as 'a fake chamber' because it was elected through 'fraudulent elections'.[14]

Many newspapers, representing a wide range of confessional allegiances, joined in the chorus of accusations of electoral fraud, representing a more populist perspective.[15] The parties that pointed out corruption in the election process were unified on that point, but shared little other consensus. Opposition came from the loyalist Maronite grouping, the Kata'ib Party, but also from the more moderate Bloc National, whose membership was not exclusively Maronite. The pan-Arabist Parti Populaire Syrien (PPS), came out in opposition, as did other parties with agendas that looked beyond Lebanon itself, including the Ba'ath and Communist parties.

These political opponents reacted even more vehemently after the Chamber passed the bill to amend Article 49 of the constitution on 22 May 1948. The bill, passed by forty-eight deputies to seven, permitted al-Khoury's candidacy at the forthcoming elections of 27 May 1949 as a 'special case'.[16] An analysis of the protests shows that the opposition's apparent unity, provided by its concern about the regime's corruption, was hardly simple. A series of self-seeking agendas limited the potential for these groups to co-operate on the issue.

This point becomes clearer if we examine the leading political figures protesting this development. Kamal Jumblat was motivated partly by principle but also by self-interest. By this time Jumblat saw 'Sultan Selim' as a threat to his power base in the Shuf because of Selim's links with the Maronites there; Jumblat did not welcome any continuation of the al-Khoury regime, which would allow Selim to continue his activities.[17]

Camille Chamoun, a member of al-Khoury's own party from 1943 to 1948, took the lead amongst Maronites unhappy with developments in 1947–8, also out of mixed motives. Chamoun had hoped to stand for the presidency himself, but, frustrated in his attempts and fearing threats to his power base in the Shuf, he shifted towards outright opposition to al-Khoury, taking a series of actions designed to give him a high profile in the opposition.[18] He publicly absented himself from the Chamber on 22 May 1948, the day the constitution was amended. This clearly established him as the leading Maronite opponent to al-Khoury, furthering his chances of succeeding in a future presidential contest.[19] But, like other opposition figures, Chamoun was also genuinely concerned that al-Khoury wanted to hold the presidency permanently and saw this renewal as the first step toward that goal.[20] Thus Chamoun and Jumblat were prepared to work together in opposition to al-Khoury – but it was an alliance of expedience and not a meeting of minds on wider political issues. With al-Khoury back in power in 1948 the third theme also became significant: the ways external powers used political figures for their own ends in the context of Lebanese foreign policy. The years just after World War II saw considerable upheaval and change in the Middle East, especially surrounding the end of the British Mandate over Palestine in 1948 and the creation of an Israeli state. After the resulting Arab-Israeli war of 1948–9, the Arab Islamic world became increasingly hostile to Western interventions in the Middle East, since Arab governments blamed the Western powers for their defeat in that war.[21] Lebanon was not immune to the effects of these upheavals, in particular the military coup in Syria in March 1949, but al-Khoury was determined that the success of military or paramilitary groupings in other Middle Eastern states would not be mirrored in Lebanon. He would take action, legitimate or otherwise, to ensure this.

He made this plain quite early. Following the Syrian example, the Lebanese PPS, led by Antun Saadeh, attempted a poorly supported coup in early July 1949. Though it failed, it showed the Lebanese opposition how the al-Khoury regime would operate. Saadeh took refuge in Syria, but was returned to Lebanon following pressure by Riyadh al-Solh.[22] Saadeh soon endured what has been described as the swiftest and most unfair trial in the history of Lebanon: he was refused the right to defend himself in any way, and was tried, convicted and executed all on the same day.[23] This drove the PPS into bitter opposition to both the al-Khoury regime and to the Husni al-Zaim regime. This position would have long-term implications for a Lebanese consensus, since the grounds on which the PPS would co-operate with any other political groupings in Lebanon depended on their attitude to the events of 1949 rather than to any broader political agenda.[24]

In the short term, however, al-Khoury's harsh reaction to the attempted coup did create an opposition alliance based on mutual expediency. Repressive policies drove the paramilitary parties like the Kata'ib Party and

*The funeral of President Emile Eddé in 1949. It was the most important funeral for any leader in Lebanese history to date. According to newspaper sources (*L'Orient, *29 September 1949) 300,000 people attended.*

The daughters of Riyadh al-Solh receiving condolences on the anniversary of their father's assassination.

its Muslim counterpart, Najjadah, into a temporary alliance with each other and other opposition groupings. In 1949, having organised his followers into a Progressive Socialist Party in direct reaction to these developments, Kamal Jumblat forged an alliance with Chamoun, apparently based on a shared socialist perspective.[25] The resultant Socialist National Front was, however, based more on mutual opposition to al-Khoury than on a real sharing of political ideology.[26] The Bloc National was still the leader in denouncing the widespread corruption of the al-Khoury regime.[27]

At this time, opposition figures also began to develop a perspective that looked outside Lebanon itself; they sought to place the republic in its regional context, and looked at how the polarisation within the Arab world between pro- and anti- Western camps could be directly relevant to the internal concerns of the various Lebanese communities.[28] Although the National Pact was supposed to ensure an even-handed attitude towards both the Western and the Arab camps, most Lebanese, at all levels of society, saw an ideal foreign policy as one that would give their own confessional grouping more security and status than the others.[29] Thus the Maronites were alarmed when al-Khoury, referring to the National Pact, refused to join the 'Common Defence' pact, conceived in 1951 as a Western project to counteract the interest in the region of both the USSR and the growing local Communist parties. But it pleased even those Muslim elements who were otherwise opposed to the regime.[30]

Despite such complications, the opposition front did eventually succeed in toppling the al-Khoury regime, helped by two linked developments. The Chamber elected in 1951 was less overwhelmingly linked to al-Khoury's interests.[31] On 16 July 1951, Riyadh al-Solh, one of al-Khoury's most significant supporters, was assassinated by the PPS.[32] This had very far-reaching results, because al-Solh was unequivocally the most popular Sunni leader of the time, and his loss further undermined the basis of support for al-Khoury's government. Immediately after al-Solh's death, however, al-Khoury saw his power increase. As one architect of the National Pact, al-Solh had effectively restrained al-Khoury; now it was impossible for al-Khoury to choose a successor who could be virtually equal to him in power. Though few recognised this at the time, al-Solh's death amounted to a breakdown in the national consensus. Influenced by his brother, al-Khoury appointed Sami al-Solh as Prime Minister. Sami al-Solh was a member of the same Sunni family, and an experienced politician at the time.[33]

It was to be the corruption issue, though, rather than foreign policy complications, that brought down the al-Khoury regime in September 1952. A series of editorials reveals the continuing significance of this factor. Kamel Mroueh, for instance, claimed in May 1952 that trust between 'governed and governors' had broken down because of corruption. In September he labelled al-Khoury's regime and its supporters, especially Selim al-Khoury, as 'arrogant thieves and profiteers'.[34] In September 1952, the opposition began to arrange a general strike 'against corruption', to call for al-Khoury's resignation.[35] A cabinet crisis resulted, as Sami al-Solh apparently broke ranks to endorse the accusations of corruption. Al-Khoury tried to create a new government, but when the strike occurred, on 15–16 September, the army refused to back the president. The crisis could only be resolved through al-Khoury's resignation and new presidential elections in May 1952.[36]

Triumphant in the election, Camille Chamoun quickly discovered the importance of foreign policy as the Lebanese reacted to the changing Middle Eastern context. As al-Khoury had discovered, despite the National Pact, foreign policy issues could still generate intercommunal tensions. In 1952, foreign policy had two main strands that would converge in the aftermath of the Suez crisis. One strand related to Syria, the other to Egypt.

The first strand, Lebanese-Syrian relations, had been strained since the separate Mandates were set up in 1920.[37] In the 1950s, the tension came mainly from the divergent economic situations of the two countries, and the question of political refugees. The Syrians had long resented Lebanon's greater economic success, with its visibly higher standards of living for most communities, including the Sunnis; the issue always had the potential to intensify short-term clashes.[38]

In the early to middle 1950s, most of these clashes resulted when Syrian political refugees fled to Lebanon and took advantage of the relative Lebanese press and media freedom to publicise their views in ways that would be heard in Syria. The number of coups in Syria after 1949 created another problem for Lebanese-Syrian relations. This crisis in relations came to a peak in 1955, when two members of the PPS, Ghassan and Fu'ad Jadid, were implicated in assassinating a prominent Syrian official, Adnan al-Maliki, in revenge for Syria's behaviour over Saadeh. Now Syria was completely hostile to the Chamoun government, which continued to tolerate the PPS and its anti-Syrian propaganda, especially since the PPS supported the Chamoun regime.[39]

The other foreign policy strand had wider dimensions, relating to the impact on the Middle East of the Egyptian coup which brought Nasser to power. In the context of the Cold War, Nasser's policy of distancing himself from the West, and seeking to persuade his fellow Arab states to do likewise had a considerable impact on political relationships within Lebanon. The West and those Arab states with a more Western orientation in the early 1950s, such as Turkey, Pakistan and Iraq, sought to develop an anti-Soviet defence strategy based on 'friendly co-operation' between the Middle Eastern states, with US backing.[40] Turkey and Iraq reached the Baghdad Pact on 24 February 1955. Iraq then took the lead in pressuring its Arab neighbours into joining.

Nasser did not welcome the Baghdad Pact. In 1954 he had succeeded in getting British troops removed from Egypt, including the Suez Canal Zone. Now he saw an Arab state, Iraq, involved with Britain in a pact that could rival his ambition to lead the Arab world. For Nasser, the pact was 'part of a Western scheme to support the creation of small, easily manipulated Arab states in order to combat the tide of Arab nationalism and perpetuate their colonial rule'; it was also a personal affront to his personal dream of Arab unity.[41] So Nasser began to pressure Arab states not to join the pact.[42] Both camps pressured Lebanon.

Chamoun's term in office started well: he made conciliatory noises to leaders of all the major political and commercial groupings in Lebanon, but by the mid-1950s the goodwill was evaporating, especially amongst the Muslim elites. Without a leader who had the stature of Riyadh al-Solh, the Sunnis felt particularly discontented, believing with some justice that their influence had lessened.[43] Thus opposition leaders were looking for excuses and opportunities to attack and undermine Chamoun. The wider Middle Eastern conflict provided just the excuses and opportunities they sought. Chamoun did turn down the opportunity to join the Baghdad Pact, but not in terms that aligned the state clearly with the opposing, Nasser-led camp. His attempt at neutrality obviously did not please the various interested parties outside Lebanon; more importantly, within the country it increased tensions along confessional lines.[44] As a result, attitudes within Lebanon toward the state's foreign policy between 1955 and 1958 related more to the perspectives dictated by confessional traditions than to the actual developments within the Middle East, such as the Suez crisis.

In the same year as the Baghdad Pact, Nasser arranged an arms deal with the Soviet bloc, signalling to the West that he was willing to work with the USSR – and causing considerable alarm in the West. The US had offered to fund the Aswan Dam, a project of huge symbolic importance to both Egypt and Nasser; now it sought to bring Nasser back into line by withdrawing the funding. But Nasser reacted promptly, negotiating Soviet funding for the dam, and also nationalising the Suez Canal Company.[45]

The 1956 Suez Crisis was a major international event, but its impact was also significant for individual states in the Middle East – including Lebanon – balanced as it was between the Western and Arab worlds through the National Pact. When the Suez Crisis was resolved in Egypt's favour, Nasser's standing within the Arab world rose enormously, alarming those not in sympathy with Arab nationalist ideas. Throughout the Arab world, popular enthusiasm for Nasser threatened the ability of any state government to take a position identified as anti-Nasserist, either explicitly or implicitly, particularly involving relations with the West or advocacy of the Baghdad Pact. This situation was crucial for Lebanon under the National Pact; it was now much harder to maintain the balance that the pact envisaged, especially in the face of pressure within Lebanon for or against either Nasser or the Western world.

After the Suez Crisis, Nasser pressured the Chamoun government to make at least a token gesture of solidarity with the Arab world by withdrawing the Lebanese ambassadors to Britain and France. Chamoun refused, invoking the terms of the National Pact to claim that he could not break with the West; instead he merely endorsed a condemnation of the actions of these powers. Even that action precipitated an internal crisis in his cabinet, indicating the existence of potentially destabilising forces in Lebanon.[46] Abdallah al-Yafi had been Prime Minister, and Saeb Salam, Minister of State from 3 June 1956, but both men were dissatisfied with the current power balance in the regime and at odds with Chamoun over economic issues relating to their communities.

The Suez Crisis offered them a chance to redress matters by asserting their power over Chamoun. So they pursued the ambassadorial withdrawals, pointing to both the policy of the Arab League, of which Lebanon was a member, and the obligations of the National Pact. On 18 November 1956 both resigned in protest at Chamoun's refusal to take 'an Arab stance', claiming he was breaking a promise he had made to them. However, they failed to bring down Chamoun himself.[47] He reconstructed his cabinet on the same day, bringing in Sami al-Solh as Prime Minister, but al-Yafi and Salam had now identified themselves with the broadly pro-Nasserist camp within Lebanon, and found it expedient to continue to do so, thereby distancing themselves from Chamoun.

Between 1956 and 1958 Nasser increasingly came to represent the ambitions and agendas of the Muslim political opposition in Lebanon. In the absence of a genuinely strong internal leader, the charismatic Nasser became a useful symbol for politicians seeking to inspire their own followers. Nasser's message was of 'dignity, social justice, development, anti-imperialism, anti-Zionism, and pan-Arabism'; all of these were already part of the Muslim political agendas within Lebanon. Thus Nasser and his words provided a useful focus through which the Muslim political leaders in Lebanon could interpret their existing agendas, giving them a higher profile and greater weight in the eyes of their supporters.[48]

The new cabinet that Chamoun chose on 18 November 1956 was not likely to increase opposition support for the regime. This was especially true of Chamoun's choice of foreign minister: the Greek Orthodox Dr Charles Malik, well-known for his pro-Western orientation. Salibi says that Malik's inclusion in the new government 'was in itself a declaration of policy'.[49]

The Eisenhower Doctrine

This background is important for understanding political debate in Lebanon over the Eisenhower Doctrine; I emphasise it over the doctrine itself and the pressures that external powers, notably Egypt and the US, were putting on the Lebanese government. The Americans intended Eisenhower's Doctrine, announced on 5 January 1957, to counteract moves towards communism in the Middle East.[50] This 'joint resolution of the United States Senate and House of Representatives', as Raymond Salame puts it, authorised 'the President to employ the armed forces of the United States to protect the independence of any nation controlled by international communism', with Egypt implicitly identified as the villain.[51]

In presenting his proposals, Eisenhower emphasised that the situation in the Middle East was 'critical', and argued that the US's global responsibilities demanded a policy that would enable it to defuse any crisis there. Consequently, the US had to be prepared to modify traditional support for national aspirations amongst states that had formerly been European colonies, judging whether or not those aspirations were tainted by communism. The doctrine aimed to go beyond merely protecting territorial integrity to providing necessary military assistance and economic aid to counter the growth of international communism. Eisenhower specifically identified Lebanon as a possible client for such assistance, describing how communists masquerading as Arab nationalists could threaten its established nationalism.[52]

Once Congress passed the doctrine and Eisenhower signed it, on 9 March 1957, the US sought – with little success – to sell it to the Arab world. Both Syria and Egypt rejected it vehemently and urged other states in the region to do the same.[53] In On 14 March 1957 James P. Richards arrived in Beirut to persuade the Chamoun government to endorse it.[54] By this time, however, there was considerable opposition resentment of Chamoun's domestic policies, linked to fears about his future political plans, and Muslim (especially Sunni) bitterness over their exclusion from real power. Any reaction to the doctrine would likely be based more on these attitudes than on a considered judgment of the doctrine's value, or threats, to Lebanon.

Even before Richards arrived, the pro-Nasserist elements in the opposition, such as the al-Yafi faction, had begun to demand rejection of the Eisenhower Doctrine. But the less ideologically aligned factions in the opposition, including those led by Christians such as Fouad Ammoun, were less decided in their stance, as a survey of reports in *al-Hayat* and other newspapers indicates. For instance, *al-Hayat* reported that both Jumblat and Bishara al-Khoury and his Constitutional Bloc saw some merits in the doctrine,[55] despite the danger of isolating Lebanon from the rest of the Arab world. Most of the opposition rejected the doctrine because it saw Chamoun's acceptance of it as linked to American endorsement of plans Chamoun might have to follow al-Khoury's precedent and seek re-election via a constitutional amendment. Chamoun's official acceptance of the doctrine was announced in the joint American-Lebanese statement of 16 March 1957, but the opposition came to believe that Richards's visit also enabled Chamoun to confirm American support for his re-election.[56]

Thus the endorsement of the doctrine divided Lebanon into two main groups, essentially those for and against government policy, whether explicitly or implicitly. Notable amongst the administration's supporters was the Kata'ib Party, with its fears of Arab nationalism and especially of Egypt and Syria.[57] The opposition included a majority of the influential Muslim leaders and several Christian leaders, especially those unwilling to see Chamoun re-elected. Furious that the government had accepted the doctrine, they also feared that it had strengthened Chamoun's own power and chances of success through electoral fraud. So they claimed that Chamoun's acceptance of the doctrine compromised the National Pact, and amounted to government corruption.[58] Facing the storm of protests against the Eisenhower Doctrine, the cabinet agreed to hold a parliamentary debate on foreign policy and to submit to a vote of confidence in the Chamber of Deputies starting on 6 April 1957. The stormy debate lasted three days, but an abiding undercurrent in that debate was the established fears and resentments of the parties involved over essentially internal matters. The government won the debate, by a majority of thirty to one, but before the vote was taken six deputies resigned in protest over government policy.[59]

One result of this debate was the formation of new opposition groupings linked primarily by their hostility to Chamoun and his regime, and focused on expressing that hostility in the forthcoming elections. The predominantly Muslim United National Front formed on 31 March 1957, and on 1 April 1957, published an agenda which summed up the range of feelings about Chamoun's policies. It contained accusations about government corruption and a commitment to the conditions of the National Pact, which it argued Chamoun had broken; thus it also mentioned the desirability of interconfessional collaboration.[60] The front included Sunni leaders like Saeb Salam and Abdallah al-Yafi, and some leading Christian figures with broadly Nasserist sympathies such as Bishara al-Khoury, leader of the Constitutional Bloc.[61] It also included political groupings such as Najjadah, the National Organisation, and the Ba'ath Party.

At the same time, a group that came to be known as the Third Force appeared on the political scene. It included political leaders from the Catholic and Greek Orthodox sects, which traditionally sought to take a neutral stance in Lebanese political conflicts. Certainly Third Force figures such as Henry Pharaon, Yussuf Hitti, Joseph Salem and George Naccache, as well as the newspaperman Ghassan Tueni, initially sought to act as a mediating element between the United National Front and the government. But as attitudes hardened on both sides, the Third Force moved closer to the Front in its views and attitudes. Eventually, little but the personalities remained to differentiate it from the United National Front in terms of relations with the government.

But as the United National Front's agenda suggests, the unity of the opposition to the Chamoun regime was again driven by expediency rather than shared agendas. Resentment that the regime had endorsed the Eisenhower Doctrine, as a symbol of the dissent on foreign policy issues, became linked to fears that Chamoun was using foreign policy for his own ends. On internal issues, the various groups had very different domestic agendas and there is no evidence of any discussions to move these agendas closer together for the longer term.[62] The doctrine retained its high profile partly because of Chamoun's plans for a new electoral law, the terms of which were first published on 18 March 1957. The new law would increase the number of deputies from forty-four to sixty-six, and change some constituencies, establishing the basis for major political changes in both confessional terms and the power bases of currently powerful leaders. This proposed law ran directly counter to opposition demands for a larger, eighty-eight-member Chamber, which it said the nation needed to provide a fairer confessional representation in the spirit of the National Pact, reversing the established bias towards the Maronite community. The opposition claimed that Chamoun's electoral reform would confirm that bias, rather than reverse it.[63]

As expected, in April 1957, the Chamber passed Chamoun's version of the new electoral law. But opposition protests continued, and increased in vehemence. The six deputies who resigned after the debate over the Eisenhower Doctrine did so largely to improve their chances of support in

Meeting at the Eddé house in Beirut. Raymond Eddé and Nohad Boueiz are carried by their supporters.

predominantly Sunni constituencies in the forthcoming elections.[64] In the election campaign, both sides adopted an increasingly common strategy of using foreign policy issues in their rhetoric; these issues tended to sum up attitudes on a range of other essentially domestic issues, including political corruption and the relative status of the various confessional communities.[65]

Michael Johnson points out one probably intended effect of Chamoun's reforms: a reduction in the power of the traditional landed classes of all communities, bolstering the power of the 'commercial-financial bourgeoisie'.[66] But Chamoun's prime motivation was probably to produce a Chamber of Deputies packed with his supporters, which he expected would come predominantly from that commercial-financial bourgeoisie, even across confessional boundaries to some extent. A Chamber favourably disposed and grateful to Chamoun would be more likely to co-operate in any attempt he made to renew his mandate by amending the constitution. Certainly by increasing the numbers of deputies by only twenty-two he reduced the power of existing strong leaders, without making it harder to keep his own majority in the Chamber.

While the first political moves in the campaign were made in March and April, official campaigning only began on 12 May 1957, with a government procession. Simultaneously the United National Front held a rally to publicise its campaign issues. Together they formed a platform on which the Front felt that political co-operation could continue within Lebanon:

1. The constitution should not be amended to enable President Chamoun to stand for re-election.
2. Lebanon should not be neutral in any dispute between foreign powers.
3. Lebanon should refuse to house foreign military bases or to join foreign military pacts such as the Baghdad Pact.
4. Lebanon should reject any aid that would restrict its sovereignty or influence its foreign policy.
5. Lebanon should pursue a policy of close, impartial and effective co-operation with other Arab states.
6. The existing government should make way for a caretaker government to supervise the elections.[67]

This list reflects the opposition's main fears, beginning with Chamoun's unspoken intention to seek another term. It also underlines the opposition's belief that the Chamoun regime was corrupt. On 20 May Hamid Frangieh alleged that Chamoun was guilty of corruption, including bribery, and also of scaremongering because he sought to use foreign policy issues for his own purposes. By trying to convince the electorate that Lebanon's very existence was at stake in the election, he was diverting attention from the real issues of his own corruption and personal ambitions.[68]

On 27 May 1957 the United National Front sought to escalate the tension and thus advance its own agenda. It gave Chamoun twenty-four hours to dismiss the Sami al-Solh government in favour of a neutral caretaker cabinet which would act to supervise the elections. If he did not act, a general strike and 'peaceful demonstrations' would begin on 30 May.[69] Similar tactics had succeeded in bringing down the al-Khoury regime in 1952, but this time the government was, or felt itself to be, in a stronger position. Thus it banned all demonstrations likely to lead to a breach of the peace and requested enforcement from the Ministry of the Interior. The army was also readied for intervention if necessary.[70]

The demonstration went ahead in Beirut on 30 May. It escalated into a fight between the demonstrators and the *gendarmerie*, though the army was reluctant to become deeply involved – as with all the fighting during this period.[71] However, it set the tone for a bitter campaign, as the press reporting indicates. The government claimed that only 4 men and 1 woman were killed, while opposition leaders maintained that more than 15 people were killed, with about 100 wounded.[72] One Sunni opposition leader, Saeb Salam, was wounded in the head and taken to hospital in custody; 350 other demonstrators were arrested and detained in a stable.

The government also sought to minimise the popular impact of the demonstration by confiscating the next day's issues of the five leading opposition newspapers;[73] the army then moved in to ensure that no more fighting began. These government actions turned a relatively minor demonstration into both a major election issue and a symbol of misuse of government power. The opposition was in fact encouraged in its defiance, and tension and disorder increased within Lebanon. As Najla Attiyah comments, 'The nature of the issues over which the government and the opposition were fighting made the election campaign a fight for survival' for the government and the policies it represented.[74]

In fact, the rest of the actual campaigning was relatively peaceful; the escalating crises for the government occurred after the election. After his arrest, Saeb Salam announced he was going on a hunger strike in an attempt to force the government, including Chamoun, to resign.[75] Chamoun wanted the army to intervene against the demonstrators, but the head of the army, General Fouad Shihab, was opposed. Shihab was a Maronite, from an important landowning family, but he did not share Chamoun's agenda. Instead, to avoid army involvement, he sought to mediate between the two sides; he won three major concessions from the government intended to appease the opposition.

From 31 May to 4 June, Shihab took over control of all the state's security forces, not just the army, relieving immediate fears that Chamoun would misuse them again. Second, he secured the appointment of two additional ministers to the cabinet, to act as neutral observers. Dr Yussuf Hitti and Muhammad Ali Bayhum were to ensure that the conduct of the elections would be fair and free. Finally it was announced that a committee would also be set up to oversee the proper conduct of the elections.[76]

Shihab's efforts did have some effect in the short term. The threatened strike was called off and Salam ended his hunger strike on 2 June. But as *an-Nahar* commented, these developments had seriously reduced the potential for any national consensus in the forthcoming elections, amounting to an effective breakdown in the National Pact.[77] Even without major violence, during the election campaign citizens certainly saw the divides deepening between politicians, often along confessional lines. For example, among the pro-government candidates were several Muslim candidates who clung to the traditional idea of intercommunal compromise, or who felt that their best chance of personal success lay in continuing support for Chamoun.[78]

On 9 June the elections began, to be held over four successive Sundays to facilitate the peace-keeping efforts of the security forces. On this first Sunday, Beirut and South Lebanon, with 11 seats each, voted. On succeeding Sundays voting occurred in Mount Lebanon, with 20 seats, then the Biqa', with 10 seats, and finally North Lebanon, with 14 seats. That the traditional Maronite stronghold of Mount Lebanon was allocated so many seats despite its relatively low population indicates how Chamoun's regime had attempted to skew the balance of constituencies in its favour.

A look at the results shows that both opposition and government succeeded, to some extent, in pressing their perspectives on their followers on issues such as corruption and attitudes for and against the Eisenhower Doctrine. In the Matn district, for instance, the electoral lists were pro-Doctrine in outlook. Chamoun calculated correctly that the Mount Lebanon district would be important to his cause: the twenty elected deputies were all 'loyalists' who supported not only the government, but also Chamoun's plans for re-election.[79] Table 2 records the results.

Table 2: Mount Lebanon[80]

Constituency	Deputy	Political Allegiance	Votes
Baabda	Elia Abou Jaoude	Loyalist Maronite	12,578
	Edouard Honein	BN Maronite	13,838
	Mahmoud Ammar	PC Shi'ite	14,891
	Bashir al-Awar	PC Druze	14,359
Matn	Salim Lahoud	Loyalist Maronite	11,172
	Assad al-Achkar	PPS Maronite	12,168
	Albert Moukheiber	BN Greek Orthodox	9,063
Baaklin	Kahtan Hamadi	PC Druze	9,074
	Henri Traboulsi	PC Maronite	1,048
	Naim Mogabgab	PC Maronite	10,153
Aley	*Amir* Magid Arslan	Loyalist Druze	14,600
	George Akl	BN Maronite	13,793
	Mounir Abour Fadel	Loyalist Greek Orthodox	13,784
Kisrawan	Nohad Boueiz	BN Maronite	16,388
	Clovis al-Khazin	Pro BN Maronite	16,375
	Maurice Zouain	Maronite Traditional Leader	16,179

Constituency	Deputy	Political Allegiance	Votes
Dayr al-Qamar	Emile Bustani	PC Maronite	11,530
	Anwar al-Khatib	Independent Sunni	11,605
Borj Hammoud	Dicran Tosbath	Armenian*	
Jbeil	Raymond Eddé	BN leader Maronite*	

Key: PC = Pro-Chamoun
      BN = Bloc National
      PPS = Parti Populaire Syrien
      *   = Candidate ran unopposed

The election results were announced in the press after each round.[81] As the pattern of results became clear, Chamoun began to be widely accused of attempting to rig the election, first through the electoral law and then through fraudulent conduct of the election campaign and the electoral process itself.[82]

Some of the most bitter of the defeated candidates were from the *zu'ama* classes in the various communities – members of the traditional landowning political elites. They claimed that Chamoun had deliberately discriminated against any potential opposition through the electoral law and had followed this up by actual electoral misconduct.[83] The evidence indicates that this was not just the rhetoric of defeat, and that the opposition candidates were seriously disadvantaged. For instance, in Beirut, both Saeb Salam and Abdallah al-Yafi were popular sitting deputies who could have expected re-election. Both lost.

The new constituency boundaries are worth examining here. To the strongly pro-Sunni and pro-opposition areas of Musaytiba and Mazraa had been added three Christian sectors: Ashrafiyyah, Rumayl and Sayfi. Theoretically such a system would be ideal in multi-confessional Lebanon, as it meant that candidates would need support from all sectors of the electorate, thus promoting consensus. However, in this case the Christian proportion now outnumbered the Muslim by a ratio of at least 60 per cent. The Christian sector could be relied on to come out in opposition to candidates taking a pan-Arabist, pro-Nasserist stance, just the position that would ensure success in the Muslim areas. The results, published by *an-Nahar* on 14 June 1957, illustrate the extent to which it had proved practically impossible for opposition candidates to succeed. However, the pro-Chamoun candidates, headed by Sami al-Solh, reaped the benefit of support from the Christian areas, as Table 3 indicates.

Table 3: 1957 Election Results[84]

District Constituencies – Beirut	Sami al-Solh	Abdallah al-Yafi	Difference
Ashrafiyyah	5,936	1,942	3,994
Rumayl	4,411	955	3,456
Sayfi	1,969	218	1,751
Total – East Beirut	12,316	3,115	9,201
Musaytiba	4,260	4,844	-584
Mazraa	2,322	8,270	-5,948
Total – West Beirut	6,582	13,114	- 6,532
Total – General	18,898	16,229	+ 2,669

This was not the only example of gerrymandering. Kamal Jumblat, another sitting deputy in the Shuf district with a significant popular following, was also defeated. His constituency had been modified to include a significant element of pro-government Christians who would not vote for a Druze leader of a 'socialist' party, even if he had supported the government on a key foreign policy issue.[85] Defeat was particularly bitter for Jumblat: though he was officially an opposition leader, and certainly opposed Chamoun on key domestic issues, he had openly endorsed Chamoun's policy of supporting the Eisenhower Doctrine.[86] He had then moved to a position of generally supporting the government in the months before the election.[87] After this defeat, he became a bitter opponent of Chamoun for personal rather than purely political reasons.

As newspaper commentary throughout June 1957 indicates, Chamoun's acts were not limited to this rigging of the constituencies to favour government-backed candidates. The actual voting figures were also open to question. Opposition leaders and newspapers pointed out that even with the constituencies rigged as described above, figures like Kamal Jumblat should have had large enough personal followings to be re-elected, though possibly with smaller majorities.[88] Instead, the government won a sweeping victory, with its candidates winning over two-thirds of the seats, and the opposition a mere eight seats. For both contemporaries and historians the results indicate some kind and amount of electoral fraud during the voting process. Though unequivocal hard evidence is not available, cumulative circumstantial evidence indicates that the elections were dishonest. Otherwise, how can we explain the defeat of so many major opposition leaders?

One explanation is that the government applied strong pressure to ensure the election of some of its candidates. Chamoun reputedly prepared to pressure candidates and voters; one tactic was issuing warnings to candidates or voters with relatives in the civil service that they should follow the government line. Another was bribery, which led some candidates to withdraw. The election of Dr Charles Malik in the Kura district of Northern Lebanon is an example. One candidate standing there was a Communist who had no chance of winning. However, the leading opposing candidate was Fouad Ghosn, a Greek Orthodox and a formidable opponent for Malik. Ghosn was summoned to the presidential palace and, after two meetings with Chamoun – said to last a total of nine hours – he was induced to withdraw and later given an ambassadorial post.[89] In Ghosn's absence the Communist candidate served merely to give the illusion of choice in an election that had already been decided in a decidedly undemocratic way.[90]

Another example of electoral malpractice was the events of 17 June, when the two 'neutral ministers' overseeing the elections, Yussuf Hitti and Muhammad Beydoun, resigned. Although they could not prove any fault with the technical conduct of the elections, they commented to *al-Hayat* on 18 June that the reality was different. They said the elections were 'superficially in order, but unfair pressures on voters were obvious on examination', and those pressures affected the way they voted.[91]

For a brief period following the elections, the tensions in Lebanon relaxed, but not for long, given the firm popular conviction – amongst the opposition at least – of electoral malpractice. Bombings, sabotage, clashes between armed bands and police in mountain areas and the resurrection of clan feuds were clearly linked to anti-government feeling. The United National Front refused to recognise the election results or the government's legitimacy. On 3 July 1957, with all the results published, the opposition finally issued a statement 'denouncing election malpractices' and accusing the government 'of trying to act unconstitutionally in order to ensure Chamoun's re-election'.[92] In this continuing tension, the various confessional factions increasingly used foreign policy issues to sum up their positions. Increasingly, therefore, these issues came to symbolise confessional discord. It was still easier to pull together a number of disparate political factions on blanket foreign policy issues, while the intricacies of Lebanese internal politics consistently tended to divide politicians' attempts at co-operation.

Feeling considerable pressure, on 25 July 1957 various government deputies, mainly Maronites, met and agreed to form a new parliamentary bloc or grouping. They issued invitations to a carefully chosen list of thirty-five deputies. Their aim was to include a range of deputies from various political parties and confessional groups by invoking their mutual support on foreign policy matters. The pro-government grouping managed to overcome its differences on internal policy by raising as an issue the need to guard Lebanon against Nasserism and Communism. Even this position posed difficulties, however, as some of the Maronites did not accept Nasserism or Communism as major threats. Table 4 lays out the confessional allegiances of the pro-government grouping in July 1957.

Table 4: Members of the Pro-Government Grouping by Constituency and Confessional Allegiance[93]

Beirut	Sami al-Solh	Sunni
	Jamil Mekkaoui	Sunni
	Fawzi Solh	Sunni
	Rachid Beydoun	Shi'ite
	Joseph Chader	Armenian
	Chafic Nassif	
	Katchik Babikian	Armenian
	Khalil al-Hibri	
	Moses Derkalousian	Armenian
South	Adel Osseiran	Shi'ite
	Yussuf al-Zein	Shi'ite
	Khazem Khalil	Shi'ite
	Muhammad Fadil	Sunni
	Reda Wadih	Shi'ite
Mount Lebanon	Emile Bustani	Maronite
	Anwar al-Khatib	Sunni
	Naim Mogabgab	Maronite
	Henri Traboulsi	Maronite
	Kahtan Hamadih	Druze
	Clovis al-Khazin	Maronite
	Maurice Zouain	Maronite
	Assad Achkar	Maronite
	Salim Lahoud	Maronite
	Albert Moukheiber	Greek Orthodox
	Dikzan Tosbath	Armenian
	Elia Abou Jaoude	Maronite
	Bashir al-Awar	Druze
	Mahmoud Ammar	Shi'ite
	Majid Arslan	Druze
	Mounir Abour Fadil	Greek Orthodox
	George Akl	Maronite

North	Charles Malik (Kura)	Greek Orthodox
	Kabalan Issa al-Khoury (Becharre)	Maronite
	Jean Harb (Batroun)	Maronite

As is clear in Table 4, most of those invited were deputies from the Maronite stronghold of Mount Lebanon. However, amongst the absentees were prominent Maronites who did not automatically follow the government line, notably Raymond Eddé and his group of deputies, including Pierre Eddé, Nohad Boueiz and Edouard Honein. Similarly, the bloc invited in several non-Maronite deputies who had regularly supported the government. They invited only those they felt would demonstrate the required group loyalty, as British observers pointed out.[94] Their intention was to counter the opposition's apparent unity after the elections, even though much of that opposition now had to be expressed outside of the Chamber, given how few opposition deputies had been elected.

Reconnecting to Foreign Powers

This lack of formal political outlets led elements in the opposition groupings to invoke external support for their position – and led to a new set of 'patron-client' relationships in Lebanon. Some political figures in the Muslim communities, especially Sunni-dominated ones, invoked Egypt and Syria to counterbalance the traditional Maronite reliance on Western powers. In the context of the Cold War, Maronite leaders and others interested in continuing a separate, non-Arab Lebanon, looked primarily to the US rather than to France. They reasoned, pragmatically, that the US would be more powerful and effective in protecting the economic and political interests of a separate Lebanon. Hence men like Chamoun became willing to endorse American policy in the region, such as the Eisenhower Doctrine.[95]

Even before the elections of 1957 the government had complained of Syrian and Egyptian interference in Lebanon's affairs, even accusing these powers of attempting to topple the Chamoun regime. On his visit to Beirut in March 1957, Richards reported being told that 'in the past few months the Syrians had sent money and arms to Lebanese tribesmen [i.e. Muslims] along the Syrian border.'[96] Government supporters used claims like these in the election campaign to attack their opponents, whom they blamed for inviting these forces into Lebanon.[97] But from May 1957 at least, it can be shown that the claims had some substance.[98]

Apart from indicating an Egyptian and Syrian willingness to become involved, this also indicates how deeply hostile some leaders of the Lebanese opposition had become towards the Chamoun regime. There is little convincing evidence that any of the political leaders of the time genuinely wished to end Lebanon's independent status. What they sought, instead, was what they identified as a return to the principles of the National Pact: a government acknowledgment that Lebanon was part of the Arab world, manifested in a policy that brought Lebanon in line with other Arab states.

To achieve this goal, some opposition figures were willing, either directly or by encouraging their followers, to use increasingly violent means to bring down the Chamoun government – which they identified as their major obstacle. Tension increased from early in 1958. On 27 January the United National Front announced that it would oppose any attempt by Chamoun to arrange his re-election.[99] On 29 January, during a debate in the Chamber, George Akl, one of Chamoun's most ardent supporters, made a speech attacking the Syrian and Egyptian governments. Sabri Hamadih, a member of the United National Front, made a counterattack on the Chamoun regime, and the hostility between the two nearly erupted into physical violence.[100]

The formation of the United Arab Republic on 1 February 1958 provided an opportunity for the wider Arab world to voice hostility to the Lebanese government that was more than mere rhetoric fuelled by Nasser's personal dislike for Chamoun.[101] During the 1957 election campaign the Egyptian and Syrian press and radio had begun a violent personal campaign against Chamoun, along with Prime Minister Sami al-Solh and Finance Minister Charles Malik, calling them, in the standard phraseology, 'traitors' and 'imperialist lackeys'.[102] The Lebanese opposition had publicised these attacks. In response the government banned all Egyptian newspapers, the major source of anti-Chamoun propaganda, until after the campaign. Still, the opposition was determined to disseminate these perspectives – which had significant potential to destabilise the government.

Tensions continued to rise. On 11 February, for example, *an-Nahar* reported that the government was continuing to investigate the importation of explosives into Lebanon to be used by government opponents.[103] On the same day the Maronite Patriarch became involved in an attempt to restore the interconfessional balance in politics. In an important speech he warned:

The *title of the Maronite Patriarch's famous speech.*

'We, the Maronites, are a ship in the Muslim sea. Either we have to co-exist with them with love and peace, or we have to leave, or else we will be annihilated.'[104] His speech touched on the traditional fear in the Maronite community, but sought to convince his fellow Maronites – especially those in positions of political power – that they had to return to a cooperative position if they were to remain in Lebanon. Despite the Patriarch's intervention, the intercommunal relations continued to deteriorate, with Maronites taking ever more rigid positions – indicating how much their widespread fear-based hostility towards the Arab Muslim world had escalated.

Further complicating the situation, Nasser visited Damascus unexpectedly on 24 February. The press despatches of the time demonstrate the enthusiasm amongst Lebanese Muslims – greater than any Lebanese political leader had expected. Thousands of Lebanese from Beirut, Tripoli, Sidon, Tyre and other towns travelled to Damascus. Taxi fares to Damascus rose to five times the normal amount and taxi drivers in Beirut, drumming up trade, chanted, 'to Damascus, to Gamal'.[105]

In addition, Nasser took the opportunity to receive innumerable official and unofficial Lebanese delegations, all congratulating him on his efforts. He spent several days addressing the cheering crowds of thousands, many of them Lebanese, who welcomed him with an enthusiasm verging on hysteria. One pro-Nasser demonstration in Damascus on 25 February numbered around 180,000.[106] To anti-Nasserist elements in Lebanon, this reaction proved that all they had feared about pro-Nasserism was true, and that the threat would materialise unless they took action to prevent it. *An-Nahar* warned that those Muslim figures like al-Solh who continued to support Chamoun would find themselves ostracised by their fellows.[107]

The Lebanese government continued trying to counteract the opposition's propaganda and demonstrations in an atmosphere of unrest, full of rumour

The Patriarch Boulos Boutros Meouchi.

and counter-rumour about plots and counter-plots. Many of these plots, real or rumoured, seemed to have little point. For example, on 25 February it was announced that a Jordanian had been implicated in a plot to plant explosives in several newspaper offices: *an-Nahar, al-Hayat* and *Sada Lubnan.* However, these were not government papers; *al-Hayat* supported the Baghdad Pact but *an-Nahar* and *Sada Lubnan* both supported opposition groupings.

Against this background, on 2 March the Lebanese government moved to prosecute two leading opposition figures, Salam and Husseini, on the charge of making defamatory statements about the Lebanese government during a ceremony Najjadah held to celebrate the Syrian-Egyptian union. The timing was clearly not ideal for such a move, but the government felt it could not afford to set the precedent of overlooking such public comments. On 3 March it adopted a new law relating to the press which it hoped would give it greater powers to control the output of journalists from abroad.[108] On 9 March, however, Ghassan Tueni, the owner of *an-Nahar*, wrote an important article. As Tueni was also a leading journalist in his own right, his comments clearly indicate that contemporaries were aware of the dangerous situation in Lebanon:

This fear over Lebanon is a danger for Lebanon. We find in the air a mixture of anxiety and stiffness in the attitudes that may lead to the ultimate danger of the disappearance of the Lebanese entity.[109]

About this time, the Maronite Patriarch's concern over the continuing situation in Lebanon also resurfaced. In a speech on 11 March, he highlighted the corruption in Lebanon's legal establishment and suggested that dealing with that corruption might make it possible to restore confidence in the government and avoid a political collapse. At about the same time, the so-called Afaf Scandal filled the newspapers: high court judges were protecting a brothel managed by a Madame 'Afaf'. While not a directly political matter, this could only discredit the administration still further at an awkward time.[110] Thus, the Patriarch hoped to galvanise the government into taking some action to improve its moral standing. But he succeeded in raising neither action nor morality.[111]

On 12 March the al-Solh government resigned. Sami al-Solh had attempted to avoid this step by enlarging his cabinet, but still failed to win his administration more support.[112] Al-Solh was not, however, disappearing from government in Lebanon. On 14 March, with Chamoun's support, he formed a new government with fourteen members.[113] On 15 March the pro-government element in the population staged a demonstration, shouting support for President Chamoun and demanding that his presidential mandate be renewed. But as no one answered the complaints of the opposition leaders, the rearrangement triggered a continuation of Muslim counter-demonstrations and fears about their impact.[114]

In this context, many of the more moderate elements in the Maronite community, and even now within the government itself, were pointing out the need for a policy of compromise. Charles Malik, for example, began to suggest that Lebanon take the initiative in arranging a *rapprochement* between the West and Nasser, instead of perpetuating the hostility between these two camps in Lebanon. Malik informed Middleton, the British ambassador, that his government favoured an end to the coolness between the UAR and Britain..[115] This step was less an indication of a fundamental change in policy than an attempt to lower the tensions surrounding Lebanon in order to decrease internal tensions and the supply of arms to the opposition.

But Ghassan Tueni pointed out, somewhat sarcastically, the dangers – even for the government – of too close an alliance with the West, especially because, as the Lebanese had learned, they could not necessarily rely on that support if the West's policies changed.[116] Overall, after the 1957 election, Chamoun faced a Chamber that was less firmly behind him and his policies than he might have hoped. Certainly he would need more support were he to be re-elected, because that Chamber increasingly faced fears about the intercommunal tensions within Lebanon, which they could not and did not want to ignore. He could count certainly fifteen and possibly up to twenty deputies who were unquestioning loyalists to his cause, the majority of them Maronites. Equally, another fifteen to twenty deputies, mainly non-Christian, could be relied on to oppose his cause vigorously. The rest were essentially uncommitted immediately after the election. A significant number, especially among the Christians, were prepared to support him on certain issues. But their support was by no means certain, especially for a strategy resulting in his re-election.

On 14 July 1957, Chamoun and members of his family met with loyalist deputies to debate the renewal of his mandate, *al-Hayat* reported. Even the loyalist deputies were split on the issue of a constitutional amendment to allow Chamoun to stand again, wondering if it was practicable and desirable. Chamoun himself tried to show that he would seek re-election not out of personal ambition, but only if pressured by his peers:

> I will not participate in the discussion, so it cannot be insinuated that I have either accepted or rejected any proposal on the matter. You are the ones who opened the topic and must close it.[117]

This ostensibly disinterested position was never likely to convince the anti-Chamoun element, or convert any waverers. Even Maronite politicians were reluctant to support this position because of the tensions it created in the overall political system.[118] Constitutional reform was a sensitive issue for them because of Maronite fears that only the constitution protected them from being subjected to the growing Muslim population in Lebanon.[119] Thus, if Chamoun were to have any chance of succeeding in his bid for a second term, he had to locate it in an atmosphere of internal crisis. Some evidence indicates that rather than making blunders in his conduct of foreign policy at this time, he was conducting a high-risk, and eventually unsuccessful, policy of creating a containable crisis.[120]

This point becomes clear if we examine the position that some Chamoun loyalists took during that period. The Kata'ib Party would ardently favour Chamoun's re-election during the summer of 1958 as a result of events then. Traditionally, the party associated itself with safeguarding Lebanese interests by preserving the pro-Western stance of Lebanese foreign policy and opposing Arab interference, by force if necessary. The party's concept of Lebanese interests was, of course, an essentially Maronite understanding of the term, as Pierre Gemayel had made plain back in 1957 at a press conference on 21 May: 'We will hold firmly to our independence and we mean by that the freedom to decide our internal as well as external fate, maintaining our relations with Arab friends on a mutual basis of non-interference in our internal affairs; and we will continue our relations with the West as long as it is in our interests to do so.'[121]

In 1957 their policy was focused on allowing Chamoun to at least finish his mandate, in order to maintain that pro-Western dimension and to prevent a victory for the Muslim elements in Lebanon. Gemayel argued that it was 'premature to think of such matters' but that he was personally against renewal because it involved a constitutional amendment and he 'would only accept this in a case where the choice was between President Chamoun and someone whom we believed would work against the interests of Lebanon'.[122] The reasons behind their change were crucial to the change in thinking amongst several Maronite political figures in the crisis.

Changes in Thinking

April of 1958 was an important month for Lebanon in terms of internal developments. Civil unrest continued, and the question of Chamoun's re-election was still important as an unconfirmed but widely believed rumour. Chamoun increasingly used the army to intervene to prevent unrest, and in several speeches he hinted at American intervention to defend his administration and Lebanese independence – justifying this development by referring to intervention from Egypt and Syria.

This was the background in April, when the question of his re-election first became a matter of open debate in the Chamber. On 10 April George Akl, a noted Chamoun supporter, announced that he intended to propose a constitutional amendment to allow Chamoun's re-election.[123] By this point Chamoun had still never explicitly stated in public – nor had he explicitly demurred – that he desired such an amendment. Both American and British sources, however, provide evidence of Chamoun's intention to stand. In March 1958 the American Embassy in Beirut reported on a meeting during which Chamoun had indicated that 'he intended to place before parliament in May the issue of amending the constitution and his subsequent re-election'.[124]

Once the question was raised openly tensions rose even higher, as it seemed to confirm all the gossip that had been circulating for months, and to raise again all the suspicions about corruption during the 1957 election. The opposition reacted immediately. On the same day as Akl made his announcement 300 Muslim leaders came out in opposition to Chamoun's re-election, including former prime ministers and speakers of the Chamber, and current opposition leaders and religious figures. But it is worth noting that they all also took pains to declare their support for Lebanon's continued independence. The *mufti*, Shaykh Muhammad Alaya, decreed that no congratulations would be offered on the Feast of the Bayram marking the end of Ramadan.[125] Instead these 300 notables attended a Ramadan dinner given by Alaya; contrary to usual practice, no Muslim members of the government were invited.[126] After the party those present issued a public statement: they opposed any attempt to amend the constitution and declared that the lack of congratulations on Bayram was a mark of mourning as Lebanon was suffering from the policies of the Chamoun administration. On 17 April the *mufti* and 200 leading Muslims declared that anyone who offered or accepted Bayram congratulations would be violating the unanimity of the Muslim community.[127]

Civil unrest continued and escalated. The army was in Tyre, a major centre of disturbance, and the announcement of 10 April did nothing to help keep the peace there. Other violent outbursts occurred throughout April.[128] Rumours began to spread that Chamoun had appealed to the US for military aid to quell the unrest; the Sixth Fleet was to arrive off the Lebanese coast. The rumour's accuracy or lack of it is less significant than the popular reaction. In a widely read editorial, full of double meanings and innuendo, Ghassan Tueni commented that 'Chamoun is not fool enough to ask for the Sixth Fleet, for he knows that the Sixth Fleet cannot stop the internal revolt'.[129] But the tension in Lebanon was so acute that even *The Observer's* foreign correspondent gave some credence to the rumour about the Sixth Fleet.[130] Thus April was a tense month in Lebanon, giving some indication of the chaos to follow. A single serious incident could spark an explosion.

Certain incidents were key. On 15 April Marouf Saad demanded that the government resign on the grounds that it was responsible for the present

Barricades in Tripoli.

chaos, which could escalate into sectarian violence; he also alleged that the government was arming its supporters.[131] On 20 April explosives were thrown near the house of Sami al-Solh while visitors were calling to congratulate him on Bayram.[132] Still, on 24 April George Akl reiterated his intention to introduce his amendment during the following week.[133]

In this atmosphere propagandists on both sides were actively looking for incidents they could interpret to their advantage. But not until May did a crucial incident occur. On 8 May Nassib al-Matni, the proprietor of the pro-Communist newspaper *Telegraph*, was murdered. According to F. Qubain, al-Matni had been at odds with the administration for some time.[134] On 22 July 1957 he had been arrested and then tried for publishing a report that allegedly defamed Chamoun. Certainly he was well known as a severe critic of Chamoun and his administration and he had come out in favour of strengthening Lebanese relations with the UAR. He was thus clearly a target because of his high-profile opposition to Chamoun. Early in the morning of 22 November 1957 al-Matni had been stabbed in the face while leaving his office.

After his murder four anonymous letters were found in his pockets threatening to kill him if he did not abandon his opposition to the government. The last letter was dated 19 April 1958.[135] It has still not been determined whether these letters were deliberately planted to lead the police astray; equally it is not known which group or even side in the interconfessional hostilities carried out the assassination. The opposition might have done it to destabilise the situation; the government might have done it to silence him. Either possibility remains credible.

American sources record that on 9 May rioting began in Tripoli in protest against the murder, and that events rapidly led to armed rebellion.[136] In these clashes with the security forces in Tripoli 15 people were killed and 150 wounded. The following day the United States Information Services Library in Tripoli was burned; 10 people died and around 100 were wounded.[137] Within days the country had become divided into a number of virtually independent sectors, each under the control of a local leader. In all these regions, most of the heavy fighting occurred in the remaining days of May.

By 20 May, western Beirut had come under the control of the opposition, and the army declared the area out of bounds to all state security forces. Tripoli, besieged by government forces, turned into a battlefield as the opposition forces holding the city had managed to get supplies from Syria. In Sidon opposition forces also assumed control, but the fighting was less intense than in Beirut and Tripoli. Fighting was heaviest and most continuous in the Shuf area, especially in the district that was home to Jumblat's followers. Here the violence was undoubtedly fuelled by the now bitter enmity between Jumblat and Chamoun as well as the traditional Maronite-Druze rivalry. In the Baalbak-Hirmel sector, and along the entire length of the Lebanese-Syrian border, independent local opposition leaders established control, maintaining separate commands and even separate systems of self-government.

According to General Shihab's summary of the military situation on 13 May 1958, the major battles occurred between 9 and 18 May. According to *an-Nahar,* over 50 people were killed and 200 wounded in the period up to 14 May.[138] Information gathered on 20 May indicated that the toll had risen to

60 dead and 300 wounded, with the major casualties in the north, especially Tripoli.[139] The fighting between the opposition and the *gendarmerie* continued after 18 May, in the Shuf district and the Biqa'.

But the fighting was not the whole picture. Various figures were making desperate attempts to reach some kind of political compromise. Many who had earlier tried to remain neutral between the hard-line pro-Chamounists and the hard-line opposition now saw the need to identify with one side or the other. In the eyes of most Lebanese, the question was now more than just a matter of renewing Chamoun's presidential mandate. In an editorial on 13 May, Ghassan Tueni said 'The question is: Lebanon's survival'.[140]

It was in these days, around 13 May, that the Kata'ib Party, for instance, not only came out in full support of Chamoun but also took to the streets to demonstrate its support, seeing that as the only way to ensure Lebanon's survival. The party's members were predominantly the Maronite petty bourgeoisie: small shopkeepers, clerks and minor officials. They saw that their livelihood and their Maronite identity were threatened if Lebanon's independence disappeared. Thus Kata'ib militias demonstrated their commitment to Lebanon's survival and accepted, however reluctantly, that this survival was now linked to the survival of Chamoun as President. Gemayel, leader of the Kata'ib Party, remained personally unhappy with Chamoun, and there is no indication that at any point during the crisis months from May to September 1958 the party's official policy changed to support the concept of Chamoun's re-election rather than merely his completion of his mandate. But the latter concept was seen as sufficiently crucial to justify armed action.[141]

A self-brokered political solution, arranged by compromise between the Lebanese communities, seemed unlikely during May and June 1958 because leading figures on both sides remained unwilling to seek any compromise and no pressure for compromise arose from the masses in either the Maronite or Sunni communities. The opposition as a whole continued to demand the resignation of the president as the basis of any solution, and Rachid Karami, based in Tripoli, threatened to seek a union between Tripoli and the UAR.

Nor was the government silent. On 13 May the foreign minister, Dr Charles Malik, announced that the Lebanese government had protested to the government of the UAR over its interference in Lebanon's internal affairs and some talked of an appeal to the Security Council.[142] Chamoun refused to bow to opposition pressure or to the public demonstrations against him by resigning, while Shihab, anxious to keep the army from disintegrating into confessional factions, used his troops to quell unrest as little as possible.

Thus it was left to individuals and groups outside the administration itself to begin the process of seeking some compromise, though they had little success during May and June. Prominent individuals involved in this process included the Maronite Patriarch; Raymond Eddé, the leader of the largely Maronite National Bloc; his brother Pierre Eddé, and Adel Osseiran.[143] Among the various plans that evolved, the most hopeful one had Shihab forming a caretaker government, which would pledge to hold elections for a president under the existing constitution and at the earliest possible date (23 July). The opposition rejected this plan, and continued to demand Chamoun's immediate resignation before it would enter any discussions. Meanwhile, Chamoun not only refused to resign but still refused to state publicly that he would not stand for re-election. Ultimately, though, the most important element in the whole mediation plan was General Shihab's refusal, during May, June and early July, to accept the office of President.[144]

On 18 May, the US Ambassador announced that the Sixth Fleet would not be visiting Beirut. As *an-Nahar* pointed out, this announcement was less of a blow for the government because the US was arranging to deliver heavy armaments to Lebanon – thus responding to a government request the same week it was made. In addition, the US had already dispatched light armaments three days earlier and on 17 May *an-Nahar* had noted that the US and British fleets in the Mediterranean were making unusual movements.[145]

Thus it is not surprising that Ghassan Tueni described that week as the most dangerous one for Lebanon's future.[146] To Tueni it seemed increasingly possible, even probable, that Lebanon's entire political structure was under threat from factions in Lebanon seeking to involve such outside forces. Foreign invasion of some kind seemed imminent. The end results of that would be horrifying; political power would collapse, leading to either a military dictatorship or Lebanon's reduction to a small Christian entity.[147] The Maronites did not take Tueni's fears lightly. They were equally alarmed by the evidence, widely accepted among fellow Maronites, that the UAR was intervening in Lebanon's affairs.

According to British sources, it was in this tense atmosphere that two neutral mediators, Raymond Eddé and Ahmed Daouk, called on Rachid Karami, the most important Sunni leader of Tripoli, on 20 May and persuaded him to come to Beirut to join their compromise discussions for ending the crisis. On 21 May, Karami ordered a largely successful ceasefire in Tripoli; although opposition rebels occupied Baalbak on that day, the ceasefire provided some optimism. In evaluating Karami's contribution to the crisis, it is worth noting Saeb Salam's claim that during the spring of 1958 the UAR had sent 5,000 pieces of armament to Karami in Tripoli, but that at no point during the crisis in the summer of 1958 did Karami use these arms in fighting the Chamoun regime.[148] While there is no proof of this claim, it does indicate the continuing Sunni perception that the Chamoun regime, and its Western backers, was responsible for the trouble, and not the Muslim or Arab world. While Karami was not willing to open discussions with Chamoun, he was perfectly prepared to do so with other Maronite figures who seemed prepared to return to the terms of the National Pact.

The optimism was premature, however: the attempted mediation failed and trouble continued throughout June. A United Nations Observation Group (UNOGIL) arrived in Lebanon in June to report on the claims of Arab intervention. Chamoun had requested United Nations intervention on 13 May 1958; the UNOGIL mission was probably an alternative worked out by Western diplomats in Beirut in response to Chamoun's personal desire for an American military intervention.[149] Whatever the mechanism, the request had been granted, and Chamoun loyalists were grateful.

Men like Raymond Eddé, however, would have endorsed suggestions from both the West and the Arab world to invite the Arab League to work out a compromise. Such a move would almost certainly have succeeded; it was widely recognised, in and out of Lebanon, that a solution from the Arab world would prove the most acceptable, and least questionable, for roughly half of the Lebanese population, whatever its terms. That would leave the issue of working out a compromise acceptable to the Maronite community – a not impossible task, given the terms of the National Pact. But the Lebanese government rejected this option on 5 June 1958, to the furious incomprehension of the Sunni opposition in particular.

Adding to the resentment at this rejection, Charles Malik did not even bother to attend the League's meeting convened to discuss the issue. Thus he not only snubbed the League but did not even give the impression that the Chamoun government was genuinely considering the proposal for Arab League intervention. Instead, Malik went directly to New York to plead for intervention at a United Nations Security Council meeting.[150] Attempting to justify his actions, Malik claimed that the Lebanese government had initially turned to the Arab League for help in solving the crisis, but had learned that the League's council would not meet in time to take action to stop the UAR intervention in Lebanon.[151] Chamoun himself had opposed any solution brokered by the Arab League because he knew it would end his hopes of re-election; on 13 May 1958, when Malik made the first request to the United Nations, he still hoped that with American support he might be returned to office.[152]

The Maronites expected that the proposed United Nations intervention would endorse their condemnations of a UAR intervention. However, as British sources reported, the Sunni opposition believed that 'Malik's real intention in going to the UN is to lay the ground for US armed intervention in Lebanon'.[153] They believed that the United Nations had a Western bias and thus could be manipulated by the Chamoun government; they thought the American government also could be manipulated in this way.

So the UNOGIL's arrival was regarded with suspicion by the Sunni opposition and elements of the opposition to Chamoun from other confessional groups including some Maronites who believed that an American intervention would be disastrous for Lebanon. On 12 June Saeb Salam issued a six-point commentary on the United Nations' Lebanon resolution; it sums up the general Sunni opposition perspective at this stage. He considered the resolution endorsing the UNOGIL to be an irrelevant and unjustified interference, since the Lebanese problem was purely internal. Highlighting Sunni fears of a Western intervention under the guise of the United Nations intervention, he stated pointedly that to prevent an infiltration of arms into Lebanon any intervention would have to stop the import of American, British, French, Turkish, Iraqi and Jordanian arms, rather than arms from the UAR – because it was interference from these countries that was aggravating the internal tension, not the friendly 'interest' of the UAR. And although Chamoun had rejected Arab League intervention, Salam argued that only through the League would it be possible to gain a solution that had the consent of the Lebanese people as a whole.[154]

According to Kamal Jumblat, this statement encapsulated the Muslim opposition position: the crisis was indeed a direct response to 'foreign influence' but the opposition did not interpret Arab intervention as 'foreign'. Moreover, Lebanon's dependence on the West was both 'unhealthy' and a betrayal of the National Pact.[155] But despite this statement, the UNOGIL was swiftly dispatched to Lebanon, making its observations during the last half of June 1958. It published its first report on 4 July, and to the delight of the opposition it minimised claims of Arab foreign intervention there, implying only a negligible infiltration of men and armaments from Syria. On 5 July the group's leader, Galo Plaza, gave a press conference in which he re-emphasised the conclusion that there was no evidence of any massive infiltration of Lebanon.[156]

The report inflamed matters once again. Both the attempts to find solutions and the fighting continued, while the observers continued to observe and compile reports, and US intelligence reports on events in Lebanon contradicted the UN conclusions.[157] As June rolled into July, few could see any prospects of breaking the stalemate. But events outside Lebanon finally made a difference. A coup in Iraq in the early hours of 14 July 1958 caused a major shift in perspectives, for the Lebanese and the US governments. Revolutionaries overthrew the Iraqi monarchy and killed the entire royal family, dragging one family member's body into the streets to be dismembered by a mob. These events rocked the Arab world generally and had an enormous impact in Lebanon. The opposition was jubilant but Chamoun was 'shaken' by the news from Baghdad, and almost certainly, by its reception in Lebanon itself.[158]

Chamoun renewed his appeal for Western, effectively American, aid to protect Lebanon and its 'legitimate' government. He demanded immediate intervention, insisting that unless this was granted within forty-eight hours he would be a dead man himself and Lebanon would become an Egyptian satellite.[159] Of course, Chamoun was not the only frightened leader in the Arab world; Jordan was simultaneously appealing for British support. Both appeals were answered and once again the scene was set for a Western-imposed solution to the crisis. On 15 July 1958 US Marines landed in Lebanon while British paratroopers landed in Jordan.[160]

In this chapter I have indicated how the political figures and parties evolved and established their positions as the crisis evolved. I have not, however, examined the position and opinions and consequent role of the major communities in Lebanon, notably the Sunni and, in reaction, the Maronite. We must consider these confessional communities in order to fully understand the crisis and its development and eventual resolution: how did these manoeuvrings affect their sense of identity and self-worth within the state? Political figures do not operate in a vacuum, and their supporters are not necessarily sheep.

In this context, it is the issue of community mythology that most clearly reveals the differences between the two communities in 1958, with

Marines purchasing souvenirs at souks *specially held for them by Sunni merchants.*

Marines touring the 'Hay al-Zeytoune' street, Beirut's red-light district.

considerable implications for political developments as the crisis coalesced. Popular perspective was clearly split on the issue of Lebanese 'national destiny'. But that split contained considerable potential for intercommunal hostility because of the way that 'the other side' interpreted these differing perspectives. Therefore the masses sought leaders who would 'protect' them and their interests from 'attack', and would support the kind of Lebanese state they found acceptable. Thus, in communal terms, the pattern of 1958 represents a return to co-habitation.

Michael Johnson points out clear linkages between issues relating to the National Pact and the 1958 crisis.[161] In this chapter I have discussed the development of the crisis at elite political levels and the stress that leaders from both Sunni and Maronite communities, from different perspectives, laid on this pact, as well as their experience of the crisis. But the impact of the 1958 crisis was not restricted to these leaders: it represented a breakdown in consensus between the communities at all levels of society. The compromise signalled by the National Pact was important not just to political leaders, but also to the masses of both communities: the people those leaders claimed to represent. These masses also had their understanding of what the pact should mean, and what it entailed in practice. They derived that understanding in part from the information their leaders provided, but also from their experience of how the state system operated, and its impact on them.

Because of the flourishing media in Lebanon, information reached the masses through a wide variety of newspapers and other publications as well as radio broadcasts, informing a popular audience on matters of interest to them from their leaderships, but also commenting on those issues in editorials and broadcasts. These media channels also give the historian a way to access comment on popular reactions to events and individuals.

I back up these media reports with comments in interviews, memoirs and the observations of the various interested external powers in their official documents. Thus, largely through media reports, I will now examine how the masses of the Sunni and Maronite communities contributed to the crisis. Like their political leaders, the masses of these communities provided the most significant polarities of opinion on the crisis. On the whole, as I will show, the mass Maronite perspective on their position was essentially defensive, a matter of their reaction to events and the agendas of other communities, notably the Sunni. Thus we must first identify what the Maronite saw themselves as reacting against. For this reason, I examine the Sunni community first, in the following chapter, and then turn to the Maronites.

Notes

1.   Theodor Hanf, *Coexistence in Wartime Lebanon*, Centre for Lebanese Studies and I.B. Tauris, London, 1993, p. 72.

2.   K. S. Salibi, *The Modern History of Lebanon*, Caravan Books, New York, 1977, p. 198; Marwan Buheiry, 'External intervention and internal wars in Lebanon 1770–1928', in Lawrence I. Conrand, ed., *The Formation and Perception of the Modern Arab World*, Darwin Press Inc., Princeton, NJ, 1989, p. 138.

3.   Marwan Buheiry, *The Formation and Perception of the Modern Arab World*, Darwin Press, Princeton, 1988.

4.   Najla Attiyah, 'The Attitude of the Lebanese Sunnis towards the State of Lebanon', unpublished PhD thesis, University of London, 1973, p. 101.

5.   This perspective was put to me by my father, Nohad Boueiz, in my youth.

6.   Michael Johnson, *Class and Client in Beirut. The Sunni Muslim Community and the Lebanese State 1840–1985,* Ithaca Press, London, 1986, p. 26.

7.   This is understandable, given that Lebanon was unique in the Middle East in having a Christian element in the population that was neither *'de jure* nor *de facto* second class citizens'. Hanf, p. 3.

8.   *Ibid.*, p. 4.

9.   Gebran Tueni, editorial, *an-Nahar*, 12 January 1946; 1 March 1946.

10. Kamel Mroueh, editorial, *al-Hayat*, 24 April 1946. Similar editorials appeared on 30 January 1946 and 11 May 1946.

11. Gebran Tueni, editorial, *an-Nahar*, 24 January 1946.

12. Kamel Mroueh, editorial, *al-Hayat*, 13 May and 24 May 1947.

13. Antun Boutros to Riyadh al-Solh, Letters, 29 May 1947, complaining about electoral fraud. These were published in pamphlet form. See *The Crime of 25 May 1947*, Bloc National Party, Beirut, 1947.

14. Augustus Moubarak, letter, 27 May 1947, archives, Bloc National Party Headquarters. The letter also appeared in print in *The Crime of 25 May 1947*.

15. These include *al-Diar, Nidal, Asia, al-Ruad, Nida al-Watan, Sada al-Ahwal, Beirut, Beirut al-Massa, Kul Shay, Telegraph, al-Hadaf, Lissan al-Hal, al-Ahrar, al-Bayrak, al-Jadid, al-Yaoum, Le Soir, L'Orient, Sawt al-Sha'b, al-Zaman, al-Dunia, an-Nahar, al-Akhbar, al-Dabur, La Revue du Liban, Zahla al-Fatat, Sada al-Shimal, Sada Lubnan, al-Afkar, al-Mustaqbal,* and *al-Safa.* See also *The Crime of 25 May 1947* for some comment on the newspaper reaction.

16. Edmond Rabbath, *La Formation Historique du Liban Politique et Constitutionnel*, Publications de l'Université Libanaise, Beirut, 1986, p. 558. Not only was this point about corruption made at the time; it was more recently given prominence in *L'Orient-Le Jour*, 16 March 1995.

17. Salibi, p. 194.

18. As with Kamal Jumblat, Chamoun feared the impact of Sultan Selim in the Shuf. See Salibi, p. 194.

19. *An-Nahar*, 11 March 1995; Salibi, p. 193.

20. The system of consecutive, non-renewable terms of office was created to prevent any one grouping in the political jigsaw from gaining too much power by establishing a monopoly over the presidency.

21. The defeat is now generally seen as resulting from Arab disorganisation, something recognised at the time by the masses if not the governments themselves. See Malcolm

Yapp, *The Near East Since the First World War*, Longman, London, 1991, p. 138.

22. Riyadh al-Solh was connected by marriage to Husni al-Zaim, the Syrian leader. See Nazir Fansa, *Ayam Husni al-Zaim*, Dar al-Afak, Beirut, 1982, pp. 75–81.

23. The records of this trial are still not to be found in the archives of the Ministry of Justice. Information beyond popular rumour has been provided by M. Chlouk, a journalist for *an-Nahar* who has researched the trial but has not yet published his conclusions; see also Salibi, p. 193.

24. In 1958, the PPS actively supported Chamoun because it refused to link itself to an opposition that included al-Khoury and had links to the Syrian regime that had betrayed them in 1949. See editorial, *al-Bina*, August 1958; Press Release No. 5, PPS, December 1958.

25. See Salibi, pp. 193–4; Johnson, p. 122; Michael Suleiman, *Political Parties in Lebanon: The Challenge of a Fragmented Political Culture*, Cornell University Press, Ithaca, 1967, p. 214.

26. Salibi, for instance, argues that the Front was partly a public relations exercise, indicating a perceived need among Lebanese politicians to take a publicly united stance where possible to maintain popular credibility for their opposition stance. See Salibi, p. 194.

27. Raymond Eddé, leader of the Bloc National in 1952, made it a matter of pride to make a stand against government corruption. He was leader of the party until his death on 10 May 2000. He has been referred to in the Lebanese press, notably by Michel Abou Jaoude in his editorials for *an-Nahar*, as 'the conscience of Lebanon'. Salim Nassar in articles to mark Eddé's eightieth birthday referred to him as 'the best president Lebanon will never have'; see *al-Hayat*, 15 March 1993; 17 March 1993.

28. See F. Qubain, *Crisis in Lebanon*, Middle East Institute, Washington DC, 1968, p. 31.

29. For instance, in 1945 the Arab League Pact had accepted the existence of a separate Lebanon. See Leila Meo, *Lebanon: Improbable Nation. A Study in Political Development*, Greenwood Press, Westport, Connecticut, 1965, pp. 90–1.

30. The proposed pact was significant because it was the first real attempt by the Western powers to get the Arab states (and Lebanon) to publicly demonstrate an alignment with the West against the USSR. Meo, p. 111.

31. On the basis of a new electoral law passed in 1950, according to Nicola Ziadeh, *Syria and Lebanon*, Ernest Benn Ltd, London, 1957, p. 111.

32. For details, see L. Yamak, *The Syrian Social Nationalist Party*, Harvard University Press, 1966; Ziadeh, p. 112.

33. Under the constitution the president had wide powers, because he inherited most of those held by the high commissioner during the Mandate period. See Malcolm Kerr, 'Political Decision Making in a Confessional Democracy' in L. Binder, ed., *Politics in Lebanon*, John Wiley, New York, 1966, p. 204; Salibi, p. 195.

34. Kamel Mroueh, *al-Hayat*, 10 May 1952; 13 September 1952. Ziadeh indicates that, as in 1947–8, accusations of corruption were widespread in the press. Ziadeh, p. 11.

35. Kamel Mroueh, *al-Hayat*, 6 September 1952.

36. Johnson, p. 122. Despite Rabbath's suggestions, there is no sustainable evidence that Western intervention engineered this development. Certainly the West had become anti-Khoury and was pro-Chamoun by 1952; but the events of September 1952 in Lebanon were internally generated. Rabbath, p. 560; Ziadeh, pp. 124–5.

37. See Inmea Sader (ed.), *Syro-Lebanese Relations 1934–1985*, CEDRE, Bayt al-Moustakbal, 1986, 2 volumes, for a chronological survey of the archival and bibliographical material charting the tensions between the two countries.

38. For the factors promoting this, see Johnson, pp. 28–9, 120–3.

39. This support had developed as a result of Chamoun's opposition to al-Khoury and the Ba'athist regime in Syria. For details of the Syrian position see Ziadeh, pp. 162–3; Itamar Rabinovich, 'Arab Political Parties: Ideology and Ethnicity', in Milton J. Esman and Itamar Rabinovich, eds, *Ethnicity, Pluralism and the State in the Middle East,* Cornell University Press, Ithaca, 1988, p. 158.

40. *Documents on American Foreign Relations,* Harper and Brothers, New York, 1955, pp. 276–8; *New York Times,* 20 September 1953. Albert Hourani, *A History of the Arab Peoples,* Faber and Faber, London, 1991, p. 365 points out that independence had not led such state governments to stop expecting that 'the former imperial rulers' would still maintain a protective military relationship with them.

41. *Al-Ahram,* 17 January 1956; *Documents on American Foreign Relations,* Daily Report, Foreign Radio Broadcasts, Foreign Daily Broadcast Information Service, 13 December 1958, A.3.

42. Meo, pp. 94–7.

43. Salibi, p. 198.

44. F0371/12605 VL1011/1 British Embassy, Beirut, to Foreign Office, 1 January 1956, highlights the dilemma the Chamoun government faced in terms of a 'choice between East and West'; it also mentions in its summary of principal events in Lebanon, the letter of appeal of the Maronite Patriarch to Chamoun, on 21 April 1955, urging Chamoun to 'remain neutral' because of fears of division amongst the Lebanese population.

45. Dwight D. Eisenhower, *Waging Peace: 1956–61,* Doubleday, New York, 1965, p. 24; Raymond Salame, 'The Eisenhower Doctrine: a Study in Alliance Politics', unpublished PhD thesis, American University, Washington, 1974, pp. 182; 192–4

46. Meo, pp. 97–8.

47. Yussuf Khoury (ed.), *Cabinet Papers, 1926–1984,* Muassassat al-Dirassat al-Lubnaniyyah, Beirut, 1994, vol. 1, p. 447, recording the events of 18 November 1956; Meo, pp. 98–9, recounts the Sunni claim that Chamoun had promised that Lebanon would sever diplomatic relations with Britain and France as an expression of solidarity with Egypt, but that he did not fulfil that promise, triggering the resignations of Salam and al-Yafi. However, as Meo also points out, Chamoun denied ever having made such a promise.

48. Michael Hudson, *Arab Politics,* Yale University Press, Connecticut, 1979, p. 243.

49. Salibi, p. 199.

50. See Paul Zinner, ed., *Documents on US Foreign Relations,* New York, 1958, pp. 195–204 for extracts from Eisenhower's speech to Congress, 5 January 1957.

51. Salame, p. 11; for the text of the joint resolution of Congress, 9 March 1957, see M.S. Agwani (ed.), *The Lebanese Crisis in 1958, A Documentary Study,* Asia Publishing House, 1965, p. 15.

52. For the full text see *Department of State Bulletin,* XXXVI, January 1957.

53. Meo, pp. 107, 115–7. She points out that Arabs had considerable justification for refusing to endorse the doctrine, as endorsement would be likely to bring the Cold War 'to their own doorstep'.

54. *Foreign Relations of the US, 1955–157,* Volume XIII, Near East, Jordan-Yemen, Department of State Publication 9665, Washington DC, 1988, p. 208.

55. *Al-Hayat,* 28 March 1957.

56. See *Foreign Relations of the US, 1955–1957,* Vol. XIII, p. 120; Meo, pp. 124–5.

57. Pierre Gemayel, leader of the Kata'ib party, spoke of his fears of being 'engulfed in

a Muslim sea' without the protection of the doctrine and of the consequent duty of supporting the government. See *al-Hayat*, 4 March 1958; Qubain, p. 84.

58. *Al-Hayat*, 19 March 1957, contains a useful summary of these opposition claims. Interestingly enough, despite its general support for Chamoun's position, the PPS could not bring itself to endorse the Eisenhower Doctrine. See Abdallah Mohsen, speech, 2 March 1958, PPS Archives.

59. *Al-Hayat*, 7 April 1957.

60. *Al-Hayat*, 31 March and 1 April 1957, gives the Manifesto of the United National Front; see also Agwani, pp. 29–33 for the full text of the Manifesto.

61. Al-Khoury's motivation was inspired more by personal bitterness than ideological convictions, though he did have some sympathies with a more pro-Arab position.

62. *Al-Hayat*, 19 March 1957; Qubain, p. 53.

63. This point was made plain in *al-Hayat*, 28 March and 29 March 1957; 16 April 1957.

64. Many Lebanese journalists discussed the reasons for their resignations and the reactions to it, making specific allusions to the debate on the electoral law. See, for example, *al-Hayat*, 7 April and 8 April 1957; *an-Nahar*, 6 April and 9 April 1957. The deputies were Hamid Frangieh, Sabri Hamadih, Rachid Abd al-Hamid Karami, Abdallah al-Yafi, Ahmad al-Assad and his son Kamel al-Assad.

65. See, for instance, editorial, *al-Hayat*, 18 June 1957.

66. Johnson, p. 123. A 1952 electoral law had broken up the large electoral districts into 22 single and 11 two-member constituencies, starting a process of undermining the *zu'ama*. The 1957 reform merely continued the process.

67. *An-Nahar*, 13 May 1957.

68. *Al-Hayat*, 20 May 1957.

69. *An-Nahar*, 28 May 1957.

70. *Al-Hayat*, 30 May and 31 May 1957.

71. F.O. 371/142208, British Embassy Beirut to Foreign Office 24 April 1959. This states, 'the Commander in Chief anxious to prevent the disintegration of the army and lacking sympathy for the President's political plans could seldom be persuaded to use his small force for offensive actions'.

72. *An-Nahar*, 31 May 1957. The full truth is not known, but it is certain that both sets of figures were inaccurate if only because accuracy in such figures on such occasions was not in the interests of any of the parties involved.

73. *An-Nahar*, 3 June 1957. One of the leading newspapers that did appear, because of its generally neutral stance, it did report this set of developments, including the figures for both sides and the censorship of other portions of the press.

74. Attiyah, p. 274.

75. *Al-Hayat*, 1 June 1957; see also *al-Hayat*, 3 June for reports on how this compromise was reached.

76. For an indication of how this arrangement was received by the opposition, see *al-Hayat*, 2 June and 4 June 1957. Hitti was an ex-deputy. He had the reputation of being an honest man, but also for being a go-between and a political 'fixer' – probably the reason he was chosen. Bayhum was a Sunni, from a traditional political family, but not a leading figure, again making him a relatively neutral choice. See FO371/134115 VL1012/1, No. 68 (Confidential) Sir George Middleton to Mr Selwyn Lloyd, No. 68, (Confidential), 2 May 1958, 'Leading Personalities in Lebanon'. See also Qubain, p. 56.

77. *An-Nahar*, 3 June 1957.

78. Saeb Salam, interview, Geneva, 4 January 1991.

79. *Al-Hayat*, 21 June 1957, made this point. Interestingly, however, some of these twenty deputies had made it public that they had reservations about government foreign policy; again highlighted in the *al-Hayat* report.

80. Figures taken from *al-Hayat*, 17 June 1957.

81. For example, *al-Hayat* provided the results, on 10 June 1957 for Beirut and the south; on 11 June 1957 for Mount Lebanon; on 24 June for the Biqa'; and on 1 July 1957 for North Lebanon.

82. Kamal Jumblat, *Haqiqat al-Thawra al-Lubnaniyyah* [The Truth about the Lebanese Revolution], Dar al-Nashr al-Arrabiyyah, Beirut, 1959, p. 115; Yussuf al-Sawda, *al-Khiyana al-'Uzma* [The Biggest Betrayal], Beirut, 1957. This pamphlet is held in the al-Sawda Papers, l'Université de St-Esprit, Kaslik, and specifically discusses the issue of Chamoun using the election in his attempt to renew his mandate. See also Farid al-Khazin and Paul Salem, *al-Intikhatabat al-Ula fi Lubnan fi ma Ba'd al-Harb* [The First Election After the War], Dar an-Nahar wa Markaz al-Lubnani lil Dirasat, Beirut, 1993, p. 29, which describes the 1957 election as 'conducted according to the plans of President Chamoun.'

83. *Ibid.*

84. *An-Nahar*, 14 June 1957.

85. This point was made very strongly in the opposition press. See *an-Nahar*, 18 June 1957.

86. *Al-Hayat*, 16 March 1957. Johnson, p. 122, points out that Chamoun had rejected Jumblat's 'moderate social democracy' on his election in 1952, though they had been in alliance against al-Khoury, placing Jumblat in the opposition camp.

87. Saeb Salam, interview, 4 January 1991, stressed this point. It was also made by Caroline Attie, 'President Chamoun and the Crisis of 1958. Referring to Foreign Service Despatch No. 487, American Embassy (Beirut) to Department of State 18 April 1957', unpublished conference paper, Austin, Texas, 13 September 192. See also *al-Hayat*, 18 June 1957 for comments on the unacceptable nature of Jumblat's defeat.

88. For example, in its analysis of the Mount Lebanon results, *al-Hayat* reported with sympathy Kamal Jumblat's accusations that Chamoun had engineered his defeat. See *al-Hayat*, 19 June 1957.

89. Ghosn's withdrawal was widely commented on at the time; he was from a landowning family with a power base in the Kura district. It was agreed that no *za'im* would choose not to stand in the elections unless something extraordinary had happened. Salim Nassar, interview, London, 20 May 1995; *al-Hayat*, 1 July 1957.

90. This point was not lost on the press, see *al-Hayat*, 1 July 1957. See also Qubain, p. 57; Salim Nassar, interview, London, 20 May 1995. Nassar was a leading newspaperman in 1958, and his comments on the public mood at the time must be taken seriously.

91. *Al-Hayat*, 18 June, 1957; see also *Mideast Mirror*, 23 June, 1957 for a repetition of the claims.

92. This was reported widely; see *al-Hayat*, 4 July 1957.

93. *Al-Hayat*, 31 July 1957.

94. FO371/134116, British Embassy Beirut to Foreign Office, 23 January 1958; 13 March 1958, commenting on the internal political situation of Lebanon.

95. Johnson, p. 126, stresses the economic dimensions behind the focus on the US.

96. *Foreign Relations of the US, 1955–1957*, vol. XIII, p. 210, footnote 3, quoting Richards's record of a meeting with Shihab, Minister of Defence.

97. Such attacks had their effect: Edward Naim lost in the Baabda district in the 1957

elections because his pro-government rivals labelled him a Communist, linking him thereby to such accusations and ensuring no Maronite voters would support him. He was, in fact, merely a socialist, with links to Jumblat's party. See *al-Hayat*, 18 June and 21 June 1957.

98. For instance, Louis de San, Belgian Consul General in Damascus, was arrested by Lebanese *gendarmes* on entering Lebanon on 14 May 1957. His car was full of a large number of weapons and a time bomb, plus a letter with general instructions for a terrorist campaign. Joseph Freiha, interview, Beirut, 14 June 1992, gave details of the case. He was the prosecuting magistrate in the case. See also FO371/134174 Tel. No. 1095, Sir George Middleton to Foreign Office, 21 July 1958. See also claims made in *al-Hayat*, 8 July and 9 July 1957.

99. No such candidacy had yet been announced but it was widely believed that this was Chamoun's intention. See K. S. Salibi, 'Recollections of the 1940s and 1950s', unpublished conference paper, Austin, Texas, 13 September 1992, p. 13.

100. *An-Nahar*, 29 January 1958.

101. *Foreign Relations of the US 1958–1960,* Vol XI, p. 2. footnote 4, makes this point: 'In a January 8 memorandum to the Secretary of Defence, the Joint Chiefs of Staff took note of political unrest and subversion in Lebanon, with probable outside Egyptian and Syrian support.'

102. *Isma'il Moussa Yussuf* [The Revolution of the Free in Lebanon], al-Zayn, Beirut, 1958. This pamphlet recirculated this phraseology, used by figures like Nasser. See also Johnson, p. 131.

103. *An-Nahar*, 11 February 1958.

104. *An-Nahar*, 12 February 1958.

105. Qubain, p. 62.

106. *An-Nahar*, 25 February 1958; Muhammad Hasanein Haykal, *Sanawat al-Galayan* [The Years of Jubilation], Ahram, Cairo, 1988, p. 319, quoting Reuters and Associated Press reports of the time.

107. *An-Nahar*, 26 February 1958.

108. A fresh ban on Egyptian papers on 6 April 1958 indicates the government's lack of success.

109. *An-Nahar*, 9 March 1958.

110. *An-Nahar*, 11 March 1958.

111. *An-Nahar*, 11 March 1958, reporting the speech, underlined its futility.

112. FO371/142208, British Embassy, Beirut to Foreign Office, 24 April 1959 reflecting back on the crisis.

113. Cabinet Papers 1926–1984, Muassassat al-Dirassat al-Lubnananiyyah, Beirut, 1994, vol. 1, p. 470.

114. *An-Nahar*, 15 March 1958.

115. *An-Nahar*, 12 April and 13 April 1958.

116. *An-Nahar*, 30 April 1958.

117. *Al-Hayat*, 16 July 1957.

118. The recent example of Bishara al-Khoury was undoubtedly influential.

119. The influx of Palestinian refugees was certainly an issue here. Johnson, p. 118 again highlights the economic dimension to these fears.

120. Johnson, p. 128, refers to Chamoun's 'tactical errors' in foreign policy, but Chamoun was a shrewd politician and his tactics make sense only if read as an attempt to create an atmosphere favourable to his re-election, although he later denied any such desire.

121. *Al-Hayat*, 22 May 1957.

122. *Al-Hayat*, 18 July 1957.

123. *An-Nahar*, 10 April 1958.

124. *Foreign Relations of the US 1958–1960*, Vol XI, Lebanon and Jordan, Department of State Publication 9932, Washington DC, 1992, p. 17, reporting the contents of Telegram 2967, 6 March 1958. See also F0371/134116, British Embassy, Beirut to Foreign Office, 13 April 1958 reporting that Chamoun had told Toufic Suwaida, Deputy Prime Minister of Iraq, of his decision to seek to renew his mandate.

125. *An-Nahar*, 10 April 1958.

126. *Ibid.*

127. *An-Nahar*, 18 April 1958.

128. *An-Nahar*, 11 April 1958. Chamoun blamed such unrest on the opposition. For example, some claimed that Jumblat was implicated in clashes at Dar al-Baydar.

129. *An-Nahar*, 13 April 1958, p, 1.

130. *The Observer*, London, 17 April 1958. See also *Foreign Relations of the U.S, 1958–1960*, Volume XI, p. 23, footnote 2, reporting Anglo-American diplomatic reactions to the situation.

131. *An-Nahar*, 16 April 1958.

132. *An-Nahar*, 21 April 1958.

133. *An-Nahar*, 25 April 1958.

134. Qubain, p. 68.

135. *An-Nahar*, 9 May 1958; Qubain, p. 69.

136. *Foreign Relations of the United States 1958–1960*, Volume XI, pp. 35–37, footnote 2.

137. *Ibid.*, p. 41.

138. *An-Nahar*, 14 May 1958.

139. *An-Nahar*, 20 May 1958.

140. *An-Nahar*, 13 May 1958.

141. *Al-Amal*, 14 May 1958; Wade Goria, *Sovereignty and Leadership in Lebanon 1943–1976*, Ithaca Press, London, 1985, pp. 45–7.

142. *An-Nahar*, 14 May 1958.

143. *Foreign Relations of the United States, 1958–1960*, Volume XI, p 35, quoting a telegram from the US Embassy in Lebanon to the Department of State, 11 May, 1958.

144. See Qubain, pp. 86–7; *Foreign Relations of the US 1958–1960*, Volume XI, p. 411, Telegram 242, Department of State, 30 July, 1958, in which he states 'Shihab ... indicated he was now ready to accept the presidency but hoped for as large a vote as possible for re-establishing a national unit'.

145. *An-Nahar*, 18 May 1958.

146. *An-Nahar*, 20 May 1958.

147. *Ibid.*

148. Saeb Salam, interview, Geneva, 4 January 1991.

149. See *Documents Diplomatiques Français*, Vol I, 1 January-30 June 1958, p. 603, Chauvel to Pineau, Telegrams nos 1633–36, 13 May 1958.

150. Bashir Awar, Minister of Justice and head of the Lebanese delegation to the Arab League, and a known moderate, resigned his office in protest. See his comments reported in *an-Nahar*, 6 June 1958; also Department of State Archives, Centre for Lebanese Studies, McClintock to Dulles, Telegram no. 4912, 19 June 1958.

151. There was also the implication, thereby, that the League would not be a neutral force. FO371/123119 VL1015/147, Middleton to Selwyn Lloyd, Telegram no. 598, 23 May 1958 passes on Malik's claims, indicating also that the intention to reject the League's

intervention had been taken long before 5 June 1958 when the League did meet and could have undertaken an intervention.

152. Qubain, p. 90.
153. FO371/123119 VL1015/147, Telegram no. 4572, British Embassy, Beirut, to Foreign Office, 9 June 1958.
154. *An-Nahar*, 12 June 1958; Department of State Archives, Centre for Lebanese Studies, Telegram no. 4664, American Embassy to Secretary of State, 12 June 1958.
155. Jumblat, p. 55.
156. Department of State Archives, Centre for Lebanese Studies, American Embassy Beirut to Secretary of State (Confidential), No. 159, 6 July 1958; Odd Bull, *War and Peace in the Middle East*, Leo Cooper, London, 1973, p. 8.
157. Qubain, p. 114.
158. *Al-Hayat*, 15 July 1958.
159. See Qubain, p. 115.
160. *Foreign Relations of the United States 1958–1960*, Volume XI, p. 245, Memorandum of a conference with the President, White House, Washington DC, 15 July, 1958, quoting the Eisenhower diaries.
161. Johnson, p. 126.

CHAPTER FIVE

The Sunni Community in 1958

Nasserism, and the revival of Arabism that it encouraged, 'crystallised latent class aspirations and grievances that had acted as a catalyst of communal feeling' in the Sunni community in Lebanon.[1] Nasserism undoubtedly had an impact on the Sunni community, but it was an essentially a local Sunni interpretation of Nasserism which acted as a major factor in creating a protective Sunni community mythology during the 1950s. Thus to merely state that Nasserism was 'responsible' for Sunni attitudes and actions in Lebanon during the 1958 crisis and its evolution, at any level of the community, is to oversimplify a much more complex scenario.[2] Nasserism, as historians of the Middle East generally use the term, was modified by factors internal to Lebanon, notably Sunni popular perspectives on how it might best be interpreted to serve their own agenda.

Raphael Samuel and Paul Thompson identify the ways social groups have used myths to compensate for their lack of confidence in, and solidarity with, a national identity that other social groups presented to them.[3] The Sunni community in Lebanon in the 1950s was one such group. Nasser was important to the Lebanese Sunnis not so much for what he actually advertised as his agenda and policies, especially in Egypt, as for what they represented him to be. As Johnson has pointed out, especially after the Suez Crisis, Nasser took on heroic stature as a *za'im* who stood above the Lebanese system and united people in admiration of his supposed, or mythical, qualities; these people were otherwise divided into 'vertically-linked clientelist structures'.[4] Such 'new' myths, especially relating to the creation of heroes, flourish when little written history is available and the community has no readily accessible alternative in the form of oral traditions that fit a particular scenario. The high levels of illiteracy in the Sunni community, which I describe later in this chapter, prevented the former; and Sunni traditions prior to the 1950s were too ill-defined to substitute for them.[5]

Nasser provided a readily accessible icon for interpretation, for two reasons: he was distant, and the Sunnis' iconography was often oral rather than written and thus subject to colder critical analysis. The growing sense of crisis in Lebanon, with the Sunni community cast in a seemingly permanent role as 'opposition' to the state's Maronite or Christian-dominated government, provided an opportunity for a 'national leader' to emerge to lead that opposition. Within Lebanon itself, no such Sunni figurehead emerged with major popular appeal, partly because so many prominent Sunnis were involved with the established order.

This left the way open for an alternative figure who could be interpreted as 'representing' the aspirations of the Lebanese Sunnis, including their aspirations to be part of a broader community than just Lebanon.[6] West Beirut's brand of Nasserism, for instance, was an 'oppositional doctrine', a protest against the dominance of the Sunni community by 'Christian Lebanon', and also a 'yearning' for 'a Sunni Arab order'. In a sense, then, Nasserism summed up what might be described as 'pan-Arabism' in a way that gave the Lebanese Sunni community a role in a wider international Sunni community.[7] Dissatisfied with their role in the country at that time, the Lebanese Sunni masses desired to play such a role. Many believed that they were exploited by 'the rich'; as Nasser Kalawoun points out, 'the rich' in this tradition were equated with the Christian, and especially the Maronite, community.[8]

Thus we need to examine the shape of the Sunni community at this point, and also to consider the impact on the community, at mass level, of a range of local issues and perspectives, including the issue of consensus or co-habitation with other confessional communities, especially the Maronites. Michael Johnson has shown a clear linkage between issues relating to the National Pact and the 1958 crisis.[9] In chapter four I discussed how the crisis developed at elite political levels and how leaders from both Sunni and

Maronite communities, from different perspectives, stressed this pact as well as their experience of the crisis.

But the 1958 crisis had an impact far beyond such leaders: it was a breakdown in consensus between the communities at all levels of society. The National Pact was also significant to the masses of both communities, the people whom those leaders claimed to represent. These masses had their own understanding of the pact, and what it entailed in practice; and it was not necessarily the same as that provided by the leaders. They had other means of gaining information and of gaining a range of viewpoints on events. The flourishing media in Lebanon allowed information to reach the population through a wide variety of newspapers and other publications as well as by radio broadcasts; thus the masses had ways to be thoroughly informed on matters they found important.

The ways that the masses of both Sunnis and Maronites contributed to the crisis is my focus in this chapter and the next. As was true of the political leaders, the general populations of these communities provided the most significant polarities of opinion relating to the crisis. On the whole, the mass Maronite perspective on their position was essentially defensive: they reacted to events and to the agendas of other communities, notably the Sunni. This perspective makes it important to identify what the Maronites saw themselves as reacting against; therefore I examine the Sunni community first.

The Sunni community had a lower level of literacy than the Maronite community; but in the 1950s the community's ready access to radio compensated for any such lack. Lebanese radio may have operated largely as a voice for the government or established elites, but Sunnis could also access broadcasts on Syrian and Egyptian radio. Only at the height of the crisis, in June and July 1958, were such broadcasts jammed, preventing their reception in Lebanon. For the rest of the crisis period, these broadcasts were a readily accessible source of anti-Chamoun and anti-government policy information and propaganda.[10]

The structure of the Sunni community did not promote conscious cohesion internally; traditional loyalties rather than deliberate decisions tended to dominate its patterns of allegiance and solidarity.[11] Like the other communities, the Sunnis had been affected by the setting up of a separate Lebanese entity in 1920. But compared to the other Muslim communities, the Sunnis may have suffered more, given their perception of the Ottoman empire and the disappearance of the wider entity to which they had given allegiance. As I have shown in chapters one and three, the Sunni community as a whole was profoundly opposed to the concept and establishment of a separate Lebanon; instead they created the vision of a Greater Syria to counter the Maronite vision of a Greater Lebanon. But as Nicola Ziadeh has pointed out, by the end of the Mandate period, the community as a whole had become accustomed to being part of an entity separate from Syria – even if they did not always like it.[12]

The Sunni elites, both the traditional landowning classes and the newer (if still small) bourgeoisie, had accepted their position in an independent Lebanon and consequently had developed common interests with, for example, the Maronites; this is clear from their co-operation in setting up the National Pact in 1943. As Michael Johnson points out, the 'Sunni notables of Beirut and Lebanon' had evolved a strategy during the Mandate, and continued to utilise it subsequently, that 'emphasised their role as communal leaders and champions'.[13] They did this by developing a rhetoric that they could use at times of potential community crisis to refer to the dream of a Greater Syria and their commitment to Lebanon's incorporation within it. However, as I indicated in chapter four, few intended to move beyond the rhetoric. The Sunni elites used the rhetoric to maintain their leadership role unchallenged by the masses, and to avoid responding directly to popular aspirations. Thus the attitude of the elites meant that at this level, the Sunni community in Lebanon had begun to feel a cultural identity that can be described as Lebanese, if it was also unequivocally Arab in nature.

The Sunni elites faced a problem, however: few amongst the masses had this sense of identification with Lebanon. Even after full independence and the creation of the National Pact, most Sunnis continued to see Lebanon not only as an artificial creation carved out of Syria, but also as a creation that brought with it no tangible benefits for them. So they had no reason to like the status quo. Hilal Khashan pointed out that it was 'common' for members of the Sunni community 'to insist, whether rightly or not, that the 1943 National Covenant had discriminated against them'.[14] In an echo of the position that Maronites often took, their grievances stemmed from the way they interpreted the past and the implications they drew from that for their present and future.[15]

What determined the attitudes – and popular mythologies – of most Sunnis during the 1950s? The main trends that shaped these attitudes can be traced back to the First World War and the Mandate period although they did not coalesce into coherent mythologies until later. The Sunnis held two major perspectives on Lebanon, along with a more minor one. First, they saw Lebanon as part of a Greater Syria in the way Faisal had outlined during his brief period in Damascus and Beirut. This perspective involved resentment against the Western powers, particularly France, which had prevented its development. Faisal's presence had had a huge and positive effect on the community at popular levels. At a time when the Sunnis were facing the uncertainty associated with the collapse of the Ottoman Empire, they were cheered at the prospect of being incorporated into Faisal's Arab kingdom, which would allow them to remain important.[16] This possibility remained a popular symbol for what the masses felt as an unjustifiable loss: a Syria, defined as a state, to be administered on decentralised lines that would echo Ottoman practice and boost Sunni importance within it. Most supporters of this idea lived in cities, especially Tripoli and Beirut, though the perspective certainly had a large following in other parts of the country.

A second perspective was represented by Arab nationalism, though it had less popular appeal because of its intellectual overtones.[17] In the decades after 1920, it was advanced by politicians from the al-Solh family of Sidon, notably Khazim, Takkieddine and their cousin Riyadh.[18] From 1943 until his death in 1951, Riyadh become the most significant Lebanese Sunni political leader. This ensured that at least the urban masses continued to be aware of the Arab nationalist agenda, even if it held less appeal than the vision of Greater Syria.

A third perspective was provided by Islamism. But without a charismatic religious leader who could inspire Sunni congregations in Lebanon, and given the Franco-Maronite domination of Lebanon, this perspective made little political headway. This situation provides a real contrast to the cohesion that the Maronite church provided for its masses.

In considering how the Sunni community made use of these perspectives on Lebanon in the 1950s, we must also consider the nature of the community. While it is possible to speak of a general Sunni attitude in some respects, that community was divided in its views and reactions, between the masses both rural and urban and those who acted as spokesmen for the Sunni community. For instance, Najla Attiyah describes 'a horizontal relationship ... between the masses and the spokesmen'; the spokesmen did not have 'a proper mandate from the masses' and were not 'accountable to them'.[19] In practical terms this meant that these so-called spokesmen made policy decisions without referring seriously to the people whose interests they claimed to represent. Shaykh Muhammad al-Jisr had been notorious for such behaviour,[20] and it continued even with a genuinely popular leader like Riyadh al-Solh.

Thus, during the Mandate period and Bishara al-Khoury's presidency, the Sunni masses had had little power to determine the political attitudes of their spokesmen. Returning to the trends identified just above, this situation attracted most ordinary Sunnis to the idea of unity with Syria; compared to the elites, they had less exposure to the material opportunities offered by the Lebanese state and even more attachment to religious issues or Islamism.[21] Over time, as I described in chapter four, the Sunni elites had become less enthusiastic about the idea of immediate union with Syria.

In considering the attitudes of the Sunni masses, we must differentiate between those in cities and the countryside. The urban Sunni masses were in the majority quantitatively; located mainly in centres like Beirut, Tripoli and Sidon, they differed significantly from the rural Sunnis, particularly in their relationships with community leaders. The urban Sunnis were reasonably independent, both economically and politically. Generally better educated, they were more open to media propaganda, especially after radio broadcasting emerged. In contrast, the rural masses were less informed and more dependent, especially financially, on their leaders, and thus were more open to their influence. These rural masses, largely located in the north and south of Lebanon, were less affected by educational developments and by the media.

Aboud Abdel Razzak, a ruler in the Akkar district, exemplifies this traditional dependency. He was essentially a feudal lord: during the 1958 crisis he was able to co-operate fully with the Lebanese state without complaints, because his followers were largely ignorant of the implications of his actions.[22] For example in August 1958 the Sunni deputies of Akkar actively testified against Syria, accusing it of causing trouble along the Syrian-Lebanese border with the aim of undermining the Chamoun regime.[23] Testifying against Syria was already, at the time, a stand the Sunni masses would not approve of.

The urban masses were less easily influenced by their elites, and were thus more likely to be critical when those elites claimed, falsely, that given views and policies represented the wishes or opinions of the masses. For instance, the 'permanent conference of the Muslim Commissions', established in 1953 to voice the ideas of the Muslim communities, 'did not enjoy great popular following', according to Nasser Kalawoun, although he does argue that it reflected 'the general mood of the community'.[24] Starting in 1954, however, the urban masses demanded a greater role in evolving the Sunni views and policies being voiced by the spokesmen, though it was only in 1957 that these views began to have a major impact on the elites.

Up to late 1957, and even into 1958, the Sunni elites could largely continue to disregard the reactions and beliefs emerging among the urban masses. Rather than listening to popular opinion, they maintained their contact with the masses by continuing to dispense patronage on a traditional patron-client basis, an approach that was less and less effective in enabling them to maintain their traditional dominance. Without any powerful populist political organisations that could act as pressure groups on the elites, at least in the period up to the 1957 elections, mass expressions of grievances against their 'spokesmen' remained incoherent and ineffective. Nor did the Sunni religious organisation offer a channel for people to express grievances with their own elites or with the state – in a direct contrast to the way the Maronite Church could act as a focus for popular opposition. Rather, the religious hierarchy of the Sunni community remained closely linked to the secular social hierarchy.[25] Moreover, no real equivalent to the Maronite Kata'ib Party emerged within the Sunni community.[26]

One factor was clearly key in these developments: without the quality of newspapers available to the Maronites, the Sunni masses had relatively little access to information that would allow them to protest as effectively as the Maronites could. In particular, without wide and consistent access to political and economic information, it was harder to develop shared attitudes and opinions and express them coherently.[27] In addition, given the lower level of education among Sunnis, including a higher level of illiteracy, the community did not demand the type of populist newspaper that could sell to the Maronite masses.

This situation had two linked effects: it helped sustain an ultimate dependence on the leaders and also ensured that few ordinary people had much detailed information about the elites' policies. Only in late 1957 did broadcasts on Egyptian and Syrian radio begin to address Lebanese policy in real detail, rather than providing rhetorically general attacks on the government. At that point radio broadcasts began to serve as an efficient alternative to newspapers for the Sunni masses. Now they could begin to develop deeper political consciousness, based on a greater knowledge of events in the Arab world and their own leaders' role in supporting the status quo in Lebanon.

It was no accident that the Sunni masses were able to have an effect on their political leadership at the same time these broadcasts occurred – as I will demonstrate later in this chapter.

It is also illuminating to look at the ways in which education was provided within the Sunni community: by doing so we can both account for the lower levels of literacy, and begin to understand some popular Sunni grievances. The Sunni masses were clearly aware, and resentful, of the imbalance in educational provision, and especially of the government's failure to remedy that imbalance. Government schools throughout Lebanon were limited in numbers, even in the 1950s, and no government worked hard to expand this provision. In the 1953 pamphlet *Moslem Lebanon Today,* Muslim leaders complained that no 'interest in Moslem education is manifested by the government'.[28]

Popular resentment over this policy was a major factor in the 1957 crisis, according to al-Jisr, and others back up this assertion. Desmond Stewart describes how the petty bourgeoisie became linked 'with the sub-proletariat under the leadership of members of the bourgeoisie' as Muslims in Lebanon sought an improved educational system through the *al-Maqassed* movement.[29] Walid Jumblat has also argued that the Muslim communities generally felt deprived of access to education in this period.[30] Thus the educational policy was a key area where the Sunni masses felt discrimination within the Lebanese state.

Government policy did not focus on educational reform because the Maronites had no need for such a policy and also, according to Jumblat, because the government found that the inadequate system permitted them to use 'the weapon of education' in their own interests, by promoting confessional differences within the system.[31] Traditionally, most education in Lebanon had occurred in private schools, notably Christian mission schools, which had understandably not attracted children from the Sunni community. The Maronites, however, made full use of this provision.[32]

Sunni political leaders did not take up the cause of improving education for their community in any serious way; doing so would only undermine their position in the Sunni social hierarchy. Although the *al-Maqassed* schools were important, their small numbers made them inadequate to meet the community's needs.[33] Moreover, the educational standards in private and especially mission schools were higher than in either the government or the *al-Maqassed* schools.[34] This was particularly so in terms of foreign language teaching, but even at the basic level of literacy it had an effect. Tables 5 and 6 illustrate some of the demographic facts that kept this problem alive.

Table 5: Percentage of Illiterate People in Lebanon's Religious Communities in 1932[35]

Shi'ite	Sunni	Maronite	Greek Catholic	Druze	Greek Orthodox
83	66	48	39	53	53

Table 6: Private Schools in Lebanon According to Confessional Orientation 1944–5[36 & 37]

	Number	Percentage of Total of Private Schools
Private Christian Schools	748	77.5
Private Muslim Schools	208	21.3

After World War II ended, state schooling in Lebanon clearly improved, with the number of state schools increasing from 238 in 1943 to 953 in 1954, according to Ziadeh. The Muslim communities in general benefited most from this development because they made use of state schooling where it was available. But most of these state schools only offered elementary education; only five provided secondary education.[38] Thus, the lack of quality education kept much of the Sunni population from pursuing career opportunities. For instance, foreign languages, essentially French and English, were available only in secondary schools, so few Sunnis could operate effectively in a wider commercial field.

As Carolyn Gates has pointed out, the Lebanese economy and economic policies focused on Lebanon's 'intermediary role between the West and the Middle East', with Beirut playing a particularly important role as a centre for trade, financial and other commercial services. This economy depended on the profits from such international trade and related services, such as expediting the passage of goods in and out of states like Syria that had more difficult contacts with the West.[39] Because governments in this period maintained open economies, the Maronite and other Christian communities faced little real challenge to their dominance of what Gates identifies as the most profitable sectors of the Lebanese economy: the 'dynamic foreign tertiary sector' and the financial and commercial services sector. According to Gates, 'The public awareness that only a very small number' were benefiting economically from Lebanon's success continually contributed to popular Sunni resentment of the Maronites and the way that community safeguarded its interests.'[40]

Economic factors also generally worked to the disadvantage of the Sunni masses in Lebanon. Overall, they had a lower standard of living than the Maronites. The Sunni bourgeois elite was economically successful in both commerce and administration, and the traditional land-based Sunni elite retained its old wealth. But the bourgeoisie was a small proportion of the overall community, particularly compared with the ratio among the Maronites.[41] The Sunni masses looking at this difference felt they were being unfairly excluded from economic as well as political and cultural power. They certainly saw discrimination in employment, as they were confined to lower paid posts with less chance of promotion to the highest levels. A writer in *Moslem Lebanon Today*, for example, complained about Christian (essentially Maronite) dominance of the civil service.[42]

The disadvantages the 'Sunni petty bourgeoisie' faced, however, were 'nowhere near as desperate as [those] of the sub-proletariat', as Johnson points out. These people not only lived in squalor but also had little opportunity to work. Johnson saw 'little doubt that the Sunni sub-proletariat recognised their relative deprivation', and certainly al-Jisr picked up this perception as he discussed the reasons for the crisis in 1958; he referred explicitly to popular consciousness of the Sunnis' 'economic deprivation' as a significant factor in their discontent.[43]

Another important contributing factor was the obviously disproportionate expenditure of government funds in the Mount Lebanon districts. From the start the Lebanese government favoured Mount Lebanon as it allocated funds for public projects, although these areas were already more developed than the mainly Muslim districts, such as the Biqa' and Akkar.[44] A simple comparison shows how this imbalance persisted even after the 1958 crisis. In 1960, these were the levels of government funding for each region, in thousands of Lebanese pounds: Mount Lebanon, 2.24; North, 2.13, South, 1.53, and Biqa', 1.69.[45] In both the South and the Biqa' the majority of the population was Muslim; the South was 70% Muslim. The government spent considerably less for public works and projects in these areas than for those areas with the highest proportions of Maronites. The Sunnis saw this situation as resulting from corruption among the Maronites at all levels of state administration.[46] This distortion in the allocation of funds added to Sunni consciousness of, and resentment over, their relatively lower standards of living compared to the Maronites. For the bulk of the Sunni community, therefore, the intercommunal compromise summed up in the National Pact had little positive impact on their lives.

For a discontented population, or a discontented portion of one, the traditional solution has been some kind of political expression of their grievances. But as I pointed out earlier, the Sunnis had no populist party in this period – at least not one willing to rework the existing system to redress Sunni disadvantages. This is not to say that the Sunni masses lacked a political consciousness. Writing in 1957, Ziadeh identified an idea 'creeping into the minds of people' in the 1950s about 'the necessity of equality and justice', which was then becoming 'more than just a cry'.[47]

But for the mass of Lebanese Sunnis, no indigenous Muslim populist political party existed that could serve as a channel for their discontent. There was the Najjadah grouping; but given its predominantly secular orientation it could not attract a substantial membership from the religiously-minded Sunni masses. The Communist Party suffered from the same disadvantage and was also tainted, in Lebanese Sunni eyes, by Soviet support for the creation of Israel. There was the Progressive Socialist Party, founded in 1949, but membership of the Druze-led party was practically confined to followers of Kamal Jumblat.[48] Even Riyadh al-Solh, with a considerable popular following amongst the masses, demonstrated little willingness to listen to their voice.[49]

Yet another complication faced Lebanese Sunnis who sought a channel to express their discontent. After Riyadh al-Solh died on 16 July 1951, al-Khoury made it clear that he would bypass the Sunni and other Muslim politicians to exercise as much independent power as possible. An editorial eulogising al-Solh described al-Khoury as 'the partner who took more than his share' and mentioned the resentment of the al-Solh family and traditional following, as well as the 'Sunni community' as a whole.[50] Certainly in 1951 and 1952, al-Khoury aroused considerable resentment amongst the Sunni elites as he tried to manipulate Sunni candidates for the premiership; his eventual choice of Sami al-Solh did not restore his popularity with that political elite.[51] Equally, al-Khoury had made no attempt to conciliate the Sunni masses, or to provide himself with a popular base in that community that would let him counteract any protests from the Sunni elites.

Al-Khoury's actions indicate how much the political establishment, whether Maronite or Muslim, believed it could ignore the Sunni masses, seeing no need to propitiate them by addressing their grievances at any level beyond the rhetorical. This situation did not change under Chamoun. If anything the issue became more acute, despite the rhetoric Chamoun used to assure Muslims that he respected Arab traditions.[52] Sami al-Solh pointed out in his memoirs that overall, Sunni participation in the state of Lebanon depended heavily on the Sunni leaders' relationships with Maronite leaders.

According to him, Sunni politicians were 'only the instruments which they set up before the eyes of the public to be held accountable for their errors and misdeeds.'[53]

Given this context, it should come as no surprise that in the 1950s the Sunni masses looked outside Lebanon for sympathy for their grievances, and for a cause to ally themselves with, if only as a source of bargaining power with which to extract concessions from their own and Maronite community leaders. In this sense, the Sunni masses began to echo the pattern the Maronites had set up under Ottoman rule. This development was ominous for the success of consensus under the terms of the National Pact, because it represented a return to the older tradition of co-habitation. True, this decision also resulted from intra-confessional strife, but the intra-communal tensions among the Sunnis would probably not have risen as high as they did in the early 1950s if most Sunnis saw the Maronites as fulfilling their side of the bargain set up in the National Pact.

I have already described how most Sunnis remained willing to identify with Syria and Syrian ambitions and interests. In the 1950s this longstanding tendency came together with another tradition in the Sunni community, dating back to the World War I: the search for inspiring heroes in the wider Arab world, given the few available within Lebanon. Up to the early 1950s, such heroes had had little direct impact on Lebanon, representing a more general sense of maintaining Arab status in relation to the West.[54] But during the1950s a new element in the Arab world began to attract the Lebanese Sunnis: Nasser. He had such a great impact on the Arab world that in Syria, for example, a majority of the population began to demand that he also become their leader. This was one factor behind the eventual creation of the United Arab Republic. When Nasser arrived in Syria in 1958, the estimated crowd of 180,000 hailed him as 'The Saviour Hero, the defender of the most sacred things'.[55]

In Lebanon the Sunni masses were also stirred to considerable enthusiasm by what he seemed to offer in the way of 'fairer' policies: Nasser seemed a model leader, one who would promote and 'protect the interests of his people' in the name of both Arab nationalism and Islam. To a community conscious of economic discrimination, his economic policies let him take on the status of a 'champion of the poor' because he gave 'a sense of dignity to people of low social status' but did so in an essentially Arab and Islamic way.[56]

The pro-Egyptian stance amongst Lebanese Sunnis can be traced back to the Egyptian Revolution of 23 July 1952, which had brought Nasser to power and eventually added a whole new dimension to Lebanese-Egyptian relations. Lebanon's Sunni masses saw Egypt as the largest and strongest Sunni Arab country; thus they felt a natural affinity for it, and Nasserist slogans calling for social justice added more appeal.[57] At the same time, American policy in the Middle East raised Sunni awareness of events in the wider Arab world and made the ordinary Sunnis increasingly dissatisfied with existing Lebanese foreign policy as well as with domestic policy. Thus the two strands that would lead to the crisis of 1958 were suddenly brought together.

Popular Sunni awareness of both these strands, and their positive reaction to Nasser's policies and rhetoric as a possible alternative to the Lebanese status quo, began to have a visible effect as the population grew increasingly annoyed with the Chamoun regime. A key event here was the visit to Lebanon in May 1953 of the US secretary of state, John Foster Dulles, who sought the Lebanese government's support for current American policy in the Middle East. This visit highlighted the differences between politicians and masses. The Sunni politicians were not enthusiastic, but were prepared to accept some compromise along the existing lines of Lebanese foreign policy. The Sunni masses felt differently, however, and demonstrated against Dulles.[58] One factor was their long-standing resentment of the West, but Nasser also played a crucial role in raising anti-American feelings. Thus the evidence is clear that Egyptian manipulation of Lebanese Sunni popular opinion started immediately after Nasser came to power and continued to significantly affect mass behaviour amongst the Sunnis throughout the rest of Chamoun's regime.[59]

Thus, a coincidence, starting in 1953, helped to promote organisation amongst the Sunni masses: the combination of Dulles's visit and Nasser's increasingly high profile in the Middle East provided a series of issues on which they could agree and begin to act. At this point several associations became more prominent, including the Najjadah grouping, the Muslim Young Men's Union, the Muslim Boy Scouts, *al-Hayat al-Watania* (the National Committee), and the *al-Maqassed* College Alumni Association. Some were already established and some were new, but all took advantage of this new discontent to recruit members.

These groupings claimed to be the 'voice' of the masses, and from 1953 very deliberately made statements, reported in periodicals such as *Beirut,* that linked long-standing domestic grievances and potential remedies with what they interpreted as the strategies of Nasserism, rather than invoking the terminology of the National Pact as traditional Sunni leaders did.[60] The organisations' names provide clues to the particular constituencies within the Sunni community (and the Muslim community generally) to which they appealed. The *al-Maqassed* College Alumni Association, for instance, brought together the more literate amongst the Sunni masses by drawing on graduates of the charitable Muslim schools.

These groupings did not have the standing or organisation within the Sunni community that the Kata'ib Party had among the Maronites. For instance, their initial statements tended to be at least somewhat conciliatory in their attitude towards the Sunni elites, and some groupings included non-Sunni members.[61] Still, they attracted enough popular support to bring about a state of tension between the Sunni community and the government in the summer and autumn of 1954.[62] The key issue was equality – confessional, cultural and economic – between the sects in Lebanon. In a letter to Chamoun, supported by the Najjadah organisation, *al-Haya al-Wataniyyah* described Sunni dissatisfaction with what it defined as contemporary 'inequality' and demanded immediate remedies. The Najjadah grouping had also re-emerged during the early 1950s, and was also claiming to be a voice of popular Sunni opinion.

These organisations were aggressive enough to alarm both the government and the Sunni community leaders, as they seemed able to orchestrate demonstrations and strikes by significant elements within the Sunni community.[63] In the end, Sunni leaders were able to diffuse this tension, as they were still able to force both the larger community and the specific organisations to accept conciliation, without really changing policy in response to their grievances.[64] Clearly these popular organisations had not yet gained significant power at political levels.

Another development came with the emergence of politicised *qabadays*, who acted as facilitators or intermediaries between the masses and the elites, providing channels for ordinary people to pass on messages to their traditional leaders or *za'ims*.[65] In the 1950s, they became an important agency for bringing pressure on the Sunni elites who relied on their services. Labib Zuwiyyah Yamak points out that even Sunni 'notables' who had become national figures, such as Bishara al-Khoury or Kamal Jumblat, relied on the 'elementary political organisation constituted by the *qabada'iyyat*' to mobilise their supporters.[66] With no alternative power structures in place, the Sunni political elite had no choice but to continue to rely on them.

They were essentially an urban phenomenon, men drawn from the masses, acting as leaders at the street level but also as channels for communication. During the 1950s, they played a dual role: they both served the elites by restraining the growing radicalism of the Sunni masses, and passed on the agendas of ordinary Sunnis to the leadership. Essentially, they were pragmatic facilitators who had no obvious ideology linking them to either side. Equally, as they were drawn from the masses themselves they could only sustain their role and influence – and thus their value to the *za'ims* – as long as they kept the support of the masses. As the masses became more unified behind Nasserist rhetoric, the *qabadays* needed to reflect that development to the Sunni elites and convince them to respond positively to the rhetoric. This became more important as the government policy seemed to be moving further and further towards a dangerously anti-Arab stance.[67]

When Chamoun came into office, Sunnis at all levels initially welcomed his advertised pro-Arab stance; he was also linked with the British position of opposing an independent Jewish state in Palestine.[68] But in 1952 he needed to conciliate Muslim opinion, and no clear breach yet existed between a pro-Arab and a pro-Western policy.[69] Given this dilemma he established some high expectations for his regime, which he never fulfilled. At first the Sunni community had had no real complaints in his handling of foreign policy. To the Sunnis, Chamoun's speeches had seemed to indicate that he was maintaining a pro-Arab policy though the substance of his policy did not bear out his fine words.[70]

As late as 1956 his claim to be a champion of the Arab cause still had an effect on Sunni politicians, even if the Sunni masses were less susceptible, given the greater appeal of Nasser's rhetoric and their own continuing discontents. Even in November 1956, *al-Hayat* did not seem ridiculous in publishing a letter from Chamoun to Eisenhower about the Suez Crisis, in which Chamoun portrayed himself as speaking in the Arab interest.[71] Although events after the Suez Crisis were to reveal very plainly the lack of substance in Chamoun's pro-Arab rhetoric, the Sunni politicians were still not willing to provoke a crisis over this issue, preferring to seek compromise instead.

Thus the attitudes of the Sunni elites and the Sunni masses were diverging clearly by the mid-1950s, with the politicians pursuing their mainly conciliatory approach, and the masses increasingly swayed by Egyptian propaganda. The general rhetoric of that propaganda allowed its listeners to interpret it as directly relevant to their concerns. The popular Sunni hostility to existing

Lebanese foreign policy developed significantly in 1955, the year of the Baghdad Pact. The pact forced Lebanon to try to negotiate its position in the new regional arena – in the context of an Arab world feeling a newfound strength. Nasserist policies had added to this sense of strength, along with the rise of a quasi-religious socialism in the Arab world.

With a cause to fight for at last, the Sunni masses began to exert concerted pressure on their leaders, and to have an impact on official attitudes towards the Sunni masses. But this impact did not lead to serious redress of their grievances. For instance, in April 1955 a new body, the Islamic Council, was set up under the leadership of the *mufti*. A government decree in January of 1955 had acknowledged the importance and religious status of the Sunni community by placing the *mufti*'s 'bureau' under the prime minister, effectively giving the *mufti* status as a government official.[72] This, in turn, gave the concept of the council some official backing. The council advertised itself as having 'a duty to defend the rights of the community, which, so it is believed, are not being given sufficient consideration by the authorities'.[73] Traditional Sunni leaders saw this council as bypassing them; for instance, Saeb Salam opposed it, fearing it would lessen his power as a *za'im*.[74] But the council was not exactly a radical body: its first genuinely radical action was participating in the 1958 boycott of the traditional government *Iftar* dinner.[75]

But some leaders of the Sunni community changed their attitudes somewhat; for example the Sunni Prime Minister Sami al-Solh opposed cabinet policy and attended the Cairo Conference in January 1955.[76] Chamoun had opposed attendance at the conference, because official Lebanese policy was pro-Iraq rather than pro-Egypt, and Iraq had not been invited to the conference. This was the first time a Lebanese prime minister acted contrary to the will of the president on such a public and important matter.[77] But this bow to Sunni mass opinion was merely a matter of appearance and did not signify any radical change in Sunni politicians' attitudes towards the status quo in Lebanon. In Cairo al-Solh tried, but failed, to work out a compromise between Egypt and Iraq, demonstrating his continuing willingness to support the official Lebanese policy line and his sensitivity to Maronite attitudes rather than taking an unequivocally pro-Nasser line.[78]

Egypt's Intervention

This attempt at conciliation had tremendous repercussions internally. Al-Solh's efforts infuriated Egyptian politicians, and made them determined to bring Lebanon's Sunni politicians into alignment with them. Through radio broadcasts, they learned that they had the basis for a propaganda campaign aimed at the Lebanese Muslim population, because the Sunni masses did not like al-Solh's conciliatory attitude at the conference. For instance, students had led demonstrations against Western alliances in general and against the Western-backed alliance between Turkey and Iraq in particular.[79] This was a good foundation for an Egyptian propaganda intervention that would force the Lebanese Sunni leaders to alter their political stance and become dependent on Egypt's goodwill.

The key was subverting the basis of public support for these leaders, a campaign that continued for the rest of the Chamoun mandate with increasing success as the Sunni masses responded positively to the rhetoric directed at them, as I will describe later in this chapter. Although some tried, with some success, to bring together those Sunni leaders in the opposition and those in the government, ultimately this Egyptian strategy seriously undermined the independence of the local Sunni leaders.[80] Though al-Solh and other Sunnis involved in government continued to support Chamoun, that support was increasingly lukewarm and hesitant in the face of Egyptian-inspired hostility to the status quo from the Sunni rank-and-file.

Between 1955 and 1958, pro-government Sunni leaders effectively ceased to carry major political weight in the Sunni community, though they gradually responded to expressions of community opinion. The growing dissatisfaction of the Sunni population, for example, led Sami al-Solh to resign on 19 September 1955 following a split in the ministerial ranks over the issue of pro-Egyptian inclination. Even Chamoun was not immune to the impact that this popular Sunni pressure was having on Sunni politicians. To defuse rising tension and the concerns of Sunni politicians, he had to appoint Rachid Karami, son of Abd al-Hamid Karami, a leading figure in the Sunni opposition, to succeed al-Solh. Needing to be conciliatory to stay on good terms with his supporters in Tripoli, Karami was not likely to take an anti-Egyptian attitude and would in fact pressure Chamoun to be conciliatory.[81] Thus 1955 was a watershed for Sunni politicians who now found themselves having to pay lip service, at least, to the pro-Nasserist Sunni popular attitudes.

Karami's period as prime minister, according to Attiyah, was a transitional period in the history of the president-premier relationship in Lebanon.[82] Early in his term he tried to interpret the National Pact along the same lines as other Sunni politicians, to retain the goodwill of the president and the support of his community. But as the two perspectives proved impossible to reconcile, Karami leaned towards satisfying the Sunni community, particularly his own constituency in Tripoli. His determination to champion a pro-Nasserist line created a new type of conflict within the government, and led to his resignation in March 1956. The pro-Chamoun element engineered that resignation, in direct response to the increasing ability of the Sunni masses to impose their agenda on their leaders. Meanwhile, the Maronites were seeing those Sunni desires as radically opposed to established Lebanese policy, while the Sunnis themselves saw them as being in line with the National Pact, as compromises to keep a Maronite agenda in check.[83]

Though Chamoun succeeded in getting Karami out of office, he had to appoint a successor. On 19 March 1956 he turned to Abdallah al-Yafi, also an admirer of Nasser with an even tougher stance.[84] To balance al-Yafi's potential impact on Lebanese foreign policy, Chamoun appointed Salim Lahoud as minister for foreign affairs, because of his rigidly traditional Lebanese views. But then Chamoun was forced to bow to Sunni popular pressure by appointing the pro-Nasserist Saeb Salam, another Sunni, as Minister of State to assist in foreign affairs to counter Sunni hostility to Lahoud. This was another clear indication of the mounting impact of popular Sunni opinion.[85] During the summer and autumn of 1956, the majority of Lebanese Sunnis continued to demand a closer alignment with Egypt and a move towards social equality along Nasserist lines, as the Sunni media indicates.[86]

This produced a dilemma for Sunni politicians. The Sunni masses would not accept anything but full support for Egypt, and wished to see this demonstrated in Lebanese policy. In terms of domestic policy, this meant Sunni politicians had to adopt a perspective and rhetoric that, superficially at least, had socialist implications. But the socialist implications of Nasserism were less important to the Sunni masses than the imagery they had evolved that associated Nasser with opposition to Christian dominance in Lebanon. So, as Johnson points out, the issue of genuine socialism in Lebanon was not central to either the elite or the popular political agenda.[87]

The real problem lay in the fact that, after the Suez Crisis, any demonstration of support for Nasser in foreign policy terms involved a formal breach with the West, which many Sunni politicians did not want to support because of its implications for the compromises at the heart of the National Pact. They would have been happy with a policy that distanced Lebanon from open support for Western policies in the region, and brought the state closer to the Arab world. After the Suez Crisis, however, the Sunni masses would no longer accept such a compromise, as they were less concerned about the nuances of the National Pact. In this attitude, they were increasingly encouraged by Egyptian propaganda reiterating Nasser's opposition to continued contact with the West, and the interpretation that such contact undermined the Arab world as a whole.

The problems this situation created for Sunni politicians are underlined by the resignations of Abdallah al-Yafi and Saeb Salam on 16 November 1956. These resignations also heightened intercommunal tensions, even though both ministers were eager to demonstrate that they left office on good terms with Chamoun.[88] On 20 November 1956, Sami al-Solh again became Prime Minister in what was intended to be a compromise move, and the new administration won a vote of confidence in the Chamber of Deputies by thirty-eight votes to two, demonstrating that a complete rift between Muslim politicians and the state did not yet exist.[89]

Indeed, the potential still existed for compromise between the leaders of the two main communities, and for this to be reflected in popular opinion. For example, after the new cabinet was formed, a demonstration in Sidon hailed both Chamoun and Nasser.[90] Aiding this continuation of consensus, the Sunni religious establishment still showed itself as willing to work with the government and accept the existence of the separate Lebanese state. For example, after Sami al-Solh formed his new cabinet on 20 November 1956, the *mufti* addressed a gathering of Sunni notables, pleading with the Muslim faithful to 'block the way of the exploiters', that is, not break their ties with the government.[91]

Sunni politicians started 1957 by seeking to maintain their neutrality between pro-Egyptian and pro-Western policies, a position they justified by referring to the National Pact. They continued this approach even after the Eisenhower Doctrine was published in the Arab world later in the year and the Lebanese government, including its Sunni members, adopted an official policy of enthusiastic acceptance.[92] In this climate, Sunni leaders looking ahead to the elections of 1957 were reluctant attack the doctrine or the government's policy of accepting it, particularly without an official Egyptian reaction to the doctrine. This conciliatory attitude began to change, however, once Sunni politicians realised how strongly the Egyptian propaganda was affecting public opinion, and especially after the elections of 1957.

In this context of growing popular support for Nasserism and the evolution of these organisations and agencies, the hierarchy of the Sunni social organisation began to change – at least temporarily. By 1957, Sunni leaders were aware of how much their hierarchy had been held together by a combination of tradition and the fact of the Sunni masses' having less access to education and thus to independent thinking. With these historical facts finally changing, the Sunni leaders began to see that they had to consider their people's wishes.[93] A 1958 pamphlet by Ismail Moussa al-Yussuf referred to the 'discontent' of the masses and their 'recriminations' against their leaders for not listening to their grievances.

By May 1958, al-Jisr demonstrated that the Sunni leadership was taking this discontent seriously. In an important speech in Tripoli in May 1958, he was willing to list what he identified as 'popular grievances' – cultural, educational and economic as well as political – as he sought to justify and explain the actions of the Sunni leadership at that time. The series of well-supported strikes by Sunni workers starting in March 1957 was another factor that Ismail Moussa al-Yussuf identified as part of the popular Sunni resentment of their leaders. He argued quite explicitly that it was 'in reaction to not being listened to' that they 'organised themselves and took up arms'.[94]

The Lebanese Sunni masses adopted a policy line that, like the Egyptian line, emphasised Nasser's influence on their thinking.[95] During 1957, this attitude was expressed largely through rhetoric reported in the media. For instance, plans for a series of strikes and demonstrations were drawn up on 29 March 1957, to start the next day. It was not until 30 May 1957 that a demonstration actually took place in Beirut. Its bloody resolution reduced the immediate popular enthusiasm for a swift repeat, and the next such expression of popular discontent was a strike on 5 November 1957, again in Beirut. During the disturbances surrounding this activity, Adnan al-Hakim, the leader of the Najjadah grouping, was arrested.[96] But as 1958 progressed, and Lebanese Sunnis became more resentful, their elites also showed themselves more ready to respond to popular concerns and to distance themselves from the government.

The Eisenhower Doctrine formed the common thread in both the Egyptian and Syrian propaganda aimed at the Sunni masses and, consequently, in the development of a closer relationship between the masses and the politicians in the Sunni community. Some idea of the initial strength of Sunni popular reactions against the Eisenhower Doctrine can be gauged by the reaction to the publication on 16 March, 1957 of the American-Lebanese communiqué implying Lebanese acceptance of the Doctrine.[97] Critical Sunni commentary was widely reported, starting immediately; it continued for over a year, encouraged by the rhetoric of radio broadcasts from Egypt.[98] This popular expression stimulated the formation on 31 March 1957 of the United National Front, a political grouping through which opposition Sunni politicians could begin to voice their hostility to the Chamoun government and its foreign policy. The Front's manifesto was signed by important Sunni figures, including predictable names such as Saeb Salam and Abdallah al-Yafi, but also some less-expected names such as Takkieddine al-Solh, one of Sami al-Solh's family members.

These figures also signed a Front petition protesting Chamoun's policies, which they presented on 12 April 1957, but it was a protest over domestic as well as foreign policy issues.[99] The Front linked these two petitions, claiming that the protests over Chamoun's domestic policy were linked to a defence of Lebanon's sovereignty. Independence could only be assured, they said, by defending the principles of the National Pact which the manifesto claimed had been 'unanimously' adopted by 'the Lebanese people' as the 'most effective means' of ensuring 'understanding, harmony and co-operation' between the communities. This element is made still clearer in Point 4 of the manifesto, which claimed that the aim was 'to ensure justice between the religious communities which form the Lebanese people so that each community may respect one another's rights and so that none should have the upper hand over the other'.[100]

Relating to this, the petition to Chamoun also stressed the need to demonstrate that the 1957 elections would be fair and honest. In order to show that their petition had popular, as well as political, support, a huge demonstration of support for the Front and the petition was organised and publicised through the media.[101] But, unwilling to seek compromise, the Chamoun government reacted by dispersing the demonstration harshly – which only increased popular Sunni disaffection. As *an-Nahar* pointed out, these events also made it more difficult for Sunni politicians to look for any grounds for co-operation with Chamoun, even if they wanted to.[102] In this context the government's high-profile pursuit of its pro-Western foreign policy was both aggressive and confrontational. It proposed a vote of confidence in its foreign policy, phrased in such an uncompromising way that even those Sunni leaders who were generally willing to accept a pro-Western policy – subject to certain safeguards – felt they could not support the vote.[103]

Still, the majority of Sunni deputies were reluctant to resign over the issue. That only a few did so demonstrated the continuing disparity between the Sunni masses and their spokesmen in parliament even at this late stage.[104] Among the six deputies who resigned were five Muslims: Abdallah al-Yafi, Ahmad al-Assad, Sabri Hamada, Abdallah al-Haj, and Kamil al-Assad.[105] Clearly, the majority of the Sunni deputies were looking ahead to the elections and thinking twice before antagonising the government or the president. But amongst the Sunni masses, especially in West Beirut, Nasserism was acting as an opposition doctrine, giving shape to a populist yearning for a Sunni Arab order.[106]

By this point, after the Suez Crisis and similar Egyptian triumphs, the Sunni masses had accorded Nasser the status of a local icon; photo posters appeared on many walls and in classrooms. On the eve of the 1957 election a popular Sunni opposition to Lebanese government policy, essentially grounded in opposition to the foreign policy, had come into existence that was endorsed by the Sunni *'ulamas* and popular organisations. One event in April 1957 indicates how attitudes amongst the Sunni religious establishment were changing, distancing them from their general support for the government in 1956. Shaykh Shafik Yamut, the head of the *Sharia* Court, held a political meeting for the opposition. Among the approximately 300 Muslim notables attending were Sunni figures such as Saeb Salam, Abd al-Hamid Karami and al-Yafi, as well as the prominent Shi'ite leaders Ahmad al-Assad and Sabri Hamadi. Reporting on the meeting, *al-Siyassa* highlighted the extent of this break with tradition by pointing out that pro-government Muslim personalities had to be excluded because of public hostility to them.[107]

At the meeting Shaykh Shafik Yamut fiercely attacked the government; its sectarian overtones indicate that his speech was clearly intended for popular consumption. He stressed Lebanon's unqualified identification with the Arab world, and called on it to pursue policies like those of the 'liberal' revolutionary Arab states. Shaykh Yamut said the meeting was called out of 'public concern' over 'Islam's honour and glory' and proceeded to describe what he saw as the role of the National Pact. He argued that for

Muslims to support the pact, government policy would have to reject pacts with foreign powers, i.e. with the West. He then advocated a 'liberal' Arab policy based on independence and neutrality between the two world camps and the continuing struggle to solve the problems of the Arab world, inside and outside Lebanon. The audience accepted this interpretation, which was later supported by the Higher Muslim Council; according to editorials, it also gained popular support.[108] Thus we can clearly see the increasing alienation of both the opposition and the Muslim religious establishment in the run-up to the elections. For example, after the government reacted harshly to the mainly Muslim demonstration on 30 May 1957, the *mufti* protested to the president about the government's actions. Soon the Higher Muslim Council joined the United National Front in demanding a neutral government in the run-up to the elections, criticising the general government attitude at this time.[109]

Still, the religious establishment did not want to totally break its ties with the government in the period before the elections. Afterwards, however, election results hardened attitudes amongst the religious establishment, as amongst the political establishment. Again, outside influences had an important impact on the Sunni masses, if only because they still had no indigenous popular leader with universal appeal. At the same time, and despite the high profile Nasser received in the absence of an indigenous leader, the leaders of the popular political opposition that did emerge at this point did not go beyond hostility to Chamoun and his policies. For instance, they did not indicate that they felt community pressure to agitate seriously for formal union with the UAR. The popular opposition concentrated on complaints about domestic policy and other local issues, given a gloss of Nasserism. As late as 16 April 1958 even the more radical of the opposition groupings, Najjadah, did not find it necessary to condemn either Lebanese sovereignty or the National Pact, as long as both were interpreted in the context of the Arab world.[110]

In the run-up to the 1957 elections the majority of traditional Sunni leaders, even those in political opposition, sought to maintain the spirit of compromise. This was not just the tradition of the National Pact in operation; it was also a fear about the impact of Nasserism on their own followers. These leaders were used to wielding considerable influence over their followers, and they feared their power would decrease in a socialist and/ or larger and essentially Arab entity. This is why, at this stage, their hostility to Chamoun's policies could not induce them to sever their ties with the state.[111] They were not nearly as annoyed by Chamoun's anti-Nasserism and his overly pro-British policy as were the Sunni voters.[112]

The events of the elections did, however, force the Sunni leaders to consider issues besides the foreign policy that had created such popular hostility; among these were the domestic grievances discussed above, which the masses saw the Chamoun government as failing to address. Some Sunni leaders had already moved slightly towards the popular position by early 1957, adopting popular mainstream slogans even when they were not willing to break with the government entirely. The president's ability to manipulate the premiership meant that ambitious Sunni politicians continued to seek both the support of their community and a compromise with the state.[113]

It was the suggestions of electoral malpractice surrounding the 1957 elections, leading to personal and communal bitterness, that finally brought men like Saeb Salam and Abdallah al-Yafi out in open opposition to Chamoun and his policies. They abandoned the search for compromise on the grounds that Chamoun had broken the terms of the National Pact first.[114] These politicians increasingly followed the example of the masses by voicing their opposition to Chamoun in terms of opposition to his foreign policy: 'The nature of the issues over which the government and the opposition were fighting made the election campaign a fight for survival on principles of consensus and within this, for a neutral foreign policy'.[115]

In addition, the media revealed how much the Sunni community believed Chamoun had broken the rules of government by consensus.[116] While opposition hostility focused ever more strongly on Chamoun and his regime, defeated Sunni leaders felt their loyalty to the Lebanese state growing weaker as they acknowledged the bitter hostility they now felt towards Chamoun. Figures both inside and outside the country attempted mediation at elite levels. For instance, King Saud, afraid of the growing regional power of Nasserism, attempted to mediate between Saeb Salam and Abdallah al-Yafi on the one hand and President Chamoun on the other.[117] The fact that these men were willing to consider ways to mitigate the effects of the elections demonstrates that even at this stage some important Sunni political leaders were not entirely focused on foreign policy.[118] For practical reasons they were more interested in domestic issues, including policies to safeguard their own personal interests in the current situation.[119]

Another factor made the Sunni elites responsive to popular pressure during 1957 and 1958: a growing consciousness that Sunni politicians could, under the right circumstances, have an impact on Lebanon's government. That is, they need not simply accept the attitude that Sami al-Solh took:

resigned acceptance to manipulation by the Maronite political and commercial establishment.[120] During the Chamoun regime, as Sunni discontent mounted, Sunni politicians began to protest collectively against Chamoun's tactics. Indeed, those politicians had played a decisive role in ending al-Khoury's regime. Remembering this, they put more emphasis on having Maronite politicians fulfil what the Sunnis saw as both the terms and spirit of the National Pact.

In the years 1952 to 1958, the National Pact was most significant because it contributed to the emergence amongst Sunni politicians of what Raghid al-Solh calls 'democracy by conciliation'.[121] These men began to see more clearly that the system of compromise provided Muslims, as well as Maronites, with the power to veto any major decisions which either side saw as dangerous to its own interests. Because using the veto would signal a national crisis, it made rule by consensus possible but, equally, made it dependent on mutual co-operation. Moreover it contained within it the potential for Sunni politicians to hinder the workings of government and even to bring down a president.[122]

This thinking leads to the conclusion that if the opposition leaders had been freed of pressures from the rest of the Arab world – even if expressed through popular opinion in Lebanon – and were allowed to work out this crisis purely in terms of the domestic issues, many would have sought a course of action less extreme than the one they eventually adopted.[123] As Attiyah has argued, the opposition would have expressed its hostility not in terms of 'a basic alienation from the state', but rather as a 'struggle for power'.[124] The attempted mediation failed because of continuing opposition to Chamoun, more than from a wish to see the end of a separate Lebanon. On 27 March 1958, for instance, eighty-two opposition politicians issued a statement emphasising the real cause of the trouble: 'the President is still determined to amend the constitution' to renew his term of office, and despite Chamoun's rhetoric, 'the signatories consider that the independence and sovereignty of Lebanon were not and will never be' under threat by elements in the Arab world while the 'Lebanese people adhere to the National Pact which has sanctified national unity since 1943'. They saw no reason for the constitutional amendment; therefore the Lebanese people would 'resist the renewal of the presidential term while pledging such support for the Pact'.[125]

The internal dimension was crucial, but equally important was behaviour by Syria and Nasser, seen as 'friendly encouragement' in the majority Sunni perspective, and as 'hostile intervention' by the government and the

Maronites. This behaviour was key in giving shape and coherence to the developing hostility of the Lebanese Sunni masses, political and religious, by the end of 1957. Nasser enthusiastically responded to Sunni dissatisfaction with the election outcome to support the political opposition and especially the Muslim religious establishment, in order to radicalise anti-government positions in Lebanon. The support was both moral and material. For example, the broadcasts about government policy provided increasingly detailed criticisms.[126] And on 25 January 1958 *al-Siyassa* reported that the Egyptian government had donated 30,000 Egyptian pounds to Lebanese mosques, information also recorded with due suspicion in the consular reports of the period.[127]

But the intervention extended beyond these peaceful examples. Several incidents beginning in the autumn of 1957 indicated, at least to the government, that Egypt was actively seeking to encourage the Sunnis and other Muslim communities to openly revolt against the state. On 3 September a Syrian driver was arrested for smuggling arms to Lebanon, leading to a heated debate in parliament the next day about a government project to place the frontiers into a state of 'emergency readiness'. On 5 October 1957, the government officially accused the Syrians of spreading disruption in Lebanon through their intelligence service.[128]

Some elements of the Muslim popular rebellion in Beirut gathered around a portrait of Nasser in 1958.

The ID of a rebel in the so-called forces of the Basta district of Beirut in 1958.

In taking up opposition to government policies, the popular Sunni (and other Muslim) organisations and religious bodies certainly stated that their opposition to Chamoun was now rooted in Arab issues which were not exclusively Lebanese and did invoke Nasser. But internal matters were also very compelling: on 8 October 1957 the opposition asked the government to try the ministers responsible for the harsh reprisals against anti-government demonstrators in Beirut, Sidon and Tripoli on 30 May 1957.[129] Thus it was largely their own doing when Chamoun and his prime minister al-Solh succeeded in alienating Sunni opinion even at elite levels, and indeed, with a few exceptions, the opinions of the Muslim community as a whole. By the beginning of 1958, the rank-and-file, the popular and religious organisations and all the prominent leaders except for Sami al-Solh, were drawn together by mutual hostility to the regime.[130] By now, this anti-government opposition within Lebanon, particularly the popular Sunni opposition, was also prepared to utilise this external intervention and other outside events to increase the impact of its opposition to Chamoun, and to take to the streets themselves in solidarity.

Taking a lead in the aggression were the Muslim associations that had significant Sunni support, such as the Najjadah grouping, the Muslim Young Men's Union, *al-Hayat al-Wataniyyah* and the *al-Maqassed* College Alumni Association. Also, a popular grouping had formed in Basta, one of the most populous Sunni areas of Beirut, primarily to pressure Muslim leaders to oppose government policy and to adopt a quasi-Nasserist perspective towards domestic grievances.[131] By 1958 these associations felt sufficiently secure of popular support, according to Ismail Moussa al-Yussuf, to declare 'popular revolution' and to 'close' key neighbourhoods such as Basta, Moussaytbe, Tarik Jdide, Mazraha and Nourieh to established authority. They marked that closure by building barricades defended by armed members of their associations.[132]

This strategy was designed to frighten the government into a 'return' to compliance and compromise. Outside forces made it possible by their willingness to see the Lebanese opposition bring down Chamoun, in order to end the pro-Western orientation in Lebanese foreign policy. They also hoped to see the Muslim masses responding to pro-Nasserist rhetoric.[133] The strategy ensured that during 1958, the opposition increasingly appeared to have a wider, Arab dimension. Predictably, the masses responded enthusiastically to the declaration of the United Arab Republic in 1958. The *al-Maqassed* association took the opportunity to declare that the day should be a national holiday. The Association of *'Ulama*, as well as the students of the *al-Maqassed* College and other Muslim schools, sent congratulatory telegrams to the presidents of Syria and Egypt, as did the Muslim Scouts and the Union of Arab students.[134] The cables themselves and the associated celebrations clearly stated the broader Islamic connotations of this Muslim jubilation; for example a quote from the *'ulamas'* cable to Nasser reads: 'The Association of *'Ulama* in Lebanon … congratulates the Arabs and Muslims in all the world on the birth of the United Arab Republic … You have fulfilled the great hopes of the Arabs and of the Muslims.'[135] Kamal Salibi recalls being told that 'the Muslim Lebanese rejoicing over the union between Syria and Egypt was running wild', and that 'mobs were clamouring for Lebanon to join the union without delay' as they 'roamed the streets of every town and city'.[136] But this popular rejoicing at the 'birth' of the UAR was interpreted through a local perspective, as it seemed likely to strengthen the Sunni position in relation to fighting the presumed Maronite agenda of divesting Lebanon of its Arab identity in favour of a Mediterranean European one.[137]

Nasser's February visit to Damascus provided another occasion for

Thousands of people from all over the Muslim parts of Lebanon went to Damascus to see Nasser.

popular Muslim celebrations with clear anti-government overtones. Popular enthusiasm, demonstrated in the trips to Damascus to view the hero of the hour, certainly alarmed the government.[138] Hasanein Haykal quoted Reuters and Associated Press estimates that half a million Lebanese – a considerable proportion of the Muslim community – went to Damascus.[139] The *mufti*, the Muslim press and the Muslim masses used the occasion to openly express their allegiance to Nasser, clearly demonstrating the degree of popular Muslim alienation from the state.

Throughout 1958 this alienation continued to grow, partly due to Chamoun's own policies but partly due to Nasser's judiciously calculated intervention aimed at the Muslim masses. For instance, Nasser addressed the Lebanese people on 2 March 1958, in a shrewdly worded letter. Without openly expressing a hope that Lebanon would join the UAR, he implied that he possessed that hope, by pointing at parallels between Lebanon and Yemen and addressing his Lebanese readers as 'fellow countrymen'. Nasser praised

Yemen for being the first country to join the UAR union: 'We welcome Yemen into our union and we feel that this unity which springs from the heart of the Arab Nation and from its will is the strength we aim at achieving.' He added that it would be the nucleus of the 'all-embracing unity we hope to see accomplished soon in every Arab country.'[140]

Conscious of support from the wider Arab world, Sunni leaders were encouraged to use tactics that reduced the immediate potential for compromise with the Chamoun government, but did seem to promise a return to the principles of the National Pact and to a greater Sunni political role within the state. Certainly these tactics won approval from the Sunni masses and thereby also brought all levels of the Sunni community closer to the Shi'a and Druze communities as they invoked both religious and Arab sentiment. On 11 April 1958 the *mufti* invited the *'ulama* and opposition personalities to an *Iftar* dinner, but contrary to usual practice, he excluded the prime minister and other government ministers.

The occasion thus turned into an opposition political rally culminating in a vote of defiance against the Chamoun government.[141] But it was not a vote against continuing Lebanese independence. Saeb Salam even claimed that 'We have made a pact with the Patriarch against Chamoun'. This snub of the government took place in the context of an opposition statement that brought Sunni leaders together with those from other Muslim communities. As I described earlier, no traditional congratulations were to be offered during *Bayram*, the feast ending *Ramadan*, as Lebanon was suffering so at the hands of her present rulers. On 17 April 200 leading Muslims declared that to offer or accept *Bayram* congratulations would mean 'violating the unanimity' of the 'Muslim community'. The Sunni masses and popular organisations applauded these moves, and the *Iftar* became a well-attended popular demonstration against the government.[142]

The prime minister responded defiantly to such demonstrations, announcing, for instance, that he would be receiving congratulations on the first day of the *Bayram* feast at his house.[143] But as the events of 20 April show, the few Muslims who remained loyal to Chamoun, including Sami al-Solh, were very isolated. At 4 AM, Sami al-Solh, accompanied by the few Muslim members of the government, attended prayers at the Omari Mosque. The religious boycott was so successful that the government had considerable difficulty in finding an *imam* prepared to officiate.[144] Later the same day, someone tossed explosives near al-Solh's house as he was receiving those visitors who did call with congratulations.[145]

The rift between the prime minister and his supporters and the rest of the Muslim community continued to grow. Al-Solh had offended the *'ulamas* by trying to stop them from attending gatherings like the *Iftar* of 11 April, so the Muslim religious establishment led by the *mufti* as well as the *'ulamas,* responded by publicly declaring him an apostate.[146] The immediate impact of the *Ramadan* events was huge and lasting. In the longer term it also served to heighten both anti-government feelings and opposition determination to increase its activities.

To bolster his re-election efforts, Chamoun portrayed these developments as evidence of a Muslim and Arab-inspired conspiracy against the state; he said the tension resulted from an intercommunal breach, rather than a simple matter of potentially political opposition.[147] Another such opportunity for Chamoun was a speech in Cairo by the spokesman of the Chamber of Deputies, Adel Osseiran. Osseiran declared that it was in Lebanon's interest to join the United Arab Republic, adding, 'I will go further than this: the day will come when everything will be achieved'. As *an-Nahar* pointed out in an editorial on 23 April, Osseiran's words could not be taken seriously as representing an opposition agenda; he was notorious for making the kind of speech his audience wanted to hear. Back in Lebanon he was to revert to support for Lebanese independence, along with the majority of opposition leaders.[148]

Chamoun's efforts to portray the growing tension as a Maronite-Sunni (or Christian-Muslim) affair did have an effect on both the Sunni and Maronite masses.[149] The Sunnis identified more strongly with the Nasser-led Arab world against the West, which was now increasingly personified by the US, as a result of both Nasser's invective against the Eisenhower Doctrine and the belief that the US government admired and supported Chamoun in his hopes for re-election.[150] But even in early May of 1958, though the Sunni political opposition disapproved of Chamoun's overly pro-Western foreign policy, it remained focused on the issue of his re-election, emphasising the need to remove him at the end of his mandate or, ideally, before.

The opposition wanted Chamoun out because in seeking to strengthen his own position he was reducing the power of the Sunni prime minister and thus the influence that the National Pact guaranteed to the Sunni community. They also accused him of manipulating the 1957 elections, which made him guilty of corruption. Only then did they accuse him, in vague terms, of following anti-Nasserist policies. Though members of the Sunni opposition had their differences with other opposition groupings, both Muslim and Christian, Chamoun's behaviours allowed them to work together: he was creating an atmosphere of emergency with his personal ambitions and his willingness to manipulate tensions in Lebanon to further them.

In this context, a temporary coalition of opposition leaders and notables emerged. They had both popular support and a single issue bringing them together: preventing Chamoun's re-election.[151] Except for Osseiran's speech, which I described earlier, no major opposition leader made any public comment or traceable private comment indicating a wish to see the end of the Lebanese entity. Looking back, Saeb Salam, for instance, stressed that throughout the crisis he remained concerned about maintaining Lebanon's independence and never supported any policy to dismantle either the free economy or the traditional political system in Lebanon.[152]

However, after al-Matni was murdered on 8 May 1958, the position of the Sunni political leadership, like that of the other Muslim communities, drew closer to that taken by the Muslim masses. At a policy meeting on 9 May 1958, the United National Front decided that open armed revolt was the only way forward against Chamoun.[153] The resulting unrest included outbreaks of violence in Beirut on 12 May, and Jumblat's forces attacked the presidential palace of Bayt al-Din. The government argued, through comments by Sami al-Solh and the Maronite loyalist press, that this violence was not internally generated but was the result of UAR intervention.[154]

But this claim is not borne out by other evidence. Unequivocal evidence shows that elements from all levels of the Sunni community in Lebanon were prepared to take advantage of the UAR's willingness to become involved in events in Lebanon. It was the availability of this support, in terms of both arms and manpower, that enabled the United National Front to launch its armed revolt after 9 May. But the UAR was not responsible for creating the hostility amongst the Sunni element in Lebanon in the first place, and it was an essentially Lebanese decision to escalate the crisis by using armed violence.[155] Still, this was not a conspiracy that aimed to destroy the state. From the perspective of Lebanon's Sunni community, the armed nature that 'intervention' or Arab aid had taken from May 1958 was justified by claims that it was a final effort to resolve, not escalate, the crisis, and that Nasser was merely showing friendly feeling in an Arab sense by providing the materials for armed revolt. For example, the pro-Sunni, Beirut-based *an-Nas* approvingly publicised Nasser's plans to propose a solution to the Lebanese crisis.[156]

The external evidence indicates that neither Nasser nor the mass of Lebanese Sunnis actually planned to incorporate Lebanon into the UAR in May 1958. It is significant that Nasser restricted himself to attacking the Chamoun regime; presumably he believed, like many in Lebanon, that Chamoun's downfall would provide the real solution to the crisis and restore a foreign policy approach in line with the National Pact, a situation Nasser would find acceptable.[157] There is no evidence that Sunni political and religious leaders would have accepted Lebanon's annexation to the UAR, and the internal structure of the Lebanese Sunni community gave such leaders considerable power over their followers. The United National Front felt able to state on 14 May 1958 that it was 'a purely national and Lebanese' movement, 'one aiming at preserving Lebanon's structure and independence and the unity of its people'; it also argued that the opposition movement would cease its activities when 'the President relinquishes the presidency and his regime vanishes'.[158]

The only Sunni leader to indicate serious support for union with the UAR in the summer of 1958 was Adnan al-Hakim, leader of the Najjadah. On 7 June he called for Chamoun to resign immediately, to be succeeded by a president who would follow a pro-Nasserist foreign policy leading to eventual union. Note, however, that al-Hakim stressed that his opposition group was not working with any other opposition group.[159] His group was indeed a minority one, largely confined to Beirut and representing a small extremist body of opinion; it had little effect on the rest of Muslim opinion at the time, especially given its secular orientation. As al-Hakim did not come from any of the traditional Sunni elites, he had comparatively little influence over the wider community.

Another indication that Lebanese Sunni leaders were using the UAR's intervention and figures like Nasser to further their own agenda is a claim Saeb Salam made in 1991: that the UAR sent 5,000 guns to Rachid Karami, but he did not use them to stir up full scale revolt.[160] In addition, while Syria's head of intelligence, Sarraj, worked to destabilise Lebanon, the Sunni leadership did not respond as Sarraj hoped. This became very clear in July 1958, when some suggested that Shihab stand for president. Sarraj sought to convince the Lebanese Sunni leadership that this would be a bad idea, but he could not move them into open opposition to Shihab.[161] Because of their established mythology, the Sunni masses were more enthusiastic about the concept of links with the UAR and were somewhat disappointed when their leaders did not respond strongly. But, as Johnson points out, any revolutionary impulses on the streets were, in May and early June, easily contained by the Sunni elites, who had an interest in counteracting such developments.[162]

On 5 June the Chamoun government rejected the Arab League's proposed mediation in the crisis. This rejection seemed illogical to the Sunni leadership, though the opposition may have come to believe that 'Malik's real intention in going to the UN' was to 'lay the ground for US armed intervention in Lebanon'.[163] But as the various foreign embassies commented, the leaders were not nearly as disappointed as the masses.[164] They reacted with surprise and incomprehension mixed with anger at the way the rejection was made; they were certainly encouraged by the astonishment and anger of the delegates to the League, who made their feelings on the issue public.[165] In what was widely seen as a snub, Charles Malik, the minister of foreign affairs, did not even bother to attend the meeting of the League to give the impression that the Chamoun government was genuinely considering the proposal. Instead he went directly to New York to attend a Security Council meeting to press for UN intervention.

Malik later tried to justify his actions by claiming that in fact the Lebanese government had from the very beginning turned to the Arab League for help in resolving the crisis.[166] However, he claimed that given the current tension in Lebanon the Council of the League would not meet soon enough to enable it to take any action which would stop UAR interference in Lebanese domestic affairs; hence the request for Security Council intervention.[167] The Sunnis were even more furious because the Council of the Arab League met within the ten-day limit its charter stipulated for setting up extraordinary sessions, while Malik continued to insist that the council was not seeing the events in Lebanon as being as urgent as the government believed.[168]

In general, the Sunnis could see no real justification for rejecting the help of the Arab League. Worse, they felt, by claiming there was serious external intervention and by calling on the UN to settle the case, the government seemed to be downplaying the internal opposition's opinion on the crisis – which could help Chamoun consolidate his position with Western support. The opposition believed that Malik's real intention in going to the UN was to lay the groundwork for American armed intervention in Lebanon.[169] The Sunni opposition did not question the assumption that the UN was a Western-dominated body that would favour the Western interpretation of events in Lebanon. So most Sunnis were hostile at when the UN Observer Group in Lebanon (UNOGIL) arrived.

On 12 June the United National Front leader Saeb Salam issued a six-point commentary on the United Nation's Lebanon resolution; it sums up the general Sunni opposition perspective at this stage. He saw international observation and intervention as irrelevant: the Lebanese problem was purely internal, a matter of needing to oust Chamoun. The UNOGIL had no role to play in that. He indicated Sunni fears of Western intervention under the cover of the UN by pointedly stating that any effort to prevent arms being infiltrated into Lebanon would also have to stop the import of American, British, French, Turkish, Iraqi and Jordanian arms, rather than arms from the UAR.

He claimed it was these countries' interference, not interest from the UAR, that was aggravating internal tensions in Lebanon. Salam insisted that any solution would require the consent of the Lebanese people as a whole; this would best be gained by the mediation of the Arab League, not the UN.[170] As Kamal Jumblat states, this encapsulated the general Muslim perception that the crisis was a direct response to foreign influence (Arab intervention not being perceived as such) and to Lebanon's unhealthy dependence on the West as a result of Chamoun's policies. This was a betrayal of the National Pact as it was a return to traditional patterns of intercommunal relations.[171] Nasser's hostility to the UN added to the widespread Sunni resentment. Thus the Sunni opposition was unpleasantly astonished at how quickly the UN implemented the resolution to send observers.[172]

The Sunni press, however, took surprised delight at the UNOGIL report of 5 July, trumpeting that the government's complaints 'have been blown up'.[173] The report undoubtedly boosted the Sunni opposition, as it seemed to indicate that Western support for Chamoun's re-election was not a foregone conclusion. The Iraqi coup further boosted Sunni hopes that Lebanon would soon return to the principles of the National Pact in terms of foreign policy. The pro-Western Iraqi government of the 1950s had provided the main rivalry to Nasser's dominance of the Arab world. Through the Baghdad Pact, the Chamoun government had linked itself with the Iraqi-led camp in the Arab world, in preference to the Nasser-led camp. The Iraqi coup thus had important implications for the Chamoun government, as it robbed it of any major Arab allies that shared Chamoun's pro-Western stance. In this context, Saeb Salam could rely on popular Sunni support for the claim that 'the coup was not just a victory for Arab Nationalism' but also for 'Lebanon and the Arab people'.[174]

The Iraqi coup certainly created further tension within Lebanon, and led to street violence. A British observer, Desmond Stewart, commented that violence was increasingly directed at the few Sunni supporters who remained loyal to Chamoun, as well as to Chamoun himself: 'an armoured car … guarding Sami al-Solh's house was then seized by the people. The President [was] still under fire, Solh's house gutted'.[175] Thus, when the Americans landed on 16 July 1958 to restore peace in Lebanon, they were far from welcome to the Sunnis, either masses or elites.[176] They were especially annoyed when Chamoun defended this development, along with Pierre Gemayel and his Kata'ib Party.[177] On 16 July, Saeb Salam expressed the political opposition's hostility, through a statement in *al-Hayat*.[178] However, unlike Osseiran, he stopped short of demanding armed resistance against the 'violation of Lebanese sovereignty'.[179]

For Salam, the landings provided an issue that could bring Chamoun down immediately. Thus he held a meeting at his home on 16 July to discuss the wording of a formal opposition response to Chamoun's welcome of the landings. Confident of support from the Sunnis and other Muslims, the opposition political leaders refused to seek a compromise with the government as long as foreign troops remained in Lebanon.[180] Ali Bazzi, the secretary general of the United National Front, declared, 'the opposition would never give allegiance to any President elected with foreign troops in the country.'[181]

More Muslim opposition to the American landings was revealed as women's organisations began issuing public protests. A group headed by Zahia Salman, and including the daughters of the great Sunni leader Riyadh al-Solh, met with figures from the Front in a move documented and publicised in the press.[182] Indeed, for the next two days, several Sunni and other Muslim delegations making protests headed for Salam's house; as the grand *mufti* of Beirut and the senior Druze religious leader Shaykh Akl put it, they were all demanding 'the immediate withdrawal of troops'.[183] Though the press was being censored by 18 July, news of the protests spread by word of mouth, keeping hostility and tensions high. All of this makes it very clear that the Sunni protests were based on their interpreting the landing as proof that the Americans backed Chamoun and wanted to see him re-elected. Apparently no significant grouping saw it as an action the Americans took to guarantee the legally constituted authority in Lebanon, let alone as part of a wider American policy in the region.[184]

The Murphy mission would profoundly change the attitude of most Lebanese, both ordinary citizens and politicians. First, as the opposition press noted approvingly, Murphy emphasised making contact with opposition and actual rebel leaders, such as al-Yafi, and was willing to listen sympathetically to their grievances.[185] He tried to provide regional context for his explanations of both the American landings and American fears about the survival of a separate Lebanon. Sunni opposition leaders were quite willing to listen to Murphy: since they had no ambitions to see the end of an independent Lebanon, American concerns carried a certain conviction, even approval. And these explanations could help the politicians save face, as they backed down from the positions they had taken after the landing, positions that threatened to bring Lebanon to a state of total civil war, beyond the familiar level of violence of May through July.

Murphy's work soon had an obvious result on the Sunni media in Lebanon. For example, in an early statement of hostility to Murphy's mission published on 18 July, the opposition had called the mission a 'useless way' to seek a compromise, and had 'great doubt of its success'.[186] An opposition statement bearing Salam's name gave Murphy forty-eight hours to produce a compromise, and warned that then 'we will ask for help from all the free countries in the world if the American troops do not withdraw', in a clear threat to escalate the crisis. But by 22 July, the opposition was willingly collaborating with Murphy, publicly stating that he could create a workable compromise. Abdallah al-Yafi and Hajj Hussein Uwayni, among others, began to suggest how this could work, and a headline in *al-Telegraph,* a leading opposition paper, announced that 'Crisis is on the Way to Solution'. *Al-Jarida* wrote that Murphy, the 'Man of Good Offices', was there to reassure the Lebanese that the Americans had landed only because of Middle East tensions resulting from the Iraqi coup, and that the US had no intentions of widening the Lebanese split 'by supporting one faction of the population against the other'.[187]

Within the Sunni community, the unity of the previous months began to break down as the traditional elites and the bourgeoisie began to distance themselves from the more radical popular elements in order to respond to the American attempts at conciliation, instead of demanding that the leaders of the Arab world arrange a compromise. In particular the Sunni leadership was reassured by Murphy's statement that the Americans had no intention of backing Chamoun's plans for re-election.[188]

Notes

1. Samir Khalaf and Guilane Denoueux, 'Urban Networks and Political Conflict in Lebanon', in Nadim Shehadi and Dana Haffar Mills (eds), *Lebanon: A History of Conflict and Consensus*, I.B. Tauris, London, 1988, pp. 186–7.

2. Nasser Kalawoun, 'The Role of the Sunni Leadership and Community towards the State of Lebanon in the 1950s', unpublished MA thesis, University of London, 1987, p. 7.

3. Raphael Samuel and Paul Thompson, eds, *The Myths We Live By*, Routledge, London, 1990, p. 84.

4. Michael Johnson, *Class and Client in Beirut: The Sunni Muslim Community and the Lebanese State 1840–1905*, Ithaca Press, London, 1986, p. 121.

5. See, for example, John Tosh, *The Pursuit of History*, Longman, London, 1984, p. 3, on this point.

6. Samuel and Thompson, p. 86.

7. Fouad Ajami, *The Arab Predicament*, Cambridge University Press, Cambridge, 1981, p. 93.

8. Kalawoun, p. 37.

9. Johnson, p. 126.

10. Anis Moussallem, *La Presse Libanaise: Expression du Liban politique et Confessionel et Forum des Pays Arabes*, Librarie Générale De Droit et de Jurisprudence, Paris, 1977, p. 20.

11. The Sunni Muslim Community, *Class and Client in Beirut. The Sunni Muslim Community and the Lebanese State 1840–1985*, Ithaca Press, London, 1986, p. 36.

12. Nicola Ziadeh, *Syria and Lebanon*, Ernest Benn Ltd, London, 1957, pp. 60–1.

13. Johnson, p. 25.

14. Hilal Khashan, *Inside the Lebanese Confessional Mind*, University Press of America, New York, 1992, p. 67. Khashan identifies other minority communities such as the Shi'a and the Armenians, who share this perspective. I do not mean to claim that the Sunni elite had come to see Lebanon as a natural entity, but simply that they had accepted its existence as being in their own interests. See also Albert Hourani, 'Lebanon: The Development of a Political Society', in L. Binder, ed., *Politics in Lebanon*, John Wiley & Co., New York, 1966, p. 25.

15. Khashan, p. 67.

16. King-Crane Commission Report on the Near East, 1920, published as a supplement to *Editor and Publisher*, December 1922; Najila Attiyah, 'Attitude of the Lebanese Sunni Towards the State of Lebanon', unpublished PhD thesis, University of London, 1973, p. 69.

17. See chapter one.

18. For a more detailed discussion of Arab nationalism and the al-Solh family's role in promoting it in the 1930s and 1940s, see Raghid al-Solh, 'Arab Nationalist Attitudes Towards Greater Lebanon', in Nadim Shehadi and Dana Haffar Mills (eds), *Lebanon: A History of Conflict and Consensus,* I.B. Tauris, London, 1988, p. 51.

19. Attiyah, p. 99.

20. See chapter three.

21. K. S. Salibi, 'Recollections of the 1940s and 1950s', unpublished conference paper, Austin, Texas, 13 September 1992, p. 6. See also Kalawoun, p. 7.

22. Attiyah, p. 133.

23. *Al-Hayat*, 30 August 1958.

24. Kalawoun, p. 26.

25. Ziadeh, p. 160.

26. Samir Khalaf and Guilaine Denoueux, 'Urban Networks and Political Conflicts', in Shehadi and Mills, eds, *Lebanon*, p. 186

27. David Vincent, *Literacy and Popular Culture*, Cambridge University Press, Cambridge, 1989, pp. 241–58.

28. *Moslem Lebanon Today*, Beiruit, 1953, pp. 7–10.

29. Desmond Stewart, *Turmoil in Beirut: A Personal Account*, Allen Wingate, London, 1958, pp. 14–15; Johnson, p. 128.

30. Nadim al-Jisr (deputy from Tripoli), speech, reported in *al-Hayat* 18 May 1958; Walid Jumblat, *Hawiqat al-Thawrat al-Lubnaniat*, Dar al-Taqadoumiat, al-Moukhtara, 1987, p. 87. This point was also made by Salim Nassar, a leading journalist for the pro-Egyptian *as-Sayyad* in 1958, in his interview with me in London, 20 May 1995.

31. Jumblat, p. 87. This point was also implicitly made by the United National Front's Manifesto, which referred to the 'propagation of the confessional spirit and its exploitation by politicians. Manifesto, United National Front, 1 April 1957, in *Cahiers de l'Orient Compemporain*, vol. 36 (Documents), 1957, pp. 139–42.

32. The factor had been formally identified back in 1938, but little, if anything, had then been done to find a solution. See *L'Orient*, 24 January 1938.

33. *Receuil des Statistiques de la Syrie et du Liban 1945-46-47*, Centre de Recherches et de Développement Pédagogique, Beirut, 1947. See also Boutros Labaki, 'L'Economie Politique du Liban Indépendant 1943–1975', in Nadim Shehadi and Dana Haffar Mills (eds), *Lebanon: A History of Conflict and Consensus*, I.B. Tauris, London, 1988, p. 177.

34. Linda Schatkowski, 'The Işlamic *Maqassed* of Beirut: A Case Study of Modernisation in Lebanon', Unpublished MA thesis, Middle East Area Program, American University of Beirut, 1969.

35. *L'Orient*, 24 January 1938.

36. *Receuil des Statistiques*, vol. 3, p. 202. See also Labaki, p. 177.

37. These percentages emphasise the overwhelming predominance of private Christian schools, at over 77% of the total of private schools in Lebanon, over the private Muslim schools in Lebanon.

38. Ziadeh, p. 250; *Moslem Lebanon Today*, p. 10.

39. Carolyn L. Gates, 'Choice, Content and Performance of a "Service-Orientated Open Economy" Strategy: The Case of Lebanon 1948–1958', unpublished conference paper, Austin, Texas, 13 September 1992, pp. 1–2.

40. *Ibid.*, pp. 36–40.

41. Johnson, pp. 30, 33, 36, 127; *Moslem Lebanon Today*, pp. 7–10.

42. *Moslem Lebanon Today*, p. 7.

43. Johnson, pp. 130–1. Nadim al-Jisr, speech reported in *al-Hayat*, 18 May 1958. The perception has been lasting: Walid Jumblat has also talked of the 'deliberate Maronite strategy to have complete control over the economic sector' in that, and later periods. See Jumblat, p. 88. A further contemporary impression in line with these comments is provided by Desmond Stewart, who also reported that resentment over their economic position seemed to be a factor with the Sunnis he encountered. Such comments indicate not so much the existence of such perceptions as their strength, in that Stewart's account suggests that they were a matter of common discussion. Stewart also seems not to need to make his own critical comments on these perceptions. See Stewart, p. 13. See also Johnson, p. 33.

44. See *Minutes of Parliament*, Beirut, 1927–8, p. 17 for an early identification of this trend.

45. Raymond Delpart, 'Liban: L'Evolution du Niveau de Vie en Milieu Rural 1960–1970', Documents, Ministry of Planning, Beirut 1970, p. 9 (roneotyped, copies in my possession and in the Bloc National Headquarters, originals apparently destroyed by shelling during the civil war). These figures are based on the study of the Institut International de Recherche et de Formation en vue du Dévelopment Intégral et Harmonisé (IRFED), *Besoins et Possibilités de Dévelopment du Liban: Etude Préliminaire*, 2 vols, I: 'Situation Economique et Sociale', II: 'Problématique et Orientation', Beirut, 1964, the key statistics for Lebanon in this period. The figures are based on a calculation of the different elements of public spending, e.g. habitation, sanitary measures, schooling, etc. This table indicates that the regions with Muslim majorities received the lowest levels of public spending when compared to the levels of government investment in areas with a Christian majority.

46. Johnson, pp. 117, 132.

47. Ziadeh, p. 257.

48. Johnson, p. 128.

49. The traditional Sunni elites were beginning to respond to pressure from the Sunni bourgeoisie in the 1950s, but relatively slightly; they also had no interest in promoting the interests of the masses.

50. Alia al-Solh, editorial: 'The Most Generous of All Who Have Left Us', *al-Hikmat*, February 1965, p. 44. Alia al-Solh was the eldest daughter of Riyadh al-Solh.

51. Attiyah, p. 197 points out that his actions made the Sunni politicians feel dependent on the whims of a Maronite president, rather than partners in government.

52. Chamoun himself claimed this. Camille Chamoun, *Mudhakkarat* [Memoirs], Beirut, 1969, pp. 262–3.

53. Sami al-Solh, *Mudhakkarat Sami Bey al-Solh* [Memoirs of Sami Bey al-Solh], Maktabat al-Fikr al-Arabi, Beirut, 1960, p. 320.

54. Attiyah, p. 69. Such heroes had included Faisal, Atatürk and King Farouk of Egypt.

55. *An-Nahar*, 25 February 1958

56. Johnson, p. 131.

57. *Ibid.*, referring to the broadcasting of Nasser's speeches and the first appearance of Nasser's photographs in Beirut.

58. *Al-Hayat*, May 17 1953.

59. Johnson, p. 131.

60. See, for instance, *Beirut*, 15 October 1953, containing a statement advocating Nasserism as the answer to Sunni domestic grievances.

61. Two populist deputies who were also members of another organisation, *al-Mutamar al-Watani*, were Abdallah al-Haj, a Christian, and Kamal Jumblat, a Druze.

62. See the tone of concern in the statement of Prime Minister Abdallah al-Yafi, 20 July 1954, *Minutes of Parliament* V, 1954–55, pp. 1300–1. Desmond Stewart also commented on this; see Stewart, pp. 13–4.

63. See, for instance, the comments in *al-Hayat*, 20 August 1954, reporting the events of the previous day; also *Beirut*, 24 August 1954. See also *Moslem Lebanon Today*.

64. Reported in debate, 9 November 1954, *Minutes of Parliament* V, 1954–55, pp. 1682–92.

65. Johnson, pp. 82–3.

66. Labib Zuwiyyah Yamak, 'Party Politics in the Lebanese Political System', in L. Binder, ed., *Politics in Lebanon*, John Wiley & Co., New York, 1966, p. 153.

67. *Ibid.*, pp. 152–4; Johnson, pp. 82–3.

68. I have already mentioned that Chamoun was seen as pro-British rather than pro-French, which was also an asset. See *Fiches du Monde Arabe*, 1. 34–8, 42–5, La Crise 1975–76 (la 9), IL 106 11 December 1979, no. 1449.

69. Chamoun, pp. 255–6.

70. *Ibid.*

71. According to *al-Hayat*, 6 November 1956, Chamoun warned the US that if the Americans did not intervene to halt the 'dangerous situation' in the region, with Egypt under attack by Anglo-French and Israeli armies, 'mass pressure' would force the Arab world to intervene on Egypt's side because hers was a 'just cause'.

72. Bishara al-Khoury, *Haqa'iq Lubnaniyyah*, vol. 3, Aurak Lubnaniyyah Publications, Beirut, 1961, p. 476.

73. *Beirut*, 17 May, 1955. The council was composed of members elected on 16 April 1955 by all Muslim bodies and organisations, and was composed of ex-prime ministers, Muslim members of the Municipality Board of Beirut, and members of the *'Ulama* Association, the *al-Maqassed* Society's committee, the professional syndicates, and popular Muslim organisations.

74. According to the British embassy, Saeb Salam 'worked against the formation of this council, as he believed that it might tend to put an end to his control of the Moslims in Beirut'. FO371/110958/1017.

75. *Al-Siyassa*, 10 June 1958.

76. *Al-Jarida*, 5 April 1956, argued that Chamoun had asked Sami al-Solh not to attend, but that al-Solh had threatened to resign if prevented from attending. Clearly he felt that his public credibility with his community depended to a considerable extent on taking such a stand. Ziadeh, p. 160.

77. Attiyah, p. 242.

78. *Ibid.*

79. *Al-Hayat*, 26 January 1955.

80. Kalawoun, p. 29.

81. Still, Karami's ministerial declaration in the assembly vote of confidence was moderate, and did not take a strong pro-Nasserite stance. *Cabinet Papers*, Muasasat al-Durasat al-Lubnanyya, Beirut, 1986, vol. I, 1926–66; Rachid Karami, Speech, 4 October 1955, p. 386.

82. Attiyah, p. 254.

83. *Minutes of Parliament* V, 1955–56, Committee Meeting, 10 November, 1955.

84. Al-Yafi took a clearer stand on foreign policy matters. He stated that he 'refused to adhere to the Baghdad Pact, and second to any Western pact' and also that he 'would try to work for the aims of the Arab League and the pact of mutual defence as well as for economic co-operation as well as any domain with the Arab brothers'. *Cabinet Papers*, Abdallah al-Yafi, 29 March 1956, p. 399.

85. *Cabinet Papers*, pp. 398–403.

86. For instance, see *Beirut*, 2 August and 5 August 1956, for articles arguing that only a domestic policy modelled on Nasserist lines would insitute a system based on equalities in political, social and economic terms between the Christian and Muslim communities.

87. Indeed, Nasser's own socialism was more rhetorical than real; see Johnson, p. 131. According to Clovis Maksoud, there were some genuinely socialist groupings within Lebanon whose members reflected socialist aspirations, notably the Ba'ath Socialist Party or *Harakat al-Qawmiyyin al-Arab*. Also, a certain intellectual constituency was

impressed by the Nasserist version of socialism and its vision of socialist justice as it was in place in Egypt. However, such groupings had 'limited' power, and were 'confined mainly to the intelligentsia with some trade union and mass following in the cities of Tripoli and Tyre'. Clovis Maksoud, 'Lebanon and Arab Nationalism', in L. Binder (ed.), *Politics in Lebanon*, p. 253.

88.   Letter of resignation of Abdallah al-Yafi as Prime Minister, 16 November 1956 in *al-Hayat*, 17 November 1956

89.   *Beirut*, 28 November 1956.

90.   *Al-Hayat*, 10 January 1957 giving the text of Charles Malik's declaration in Rome, 9 January 1957, on the Eisenhower Doctrine.

91.   *Beirut,* 14 December 1956.

92.   Charles Malik stressed this point in Rome, 9 January 1957; see *al-Hayat*, 10 January 1957.

93.   Khalaf and Denoueux, p. 187.

94.   Ismail Moussa al-Yussuf, *Thawrat al-'Ahrar fi Lubnan*, n.d. (but internal evidence, notably reference to recent strikes in May 1958, makes it plain that it dates from the late spring or summer of 1958), pp. 36; 135; Nadim al-Jisr, speech, reported in *al-Hayat*, 18 May 1958. *Al-Hayat* reported that a decision to go on strike to highlight a range of popular grievances was taken on 29 March 1957, and was swiftly followed by demonstrations on 30 March. A demonstration on 30 May 1957 ended in violence with 7 dead, 73 wounded and 400 arrested. Another strike on 5 November 1957 involved the populist Najjadah grouping, and saw the arrest of its leader, Adnan al-Hakim. See *al-Hayat*, 30 March 1957; 31 March 1957; 31 May 1957; 5 November 1957.

95.   A point consistently brought out in *Beirut*, see for instance the article of 21 December 1956.

96.   *Al-Hayat*, 30 May 1957; 30 May 1957; 31 May 1957; 1 June 1957; 5 November 1957; 6 November 1957.

97.   For the text of the communiqué of 16 March 1957, see M. S. Agwani, *The Lebanese Crisis 1958: A Documentary Study*, Asia Publishing House, New Delhi, 1965, p. 16.

98.   See, for example, *al-Hayat*, 11 April 1957, making mention of such broadcasts.

99.   See Agwani, pp. 29–33, for a translation of the full text of the petition and the manifesto of the United National Front. This grouping also included figures from other Muslim communities, such as Kamal Jumblat, and even a number of noted Maronite opposition figures such as Fouad Ammoun, Phillippe Takla and Ilyas al-Khoury.

100.   Agwani, p. 30.

101.   See, for instance, reports in *al-Hayat*, 1 April 1957; *Beirut*, 3 April 1957.

102.   *Al-Hayat*, 13 April 1957.

103.   *Beirut*, 3 April 1957.

104.   Attiyah, p. 269.

105.   *Al-Siyassa*, 7 April 1957.

106.   Fouad Ajar, *The Arab Predicament*, Cambridge University Press, Cambridge, 1981, p. 93.

107.   *Al-Siyassa*, 25 April, 26 April and 27 April 1957.

108.   See, for instance, editorials in *al-Siyassa*, 25 April and 27 April 1957.

109.   *Al-Siyassa*, 31 May 1957.

110.   *Al-Hayat*, 15 March 1958, reported an appeal – rather than a warning – from Najjadah

to the government to moderate its policy towards the Arab world; *al-Hayat*, 16 April 1958. See also Agwani, pp. 42–3.

111. *Minutes of Parliament* V, 1955–56, meeting, 26 November 1956, pp. 107–9; 111–2.

112. *Beirut*, 14 December 1956.

113. After the resignation, Sunni politicians generally sought to remain on good terms with Chamoun if they wished to return to office. Hence al-Yafi's declaration that 'We have not and never shall stab a Lebanese President in the back', *Minutes of Parliament* V, 1955–56, meeting, 26 November 1956, pp. 107–9; 111–2.

114. *Beirut*, 3 April 1957.

115. Attiyah, p. 274.

116. It was sufficiently acute to be noticed even in the Maronite press, see, for example, *al-Hayat*, 31 May 1957; *al-Hayat*, 19 June 1957.

117. *Al-Siyassa*, 14 June, 15 June, and 3 July 1957.

118. *L'Orient*, 3 July 1957.

119. *Al-Hayat*, 3 June 1957.

120. Sami al-Solh, p. 320.

121. Raghid al-Solh, 'Lebanon and Arab Nationalism, 1936–1945', unpublished PhD thesis, St Anthony's College, Oxford, 1986, p. 277.

122. Kalawoun, p. 37; Chamoun, pp 262–3.

123. Attiyah, p. 275.

124. *Ibid.*, p. 276.

125. *Al-Hayat*, 28 March 1958.

126. See, for instance, *al-Hayat*, 23 December 1957, 16 March 1958; *al-Hayat*, 29 January, 9 February and 16 March 1958, all mentioning such criticisms and relating them to popular disturbances of a pro-Nasserist description.

127. FO 371/1134116, Telegram no. 477, Middleton to Selwyn Lloyd, 13 May 1958; FO 371/134127, Telegram no. 956, British Embassy, Beirut to Foreign Office, 9 July 1958; FO371/134130, Telegram no. 991, British Embassy, Beirut to Foreign Office, 14 July 1958.

128. *Al-Hayat*, 3 September 1957; 4 September 1957; 13 September 1957; 19 September 1957; 5 October 1957; 6 October 1957.

129. *Al-Hayat*, 8 October 1957.

130. Agwani, pp. 35–41.

131. Moussa al-Yussuf, p. 135.

132. *Ibid.*

133. Still, Lebanese Sunni and other opposition politicians gave little indication in their speeches, etc, that they wanted to abandon the National Pact to the extent of a complete break with the West, for practical economic reasons if for nothing else.

134. *Al-Siyassa,* 2 February, 4 February, 5 February, and 7 February 1958.

135. *Al-Siyassa*, 4 February 1958.

136. Salibi, p. 15.

137. Muhammad Hasanein Haykal, *Sanawat al-Ghalayan*, p. 319.

138. *Al-Hayat*, 4 February, and 16 March 1958, for instance.

139. Haykal, p. 319.

140. *Al-Siyassa,* 4 February 1958; this provided a laudatory survey of Nasser's speeches and press interviews.

141. *Al-Hayat*, 10 April and 11 April 1958.

142. *Al-Siiyassa*, for instance, reporting these developments on 11 April, 12 April, 17 April and 18 April 1958.

143. *L'Orient,* 21 April 1958.

144. *Ibid.*

145. *Al-Hayat,* 21 April 1958, provided a graphic report of this incident.

146. *Ibid.*

147. *Ibid.*

148. *Al-Hayat,* 23 April 1958.

149. See chapter six.

150. Saeb Salam, in our interview in Geneva on 4 January 1991, spoke of a growing anti-Western feeling amongst the Sunni and other Muslim groups in Lebanon. See, also for example, Telegram Nos. 328, 529 Beirut, 4 May 1958, pp. 555–556, *Documents Diplomatiques Français,* vol. I, 1 Jan–30 June 1958, Telegram nos. 328 and 529, French Embassy, Beirut to Ministry of Foreign Affairs, 4 May 1958, pp. 555–6; Department of State Archives, Centre for Lebanese Studies, American Embassy, Beirut to Department of State, Confidential: 'The Crisis in Lebanon', 9 May 1958, pp. 1–3.

151. FO371/134116, Telegram no. 433, British Embassy, Beirut to Foreign Office, 5 May 1958. It is interesting here to note the parallels with the downfall of Bishara al-Khoury in 1952. For comments on the temporary nature of this unity see Kalawoun, pp. 43–4.

152. Salam, Interview, 4 January 1991.

153. *Al-Hayat,* 10 May 1958. See also Agwani, pp. 57–8 for the full text of the statement by the United National Front.

154. *Al-Hayat,* 17 May 1958 contained claims from al-Solh to this effect, for instance.

155. *Al-Amal,* 11 May, 12 May and 13 May 1958; *al-Hayat,* 12 May and 14 May 1958. See also the summary of Lebanese opinion in *Documents Diplomatiques Français,* vol. I, 1 Jan–30 June 1958, Telegram nos 579–588, Roche to Pineau, 12 May 1958.

156. *An-Nas,* 29 May 1958.

157. Salam, interview, 14 January 1991. It is worth noting here that it was Syria that had initiated moves to create the UAR and not vice versa. Nasser had been less eager because of what he perceived as the problems of a union that he could only control with difficulty, if only because of the distances involved.

158. *Al-Hayat,* 14 May 1958, reporting a United National Front press conference and press release from Saeb Salam

159. Department of State Archives, Centre for Lebanese Studies, Telegram no. 4532, McClintock to Dulles, 7 June 1958, reporting an interview with al-Hakim.

160. Salam, interview, 14 January 1991.

161. *Ibid.*

162. Johnson, p. 134, Salam, interview, 14 January 1991.

163. FO371/134119, UL1015/147, Telegram No. 4572, Middleton to Selwyn Lloyd, 9 June 1958.

164. *Ibid.*; Department of State Archives, Centre for Lebanese Studies, Telegram No. 4912, McClintock to Dulles, 19 June 1958. See also *an-Nahar,* 6 June 1958, giving an account of the reactions of Bashir Awar, a known moderate, who resigned his office in protest over this.

165. Department of State Archives, Centre for Lebanese Studies, Telegram No. 4664, McClintock to Dulles, 12 June 1958, reporting Saeb Salam's statement that no solution would be possible without the consent of the Lebanese people as a whole, and that this could only be gained through the mediation of the Arab League rather than the UN. See also Telegram no. 4912, McClintock to Dulles, 19 June 1958.

166. FO371/134119, UL1015/147, Telegram no. 598, British Embassy, Beirut to Foreign

Office, 23 May 1958; M. S. Agwani, *The Lebanese Crisis*, pp. 1–22 for the text of Charles Malik's speech of 6 June 1958.

167. *Ibid.*

168. *Ibid.*

169. FO 371/134119, UL1015/147, Telegram no. 4572, Middleton to Selwyn Lloyd, 9 June 1958.

170. Statement, Saeb Salam, reported in Department of State Archives, Centre for Lebanese Studies, Telegram no. 4664, American Embassy, Beirut to Secretary of State, 12 June 1958.

171. Kamal Jumblat, *Hagigat al-Thawrat al-Lubnaniat*, al-Dar al-Takadoumiat, Beirut, 1987, pp. 44–55.

172. Department of State Archives, Centre for Lebanese Studies, Telegram no. 4696, McClintock to Dulles, 13 June 1958.

173. *An-Nas*, 5 July 1958.

174. *Al-Hayat*, 15 July 1958, reporting Saeb Salam's perspective and similar ones from leading figures like Taki al-Din, al-Solh, Anwar al-Khatib, Nazem Akkarl and, predictably, Adnan al-Hakim. It also reported popular Sunni enthusiasm for the coup.

175. Stewart, p. 101.

176. See, for example, *al-Hayat*, 16 July 1958.

177. *Ibid.*

178. *Al-Hayat*, 16 July 1958.

179. *Al-Hayat*, 16 July, 17 July, and 18 July 1958.

180. *Al-Hayat*, 17 July and 19 July 1958.

181. Department of State Archives, Centre for Lebanese Studies, Telegram no. 496, McClintock to Dulles, 18 July 1958.

182. See for example, *al-Hayat*, 17 July 1958.

183. Department of State Archives, Centre for Lebanese Studies, Telegram no. 4194, McClintock to Dulles, 18 July 1958. It is necessary to turn to these sources because of press censorship in Lebanon.

184. *Al-Hayat*, 18 July 1958.

185. *Al-Hayat*, 22 July 1958.

186. See, for example, *al-Hayat*, 18 July 1958.

187. *Al-Telegraph*, 22 July 1958; *al-Jarida*, 22 July 1958; *al-Hayat*, 22 July 1958.

188. Robert Murphy, *Diplomat Among Warriors*, Greenwood Press, Connecticut, 1976, pp. 405–6.

CHAPTER SIX

The Maronite Community in 1958

Sunni mythology located Lebanon as a politically independent entity that was an integral part of an Arab, and Muslim, world, and used the rhetoric of Nasserism to express this perspective. But the Maronite masses, watching Arab power increase at the expense of Western influence in the Middle East, interpreted these statements as Arabs rejecting Lebanese sovereignty, rather than as offering an alternative. To the Maronites, the Sunni mythology negated the essence of Lebanese 'nationalism' contained in Maronite mythology about the state and about their own role within that state. Thus the Sunni mythology that evolved around the figure of Nasser and placed Lebanon alongside Arab states such as Syria and Egypt directly challenged the established notions of sovereignty and Maronite interpretations of Lebanon's history.[1]

Some intellectuals appealed to the Maronites to grasp the reality: no major Muslim community threatened Lebanon's existence or the position of the Maronite community as established by the compromise of the National Pact. For instance, on 16 March 1958, an editorial in *L'Orient* reported that Nassib al-Matni, the journalist whose murder probably started the actual 1958 crisis, had tried to calm Maronite fears. He was claiming that 'Some Christians [i.e Maronites] are frightened ... [but] All the Christians desire is to be told that the independence and sovereignty of Lebanon are not being threatened; then the present atmosphere of apprehension and mistrust will disappear completely'.[2] Despite his attempts to reassure the Maronite readership, this Muslim opinion stood little chance of having a positive impact on the Maronite masses.

The reality was that by March 1958, the Maronite masses were reacting to several events, any one of which would have made them uneasy; cumulatively, they created a mood of general alarm. As reports in the more populist Arabic-language, pro-Maronite newspapers indicate, these events included the formation of the UAR, the reports of Nasserist-inspired help for malcontents (mainly Sunnis) within Lebanon to demonstrate violently about their grievances, and the anti-government propaganda they heard on their radios coming from Syrian and Egyptian newspapers.[3] As the Muslims elevated Nasser to heroic status, Chamoun assumed equivalent status as an iconic figure who embodied and championed 'le Libanisme', an ideological doctrine that placed the Maronite community at the heart of Lebanon, as its core and its *raison d'être*.[4] As Chamoun adopted policies that brought him into direct conflict with Nasser, his heroic stature increased along with the popular will to equate him, and his continued hold on office, with the maintenance of Lebanese independence.[5]

The Maronite-oriented press played a significant role in formulating the nature of this mass reaction to events and opinions inside and outside Lebanon; on the whole, radio was less important to this community. Readership figures, so far as they exist, as well as general anecdotal evidence, suggest that the Maronite masses, at least, took some pains to be well informed about political matters.[6] As I described in chapter two, the Maronites held a very specific vision of Lebanon, related to myths about an ancient Maronite inheritance and the consequent 'right' this conferred upon them to identify themselves as being at the core of a Lebanese national identity.

That vision was not restricted to an intellectual community. As these myths were repeated in the basic education provided for most Maronite children, they had a wide popular currency.[7] And at the popular level, few thought critically about the validity of such myths. Indeed, the fact that academics dismiss the myths has been irrelevant to the popularity of perceptions that Maronite culture and beliefs are individual and superior. At the popular level the myths were established and rarely questioned 'truths'.[8] Central to a popular Maronite consciousness of what made the Maronites so different, they provided 'proof' of a genuine difference between the Maronites and other communities that could not be undermined without affecting the popular self-identity of the Maronite masses.[9] This 'proof' of difference, and of a more ancient existence in Lebanon than any other community, justified the Maronite 'right' to claim that without them there was no Lebanon.[10] Thus the continued existence and interests of the Maronites were inextricably bound up with the continued existence and interests of the state of Lebanon. From the Maronite perspective, however, the same was not true of any other community.

Because of this perspective, and because a popularly available Maronite historiography stressed Maronite trials, especially under the Ottomans, the Maronite masses in the 1950s tended to be easily alarmed into the defensiveness identified in *L'Orient*. This defensiveness was most easily aroused when the Lebanese entity, and the Maronites' privileged position within that entity, seemed to be threatened. In the past such threats had come from the Ottoman empire; they now came from those within Lebanon itself who sought to link Lebanon too closely with Syria and Egypt. The threats, then, came from quarters identifying themselves not only with the traditional threat from Islam, but also with the newer threat of Arab nationalism. Opinions among Maronites at all levels stressed Lebanon's links with the West, rather than with the Arab world. To fully understand Maronite mass reactions to the evolution of the 1958 crisis, and elements in that crisis such as the question of Chamoun's re-election, we must first understand how those reactions developed out of the Maronites' long-established concerns about their own, and Lebanon's, security and rightful place in the world.

The masses reacted less out of a sense of economic self-interest than from their central core of understanding what made them different from Lebanon's other communities. They became conscious of this reaction only after they felt their truths being 'attacked' by the Muslim communities seeking to align Lebanon with the Arab world. In terms of difference, the Maronites felt the impact of the West most strongly not in material aspects, which other communities shared, but through religion and ideas of what constituted 'civilisation'. Thus we must not underestimate the popular significance of traditional Maronite links with European Christianity and the civilisation it produced.

A major part of the Maronites' sense of 'difference' was bound up with their religious heritage. That heritage distinguished them not only from Muslim communities but also from other Christian communities within

Lebanon, because the Maronite Church was not an Eastern Christian church. Thus, theologically, the Maronite community was not just another Christian community in the Middle East; it was a community in official communion with the Roman Catholic Church that set its religious calendar in accordance with Rome.[11] Nor was the difference merely theological; it also extended to popular political and cultural loyalties. This is clearly demonstrated by popular Maronite affection for Roman Catholic-inspired French culture, if not always for France itself, during the 1950s.[12]

Although French rule was unpopular during the Mandate period, pro-French feelings could arise again in an independent Lebanon, especially in the context of threats from Arab nationalism. Maronite education continued to be modelled on French education, and to be conducted predominantly in French; many of the better-educated Maronites frequently spoke in French. Moreover, Maronites generally retained a pro-Western orientation, with English and American culture having a continuing impact within Lebanon.[13] This is a striking contrast to the pattern in other post-colonial states in the region at this time, where one could sense opposition to Western 'colonialism' throughout the population.

These pro-Western feelings within Maronite thinking, which led the government to oppose breaking ties with the West and to accept the highly contentious Eisenhower Doctrine, were not confined to elite levels. They were publicised widely in the Maronite press, and I find no evidence that ordinary Maronites opposed the government's reasoning. The systems of education in place within the community, and the tone of the popular press, all helped to reinforce pro-Western attitudes within the community at all levels.

This Maronite tendency to think in terms of relations with the West also had economic consequences. By introducing Western ideas, the missionary schools had contributed not only to Maronite political development but also to more Western and capitalist attitudes towards economic development.[14] The Christian part of Beirut and Mount Lebanon had more developed economic infrastructures in capitalist terms than the largely non-Christian regions of the North, South and the Biqa', though these regions had an affluent Muslim upper class. Trading and other links with the Western world produced a self-consciously Western consumer culture within the Maronite community; people valued Western commodities and cultural products because they identified their community orientation.[15]

This is not to suggest a simplistic economic division within Lebanon where the poor were Muslim and the rich were Christians or even Maronites. The crisis of 1958 cannot be explained as a situation where the loyalist Maronites were defending the developed areas of Lebanon against rebel Muslims controlling the poor areas. The division is far more complicated. All confessional groups, including the Maronites, had their social classes and economic divisions. However, as far as their finances allowed, the Maronite masses demonstrated a loyalty to Western consumerism and capitalism at a time when it was being attacked by Arab nationalism for its imperialist connotations. For those whose finances permitted little display, religion was the cultural product they clung to most strongly. Religion provided the most prominent and uniformly held dimension of communal identity amongst the lower strata of the Maronite masses. For those with less limited access to education, religious belief and its associated rituals and popular myths remained more important than they did amongst the relatively better-off, more educated strata where access to a more sophisticated community identity evolved.[16]

Traditionally, these ideas of Maronite identity among the masses had been expressed through the Maronite notables, both the traditional landowning class and the newer commercial and administrative bourgeoisie. These elites had generally produced the community's political leaders, and also many of the leading newspapermen and journalists.[17] The community's exposure to Western ideas of education and consumer culture also had a political impact, as the Maronites were the most politically conscious of the communities in Lebanon, in a sense comprehensible to Western perspectives. That is, their education allowed the Maronite population to understand what the West meant by a political party system in a democratic state.[18]

The Political Parties

The Maronite political parties were certainly not as developed as twentieth-century political parties in the West. Indeed, during this period the Maronite political parties looked more like political parties in Britain in the late eighteenth and early nineteenth centuries, given the importance of affiliations based on land and kinship.[19] But this situation was changing. For instance, after the Kata'ib Party reorganised itself in 1949, it become a political party in this modern sense rather than just a traditional clan grouping.[20] Also, given the variety of parties in the Maronite community, voters had a range of political choices. For example, a disgruntled voter could find a party to vote for that did not require an alliance with traditional clan hostilities. And in times of crisis Maronite political parties such as the Kata'ib Party were able to mobilise their membership quickly and coherently, because they had set up their internal organisations, as in the West, to encourage precisely that flexibility.

The Kata'ib Party originated as a Maronite boy-scout movement during the Mandate period. But its constituency included students and minor civil service officials as well as schoolboys, apprentices and men drawn from the Maronite petty bourgeoisie. This constituency promoted the development, from 1949, of a sophisticated and effective political party organisation that reflected political developments in the West, familiar especially to students and officials through their education and employment.[21] It was a popular party in that it was funded primarily through membership dues, and its most of its leaders were members promoted through the ranks. Thus it saw itself as having a constant political role in the state, holding regular membership meetings to discuss policy and promote local participation and interaction between party members and elected Kata'ib politicians. According to Entelis, the party was 'the major instrument for guaranteeing Lebanese-Christian interest in the state'.[22] This was true until the Ta'if Accord.

In this sense the Kata'ib Party was unlike the Bloc National, a 'cadre' party that brought together at leadership level individuals from the established Maronite elite. Moreover, as the Bloc National was mostly concerned with campaigning, it met with its supporters mostly in anticipation of forthcoming elections. At other times, it emphasised interaction at leadership levels.[23] The available data on party membership indicates that, particularly at times of perceived crisis for the Maronite community and 'Lebanon', the Kata'ib had substantial support from the community's masses. Moreover, its ability to recruit extra members at such times indicates a voluntary level of support. It also shows how much the party had established itself as the 'focal point' through which ordinary community members could express their concerns and seek advice and guidance on their reactions.[24] By contrast, during this period the Bloc National had a significantly smaller support base, drawing on more automatic, or involuntary, support from the followers of the party's essentially *za'im* leadership.[25]

It is worth noting here that at the point in 1958 when elements of the Maronite community finally felt compelled to take up arms, they generally did so under the auspices of the Kata'ib Party. The only populist alternative

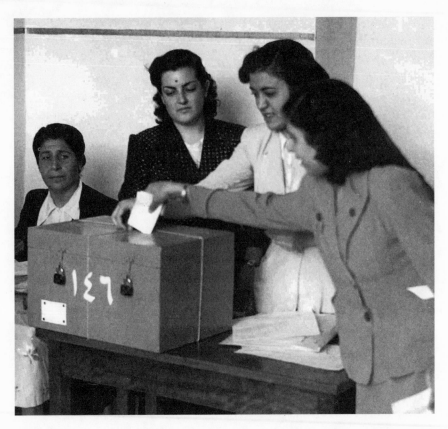

Lebanese women in 1953 participate in elections for the first time. The Bloc National had introduced legislation for women's suffrage in 1945. (The BN under Raymond Eddé also proposed legislation in 1958 granting women equal inheritance rights, which was passed that same year by Parliament.)

was the PPS, but PPS members did not take to the streets as an unorganised mob.[26] Equally, the Maronites were unlike the other confessional groups in that their traditional leaders, whatever their formal political profile, took no part in the actual fighting, except in Zgortha, in the north. This one exception underscores how much the leaders and members of other Maronite political parties had moved in their politics to a level of complexity beyond traditional clan reactions.[27]

The Kata'ib Party was certainly not the only important political or quasi-political grouping in the Maronite community. Among the others were the Bloc National, led by Raymond Eddé; the Constitutional Bloc, led in the 1950s by Bishara al-Khoury; and Camille Chamoun's Liberal Nationalist Party. In addition, other elements and institutions, such as the Maronite Church and individual clergy, had traditionally played a political role in the community. Overall, then, the Maronite community had a considerable level of political awareness, and a range of options for expressing its political opinions. Equally, however, part of that political awareness was demonstrated as a commitment to maintaining the political status quo and its institutions, established under the National Pact. Thus the community tended to show its political opinions through more organised political channels.[28]

Leadership style was another difference between the more 'modern' Maronite and the Muslim political groupings.[29] In general, the Maronite leaders had become involved in the 'modern', or Western, economic world through their careers, but often in ways that also maintained their traditional family and clan links. Arnold Hottinger has identified Maronite political leaders from traditionally powerful backgrounds who also had the support of a 'locally circumscribed' community, and who nurtured their followers, or 'clientele', through a traditional kind of patronage system. A leader such as Pierre Eddé, from a traditional background but with a career in banking, was able to combine the old methods of community leadership with more modern ones, as he dispensed 'patronage' to political followers who also had clan or kinship affiliation to him.[30]

But other Maronite leaders were either newcomers, like Emile Bustani, or like the Shuf deputy Chamoun himself. They came from commercially or professionally successful families and lacked the traditional landed base. Such leaders used the patronage available through their commercial or professional connections to build up a following that enabled them to figure in the Maronite political world. Chamoun's success in 1952 shows clearly that it had become possible for a non-traditional Maronite leader to achieve political power that drew on support from all levels of the Maronite community.[31]

Populist Maronite political thinking did derive from the traditional Maronite focus on the community's interests, but, developing out of that, it came increasingly to focus on the community's interpretation of the president's political role because he was responsible for foreign policy.[32] In this period of Middle Eastern Arab nationalism and anti-Westernism, the Maronite masses saw foreign policy as the key to their security, indeed to the very survival of Lebanon as a separate entity.[33] Thus the 1958 crisis came to demonstrate popular Maronite willingness to co-ordinate political support around the institution of the presidency when its essentially Maronite character seemed threatened, along with the existing pro-Western foreign policy.

Chamoun certainly understood how much the Maronites stressed foreign policy issues. A shrewd politician, he monitored popular Maronite reaction to his rhetoric rather than the reaction of fellow politicians. Thus he sought to appeal directly to the community as a whole, giving public speeches that were reported in the Maronite or pro-Western media, hoping thereby to pressure the less committed Maronite politicians to respond directly to the concerns his rhetoric raised among their electoral following. In bypassing the Maronite political elite in this way, Chamoun apparently hoped to develop such a powerful base of popular support that the other Maronite politicians would find it expedient to listen to the opinions of their own followers and support Chamoun's re-election hopes.[34] Thus it is useful to examine his rhetoric, seeking clues to the state of popular feeling, or alarm, amongst the Maronite masses.

Chamoun's Rhetoric

In 1957 and 1958, Chamoun's political rhetoric, aimed at the whole Maronite community, almost invariably connected internal policy matters – especially potentially unpopular ones – to foreign policy statements. Thus he played on the readiness of the Maronite masses to respond to any implication that Lebanese sovereignty was in jeopardy. For example, in March 1958 he spoke of Lebanese finances in a widely reported speech at Bkirki; he related the economic issues to his reassurances that under his leadership, the Lebanese people would contrive, as they always had done, to resist 'the conquerors and invaders'. In April, speaking during a *Ramadan* feast at the house of Sami al-Solh, he linked internal stability and the Eisenhower Doctrine with a justification of his policies towards the Arab world.[35]

Though they undoubtedly had their fears about the threat of Nasserism and the importance of foreign policy issues, the Maronites were not so easily manipulated by a superficial assessment of their undoubted fears about the threats posed by Nasserism and Arab nationalism.[36] Their level of political sophistication showed in their ability to act as a community despite, rather than because, of Chamoun and his rhetoric. They responded to that rhetoric because it did echo their genuine fears, but their community identity was long-established and all Chamoun did was to create a situation in which they readily expressed their communal feeling.[37]

We must also examine Chamoun's attitude towards other Maronite leaders with a substantial following. Did he attempt to make alliances with such leaders in order to widen his base of support within the Maronite community, even to extend that base to other Christian communities? Did he try to address the agendas of political leaders within these communities which, unlike those in the Sunni community, reflected community opinion rather than merely the leaders' self-interest? I have found no direct evidence that Chamoun was conscious of the difference between the Maronite and other Christian communities. But he was apparently aware of the difference, to judge from his direct rhetorical appeals to the Maronite community as a whole and not just to leaders or particular groups, and his policy during the 1957 elections undermined traditional leaders.

The difference was between the operation of 'modern' Maronite political parties and traditional community powers; thus he must have realised what importance that gave to the reactions of the masses. In their capacity as voters, rather than loyal followers of traditional leaders, the Maronite masses could be susceptible to appeals that touched on issues of popular concern regardless of the leaders' opinions on them. As the fluctuating membership of the Kata'ib Party indicates, Maronite voters in the 1950s clearly were prepared to respond more directly to issues than to traditional loyalties when a crisis seemed threatening enough.

I suggest that Chamoun simply recognised instinctively that a 'modernisation' of the Maronite community had undermined the power base of the traditional community leadership, and he sought to use this change for his own ends. As Johnson points out, 'Chamoun's political moves against the landlords reflected the dominance of the bourgeoisie at a time when urban businessmen, lawyers and other professionals increasingly represented rural districts in Parliament'.[38] But Chamoun certainly seemed to understand how to arouse concerns in the Maronite community through rhetoric designed to invoke concerns that were intrinsically part of Maronite mythology – in an interesting contrast to his apparent position at the start of his mandate.

President Chamoun had taken up his mandate as a popular figure seen, in the spirit of the National Pact, as attractive and friendly to Christians and non-Christians alike. Born in Mount Lebanon into a professional, not a political, family, he had trained as a lawyer before entering politics in the 1940s.

Despite his lack of elite or political family connections, Chamoun's talents had ensured his rise – a factor that emphasises the evolution of Maronite political perceptions beyond dependence on traditional loyalties. He worked actively, and successfully, to shorten al-Khoury's mandate.

But while Chamoun was popular, that popularity had limits. In the 1952 elections, he had stood against a traditional Maronite leader, Hamid Frangieh, defeating him by a narrow margin. In office Chamoun was unable to consolidate his popularity through his own personal qualities. As I described in chapter five, in the context of the Sunni community's reaction to his policies Chamoun failed to institute domestic policy programmes that addressed existing problems in Lebanon. His domestic policies had the most negative impact on the Sunni and other Muslim communities.[39]

Nor could Chamoun rely on the uncritical support of other Maronite politicians, as I pointed out in chapter four. Indeed, he became 'the despair of' the traditional Maronite political leaders. As the British ambassador George Middleton observed, instead of building up his connections, Chamoun preferred to rely mainly on 'his talent for intrigue' and his 'personal popularity' – a diminishing asset, even among the Maronite community.[40] By 1958, it was only the perceived international crisis that kept Chamoun's popular credit as high as it was.[41]

In maintaining his popular support, Chamoun was fortunate that his most outstanding feature, to both the Maronites and the West, was his strongly pro-Western orientation. Despite his reservations, Middleton commented approvingly on Chamoun's 'strong line' in refusing to break with the West in 1956.[42] Even here, however, he faced a potential problem given the Maronite community's traditionally pro-French line. Chamoun was, in fact, anti-French, having been arrested by the French in November of 1943. This experience had left him out of step with many people whose support he needed.

His pro-British sympathies made his anti-French stance even more prominent.[43] Significantly, his wife, Zelfa Tabet, was of mixed Lebanese and Irish extraction and supposedly encouraged him to develop a more British orientation.[44] As ambassador in London from 1944 to 1947, he had made a number of connections, especially with the Foreign Office, on which he would later draw. In addition, he was later remembered for having strongly opposed the French presence in the Middle East, which certainly increased his popularity with that office.[45] However, his close identification with the British left him open to the charge of being a Foreign Office tool, a factor with some potential to undermine his personal popularity in a community that was traditionally more French-oriented.[46] Certainly when Chamoun did stand for office in 1952, other elites saw the contest between him and Frangieh as a battle between the interests of the Quai d'Orsay and Downing Street. And the latter came out on top.[47]

The Maronites certainly recognised, and even admired, Chamoun's perceived talent for intrigue. General Bustani referred to the popular perception of Chamoun as an 'astonishing political manoeuverer', and listed several points to support his claim. For instance, during the late 1940s Chamoun had been seen as one of the most pro-Arab of the Christian politicians; perhaps, given his pro-British orientation, this was a simple matter of links to the British (Foreign Office) position. In the UN in 1946, Chamoun had linked the cause of Lebanese independence with the cause of 'the liberation of the Arab world from all foreign and colonial intervention'.[48] During his period of opposition to al-Khoury in 1948–52, he had courted those Arab leaders and governments that might have an impact on a presidential election in Lebanon, notably those based in Cairo, Baghdad, Riyadh and Amman, reinforcing perceptions of him as a pro-Arab Maronite.[49]

Chamoun was also shrewd enough to realise that achieving his presidential ambitions required Muslim/Arab support, so he portrayed himself as a supporter of themes popular with these groups. Once elected, he saw less need to cultivate that support. Thus he found it easy to abandon a pro-Arab stance when doing so suited him better, after the events of 1955–6, because it was based on expediency rather than personal conviction. General Bustani believes that Chamoun personally placed the highest priority on his pro-British stance and his commitment to protecting the Maronite community.[50]

While Chamoun alienated many of the traditional landowning and political elites, he did not succeed in replacing them with other political figures who were loyal to him. Arguably, this is why he went over the heads of Maronite politicians, speaking directly to the Maronite masses in his public rhetoric. He succeeded to some extent: as the 1957 election results show, he did replace the traditional leaders in the loyalties of a significant proportion of the Maronite voters. Still, his popularity within Lebanon was already waning by the 1957 elections; after the elections he sustained it at popular levels only by developing the crisis and identifying publicly with the cause of Maronite and Lebanese survival.

By 1957 Chamoun had developed both an ambition to seek a fresh mandate, and the problem of how to achieve it. Electoral manipulation was his only practical option. In the 1947 elections, al-Khoury had been able to draw on his links with the traditional *za'im* class. Lacking such links and having undermined *za'im* power, he probably believed that he could guarantee his position only by identifying his mandate with Maronite consciousness of Lebanon's future security. Events after the elections of 1957 then played into his hands, enabling him to sustain that perception. The new electoral law of 1957 increased the power of the electorate in many of the new, smaller constituencies. Certainly the changes in constituency boundaries should have allowed most Maronites to raise their voices more powerfully. In many cases they actually did so, but in some constituencies those voices were not properly heard. In chapter four I discussed the evidence that some of the elections were fraudulent.[51]

Comments in the press by some populist Maronite leaders reflect the community's anger at the suggestions of election fraud. *Al-Hayat* had challenged the Kata'ib leadership: 'Does your party believe in the legality of the parliament of 66 and in its representative character?' The appeal was made, of course, because the party had a wide base of popular support amongst ordinary Maronites. Though he officially supported the government, however, the leader of the Kata'ib Party, Pierre Gemayel, replied in a letter published in *Le Soir* that 'the parliament which has just been given to us represents, in my opinion, only ten per cent of the population of the country. At the moment the real parliament is in the street.'[52] Nor was Gemayel the only Maronite leader to admit in print that the election had been rigged. Alfred Naccache also went on record in *al-Hayat*, agreeing that the elections were dishonest.[53]

On 20 June 1957, two of Chamoun's main Maronite opponents – both candidates in the general election – Dr Elias al-Khoury and Fouad Ammoun, had held a press conference. In it, they openly accused Chamoun of personally interfering in the elections, and of using the state apparatus to ensure that his own supporters won. According to al-Khoury, government employees were going to the villages and trying to persuade voters not to vote for him. Ammoun also accused the president of direct interference, alleging that in some cases violence was being used in the final hours of the hustings.[54] While both these men had personal reasons for accusing Chamoun of political corruption, it is significant that they not only felt able to voice these accusations, but could do so without condemnation from the Maronite press that published their comments; apparently readers of newspapers like *al-Hayat* were prepared to accept this perspective.

Even these accusations did not succeed in creating a serious popular crisis of confidence in Chamoun's leadership amongst the Maronite masses, probably because the flow of rhetoric from Chamoun and his immediate followers was sufficiently successful in creating a sense of a broader, impending national crisis. If he did not entirely stifle criticism, he managed to make it seem less significant than it might have been otherwise. Thus, the rhetoric coming from this quarter, invoking established mythology, corroborated by other evidence (including newspapers and the oral commentary of journalists like Ghassan Tueni) provides a useful indication of the popular mood amongst the masses.

Because Maronite candidates, including some opponents of Chamoun, did quite well in the 1957 elections, Chamoun apparently believed he could rely on a degree of genuine support from the Maronite voters. Those were the voters, of course, who were most likely to be concerned about developments in the region and about local Sunni reactions to them. In Maronite strongholds like Mount Lebanon, therefore, Chamoun had less need for electoral fraud than in other areas, though even in Mount Lebanon some notable Maronites lost their seats.

Thus, at least during his mandate, no other Maronite figure also endorsed a pro-Western stance or had a more appealing or convincing internal agenda. This fact was sufficiently acute to be noted by the interested Western powers. For example, American reports on the attitude of the Maronite community stressed that 'the crux of the problem ... is whether or not there is available a suitable replacement for President Chamoun', who would safeguard their interests.[55] Equally, Chamoun benefited from the high profile of foreign policy issues after the Suez Crisis and during the ongoing negotiations for union between Syria and Egypt. Indeed, during late 1957 and the first months of 1958, membership in the Kata'ib Party increased significantly.[56]

In a sense, Nasser himself boosted Chamoun's standing with the Maronite masses by expressing personal hostility towards him. Thus, unlike any other prominent Maronite figure, Chamoun came to personify resistance to Nasserism and its expression in Lebanon. Even the more modern elements of the Maronite community feared Nasserism, seeing its overtones of socialism. The popular attitude of the community towards Chamoun, then, was based not on a spontaneous popular endorsement of him but rather on the defence of Maronite interests that he appeared to represent for the time being. Indeed, the community would have been equally prepared to support another president who could guarantee maintaining the same line of defence. Thus, if Chamoun was to renew his mandate, he had to create a widely believed scenario in which he was the only Maronite figure who could be relied upon to do this successfully.

The elections themselves also indicated that this situation was not entirely straightforward. In constituencies where the contest was between Maronite candidates, it was fought on issues that did not relate to Chamoun and Nasserism. Instead, internal issues were crucial, including the prospect of an amendment to the constitution to permit Chamoun's re-election. The edition of *al-Hayat* that discussed the question of electoral fraud and the resignation of the ministers entrusted with conducting the elections framed its discussion in the context of internal issues, rather than foreign policy ones.[57] The issue of constitutional reform that would permit Chamoun to run for office again was a sensitive one for all levels of the Maronite community, not just for the deputies and other political leaders. As Pierre Rondot points out, the fact that 'the President of the Republic is not immediately eligible for re-election to this office was initially designed to prevent one community or clan from perpetuating itself' in power at the expense of others.[58]

Under the terms of the National Pact, the presidency would always be held by a Maronite; thus it was redundant for the constitution to prevent a particular community from developing a monopoly over the office. But Maronites thinking about community unity felt it important to ensure that no particular family or clan developed a hold over the office. Given that sectarian and clan affiliations are at the heart of Lebanese political life, any such monopoly could be deeply divisive.[59] Such divisions in the community might threaten community security by promoting intracommunal disputes, leaving the Maronites more vulnerable to attacks by other communities jealous of their superior position.[60] Popular attitudes on the constitutional amendment become clear if we examine the attitude of the Kata'ib Party towards this issue in 1957 and 1958. As late as 29 May 1958, the party was opposed to such manoeuvring: Pierre Gemayel stated bluntly, 'We have always been against renewal [of the president's term] and we remain so today as well as in the future'.[61]

Thus Maronites were reluctant to see any amendment. In addition, some feared that amending the constitution could establish a precedent that would allow Nasserist-inspired amendments that could undermine the Maronite community. In this context, the community reacted instinctively, urging maintenance of the status quo rather than risking a collapse of the formula established under the National Pact. Despite this refusal to endorse an amendment, the Kata'ib Party was insisting that it supported Chamoun's present policies, especially his foreign policy; its increased recruitment of members indicates that this position was popular with the masses.

An examination of the Kata'ib position also indicates that as the crisis developed, the Chamoun question for the Maronites became two questions: Should Chamoun finish his mandate? And should he stand for re-election, requiring a change in the constitution? These two questions were understood separately at the time. However, even though the question of Chamoun completing his mandate was not articulated until later, to the Maronites it was dominant, and they were nearly unanimous.[62] Even those in the Third Force, and individuals personally opposed to Chamoun like General Shihab or the Patriarch, supported the idea that Chamoun should stay in office until the end of his mandate.[63]

The issue at stake here was a broad question of principle that had little to do with Chamoun himself. The issue was that a Maronite president should never be forced to step down before he had fully completed his mandate for any reason that Maronites could perceive as being linked to foreign interference. Salibi, for instance, remembered the widespread Christian concern that under 'popular pressure' Muslim leaders might be forced to 'surrender the sovereignty of Lebanon to Nasser' if Chamoun was 'to step down before the end of his constitutional term', thereby 'giving the leaders of the Muslim opposition the victory they wanted'.[64] True, in 1952 Bishara al-Khoury had been forced to step down early from his second term. However, that situation included no foreign policy dimension with a popularly perceived threat to the very existence of Lebanon; a purely internal issue of government corruption had brought about his fall, and the fall was engineered as much by Maronite as by Muslim opponents. In 1957–8, the only groups wishing to force Chamoun into early resignation were elements the Maronites saw as Arab nationalist at best, and pro-Nasserist at worst.[65]

The private correspondence of Moussa Moubarak, the Lebanese ambassador to Paris in 1958, contains a letter to Pierre Bart, the French ambassador, analysing the situation and popular reaction to it, and he highlights this point. Moubarak emphasises the foreign dimension of the question in the popular perception, and thus its popular importance to the Maronite community:

The loyalists consider that it is important to support the state authority against the pressures of the people on the street [Muslim demonstrators presumed to be inspired by Nasserism] in order to ensure that M. Chamoun finishes his term of office. Even the Christian elements of the Third Force share his [Chamoun's] opinion on the deadline for the presidential term of office, in other words, until 24 September.[66]

And thus, two issues became inevitably linked in the Maronite mind: that of a president completing his mandate in defiance of what was popularly interpreted as foreign, not indigenous, pressure, and the equally broad issue of Lebanese independence from any foreign pressure, especially if that pressure was pan-Arab in nature. Thus the issue was rooted in traditional Maronite thinking, but in the context of 1958 it was exacerbated by the perceived danger of Nasserism imposing its will on Lebanese politics.

The strike of 9 May 1958 that took place in Sunni strongholds such as Beirut and Tripoli, in reaction to the assassination of journalist Nassib al-Matni, led the opposition to demand Chamoun's resignation. But the Maronite mainstream interpreted this incident as having far-reaching connotations that linked the calls for resignation to foreign intervention, as reports in *al-Hayat* reveal. Government reaction made these claims more credible. For instance the prime minister, Sami al-Solh, accused the United Arab Republic of sending arms to Lebanon to fuel rebellion on the streets; these accusations were heavily reported in the press.[67] Thus the issue of completing the presidential mandate developed into another one, as the Maronites saw a Lebanese and Maronite president, whatever his merits, being pressured to resign by Nasser's forces.

In response, the Maronite community developed a position of being prepared to resist that pressure vigorously, as a matter of principle entirely separate from any question of re-election and constitutional amendment to permit a renewal of Chamoun's mandate. Their alarm rose further when Muslims began to demand a new census. As a British Foreign Office despatch pointed out, the Maronites saw this demand as threatening the National Pact because it might well upset 'the foundation of the existing system of carefully calculated balances between the various sects and sections of the population'.[68] The Maronites felt it was up to them to decide the fate of their president because under the terms of the National Pact, he was first and foremost their representative in the state, and a threat to his position from outside the Maronite community seemed a threat to their interests.

One prominent Maronite political figure did react positively to the question of Chamoun's early removal and sought to win support for his position: Bishara al-Khoury. His motives are open to question of course, given Chamoun's role in removing him from office in 1952. Nor was he likely to have seen the possibility of Chamoun's fall as a potential constitutional crisis! Al-Khoury made his public position plain on 20 May 1958, in a statement on Damascus radio. This was in itself a provocative act, and indicates how much he was out of step with general Maronite opinion. A report to the British Foreign Office recorded him as stating, 'The only solution to the Lebanese crisis is the resignation of the President.' He also rejected the allegation that removing Chamoun would 'open Lebanon to President Nasser'. He concluded: 'I must say that had a word been said by the Lebanese President a month ago, the country would have been saved the present tragic situation. But unfortunately he did not say such a word.'[69]

In general, Maronites reacted to this broadcast with hostility, indicating that the community continued to fear the threat to Lebanese integrity posed by Nasserism. Thus an attack on Chamoun's right to complete his mandate was an attack on them as well.

Chamoun's re-election was another matter; for most Maronites it was not automatically linked to the first question. Experience now showed that such a scenario created a tension in the Maronite community.[70] As the Patriarch made plain in his published comments on the issue of a constitutional amendment in March 1958, it would be acceptable only if it concentrated on the merits of Chamoun's candidacy itself, and less on any broad issue of principle, since no precedent would be set in this respect. In March of 1958 the Patriarch saw no reason to advise the Maronite community that he saw no realistic alternative to Chamoun.[71]

For the Maronite masses, however, wholehearted support for Chamoun was increasingly becoming linked with the question of their political survival. Support for Chamoun's re-election could be seen as support for the kind of Lebanon the Maronite masses wanted, linked with a refusal to submit to Nasserist dictates. This link became clear in the period after the UAR was formed on 2 February 1958, and especially after Nasser visited Damascus. When the Maronite community saw just how powerful an effect Nasser had on the Muslim community in Lebanon, and they heard his rhetoric, 'Chamoun came to embody for the Christians of Lebanon the symbol of resistance to Nasser', according to a French source.[72] Georges Naccache, a journalist on the moderate wing of the opposition, commented rather acidly on the Maronite reaction during the negotiations leading up to the creation of the UAR, and before the hysteria surrounding Nasser's visit:

> *Un nouveau credo est proposé depuis huit mois aux Libanais; si vous n'êtes pas Chamounien, c'est que vous êtes un traitre et un Syro-Bolchevik.*[73]

> [A new credo is proposed to the Lebanese since eight months ago: if you are not Chamounist, it must be because you are a traitor and a Syro-Bolshevik.]

Chamoun was certainly working behind the scenes to create an atmosphere of crisis in which the public would demand that his mandate be renewed. Having decided that his most effective course was not to show his hand, he avoided as long as possible making any public stand on the issue of seeking a constitutional amendment and a fresh mandate. Of course, Lebanese tradition dictates that a politician not announce his own personal ambitions, but rather give the impression that he is standing for office because of pressure from friends and supporters. Thus it was not unusual in itself that Chamoun relied on hints rather than clearly stating his intentions. For instance, he made this comment in *L'Orient* in December 1957:

> I have my reasons. I will let my opinions be known in due time. It will be in May, June or July ... I fully understand the worries that the amendment of the constitution can give you. I am myself against the amendment in principle. But there is a point I don't want to leave ambiguous. If at the due moment I am not sure of finding a successor who will ensure the continuity of my policies, I am declaring already that it means that I will reconsider my position.[74]

While this is a fairly clear hint that re-election was on his agenda, Chamoun was still being deliberately ambiguous. He was not clearly stating his position or policy but was leaving the way open for others to 'pressure' him to stand again. He continued to leave his position publicly ambiguous. British Foreign Office sources of 13 April reveal that Chamoun had told Tufic Suwaida, the deputy prime minister of Iraq, that he had decided to stand again for the presidency. This statement was important in signalling his intentions to the

West, given Iraq's pro-Western stance at the time. Still, he made no public statement.[75]

While this game was part of Lebanon's political tradition, it was not usually played against such a tense background. Thus it created a problem: rather than increasing Chamoun's own chances of success, as he intended, it increased the tensions within Lebanon itself. It also heightened the uncertainty in the Maronite community: while many Maronite political figures had the ambition to become president, there was no single obvious candidate, as Moussa Moubarak commented.[76]

This popular insecurity about prospects for the future worked to Chamoun's advantage: by April 1958, a significant proportion of Maronites, possibly a majority, had come to favour Chamoun's re-election primarily because of fears associated with Nasser's high profile. As Ghassan Tueni commented, Chamoun had become a symbol of resistance to Nasserism.[77] *Amir* Farid Shihab, head of the Lebanese police, wrote a top secret letter to Sir Peter Coghill that sums up popular sentiments.[78] He remarked that the masses considered Chamoun 'a god' for his foreign policy and his patriotic sentiments; he also claimed that Chamoun was the reason why Egypt, Syria and Russia were helping the opposition.

He added that elements in the Maronite community planned to help Chamoun 'because of his sound external policy and because Lebanon cannot run the risk of having either a weak President or a man won to the enemy'. They were especially eager to help 'because the other candidates are either dangerous like Bishara al-Khoury or very weak ... There is a big gulf between him and all those men. He is far better than any one of them.'[79]

Watching Nasserism gain popularity in the spring of 1958, the Maronite masses were afraid of the outcome if a president acceptable to the opposition were elected, as that would have considerable implications for the survival of the National Pact. Thus, in February 1958, the Kata'ib Party came out in open support of Chamoun's foreign policy after meeting with him at the presidential palace.[80] Salibi also recalls 'the Christian whispers' that Shihab, the obvious candidate who did enjoy some opposition support, 'actually wanted Chamoun brought down, so he could get the presidency for himself with Muslim support'; and the rumours that 'the man was reverting to type ... Had not his ancestors at one time been Muslims?'[81] Once again, then, a co-habitational pattern of behaviour expressed itself as public opinion in the Maronite strongholds; public opinion was becoming well-disposed towards the idea of an actual Western intervention if Nasserist forces were seen to intervene in Lebanon. In Chamoun, it seemed, they had a president who could guarantee opposition to Nasserism, continue Western support at a time of increasing crisis and even arrange Western intervention as in the past if that became necessary.[82]

With Chamoun seeking to escalate rather than to defuse the crisis, relying on increasing popular Maronite support and the promise of support from Britain and the US, it is not surprising that by the spring of 1958 his re-election had become a major issue.[83] After Chamoun's speech of 20 April, in which he made a spirited defence of his policies and attacked those of others, Moussa Moubarak claimed that re-election 'dominates the political scene and agitates public opinion. The opposition has taken direct action and the loyalists are continuing their propaganda campaign'.[84]

The Patriarch Flexes His Muscles

Despite the pro-Chamoun stance of the Maronite masses, Maronite political leaders remained far from united in their willingness to endorse Chamoun in running for office again. Complicating their stance were the attitude of the Maronite Patriarch and the Maronite chief of the army; both held important roles within the Maronite community. The Patriarch's attitude was especially important, given the church's defining role in the community's identity. The Patriarch at this point was Boulos Boutros Meouchi, a relative of Chamoun's enemy Bishara al-Khoury and one of al-Khoury's strongest supporters. Not surprisingly, he personally opposed Chamoun.[85]

Meouchi did genuinely identify with those Maronites who believed that the only permanent safeguard for an independent Lebanon was an explicit consensus with the Muslim elements there. He also believed that it was in Lebanon's best interests to maintain good relations with the Arab world. On 13 February 1958, for instance, he stated that 'the Maronite community was Arab before the advent of Islam, and will always remain faithful to Arab Nationalism'.[86] Not only was the church still a powerful force in Maronite popular thinking; Meouchi also had a very powerful personality. Using his authority, he assured his flock that closer links with the Arab and Islamic world would not threaten the integrity of the Maronite Church. In a sense, he was trying to step outside his role as a 'Christian religious chief' to intervene in politics to promote closer links with Muslim/Arab leaders.[87]

Thus, Meouchi's intervention in the spring of 1958 is worth examining in some detail to assess its impact on Maronite thinking. On 30 May, for example, Meouchi gave a press conference at his residence, in Bkirki. Asked whether he believed that the opposition leaders were acting in good faith, he replied, 'Without the slightest doubt they are intelligent men who know well that to sacrifice the Lebanon would be against their own interests. Their aim is simply to rid the Lebanon of the ruffians who govern it'. Another sensitive question was whether he approved of the Lebanese government's complaint, filed with the UN Security Council, against the United Arab Republic.

In his response, he cautioned against washing 'our dirty linen in public', and continued, 'The crisis is internal and no other country is involved. We do not want the Lebanon to be a slave to anyone. It should co-operate with all countries, especially its neighbours and brethren.'[88] Thus he believed that the opposition contained worthy men who aimed to serve their country both by ridding it of a bad government, and working towards good relations with her neighbours, but he felt they had no intention of supporting a union with the United Arab Republic.

This leaves open the question of how Meouchi developed his ideas, which were demonstrably out of step with majority opinion in the Maronite community. Bustani has suggested that the Holy See, in Rome, may have inspired the Patriarch's policy; aware that an isolationist policy could endanger the Christian communities in Lebanon, it may have suggested Meouchi's conciliatory line. Bustani's reasoning was based on the fact that the Patriarch was appointed by Rome and at that time may have been particularly dependent on Rome.[89] Some support for this view is contained in an April 1958 telegram to the Foreign Office containing Tufic Suwaida's views on the subject. Suwaida also expressed concern at Meouchi's attitude, and suggested that he was receiving misguided support from the Vatican. Alternatively, he reasoned, the Vatican was being culpably weak in its handling of the Patriarch.[90]

The reality was rather more complicated than either Bustani or Suwaida suggests. We must remember that while the Maronite Patriarch is appointed by Rome, it has long been a special relationship.[91] At this point, apparently, Meouchi was in conflict with the Vatican rather than being controlled by it, as the Vatican stressed good relations with its congregations over the benefits of international diplomacy. Certainly some European diplomats were aware of a cold war between the papal nuncio and the Patriarch, with the nuncio reporting back to Rome on what he termed the 'unsatisfactory' nature of Meouchi's behaviour, which seemed to mean his anti-Western and pro-Nasserist stance. Thus the Vatican was aware that the Patriarch was playing a 'dangerous' role in Lebanese politics, but was limited in its power to do anything effective.[92] In 1958 the British embassy in Beirut commented that Meouchi 'has been an absolute headache to the Vatican for many months'.[93] This all seems to indicate that the Vatican cannot be held responsible for Meouchi's stand and turns the focus back onto Lebanon itself: the interplay of personalities there, and the impact that had on popular reactions.[94]

The Maronite masses reacted to Meouchi's position on Nasserism and Arab nationalism with hostility and incomprehension. In a November 1957 editorial, *al-Hayat* commented on Meouchi's complaint that his own clergy was 'rebell[ing] against him', including his clash with the Archbishop of Byblos, Yussuf Akl, because of 'his political stance' in relation to Nasser.[95] This hostility grew after February 1958, when Meouchi sent personal representatives to Nasser to congratulate him on the birth of the United Arab Republic and his election as its president. A March 1958 editorial by Adli al-Hajj, in *an-Nahar*, attacked the Patriarch and accused him of failing to follow the edicts of the Gospel in seeking to conciliate the Arab world. Soon the Maronite community was calling him 'Muhammad al-Meouchi' and openly venting resentment.[96]

These comments indicate just how unwilling the Maronite masses were to seek consensus with the Lebanese Muslims, in line with the National Pact. The Patriarch was the head of the church, but even he could not command their obedience to an approach that seemed to contradict everything the Maronites thought they stood for. The Maronite accusations against him focused on his being pro-Muslim. Father Antoine Qurtbawi, a Maronite priest, wrote an article for a Maronite periodical that likely had close connections with Chamoun; Qubain sees it as a response to Meouchi's delegation to Nasser. Father Antoine reminded the world that 'Lebanon is not Arab, but is the Lebanon: a Mediterranean country whose language is Arabic'.[97]

But Nasser's speech of 2 March in Damascus, which the Maronite press interpreted as indicating a desire to incorporate Lebanon into the UAR, triggered considerable fear among Maronite readers.[98] The same day, Pierre Gemayel wrote an open letter to the Patriarch asking him to explain Nasser's speech and justify his claim that the wider Arab world presented no threat to the integrity of the Maronite community or church. In his letter, which sums up the basis of the fear, Gemayel stressed that Lebanon had been subjected to intense propaganda by forces asking the Lebanese to join their nations. Gemayel asked the Patriarch 'to put an end to the equivocation (caused by his pro-opposition position) from which only the enemies of Lebanon stood to gain'.[99]

In response, Meouchi sought to alleviate these fears, but also to maintain good relations with Sunni community leaders. He replied to Gemayel on 4 March 1958, insisting that his words were intended 'for Sunni as well as Maronite consideration', He wrote,

> To our Arab brethren, wherever they may be, we say that whatever is for the good of Lebanon is also for the good of the Arabs.[100]

He went on to claim that 'The independence of Lebanon has to be preserved and strengthened', and invoked 'profound love' as he said, 'Let us not reconcile ourselves to any unity or union which accepts anything that may weaken the sovereignty and independence of Lebanon'.[101] Then, on 9 March he sought to reassure the Maronite community:

> My dear sons, I have a letter from President Gamal Abd al-Nasser, the President of the United Arab Republic and an old friend of Lebanon saying that Lebanon as it stands at present is a structure with complete sovereignty and independence and these will not be threatened.[102]

Meouchi's efforts had the opposite effect of what he intended, to judge by the popular reaction within the Maronite community. For instance, many people believed Saeb Salam's widely reported claim on 10 April 1958 that the Muslim opposition had 'made a pact with the Patriarch against Chamoun'.[103] The popular resentment this stirred up further increased popular support for Chamoun. On 11 March 1958, two days after Meouchi had attacked the corruption of Chamoun and his regime, and the day after Salam's declaration about the Patriarch, Chamoun attended mass at Antelias. This was the seat of the Armenian Patriarchate, and Chamoun had come to congratulate the new Armenian Patriarch on his election. But, according to *an-Nahar*, Chamoun was 'welcomed by huge crowds' from all over Mount Lebanon. In other words, Maronites had turned out to attend a ceremony at a rival religious centre to demonstrate opposition to their own Patriarch and support for Chamoun. *An-Nahar* used its editorial columns to describe the wide public support for Chamoun, and corresponding hostility to Meouchi, while pleading with Meouchi to change his stance on these issues.[104]

These developments distanced the Patriarch from the rest of the Maronite church. Rather than use the pulpit to persuade congregations to follow Meouchi's views, his clergy began preaching sermons that were implicitly hostile to him. At his press conference in May 1958, he was asked if the bishops had indeed broken with him. His answer was 'a few', but he attempted to defuse this by claiming that 'they are in the pay of the Government'.[105]

Whatever the truth of his claims, the Maronite bishops were clearly under some public pressure to cut their ties with Meouchi. Editorial comments on the press conference also emphasise how much he was alienated within the church, and comment satirically on his refusal to modify his stance.[106] Whatever the majority of Maronite clerics may have felt personally about Meouchi's statements on Chamoun and on maintaining a friendly attitude towards the Arab world, we can reasonably infer that they were not prepared to risk their hold over their congregations by supporting their Patriarch on an issue where popular feeling was so demonstrably against him. It is also worth noting that by the 1950s the majority of parish priests came from the lower levels of the population, not the elites.

The popular Maronite refusal to compromise in 1958 was undoubtedly heightened by the popular, if unfounded, Lebanese belief that the Western powers were willing to repeat old patterns and take action to support Chamoun's re-election if the tension rose high enough. Some leaders of the Maronite community, such as the Eddé brothers, feared that Chamoun's re-election and/or any Western intervention would destabilise Lebanon itself. The evidence is that overall Maronites were more worried about an external Arab threat. They saw the UAR encouraging the Muslim opposition to be uncooperative towards Chamoun and thus toward their own community, for reasons of UAR policy and ambition. In other words these loyalists saw the possibility of Western intervention against the background of an already existing hostile, external intervention.

Chamoun and his closest supporters did their best to foster this popular perception that an intervention was likely. On 13 May, Charles Malik spoke at a press conference in Beirut, openly accusing the UAR of intervening in Lebanon, and thus causing Lebanon's problems. This was the first public statement to claim an intervention and it was well-received by the Maronite masses. Malik insisted that because of this intervention, Lebanon must abandon any policy of conciliation towards the UAR. He listed various incidents to support his thesis of UAR interference, calling them 'only the latest manifestations of a concealed movement that has been going on for months and indeed for years, designed to undermine and destroy Lebanon as a free, independent and sovereign state and bring about a radical modification in her fundamental orientation'.[107]

Malik's points were reinforced at a press conference on 4 June by Pierre Gemayel, the Kata'ib leader. Gemayel argued that the tensions of 1958 were not internal in origin, but dated back to November 1956, when, he said, Lebanese opposition leaders had taken up the Nasserist option and invited Nasser's intervention, regardless of the Lebanese nation's legitimate interests, its independence and sovereignty. In other words, he argued, the opposition's electoral battle had been and was still being waged under Nasser's banner. Underlying Gemayel's statement was his belief that the Lebanese were unwilling to fight fellow Lebanese. He explained the recent violent incidents as armed UAR interventions, not as expressions of internal dissent. Ending this intervention, he said, would lead to a prompt reconciliation between the divergent Lebanese elements.[108] All this helped to reinforce the Maronite perspective of an external intervention that was hostile to them and Lebanon.

These beliefs were undeniably popular among some Maronites. Those who supported an extension of Chamoun's mandate were attracted to the theory that Lebanon's troubles were generated externally and not internally. The Kata'ib Party strongly supported this theory, and it gained an audience amongst the Maronite masses as a whole, especially after speeches like that of Sami al-Solh, on 17 May 1958. He spoke in alarmist terms about attacks on frontier posts, etc, as evidence of UAR interference and incitement to revolt.[109] This does not indicate, however, that the Maronite masses universally shared the loyalist opinion on the best solution to the problem. Gemayel's views also found a sympathetic echo among the Western powers; certainly the US embassy generally supported his analysis of causes behind the crisis. Even so, it cautioned that he should have placed more emphasis on the role of local politicians' ambitions.[110]

A few incidents justifiably reinforced the loyalists' perspective, including some deliberate physical intervention by Syria and Egypt. We must take seriously the evidence from contemporary newspapers and diplomatic archives for the UAR supplying arms and men to participate in demonstrations in

Lebanon.[111] Also heightening tensions was the Maronite reaction to media reports of Sunni feelings. What the media identified as popular Sunni resentment of Maronite pro-Western attitudes expressed itself in accusations of Maronite insensitivity to pan-Arab aspirations in the interest of total submission to the West.[112] But the Maronites generally did not understand Sunni fears about becoming alienated from the Arab world if the Maronite policies were continued. Instead the Maronite masses generally understood Sunni sentiments as confirming Sunni involvement with what the Maronites accepted as UAR ambitions to absorb Lebanon. Thus to a considerable degree, the Maronites' paranoia was based on their not understanding why the Sunni community was upset, and why they might take action to reduce the reasons for their discontent.

From simple misunderstanding, the Maronites moved to a feeling of being under siege, exacerbated by their fear of an enemy within the walls.[113] We must remember that fear of being ruled from outside was always a sensitive issue for the Maronite community.[114] Nor did the Maronite attitudes react uniformly, especially as the crisis intensified. As the crisis proceeded, however, the popular Maronite attitude towards Chamoun's re-election became more uniformly positive out of a spirit of sheer defensiveness, as Maronite paranoia in 1958 was heightened by the comments of the Sunni prime minister, Sami al-Solh. His words seemed to reinforce their perspective that the UAR presented a threat. Undoubtedly the loyalists took him more seriously because of his Sunni background, which seemed to give him extra credibility.

Through radio broadcasts and newspaper articles, al-Solh tried vigorously to inform the Lebanese people of his belief that the UAR was intervening in Lebanon.[115] He seems to have intended to create a broad consensus in Lebanon as a whole, generally supporting the government and Chamoun's cause, by raising fears about the collapse of Lebanese independence. For example, in his broadcast of 5 June, he raised the spectre of foreign-inspired opposition leaders who falsely claimed that the Lebanese people wanted Lebanese policy to be 'evolved on the banks of the Barada [i.e. Damascus] or the Nile [Cairo].'[116]

But al-Solh's words undoubtedly reinforced the already existing alarm amongst the majority of Maronites,[117] who were increasingly convinced of the reality and the dangers of foreign intervention in Lebanon. Still, we must be cautious here. I found no evidence that the logical corollary to all this agitation was for all of the Maronite community to support Chamoun's re-election.

To sum up, the attempts to inspire alarm succeeded amongst the Maronites. Fear that the UAR would annex Lebanon, whether real or imaginary, did inspire some elements in the Maronite community to support Chamoun's re-election as part of a defensive reaction, something they otherwise would not have done. But this reaction was not universal. Even at the end of May 1958 the alarmist words of men like Gemayel and al-Solh did not convince loyal followers of Bishara al-Khoury or the Patriarch that there was a real threat. If they accepted the reality of the intervention, they interpreted it as being provoked by Chamoun's policies. The solution to the crisis, therefore, was Chamoun's retirement, not his re-election.

Reasons for the Crisis

By the summer of 1958, several prominent Maronite leaders, including the Patriarch, believing in the compromise encapsulated in the National Pact, were convinced that the heart of the crisis was Chamoun and his policies, not inter-community relations. These men sought to convince not only their own followers but also the majority of Maronites that Chamoun was destroying the National Pact and thereby dragging Lebanon down a path leading to the kind of confessional conflict that had marked the darkest periods in Lebanon's history.[118] They used opportunities for speeches in both the press and the pulpit to stress that immediately removing Chamoun was key to restoring peace in Lebanon.

Papers like *an-Nahar* carried articles arguing that by turning to the West and seeking its active intervention, Chamoun and his supporters unacceptably endangered the current, compromise-based political system.[119] Indeed even before the Patriarch had made his public statement, pro-Patriarch elements in the Lebanese press had come out against the Chamoun policy which saw the possibility of Western intervention as desirable. One said, 'It is about time that the USA and Britain stopped smearing Lebanon's reputation by movement of planes and ships and by the misrepresentations they spread about military movements'.[120]

On 19 May, in his column in *L'Orient*, René Aggiouri added another fear for those Maronites who did not support a Western intervention despite the 'reality' of the UAR one. The idea of such an intervention must be dispelled, he argued, because of what it implied: the American and British governments could be planning to use the Lebanese situation as a pretext for military action that could involve the entire Middle East.[121]

It is significant that Aggiouri wrote for *L'Orient,* whose publisher was Georges Naccache, a prominent member of the Third Force. *L'Orient* also published the comments of journalist Charles Helou, another Third Force member, calling for international recognition and guarantees of Lebanon's neutrality, in a conscious imitation of Switzerland's position, a stance that aimed to prevent either Western or UAR intervention.[122] Given such comments in the press, we must see the anti-Chamoun reactions amongst some Maronites as reflecting their unease that Chamoun's manoeuvrings were endangering the fundamental compromise in Lebanese politics. For instance, I believe that Aggiouri's main aim in his statement was to defuse what he saw as the unthinkingly extreme reaction of Chamoun loyalists to their fear of an Arab threat to Lebanon's stability. Thus, to reduce loyalist support for a policy that could destroy the compromise and thus Lebanon itself, Aggiouri sought to show how little Lebanon mattered to the US, for example, in its dealings with the Middle East as a whole.

Other evidence, however, including further comment in papers such as *an-Nahar,* indicates that these anti-Chamoun reactions found little popular following. Essentially appeals on behalf of the National Pact, these comments did little to shift the fears of large numbers in the community. *Al-Amal,* a voice for the Kata'ib Party, continued to advocate for active Western intervention to secure Chamoun's re-election, although Gemayel was still not willing to formally endorse such a policy.[123] *Al-Amal* argued that anything was better than Nasser, showing now deeply the paper's readers believed in the potential of a Nasserist intervention.[124] In terms of its impact on the Maronite community, therefore, when we consider the UN intervention in the summer of 1958 we must remember how deeply that community was divided over Chamoun's policy of invoking the West.

The UN intervention occurred as tensions heightened in Lebanon after the murder of Nassib al-Matni.[125] Initially Chamoun had sought to use the street violence occurring after the murder to invoke US military intervention, but UN intervention had been agreed on instead.[126] To assess the perspective of the Maronite masses on the intervention, it is useful to consider their reactions, indicated through the press. Maronites generally supported the concept of the intervention even though the alternative was intervention by the Arab League.[127] Significantly, the Maronites did not criticise the government for rejecting the Arab League intervention, which would have been in the tradition of compromise in the National Pact.[128]

Many Maronites, even those who did not support Chamoun's current policies, expected that the UN Observer Group in Lebanon (UNOGIL) would endorse Chamoun's claims, because the UN was popularly seen as a Western body that would naturally favour the Maronite community.[129] One presidential heir-apparent, Selim Lahoud, publicly described the United Nations' action as 'good and reasonable'.[130] Another would-be, if less likely, presidential candidate – Jawad Boulos – declared that the UN intervention was a 'good omen' for the future.[131] Opposition Maronite elements were rather more gloomy, expecting a predictably pro-Chamoun result.[132] Adel Osseiran, speaker of the Chamber of Deputies, told an American embassy employee that when UN observers arrived, the splits between the government and the opposition and between Lebanon and the UAR would be increased.[133]

When the Maronite community realised that it was mistaken to believe in a UNOGIL report endorsing claims of UAR intervention, an acute popular reaction occurred, leaving a permanent change in Lebanese opinions and alliances. At the end of June 1958, the first hints appeared that the UNOGIL report would not be to the government's liking, and the pro-Chamoun press began to attack the observers.[134] These attacks peaked with the issue of the first report on 3 July 1958. The headline in *al-Amal* read 'Observers Failed Their Mission'.[135] The headline in the pro-Chamoun *al-Ahrar* read, 'Observers Unable to Discover Infiltration Because Barred from Insurgent Controlled Areas.'[136] *An-Nahar*, *al-Amal* and *al-Ahrar* all quoted Lebanese government officials as being 'bitter' and 'worried' about the outcome.[137] The UNOGIL assessment of no massive infiltration from Syria created a panic in the Maronite community; it related as much to the 'betrayal' of Maronite expectations of Western support in times of need as to the actual content of the report.[138]

In summing up the report to consider its impact on Maronite opinion we must remember that from a Maronite perspective it did not assess the situation adequately or coherently. It claimed that the rebellion was indigenous in origin, and did not deny some UAR intervention.[139] However, it made no attempt to define the scale of the intervention – which was the main point of controversy within Lebanon itself. Thus the questions that had dominated Lebanon before the United Nations' involvement still remained: could radio and press attacks against the Lebanese government count as intervention? Was the quantity of arms smuggled into Lebanese territory enough to prove a physical UAR intervention? Many Maronites insisted they could and did, thereby justifying the generation of more fear, tension and resentment in the Maronite community, and therefore its defensive reaction.

Thus, Maronite disappointment with the UNOGIL's conclusions was acute enough to make their position even more extreme.[140] The community now felt a vulnerability that was broadly destabilising. Even those who did not support Chamoun shared the general alarm that, according to the report, the community was losing ground both internally and internationally.[141] This was particularly significant given the traditional Maronite belief that the West represented the only final security they could depend on. If that failed, what other hope had they? This alarm made people more willing to listen to figures like Chamoun and Charles Malik when they claimed that the only solution lay in a military intervention by the Americans, as if to demonstrate that the US was still committed to the Maronite cause, if the UN was not.[142]

Many Maronites felt that the compromise underpinning the National Pact would be destroyed if the Sunni opposition, supported by the UN, could impose its interpretation of events, since the Arab world would also line up behind the Muslim community. Externally, the community felt deserted and isolated as never before. In its vulnerability it was undoubtedly more willing to seek a Maronite unity in the face of an external threat that seemed worse than the possibility of Chamoun's re-election. Or, at least, it made that possibility less immediate, capable of being deferred until later.

Popular attitudes shifted significantly after the UN report was published, even if the cause was the popular fears outlined above more than intrinsic support for Chamoun and his policies. Many believed that Chamoun was still trying to involve the West in order to secure his re-election, but many Maronites who had previously opposed intervention were now prepared to welcome a demonstration of pro-Maronite Western feeling. Thus it was significant that the loyalist Kata'ib Party added still more members at this stage, because of its role as an indicator of mass Maronite opinions.[143] It can be said to have represented the hard-line core of Maronite feeling in the community.[144] In late 1954 Kata'ib members had numbered around 26,000; by July 1958, according to *L'Orient,* this number had risen to 62,200, making it the largest political party in Lebanon.[145] Indeed, Kata'ib numbers had been growing even before the report, inspired by events like the destruction of Lebanese flags during Muslim demonstrations in Tyre and Tripoli, which gave popular colour to the rhetoric of UAR intervention.[146]

Even so, we cannot claim that attitude was universal amongst Maronites at this stage, though tension was increasing in Lebanon and Maronites were feeling more isolated in and out of the country. Most of the tension was generated internally, and the community interpreted external factors to fit in with these internal explanations. During the summer of 1958, Chamoun continued to tell the West that the conflict in Lebanon was part of the wider problem of the Middle East. He described it as a struggle between a pro-Western Lebanon and an external radical Arab nationalism, allied with Communism and with dissident Muslim elements in Lebanon aiming to stage a takeover. He realised he did not have enough support within the Maronite community, let alone with other Lebanese, to secure his re-election by straightforward means; nothing he did seemed to increase his support internally. So, to continue in office he would need active intervention by the West: essentially, the Americans. Chamoun was clearly insecure; he sent his wife's jewels and his grandson out of the country in July 1958.[147]

Reports like this certainly increased tension within the Maronite community. However, despite the Maronite tendency to paranoia caused by the West's apparent desertion, indicated in the UNOGIL report, prominent Maronite figures such as General Shihab and the Patriarch continued to oppose Chamoun – with community support. This ensured that some important, if fewer, Maronite elements continued to see Chamoun as the cause of, not the solution to, the crisis. Shihab consistently maintained that Chamoun could best settle the crisis, openly stating that he would retire from the presidency at the end of his term of office.[148] There is no indication of any widespread dissatisfaction with this position among the Maronite elements within the armed forces.[149] Equally, the Patriarch continued to draw support from elements within the Maronite community, in and outside Lebanon, even if he did not have all the officials of his church solidly behind his position.[150]

In negotiating with the Western powers to intervene, Chamoun had done his best. He succeeded somewhat in alarming these powers into a sense of crisis relating to the internal situation of Lebanon, and Lebanon's position within the Middle East as a whole, hoping to convince them to overlook or misinterpret any lack of internal enthusiasm for his re-election.[151] But the Western powers also had access to the opinions of men like the Meouchi and Shihab.[152] The UNOGIL report also strengthened Western belief that military intervention in Lebanon would be counterproductive, both for Lebanon and the Western position in the Middle East.[153] Thus it cannot be argued that

Maronite alarm actually galvanised the West into interventionist action, or that Western alarms created an atmosphere of universal Maronite hysteria even in the days immediately after the UNOGIL report was released.

But then, on 15 July 1958, US Marines landed on the beaches of Beirut, to the surprise of most Maronites. Lebanese reaction to this American intervention was mixed. Most Maronites apparently greeted it with initial enthusiasm, if only because it showed that the Americans did support Lebanon, while the revolution in Iraq had increased popular fears (perhaps with some basis) that Nasser aimed to take over the entire region and that he had the capacity to do so without American intervention.

In this context, the prospects looked bleak for the survival not just of Chamoun but also of any pro-Western Lebanese government that the Maronite community could support. Even if Chamoun's re-election had not been secured, up until then the Maronites had seen him as having good prospects of completing his term of office and retiring on 23 September 1958. Even people like Shihab who opposed his re-election had generally supported his completing his term, seeing that as important to maintaining the current balance in the political system.[154] But the events in Baghdad made the prospect of this seem bleak. Many feared that his government might fall before he ended his term in office, and even that he might be assassinated, making the Maronite community deeply vulnerable to Muslim and pan-Arab ambitions.[155]

It was these fears that caused Maronites to fire bullets for joy in the streets of Beirut just after the Americans landed. Even if these expressions of support were mainly confined to Chamoun loyalists, no Maronites expressed serious hostility to the loyalists who were showing pleasure in this way.[156] True, the majority of Maronite political leaders remained silent immediately after the landings, the only exceptions being government spokesmen. This was partly a matter of political astuteness among men who feared creating resentment and hostility amongst the Muslim community that could result in open civil war if they openly expressed support for the landings. But despite the pressure of the Iraqi coup, those Maronite politicians who were not Chamoun loyalists were equivocal about the landings.[157]

On the one hand they hoped that the American presence would allow the general election to be held at the appropriate time, and would also help safeguard the Maronite role in the political system; on the other hand they were aware of the growing hostility voiced by Sunni politicians.[158] Essentially, these men were aware that they depended on Muslim support within the current Lebanese political formula, and they had no wish to change that formula.

It is instructive to contrast the moderation Selim Lahoud displayed at this point with the belligerent mood of Pierre Gemayel. Gemayel and his followers in the Kata'ib Party were Chamoun loyalists, and supported the American presence unquestioningly, stating that the actions of the Muslim opposition had obliged them to take this position.[159] Lahoud had come out in support of Chamoun's re-election but now, with presidential hopes of his own, he felt able to seek moderate Maronite backing for a personal position based on compromise.[160] This underlines the fact that many Maronites still saw the Kata'ib Party and its position of support for Chamoun's re-election as being too extremist to gain universal support, even in this time of crisis. Yet increasingly, even the Chamoun loyalists, who favoured his re-election, came to see the American landings as obstacles to any resolution of Lebanon's internal crisis. They began to join with the opposition to seek a withdrawal of the troops as a preliminary to arranging a compromise that would safeguard the Lebanese compromise and the Maronite role in the Lebanese state.[161]

From the perspective of the Maronite masses, however, the solution was not so straightforward. In the tense atmosphere of late July 1958, simply removing the troops and arranging a compromise looked like it might endanger, rather than protect, the Maronites' privileged role in the state. In addition, some feared that such a compromise might depend on the Maronites breaking their relations with the West, which would of course have profound economic as well as cultural implications. It must be remembered that Nasser continued to have an impact on Maronite thinking, as he personified the Maronite nightmare of Arab intervention in Lebanon's affairs. Thus it was Nasser, not Chamoun, who got the popular blame for the crisis. As Moubarak commented, the troubles that had occurred in some cities like Tripoli and Beirut were not only caused by the proposal to re-elect President Chamoun but were also provoked by Nasser's agents.[162]

Throughout the crisis, the press had evoked memories of past massacres of Maronites at the hands of 'Muslim oppressors' and the need to resist foreign domination if the community was to survive. These ideas first crept into public rhetoric as early as 1956, when Pierre Gemayel argued for the need to value 'our relations with France', because France had 'helped to free us from Ottoman oppression and made us part of the civilised world'. Later that year, against a background of some local Sunni unrest and the imposition of newspaper censorship, Ghassan Tueni justified government policy and exhorted Maronites to 'Remember 1840, 1848, 1860, 1936'.[163] By 1958, the invocation of this dark mythology had become more frequent and sometimes more cryptic or implicit, as if there was no need to explain such references in detail.

Indeed, reference to this 'history' was not restricted to the Maronites, further indicating how widespread this perception was. On 17 May 1958, Nadim al-Jisr said that the reasons for the Maronite tension 'are the reasons of 1860', explaining that 'once again, the Christian minority refused to live accordingly'.[164] Shortly afterwards, during a press conference, Ghassan Tueni described 'this week' as 'the most dangerous for Lebanon since 1860', saying that 'neither World War I nor World War II had been as dangerous'. In justifying his stance, he referred explicitly to the 'past Maronite-Druze massacres in Lebanese history', hoping that 'these would not be repeated' and a 'solution' would be found.[165] Pierre Gemayel used more inflammatory rhetoric, linking the events of 1860 and other crises during the Ottoman period to the choice that 'Christians' in 1958 again had to make between 'liberty and slavery'.[166]

Such statements did not create a popular mood that favoured consensus; rather they urged a return to the old habits of co-habitation and mutual suspicion. After all, the Maronite masses themselves had never been consulted on the National Pact and its terms. As long as the pact had seemed to work in Maronite interests, most had accepted it. But many amongst the masses interpreted the events of May, June and July 1958 as signs that the Muslims were seeking to reassert their old domination, which would lead to Lebanon disappearing in any meaningful sense. For the Maronite masses to willingly support a restoration of the National Pact, they needed some real demonstration that it was not a disguised Sunni triumph. As the Muslim population reacted with joy to the Iraqi coup, they seemed to expect such a triumph.[167] Thus, even if many Maronite politicians had a more sophisticated view of events and saw the potential for a return to consensus, a majority of Maronites was increasingly exposed to rhetoric that linked fears of Arab intervention in its affairs to experiences in its past that had supposedly threatened its very existence.

Not surprisingly, then, many came to believe that they were protected only by Chamoun's hard-line stance and the presence of American troops.

Despite the UNOGIL report, they felt, the West was still prepared to protect Maronite interests. For instance, on 18 July Pierre Gemayel spoke to his followers, stating his 'unquestioning support of the US presence' because 'the actions of the Muslim opposition and their friends had obliged them to take this position.'[168] *Al-Hayat* also referred to 'popular panic' in discussing how the general Maronite community and the political establishment diverged in their understanding of the Iraqi coup's implications.[169]

The upsurge in popular support for the Kata'ib Party, representing unwavering support for Chamoun and the American landings, continued at the end of July. This encouraged Chamoun to believe that he could at least complete his mandate, however remote the prospect of re-election. However, the Maronite leaders – except for a small core including Gemayel – now saw compromise, rather than violence, as a first step in solving the crisis by removing both Chamoun and the American troops. They now found themselves effectively out of step with probably the majority of the Maronite masses.[170] Leaders such as Farid Kozma appealed for a return to consensus and urged the community to downplay historical mythologies: 'Let us not remember the dark past except to learn a lesson and so work together in unity, instead of being tied up in fear'.[171] But the 'dark past' did not go away, either in popular memory or in the rhetoric of leaders, as Bashir Gemayel's comment of 1975 indicates.

Even so, the tension lessened. Starting in late July, popular Maronite perceptions changed, beginning amongst the Lebanese army, including its Maronite elements, and encouraged by Maronite political leaders and the interested Western powers. The army's reaction to the American landings had been hostile from the start; on a few occasions the two armies had been on the verge of clashing physically. The Lebanese army was deployed to resist any attempt by American forces to enter Beirut itself, and only the efforts of McClintock and Shihab prevented a direct clash.[172] Shihab himself had been against the landings, which he saw as having the potential to split the army and so lead to a full-scale civil war, and then to the nation's complete disintegration. Involving the army, Shihab felt, would risk its collapse along confessional lines. The general preferred to leave the police and the *gendarmerie* to tackle these internal problems.[173]

By the summer of 1958, Shihab had a high, if not necessarily popular, profile in Lebanon. He was extremely popular with his troops, and he commanded respect, if not popular liking, for his determination to keep the army out of

Demonstration held during the 1968 election campaign. Note the placards bearing portraits of the three Maronite leaders of the so-called 'Helf Coalition': Eddé, Chamoun and Gemayel.

intercommunal and political disputes.[174] From quite early on in the crisis he had been one figure suggested as a possible alternative to Chamoun, though he had been reluctant to consider it.[175] The Maronite masses, however, were not especially eager to see Shihab replace Chamoun immediately after the American landings, given that since May Shihab had consistently refused to commit the army to support Chamoun. During June and July, elements in the pro-Chamoun camp, including Kata'ib Party members, had been demanding that the army actively intervene to deal with Lebanon's 'enemies' in the interests of state security.[176] True, the army had undertaken some limited action, such as that in Sidon on 28 May 1958 against pro-UAR demonstrators, on the few occasions when state security did seem threatened.[177] Indeed, since Shihab was known to personally dislike Chamoun, some saw the suggestion that Shihab should replace him as 'evidence' that Shihab had been plotting and manoeuvring for political power for himself.[178]

Meeting at the Bloc National party headquarters following the 1968 victory of the Helf Coalition. On the wall are photos of Raymond Eddé and MP for Kisrawan Nohad Boueiz.

However, by 30 July, even Chamoun had accepted the American view that Shihab should succeed him. But Chamoun still intended to complete his mandate, and Shihab refused to confirm he was willing to stand. McClintock reports that Chamoun told the loyalist deputies that they would have to 'accept his advice, meet tomorrow and elect Shihab', or he would resign.[179] But what was popularly seen as Shihab's 'indecision' and 'inactivity', including his refusal to confirm his position on the presidency, helped to sustain Chamoun's mass appeal and popular Maronite support for him to complete his mandate. Thus, in the end, the Maronites acquiesced to the arrangement that Chamoun effectively be sidelined for the remainder of his mandate and be replaced by Shihab, simply because Chamoun himself acquiesced. With the Americans refusing to support any other solution, Chamoun had no practical choice in the matter.

But for the Maronite community, the return to the consensus arrangements

Celebrating the landslide victory of 1968; from second left: Ghassan Tueni, MP for Byblos Gaby Germanos and Raymond Eddé. Second from right is Samia Shami, Tueni's assistant.

of the National Pact was simply a cover for them to hold perspectives based on the old patterns of co-habitation. The majority did now accept that Shihab would safeguard the community's traditional pro-Western stance, but they still saw no problem in continuing such links, and accepted none of the shame that the Arab world assigned to them. To abandon them would imply abandoning the mythology that lay at the heart of their feeling of national identity, and their claim to be, morally at least, the most significant of the confessional communities in Lebanon. This perspective ensured that they would remain suspicious of those in Lebanon – including some in the Sunni community and many Sunni political leaders, but also leaders like Walid Jumblat – who tried persuading them to modify this mythology.

Thus, the events of 1958 did not alter Maronite community mythology in any fundamental way.[180] The National Pact was restored with support from Maronite politicians, but many amongst the masses remained suspicious of that compromise, as their political perspective was still dominated by confessional and clan considerations. This is indicated by the extent to which Chamoun maintained his own status as a symbol of '*le Libanisme*', and his personality was invoked in later crises. In 1968, for instance, when Maronites again believed that Nasser was interfering with Lebanese internal politics over the status of the Palestinians, Chamoun enjoyed a surge in popularity. An attempt by the security police to curtail his public appearances indicates how much public support he could still invoke. News of this attempt spread within an hour, and Maronites from the Mount Lebanon region and some from the North converged on Jounieh, where Chamoun was appearing. In my own memory it looked like the whole mountain had come to demonstrate support. In the elections of 1968, the Maronite candidates he backed swept to victory with the majority of contested seats.

Notes

1.   Selim Abou, *L'Identité Culturelle. Relations Inter-ethniques et Problèmes d'Acculturation*, Editions Anthropos, Paris, 1981, p. 160, highlights the links between concepts of nationalism and 'collective popular myths' evolving around the 'notion of sovereignty.

2.   *L'Orient*, 16 March 1958.

3.   In the introduction, I mentioned the extent to which the Lebanese press reflected popular opinion. See also *Foreign Relations of the United States, 1958–1960*, Vol. XI, Lebanon and Jordan, Department of State Publication 9932, Washington DC, 1992, pp. 196–7.

4.   For a discussion of 'le Libanisme', see 'Le Libanisme, Une Doctrine', *Action*, December 1956, pp. 11134–9. This doctrine was particularly associated with the Kata'ib Party, the largest and best organised of the political groups in Lebanon, which took '*le Libanisme*' as its central ideology.

5.   K. S. Salibi, 'Recollections of the 1940s and 1950s', unpublished conference paper, Austin, Texas, 13 September 1992, pp. 14; 15; 17. At the time Salibi, and his students at AUB, saw Chamoun as 'the national hero', who had gotten away with 'defiance of Nasser', and in so doing, 'saved' Lebanon.

6.   Anis Moussallem, *La Presse Libanaise: Expression du Liban Politique et Confessionelle et Forum des pays Arabes*, Libraire Générale de Droit et de Jurisprudence, Paris, 1977 pp. 1–16; Desmond Stewart, *Turmoil in Beirut: A Personal Account*, Allan Wingate, London, 1958, p. 20. Stewart states 'that in Lebanon even the uneducated followed each [radio] news bulletin with close attention.'

7.   Jean Hayek, *al-Tarikh al-Ilmi, al-Jizq al-Awwal*, Maktabit Habib, Beirut, 1994.

8.   Hilal Khashan, *Inside the Lebanese Confessional Mind*, University Press of America, 1992, p. 11, quoting Bulus Naaman, a former head of the Federation of Lebanese Monks who was a leading figure in the 1975–85 years. Naaman states, 'Lebanon is synonymous with Maronite history and ethos: Maronitism antedates the Arab conquest of Syria and Lebanon and Arabism is only a historical accident'. He describes the Maronites as the owners of their history 'because they are attached to their land'.

9. See Khashan, p. 11, quoting Ibrahim Najjar, a member of the Phalange Party political bureau who was explicit about this: 'in order for the two civilizations to meet, we want the Muslims to concede the superiority of the Christians'.

10. Amine Gemayel, *Peace and Unity*, Colin Smythe Ltd, Gerrards Cross, 1984, p. 18. This gives extracts from his speech of 18 October 1982 to the UN General Assembly. Grandly titled 'Give Us Peace and We Shall Again Astound the World', it touched on important themes in Maronite thought, including the ancient heritage of the Maronite community and its identification with Mount Lebanon, essentially indicating that these ideas are mutually interdependent.

11. This is not a minor point: it means that the Orthodox and Catholic communities popularly celebrate the Christian festivals of Christmas and Easter on different dates.

12. Stewart, p. 12. The people in the Maronite areas referred to France as *al-umm al-hanoun* [the nourishing mother].

13. For example, the American University of Beirut (AUB) has remained one of the leading university institutions in Lebanon, and university sector education has retained strong links with Western institutions.

14. Michael Johnson, *Class and Client in Beirut: The Sunni Moslem Community and the Lebanese State, 1940–1985*, Ithaca Press, London, 1986, p. 125.

15. The advertisements in the Maronite-oriented media of the period underline this aspect. See, for example, French-language publications like *L'Orient*, but also Arabic language ones such as *an-Nahar*. For comments on commodity culture see Thomas Richards, *The Commodity Culture of Victorian England, Advertising and Spectacle 1851–1914*, Verso, London, 1991, pp. 1–3, 10. 128, 140.

16. Max Weber, *The Sociology of Religion*, Methuen, London, 1965, chapter 8.

17. There was considerable intermarriage at elite levels between the Maronite landowning and commercial classes, creating kinship alliances at the least.

18. Johnson, p. 99.

19. Arnold Hottinger, 'Zuama in Historical Perspective', in L. Binder, ed., *Politics in Lebanon*, John Wiley & Co., New York, 1966, pp. 98–100.

20. Not all members of the Kata'ib Party were Maronite Christians. Joseph Chader, an Armenian Christian, elected to the Chamber in 1951, was a Kata'ib member and its parliamentary spokesman. See K. S. Salibi, *Modern History of Lebanon*, pp. 193–4. Johnson comments 'the Kata'ib Party's formal organisation can be attributed to the highly political salariat it drew on'; see Johnson, p. 99.

21. John Entelis, *Pluralism and Party Transformation in Lebanon: al-Kataib 1936–1970*, E.J. Brill, Leiden, 1974, pp. 9; 44; Hazem Saghieh, *Ta'rib Hizb al-Kata'ib al-Lubnaniyah*, [The Arabization of the Lebanese Kata'ib Party] Dar al-Jadid, 1991, p. 50. See also Joseph Abou Jaoude, *Les Partis Politiques au Liban*, Bibliothèque de l'Université Saint-Esprit, Kaslik, 1985; Boutros Khawand, *al-Quwat al-Nizamiat al-Kata'ibiat*, Publication of the Kata'ib Party, Habib Eid Publishing, Beirut, 1986.

22. Entelis, p. 10.

23. *Ibid.*, p. 101.

24. *Ibid.*, p. 10; Amine Gemayel, interview, Paris, 27 March 1992.

25. *Ibid.*, pp. 101, 142–4; Gemayel, interview, 27 March 1992; Raymond Eddé, interview, Paris, 19 July 1994.

26. The Kata'ib Party was the single largest Christian party, and predominantly a Maronite one. Indeed, it was the largest single political party in Lebanon, something the party itself was very conscious of in the 1950s. 'Le Libanisme, Une Doctrine', pp. 1134–39.

27. The event in Zgortha was traditional bloody village feud between the two historically prominent families of the region, the Fangieh and the Duwaihi. The feud spilled over into the wider conflict of 1958, but actually had little do with the modern face of the Maronite community. See Johnson, p. 125; Hottinger, p. 99.

28. Several of the people I interviewed stressed this point strongly, especially Amine Gemayel, in Paris, 27 March 1992; Ghassan Tueni, in Beirut, 30 July 1992; and Sofia Saadeh, in Beirut, 2 January 1993. General Bustani also mentions this in his 'Memoirs', an unpublished typescript in my possession.

29. I do not intend to suggest that the other Christian communities in Lebanon, such as the Greek Orthodox, had not developed along similar paths. However, that community is not my focus in this chapter.

30. Hottinger, p. 99.

31. He even developed something of a power base in a locality, the Shuf; Camille Chamoun, *Crise au Moyen Orient*, Gallimard, Paris, 1963, pp. 20–30.

32. *Al-Hayat*, 4 March 1958.

33. Chamoun, p. 7, recounts how the Maronite crowd shouted to him at the end of his mandate, 23 September 1958, 'you saved Lebanon, don't abandon us'. This emphasises how such fears continued at popular levels in the Maronite community.

34. Several of the people I interviewed emphasised Chamoun's reliance on public reporting of his words. For instance, Ghassan Tueni commented on his 'advanced consciousness' of the value of the media for getting the popular ear, for instance. Tueni interview, July 1992. Also Salim Nassar, interview, London, 20 May 1995; Dr Albert Moukheiber, interview, Bayt Meiri, 15 April 1995.

35. For instance, *an-Nahar*, 11 March and 23 April 1958; *al-Hayat*, 11 March and 23 April 1958.

36. If the Maronite community commonly agreed that Nasserism was a threat, the community was clearly divided over how best to cope with it to preserve its interests by preserving Lebanon's independence. For example, in *al-Hayat*, 29 March 1957, this debate is highlighted, and the discussion refers to public opinion amongst the Maronites.

37. Gemayel interview, 27 March 1992; Entelis, p. 175.

38. Johnson, pp. 123, 125.

39. Sofia Saadeh made this point in our interview, 2 January 1993.

40. Salibi, who recalls positive feelings towards Chamoun in this period, identified 1956 as 'the height of [Chamoun's] popularity', but also identified growing disappointment with him. K. S. Salibi, 'Recollections of the 1940s and 1950s', p. 13.

41. FO371/134115, UL1012, Sir George Middleton to Selwyn Lloyd, Confidential, Beirut, 12 May 1958, p. 5. This despatch was a discussion of Lebanon's leading personalities; for further comment on Chamoun's policies and character see Johnson, p. 123,

42. *Ibid.*

43. Salibi recalls a widespread popular knowledge of Chamoun's 'pro-British leanings' and the fact that 'it was generally believed that his British friends had actually helped him come to power, so he could contribute to the promotion of their policies in the area.' K. S. Salibi, 'Recollections of the 1940s and 1950s', p. 13.

44. For instance, Chamoun's sons were educated in Britain, which was most unusual for Maronites in this period; Wade Goria, *Sovereignty and Leadership in Lebanon 1943–1976*, Ithaca Press, London, 1985, p. 37, quoting Sir Edward Spears on this point.

45. FO371/134115, UL1012, Sir George Middleton to Selwyn Lloyd, Confidential, Beirut, 12 May 1958, p. 5; Bustani, p. 213.

46. Bustani's memoirs indicate the impact this reporting had on the popular belief that the British had sought to get Chamoun elected in 1943; there is no supporting evidence but it was widely believed. Bustani, p. 213.

47. *Ibid.* There is, however, no suggestion that either the Quai d'Orsay or Downing Street tried to affect the outcome of the election.

48. *Ibid.*

49. *Ibid.* It could certainly be argued his British connections gave him a better basis understanding Arab issues than other Maronite leaders had.

50. *Ibid.*

51. See chapter four.

52. *Al-Hayat*, 18 June 1957; *Le Soir*, 15 July 1957.

53. *Al-Hayat*, 28 May and 10 June 1957.

54. *Al-Hayat*, 21 June 1957.

55. *Foreign Relations of the United States, 1958–1960*, vol. XI, p. 6, American Embassy, Beirut to Department of State, Memorandum, 17 January 1958. American concern in this respect, of course, was based on identifying the community's pro-Western orientation.

56. Gemayel, interview, 27 March 1992; he drew a clear linkage between popular perceptions of the crisis and increased party recruitment. See also Entelis, pp. 142–4.

57. *Al-Hayat*, 18 June 1957.

58. Pierre Rondot, 'The Political Institutions of Lebanese Democracy', in L. Binder, ed., *Politics in Lebanon*, John Wiley & Co., New York, 1966, p. 129.

59. This is not to say that such affiliations were not equally important in the political life of other Lebanese communities. On this point of affiliations see Michael Hudson, *The Precarious Republic: Political Modernisation in Lebanon*, Random House, New York, 1985, p. 111; Michael Hudson, *Arab Politics*, Yale University Press, 1979, p. 238; Entelis.

60. External sources emphasise that opposition to Chamoun was found within the Maronite community. See *Documents Diplomatiques Français*, Vol. 1, 1 Jan - 30 June, Telegram No. 328, 529, Beirut 4 May 1958, pp. 55–6.

61. Pierre Gemayel, Article, *al-Amal,* 29 May 1958.

62. Salibi comments on the widespread popular perception of this point: 'his partisans as well as his opponents were convinced that he intended to seek a second term of office', but while that prospect was not widely welcomed, 'who could tell what would happen to Lebanon if Chamoun did step down'. Salibi, 'Recollections', pp. 15–16.

63. See *al-Hayat*, 23 July and 18 August 1958; *Foreign Relations of the United States 1958–60* Vol. XI, p. 38, 11 May 1958, American Embassy, Beirut to Department of State, recording that Shihab 'Vigorously reaffirmed his support for the President for legal time in office'; and 2 June 1958, American Embassy, Beirut to Department of State, that 'the Patriarch stated his support for Chamoun so long as he did not run for a second term'.

64. Salibi, 'Recollections', p. 16.

65. Nicola Ziadeh, *Syria and Lebanon*, Ernest Benn, London, 1957, p. 125.

66. Moussa Moubarak to Pierre Bart, April 1958, Moussa Moubarak papers, copies in my possession. Further dating of even the original is impossible as the date on the letter is blurred.

67. *Al-Hayat*, 10 May and 17 May 1958.

68. FO371/13422 UL1015/238, British Embassy, Beirut to Foreign Office, 11 June 1958, p. 4.

69. FO371/134118 UL1015/129, British Embassy, Beirut to Foreign Office, 20 May 1958, citing as source BBC monitoring reports.
70. See chapter four.
71. *An-Nahar*, 11 March 1958. Among the alternative Maronite presidential candidates that Maronite political leaders were considering between March and July 1958 were Alfred Naccache, Jawad Boulos, Hitti and even Bishara al-Khoury. There was no clear candidate as late as July 1958. See *al-Hayat*, 25 July and 26 July 1958 when all these names were still being publicly put forward as potential presidential candidates.
72. *Documents Diplomatiques Français* 1958, vol. I, 1 Jan–30 June, nos. 530–7, M. Roche, French Ambassador to Beirut, to M. Pineau, Foreign Minister, p. 556.
73. George Naccache, 'A l'heure de Mme Afaf', *L'Orient*, 17 January 1958.
74. *L'Orient*, 31 December 1957.
75. FO371/134116, British Embassy, Baghdad to Foreign Office, 13 April 1958. As late as May 1958, Chamoun was still thinking of seeking re-election; see *Documents Diplomatiques*, vol. I, 1 Jan–30 June, Telegram, nos. 328, 529, Beirut, 4 May 1958, pp. 555–6.
76. Moussa Moubarak to Pierre Bart, 28 April 1958, Moussa Moubarak Papers.
77. *An-Nahar*, 2 April, 1958. The Tueni editorial argued that Chamoun, Malik and the US were symbols on one side and Nasser on another. It is a measure of Chamoun's success in establishing himself as a popular icon symbolising resistance to Muslim/ Arab designs on Lebanon that he remained a popular figure even after he left office, as a survey carried out in Beirut in 1972 indicated. David Smock and Audrey Smock, *The Politics of Pluralism*, Elsevier, New York, 1975, p. 136.
78. As Lieutenant-Colonel Sir Peter Coghill, he had been head of the British Security mission in Lebanon 1941–5 and maintained contacts there with people like *Amir* Farid Shihab.
79. *Amir* Farid Shihab was not related to General Shihab. In his letter, *Amir* Farid Shihab stated that he feared that if his writing to the British became known he would probably be killed. See FO371/13116, containing extracts from a letter of 26 February 1958, from *Amir* Farid Shihab to Sir Peter Coghill, p. 102.
80. This endorsement was reported in *al-Hayat*, 12 February 1958. According to Mrs Geneviève Gemayel, the meeting was held because Chamoun was seeking to assess official Kata'ib reaction to the prospect of his re-election, but conclusions were limited to endorsement of his foreign policy and a completion of his mandate. Mrs Geneviève Gemayel, interview, Beirut, 1 March 1996.
81. Salibi, 'Recollections', p. 16. Mrs Gemayel also endorsed the existence of such popular concerns amongst the Kata'ib membership; interview, 1 March 1996. See also *al-Amal*, 17 June 1958, discussing such concerns.
82. Salibi, *ibid.*, pp. 16–17, comments on the growing popular acceptance amongst Christians that Western intervention was both desirable, 'A solicited political intervention by the United Nations having proved useless', and likely, with Chamoun invoking, very properly, the Eisenhower Doctrine 'to which he had earlier subscribed'. See also *Foreign Relations of the United States 1958–1960*, vol. XI, p. 149, reporting that Chamoun had been given assurances of intervention on 13 May 1958. It seems probable that such assurances had been 'leaked' to Chamoun's supporters at least.
83. FO371/134122 UL1015, British Embassy, Beirut to Foreign Office, 11 June 1958, p. 3.
84. Moussa Moubarak to French ambassador Pierre Bart, 28 April 1958, Moussa Moubarak papers. Also, *al-Hayat*, 6 April 1958, reported that Chamoun won a vote

of confidence in the Chamber with the support of all Maronite deputies.

85. FO371/134115, Sir George Middleton to Selwyn Lloyd, 2 May 1958, on Leading Personalities in the Lebanon, p. 16, describing Meouchi as a 'vindictive and intriguing leader'.

86. Boulos Meouchi, *L'Orient*, 13 February 1958.

87. *Ibid.*, p. 16.

88. FO131/134120 UL1015, Telegram no. 642, Sir George Middleton to Selwyn Lloyd, 31 May 1958.

89. General Bustani, 'Memoirs', p. 216.

90. FO371/134116, British Embassy, Baghdad to Foreign Office, 13 April 1958.

91. See chapter one.

92. FO371/134184, Sir William Hayter, deputy undersecretary, to Levant Department, 17 April 1958, containing information gleaned from the Italian embassy, Beirut.

93. FO371/134184, British embassy, Beirut to Sir William Hayter, deputy undersecretary, 13 January 1958, p. 1; see also Pierre Bart to Moussa Moubarak, 7 June 1958, Moussa Moubarak papers, for his comments on the Patriarch's policies.

94. FO371/134184 British embassy, Beirut to Sir William Hayter, deputy undersecretary, 13 January 1958, p. 1, commenting that 'The president was as obstinate and pig-headed as the Patriarch!'.

95. Al-Hayat, 29 November 1957.

96. Several of the people I interviewed recall the use of this term, including Mrs Gemayel, 1 March 1996; Amine Gemayel, 27 March 1992; and Sofia Saadeh, 2 January 1993. It also appears in print; see *an-Nahar*, 12 March 1958.

97. F. Qubain, *Crisis in Lebanon*, The Middle East Institute, Washington DC, 1961, p. 63.

98. *Al-Amal*, 3 March 1958; *an-Nahar*, 3 March 1958. See also chapter five. An invitation to join the UAR was never actually explicitly given, and the likelihood is that Nasser never intended to do so, but simply to stir up anti-Chamoun feeling.

99. *Al-Amal*, 3 March 1958.

100. *Oriente Moderno*, March 1958 (translated from the Italian from a copy in AUB Library); *al-Amal*, 5 March and 6 March 1958. See also M. S. Agwani, *The Lebanese Crisis 1958: A Documentary Study*, Asia House, New York, 1965, p. 46.

101. *Ibid.*, pp. 46–67.

102. *Ibid.*, pp. 47–8, quoting summary of world broadcast, part IV 2–3, 12 March 1958.

103. Saeb Salam, Speech, 10 March 1958, reported in *an-Nahar*, 11 April 1958; *al-Amal*, 11 March 1958; *al-Hayat*, 11 March 1958.

104. *An-Nahar*, 11 March 1958.

105. FO371/134120 UL1015, Telegram no. 642, Sir George Middleton to Selwyn Lloyd, 31 May 1958. *al-Amal*, 25 May 1958; *an-Nahar*, 25 May 1958.

106. For instance, *an-Nahar*, 26 May and 28 May 1958; *al-Hayat*, 27 May 1958.

107. FO371/134120 UL1015, Telegram no. 642, Sir George Middleton to Selwyn Lloyd, 31 May 1958; *an-Nahar*, 14 May, 1958; *al-Hayat*, 14 May 1958.

108. *An-Nahar*, 5 June 1958; Department of State Archives, Centre for Lebanese Studies, Telegram No. 4457, McClintock to Dulles, 5 June 1958, reporting the press conference and Gemayel's views; *The Times*, 6 June 1958; Raymond Eddé, interview, Paris, 14 July 1993; Albert Moukheiber, interview, 15 April 1995.

109. *Al-Hayat*, 17 May 1958, for instance. See also Qubain, pp. 83–4.

110. See Department of State Archives, Centre for Lebanese Studies, Telegram No. 4457, McClintock to Dulles, 5 June 1958; Department of State; *Foreign Relations of the United States*, vol. XI, p. 41, recording Telegram no. 3286, McClintock to Dulles, 13 May 1958.

111.   *Al-Hayat,* 20 July 1958.

112.   *Al-Hayat* is a particularly fruitful source on this issue. It was apparent from 1957, but particularly acute in 1958. See *al-Hayat,* 10 May and 11 May, 1957; 20 July 1958.

113.   As early as May 1957 'groupings' such as the Kata'ib Party were holding demonstrations to 'counter' rallies organised by the Sunni. See *al-Hayat,* 7 May 1957.

114.   Albert Moukheiber, speech, reported in *al-Hayat,* 7 September 1995, claiming that the present rulers of Lebanon are 'Damascus puppets' who have stripped Lebanon of its independence.

115.   See, for example, *al-Hayat,* 7 May 1957.

116.   See Department of State Archives, Centre for Lebanese Studies, Telegram No. 4512, McClintock to Dulles, 7 June 1958, for a report of al-Solh's broadcast.

117.   Raymond Eddé, interview, Paris, 20 March 1991; Albert Moukheiber, interview, 15 April 1995.

118.   Letters from the Patriarch are in existence addressed to various members of the Maronite congregation outside Lebanon. See, for example, Boulos Meouchi to Father Elias Maria Garib, Head of the Maronite Lebanese Mission, Brazil, 4 June 1958; Boulos Meouchi to Mary Moukarzel, proprietor of *al-Hoda,* a New York-based Lebanese newspaper, 5 June 1958; Boulos Meouchi to George Toufic Mouffarege, Cambridge, UK, 11 June 1958, Meouchi Papers, Maronite Patriarchate Archive.

119.   *An-Nahar,* 1 June 1958. See also articles in *an-Nas,* especially 1 June 1958; *al-Yom,* especially 3 June 1958, and even *al-Hayat* on 1 June 1958.

120.   *Al-Hayat,* 18 May 1958, translated and reported in Department of State Archives, Centre for Lebanese Studies, Telegram No. 4032, McClintock to Dulles, 19 May 1958.

121.   *L'Orient, 19* May 1958. René Aggiouri was a leading Maronite journalist.

122.   *L'Orient,* 19 May 1958. Naccache is significant because he was not only a leading pro-French newspaperman, but also was to become a minister in later governments.

123.   *Al-Amal,* editorials in May and June 1958.

124.   *Al-Amal,* 18 June 1958.

125.   See chapter four.

126.   See chapter five; *Documents Diplomatiques,* vol. I, 1 Jan–30 June, Telegram nos. 1633–36, Chauvel to Pineau, London, 13 May 1958, p. 603.

127.   See chapter five.

128.   Qubain, p. 90.

129.   General Odd Bull, *War and Peace in the Middle East,* Westview Press, Bristol, 1973–1976, p. 9. McClintock was made aware of this expectation, see his report in Department of State Archives, Centre for Lebanese Studies, Telegram No. 4696, McClintock to Dulles, 13 June 1958. Even so, Chamoun still hoped for American involvement, see also Department of State Archives, Centre for Lebanese Studies, Telegram No. 2958, giving memorandum of a conversation between Malik and J. J. Sioco, First Secretary, 18 June 1958, in which Malik expressed concern that only military intervention would act as a real deterrent to UAR intervention.

130.   *Ibid.*

131.   *Ibid.*

132.   *Ibid.*

133.   *Ibid.*

134.   See Bull, p. 9, for a discussion of this; see *ibid.,* p. 69 for the impact of continuing opposition to the United Nations Observer Group.

135.   *Al-Amal,* 5 July 1958.

136. *An-Nahar*, 5 July 1958.
137. See *an-Nahar; al-Amal; al-Ahrar*, 5–6 July 1958; see also Department of State Archives, Centre for Lebanese Studies, Telegram No. 320. 5783a/7.2258, American Embassy, Beirut to Department of State, 22 July 1958.
138. There were five reports in all: 3 July 1958; 30 July 1958; 14 August 1958; 29 September 1958; 17 November 1958
139. Robert Murphy, *Diplomat Among Warriors*, Collins, London, 1964, p. 402; Bull.
140. An example is Albert Moukheiber's bitter complaint to the American Embassy. See Department of State Archives, Centre for Lebanese Studies, Telegram No. 320, American Embassy, Beirut to Department of State, 22 July 1958.
141. The Americans picked up on this feeling: 'no-one here can understand how UNOGIL could so far imply non-existence of intervention'. See Department of State Archives, Centre for Lebanese Studies, Telegram No. 137, McClintock to Dulles, 5 July 1958, warning of Maronite bitterness over the report.
142. *Al-Hayat*, 15 July 1958, for example.
143. Mrs Geneviève Gemayel, interview, 1 March 1996; Amine Gemayel, interview, 27 March 1992. Both commented on the increased recruitment in the summer of 1958, when there was, according to the latter, a feeling that the situation had developed into a choice between pro- and anti-Lebanese forces.
144. Amine Gemayel, interview, 27 March 1992.
145. Figures taken from the survey conducted by *L'Orient,* 11 December 1958.
146. *Foreign Relations of the United States 1958– 1960*, vol. XI, p. 35, reporting Telegram no. 3826, from McClintock to Dulles, Beirut, 11 May 1958.
147. An alternative interpretation of this might be that Chamoun himself genuinely believed in the possibility of UAR-backed civil war in Lebanon if the West did not intervene. He was a product of Mount Lebanon, after all. However, this seems the less likely interpretation. See Murphy, p. 397.
148. Bustani, p. 189; *Foreign Relations of the United States 1958–1960*, vol. XI, p. 55, Telegram nos. 3949 and 3958, 16 May, 1958, on Western efforts to get Chamoun to announce his retirement.
149. Bustani, pp. 189–90.
150. See, for example, Boulos Meouchi to Brendan A. Finn, Maronite emigrant in the US, 11 July 1958, Meouchi papers.
151. For an indication of Chamoun's success in this respect see FO371/134124, Telegram No. 775, British Embassy, Beirut, 16 June 1958; FO371/134117 UL1015/62, Telegram no. 1151, British Embassy, Beirut, 15 May 1958; and FO371/134124 Telegram no. 1624, Sir Harold Caccia, British Ambassador, Washington, to Selwyn Lloyd, 19 June 1958, for example; also *Foreign Relations of the United States, 1958–1960*, vol. XI, p. 71, recording Dulles's acceptance of Chamoun's fears that Lebanon was in danger of being 'lost to Nasserism'.
152. See FO371/134124, Telegram no. 775, British Embassy, Beirut to Foreign Office, 16 June 1958, for example.
153. See, for example, *New York Times*, 7 July 1958.
154. Bustani, p. 223.
155. *Al-Hayat*, 16 July 1958.
156. *Ibid.*; see also *Foreign Relations of the United States 1958–1960*, vol. XI, p. 389, Telegram no. 658, 24 July 1958, in which McClintock reported 'I also have feeling most Lebanese welcome our presence here and feel it will make it possible for them to reach a political solution'.

157. Raymond Eddé, interview, 20 March 1991.

158. Eddé, interview, 20 March 1991; *Foreign Relations of the United States 1958–1960*, vol. XI, p. 241, reporting Telegram no. 290, indicating that McClintock believed that Pierre Eddé, Raymond's brother, was, despite his pro-government inclination, hostile to the landings.

159. See Pierre Gemayel, speech, *al-Hayat*, 18 July 1958.

160. See *al-Hayat*, 19 July 1958.

161. See, for example, *al-Hayat*, 19 July 1958.

162. Moussa Moubarak to Charles Malik, Letter, 12 May 1958, Moussa Moubarak papers.

163. Pierre Gemayel, speech, *al-Amal*, 10 April 1956; *al-Hayat*, 10 April 1956; Ghassan Tueni, speech, *al-Hayat*, 27 November 1956. The latter is an interesting perspective for a supposedly moderate newspaperman to maintain in justifiying government policy as early as 1956; thus it indicates how instinctive this appeal was to the Maronites' mythology of past calamity.

164. Nadim al-Jisr, *al-Hayat*, 17 May 1958. Al-Jisr was a deputy.

165. Ghassan Tueni, *al-Hayat*, 20 May 1958. According to Tueni, however, such a solution did not lie in abandoning either Chamoun before the end of his mandate, or to breaking ties with the West.

166. Pierre Gemayel, speech, *al-Amal* 25 June 1958; *al-Hayat*, 25 June 1958.

167. *Al-Hayat*, 15 July 1958.

168. Pierre Gemayel, speech, 18 July 1958, PPS papers, Beirut. Salibi, 'Recollections', p. 15, commented on his memory of being informed of 'a full-scale Muslim insurrection enjoying the personal backing of Nasser, and provided with arms and other assistance from the UAR'. Mrs Geneviève Gemayel, in our interview, 1 March 1996, also commented on her memories of Maronite panic, and her belief that it was a factor in sustaining recruitment to the party at this point.

169. *Al-Hayat*, 16 July 1958.

170. In the interests of trade and commerce, the bourgeoisie tended to support a peaceful compromise. There is no way of getting satisfactory statistics to confirm the impression given in the press and by commentators such as Moubarak and Bustani that the majority of the Maronite masses were, towards the end of July, still firmly behind Chamoun, at least in terms of his completing his mandate. However, there is no useful evidence to contradict this perspective.

171. Karid Kozma, *al-Hayat*, 17 October 1958. This, again, emphasises the contemporary recognition of a popular reliance on mythology in the interpretation of contemporary events.

172. *Foreign Relations of the United States 1958–1960*, vol. XI, p. 254, Telegram no. 428, 16 July 1958, recording McClintock's account for Dulles of the reaction of the Lebanese army.

173. It must not be forgotten that the army was interconfessional in composition. See Bustani, p. 89

174. Western observers shared this respect, at least to some extent; the British considered him to be 'honest and loyal' though they doubted his 'intelligence'; the Americans commented 'All he has is common-sense – but a great deal of that', while fearing that he was 'too apolitical' to be as pro-Western as they would like. See FO371/134115 UL1012, British Embassy, Beirut to Foreign Office, 12 May 1958, on Leading Personalities in Lebanon, p. 6; *Foreign Relations of the United States, 1958–1960*, vol. XI, p. 12, American Embassy, Beirut to Department of State, 21 February 1958.

175. *Al-Hayat* made this point in May, reiterating it again in July 1958, claiming it was the only acceptable solution if internal stability was to be sustained. *Al-Hayat*, 17 May 1958; 31 July 1958. Moussa Moubarak, letter, 2 August 1958, Moussa Moubarak papers, commenting on Shihab's 'obstinately refusing' to put himself forward. The addressee is unclear, but is possibly Pierre Bart.

176. Bustani, pp. 188–9.

177. *Al-Hayat*, 29 May 1958.

178. FO371/134110 UL10115/1741, British Embassy, Beirut to Foreign Office, 18 May 1958, Memorandum, making an early comment on this factor. It may well have been a factor in Shihab's failure to win real liking outside the army that, in contrast to Chamoun's handsome and charismatic appearance, Shihab looked forbidding and behaved in a stern manner.

179. *Foreign Relations of the United States 1958–1960*, Vol. XI, p. 411, Telegram No. 836, 30 July 1958.

180. Its backing of Chamoun remained until the last day of his mandate and weeks afterward. See *Foreign Relations of the United States 1958–1960*, vol. XI, p. 593, Telegram no. 342, 2 October, 1958, recounting McClintock's informing Dulles that 'I took half an hour to move half a mile where a helicopter landed at Chamoun's villa as the road was blocked filled with cheering adherents of the ex-President'. An estimate of average daily visits by adherents to Chamoun's residence was recorded as around 5,000.

Conclusion

In essence, the 1958 crisis developed out of the established pattern of Lebanon's communal politics, a pattern based in turn on conflicting community mythologies that anchored distinct community identities. These essential community identities were, however, interpreted by their adherents as being the core of 'national' identity within Lebanon; this led to them establishing divergent visions of Lebanon's destiny, leaving them little opportunity to generate a compromise and return to the consensus that the National Pact had envisioned.

In this context, it was the interaction with the regional, as well as the international, political scene that made it possible to resolve the crisis and restore some semblance of consensus. This crisis marked a total, if temporary, breakdown of the political compromise that had been intended to stabilise an independent Lebanon, making it a crucial event in Lebanese history. This is why it is impossible to explain the collapse of that compromise simply in terms of external pressures – though external sources certainly brokered the restoration of that compromise.

In this book I have tried to show how much the Lebanese themselves brought about their own crisis: differing agendas and perspectives had become institutionalised in the Lebanese political, social and cultural systems because they earned such high popular status, particularly the reactions to the Maronite versions of Lebanon's history. Thus my argument contradicts the air of inevitability about Lebanon's role in Middle Eastern events after Nasser's rise – an air often assumed by those examining events from an external perspective.

Observers could have predicted that crises were constantly likely, but not that they would inevitably be linked to Nasserism and wider events in the Middle East. It was the existence of a vacuum within the Sunni community, the lack of an acceptable local popular champion, that enabled Nasser and Nasserism to assume the profile they did in the 1958 crisis. It is also worth noting that the pro-Western state of Jordan did not collapse despite considerable pressure from pro-Nasserist elements in the Middle East. Thus, I argue that Lebanese factors were primarily responsible for creating the Lebanese crisis of 1958.

One of these factors is the extent to which elements in Lebanon were responsible for accepting, reinterpreting and manipulating external pressures and interests to promote the ambitions of their own communal groups, and themselves, within Lebanon itself, by consistently invoking the rhetoric of their respective mythologies. By August 1958, the outcome of a presidential election was being advertised as the way forward: choosing a president who would be acceptable to all elements in Lebanon, thus reconstructing the National Pact. Consensus increasingly focused on the issue that people and politicians on all sides were now seeing as all-important: withdrawal of American troops from Lebanon. The end result – withdrawal and the election of an acceptable candidate – did appear to restore the Lebanese political compromise, as the politicians, if not the people, on all sides supported it.

In reality, however, it was once again a compromise arranged by outside powers, in an echo of 1860 and so many other crises in Lebanon's past. Unlike the crisis itself, the solution was not internally generated. Because it originated outside Lebanon, the compromise remained a fragile one and did not tackle the fundamental problems that underlay the National Pact. Because the solution was largely brokered by external powers, many observers of the 1958 crisis have presumed, mistakenly, that its origins were also mostly external. Instead, the origins of the crisis lay primarily in the reluctance of most Lebanese, especially community leaders, to confront the real differences between them, to work through them and then to seek an honest basis for intercommunal consensus.

In this process, the various communities made it harder to develop that crucial honesty by relying so deeply on their own mythology and categorising themselves and others in confessional colours, even at the highest levels of community hierarchies. By associating religious belief with communal identity, they worked against any potential for compromise between communities. This becomes even clearer as we examine the aftermath of the crisis and each community's reactions to the solution, which had in themselves become part of the mythology of different communities, and thus were also open to consistently different interpretations.

By the summer of 1958, the traditional system of inter-communal compromise had been strained to the breaking point. The panicked Maronites were interpreting the combined pressures of Chamoun's personal ambitions, and his publicly pro-Western and anti-Nasserist stance, as an attempt to protect their interests, not his own. This increased the hostility toward anti-Chamoun elements, even those who supported the continuation of an independent Lebanon. Equally, the Sunni and other Muslim communities increasingly feared that Chamoun intended to use the crisis not only to renew his mandate, but also to strengthen the position of the Maronite and other Christian elements over the Muslim position.[1]

When the Muslim opposition's greatest fear – an American military intervention – actually occurred, their hostility was fervent. But at least the opposition's leaders realised that they were not alone in opposing the landings. Leaders of the various Christian communities, including the Maronites, agreed with them that Chamoun was becoming politically isolated and therefore weak. Initially, the Sunni political leaders protested, interpreting the landing as proof that the Americans backed Chamoun and wanted him re-elected, and believing that Maronite politicians would seize the opportunity to bring about that scenario. Their fears on this score decreased as the politicians demonstrated both their opposition to the landings and their willingness to seek a compromise that would not be based on renewing Chamoun's mandate. This created a basis on which they could negotiate with the Murphy mission.

The Lebanese army's reaction to the American landings led to an interesting short-term result: it actually united the communities in Lebanon, in their hostility to the American action. To the surprise and dismay of both the troops and the American leadership,[2] there was a real danger that the Lebanese and American soldiers would engage in hostilities.[3] Fouad Shihab, however, insisted to Robert McClintock that his troops were not part of some 'conspiracy' by Lebanese elements who intended to overthrow the Lebanese government. Rather, he said, it was a 'spontaneous' reaction that crossed confessional boundaries and was simply focused on removing American troops from Lebanese soil.

This reaction certainly included both Maronites and Sunnis, officers and soldiers. It is generally accepted that the ordinary and mainly Muslim soldiers, were prepared to die at their guns as a symbolic gesture of patriotic defiance; this patriotism, in turn, inspired the mainly Maronite officers to follow their lead.[4] American sources describe the seriousness of this reaction: even on 16 July, Shihab himself did not know how much his staff and men were prepared to engage in hostilities with the American troops.[5] Equally, the American sources said the mood of the Lebanese army was in tune with the mood of the larger Lebanese population.[6]

Given this background we see the significance of Robert Murphy's attempts to appeal to all elements within the Lebanese political dimension, especially the opposition, and to explain American motivations in making the landing. By talking sympathetically to all leaders in the Lebanese political arena, Murphy succeeded in defusing the situation. He emphasised making contact with opposition and with actual rebel leaders, such as al-Yafi, and showed himself willing to listen sympathetically to their grievances. By explaining both the American landings and the American motivation in terms of the wider regional issues, he defused the issue for the Sunni leaders, few of whom had any wish to see the immediate end of an independent Lebanon.

In this context, then, the US's regional concerns carried a certain conviction; whether or not they approved, the Sunni politicians could at least use them to save face – backing down from the sometimes extreme positions they had taken after the landings which now threatened hostilities with the US. Murphy reassured the Sunni leadership that the Americans had no intention of backing Chamoun's plans to arrange his re-election. Also reassuring to the Sunni leaders, the Americans had begun discussions with Nasser, and so could be popularly seen as working to restore good relations in the Middle East.[7]

Indeed, these perceptions began to affect Muslim public opinion through the press in Lebanon, starting on 18 July when an opposition statement professed 'great doubt' that the Murphy mission would succeed.[8] The press reports of 19 July began to mention the opposition waiting 'in expectation' for the mission's result.[9] On 22 July the opposition was said to be collaborating voluntarily with Murphy because they believed he could create a workable compromise; a headline in *al-Telegraph*, a leading opposition paper, announced 'Crisis is on the Way to Solution'. *Al-Jarida* wrote that Murphy, the 'Man of Good Offices', was there to reassure the Lebanese that the Americans had landed only because of Middle East tensions resulting from the Iraqi coup, and that the US had no intentions of widening the Lebanese split 'by supporting one faction of the population against the other.'[10] Equally significantly, Maronite politicians increasingly supported Murphy's suggestions for a compromise based on immediately replacing Chamoun. Of course the Chamoun government and its hard-line supporters were hostile, seeing Murphy's mission as the end of their hopes for keeping Chamoun in power. But this group was losing both members and impact as it became more isolated. Those Maronite politicians who had only supported Chamoun in finishing his mandate swiftly changed to a position of favouring Murphy's efforts. However, more than a few moderates, even some who supported his re-election, were publicly supporting a compromise like the one Murphy was brokering.

In agreeing on Shihab as a compromise candidate, however, the Maronite politicians were moving ahead of the Maronite masses, by being willing to accept him as a substitute for Chamoun, who was so closely identified with protecting Lebanese/Maronite integrity.. The brokers of the compromise had thought the only hope of a solution lay in immediately replacing Chamoun, and Shihab was the obvious choice. He was acceptable to the Americans, and apparently to the elites of the two main sides of the political equation within Lebanon. Given the powers that Sunni political leaders had over their followers, no major dissatisfaction with the compromise was voiced from that quarter because removing Chamoun had become their main goal.

The Maronite masses did feel they were the losers when Shihab was installed as President, because, at the height of the crisis, they had seen him as being in the opposition camp. Worse, Shihab appointed an ex-rebel leader, Rachid Abd al-Hamid Karami, as his prime minister. That move made political sense in terms of Lebanon's overall political map, but created great resentments amongst the Maronite masses, who saw it as an affront because it conflicted with their established mythology about their role in the state. Thus, given how independent the Maronite community was from its political leadership, many Maronites did not see the crisis as being resolved. This opinion would have repercussions after the American troops withdrew.

Perhaps this outcome, generated from outside and not unanimously agreed upon from within, was as doomed as all the other 'solutions' to Lebanon's past problems. The crises of 1860 and 1958, as well as 1976, all are strikingly similar in having been internally generated, with solutions brokered from outside Lebanon that did not address the roots of the crisis, and so were vulnerable to breaking down. The Lebanese did not seem willing to pinpoint the shortcomings of their system of administration and government as a first step in evolving a solution. Amine Gemayel's draft plan of 1987 is one such compromise agreement that could not be developed into a document generating consensus, although Walid Khalidi says it incorporated a formulation of Lebanese Arab identity as well as dismantling the sectarian system within ten or fifteen years.[11]

The 1990 Ta'if Accord, solution to the most recent crisis, was also based on the 1943 pact and the communal divisions incorporated in the heart of that pact, even if it was modified in certain significant ways. But it failed to confront the issue of reworking the different community mythologies. The Ta'if Accord placed the Muslims and the Christians – essentially

Raymond Eddé following an assassination attempt in 1975 by members of the Kata'ib party at Nahr Ibrahim (Jbeil). His moderate approach threatened their power.

the Maronites – on an equal footing within the state, after the Maronite community in particular was weakened in the recent civil war. The accord thus took several constitutional prerogatives of the president's office and shared them out to the entire ministerial cabinet. The parliament also gained some power, especially in the office of the speaker of the house. But these new arrangements still enshrine the idea of a relatively static communal base for Lebanon's administration and government, even if the communal balance of power is now rather different. Effectively, the state is now led by three heads in what has come to be termed popularly the 'three presidents'. The president is still a Maronite, and the prime minister a Sunni, but the recent changes added a Shi'ite speaker of the house, and all three must be consulted on every decision. In theory, even in practice, this means that the Maronite/Christian position can now be outvoted by a Muslim combination.[12]

Outside powers might be forgiven for not recognising the fundamental flaws of that pact and the implications of assuming an essentially static communal mix. But few Lebanese of any real influence, except for new actors like the Shi'ites, have been willing to point out the new situation: that new actors in the Lebanese drama have arrived and gained importance.[13] For reasons of individual and communal self-interest, the protagonists do not notice that these solutions are essentially temporary, and the entire community postpones the process of creating a genuinely national identity. Ever since 1943, and more than ever in 2004, the Lebanese have been running in circles, with each community attempting to gain an advantage in power over other communities, while still preserving the fiction of the 1943 compromise.

In operation, the Ta'if Accord reveals the disadvantage of seeking consensus in Lebanon by continuing to use confessionally-based communities as the basis for administering the state. One indication is the perception that the communities still need threats or even actual force to enforce that consensus. Perhaps more importantly, 1990 saw a repetition of the chronic 'mistake' of Lebanese presidents: trying to break the constitution in order to renew their six-year term of office, leading to crisis. If not all those crises have been on the scale of that in 1958, no renewal has been devoid of problems. Bishara al-Khoury falsified the parliamentary election of 25 May 1947 in order to gain enough support to amend Article 49 of the constitution. President Chamoun raised the number of deputies from forty-four to sixty-six and rigged their election. Fouad Shihab did, in fact, leave at the end of his term, but allowed tensions to rise in Lebanon as people speculated that he intended to seek an amendment of Article 49.

In 1976, President Sulayman Frangieh also tried to renew his term of office. In 1995, President Elias Hrawi sought to follow in the path of his predecessors, seeking to amend Article 49 so he could renew his term – though Lebanon urgently needed to end his corrupt regime. Most Maronites, including the Patriarch, greeted his actions with despair and resentment. Nor did other community leaders welcome it universally. The Lebanese press underlined these reactions, for example in *L'Orient-Le Jour* of 16 March 1995. All these events indicate that the communal basis of rule in Lebanon, surrounded as it is with the emotions generated by confessional loyalties and prejudices, cannot be flexible enough to allow the state to evolve and modernise. Thus, when stresses and tensions arise, especially those that are internally generated and bring along economic and social hardships, the political dimension is strained and the political formula for government put under pressure. Sometimes that pressure is strong enough to provoke outright crisis to the point of civil war; at other times, it proves able to defuse it internally. Partly, this is regulated by the various communities' will to invoke outside intervention in times of crisis, and their success in doing so. In so doing, they replay the 'patron-client' game Buheiry identifies.

Each confessional community in Lebanon has identified its external patron; sometimes these may change, but often they carry the considerable baggage of history along with that patron-client relationship, as in the case of the relationship between the Maronite community and France. Given the baggage of history, during any given crisis the Lebanese clients at least bring an emotional, rather than a logical, dimension of the patron's self-interest in becoming involved, or abstaining from becoming involved. Therefore whenever the Lebanese clients accurately assess the potential of a crisis escalating because of outside intervention, they justify their decision by claiming to be responding to an internal request for help.

In this light I argue that the only lasting solution for the Lebanese is likely to lie in building a state, instead of continuing a consensus. A secular base for the state is the only likely remedy for all the problems of sectarianism.[14] For instance, a state would promote a uniform system of education, which could possibly include not only the influences and learning of the West, but also key ideas of Arab culture and thinking. According to Amine Gemayel, today Lebanon needs a common political culture based on a historical Lebanese identity, one that can outweigh any other source of identification for Lebanese citizens.[15] While in office, however, Gemayel could not implement any such solution.

Despite the continuing confessional and political divisions, a process has recently emerged, and attitudes are changing: Christian communities accept more readily their Arab appurtenance while Muslim communities are becoming more aware of their Lebanese identity. This change is particularly significant because it comes from the base as a genuine movement not imposed by the political elites. Is this the germ that will eventually lead to the transformation of Lebanon into a nation in the proper sense?

Notes

1. See, for example, *al-Hayat*, 16 July, 1958.
2. General Bustani, 'Memoirs', p. 200.
3. *Ibid.*
4. See, for example, *ibid.*
5. Department of State Archives, Centre for Lebanese Studies, Telegram No. 496 (Section Two of Two) Robert Murphy to Secretary of State, 18 July 1958.
6. Department of State Archives, Centre for Lebanese Studies, Telegram No. 618, McClintock to Secretary of State, 22 July 1958.
7. See R. Murphy, *Diplomats Among Warriors*, Greenwood Press, Westport, p. 19.
8. See *al-Hayat*, 18 July 1958, for example.
9. See *al-Hayat*, 19 July 1958, for example.
10. *Al-Telegraph*, 22 July 1958; *al-Jarida*, 22 July 1958.
11. Walid Khalidi, (ed.) Leila Fawaz, *State and Society in Lebanon*, The Centre for Lebanese Studies, Oxford, 1991, p. 34.
12. For the Ta'if Accord see *Lebanon: Official Gazette, Special Issue No. 39, Constitutional*

Law, no. 18, 27 September 1990, p. 2.

13. Nabih Bezzi, the Shi'ite speaker of the House on the main current political issues, *al-Hayat*, 31 August 1995, and 1 September 1995.

14. See Dominique Chevallier, 'Comment l'Etat a-t-il été compressé au Liban', in Nadim Shehadi and Dana Haffar Mills (eds), *Lebanon, A History of Conflict and Consensus*, I.B. Tauris, London 1988, p. 222.

15. The Lebanese generally recognise the need for a new National Pact, but no leaders or communities seem willing to work out its terms.

Bibliography

Primary Sources

Documents and Other Unpublished Sources

Official
US Department of State papers, held at the Centre for Lebanese Studies, Oxford, largely
   unclassified.
UK Foreign Office papers, Public Records Office, Kew, London.
Quai d'Orsay Archives, Paris and Nantes.

Unofficial
Correspondence between Moussa Moubarak, the Lebanese ambassador to France in 1958,
   to Pierre Bart, the French ambassador to Lebanon in 1958, in the possession of Samir
   Moubarak, the former Lebanese ambassador to the United Nations. Photocopies retained
   by this author.
Memoirs of General Emile Bustani, head of the Lebanese Air Force in 1958 and subsequently
   General-in-Chief, Lebanese Army, 1964–70, unpublished typescript retained by this
   author.
Personal papers, al-Khazin family, unpublished and unclassified, in the possession of Shaykh
   Clovis al-Khazin, Lebanon.
Personal papers, Yussuf al-Sawda, unpublished and unclassified, logged at the Université St
   Esprit, Kaslik.
Personal papers, Kazem al-Solh, unpublished, in the possession of Raghid al-Solh, Oxford,
   consulted with kind permission of the author. This holding includes an unpublished
   manuscript, *Mu'tamar al-Sahil* (Conference of the Coast).
Papers, Bloc National, archives, Bloc National headquarters, Beirut.
Papers, Parti Populaire Syrien (PPS), archives, PPS headquarters, Lebanon. Copies kindly given
   by Yussuf al-Achkar, the president of the party in 1994, retained by this author.
Papers of the Maronite Patriarchate, archives, Maronite Patriarchate, Bkirki. Currently closed
   for sixty years, access with kind permission of the Patriarch.

Newspapers, Journals and Other Printed Sources

Newspapers and Journals (All titles are daily publications unless otherwise noted.)
Al-Akhbar, official newspaper of the Lebanese Communist Party, archives, AUB Library.
Al-Amal, official newspaper of the of the Kata'ib Party, Kata'ib Party headquarters.
Al-Anba, official newspaper of the Progressive Socialist Party, archives, AUB Library.
Al-Jarida, weekly journal, centrist affiliations, archives, AUB Library.
Al-Hawadith, monthly review, Nasserist tendencies, archives, AUB Library.
Al-Hayat, newspaper, pro-Maronite, hostile to Nasserism and pro-Iraq during the 1950s, currently pro-Saudi, archives, *al-Hayat,* London.
Al-Hikmat, monthly review, special issues for January, February, June, July 1965, from this author's collection.
Al-Sharq, newspaper, Nasserist tendencies, archives, AUB Library.
Al-Siyassa, newspaper, outlet for the United National Front in 1957–8, archives, AUB Library.
An-Nahar, newspaper, centrist, linked to Gebran Tueni's Third Force in1957–8, *An-Nahar* archives, Beirut.
An-Nas, newspaper, pro-Sunni tendencies, archives, AUB Library.
Beirut, monthly review (ceased publication in 1957), popular, pro-Sunni, from the collection of M. Mokaddem.
Beirut al-Massa, monthly review, not published from 1950–8, popular, pro-Sunni, from the collection of Muhammad al-Mashnuk, also in archives, AUB Library.
Le Jour, French-language newspaper, pro-Maronite, linked to Bishara al-Khoury's Destour Party in the 1950s, archives, AUB Library.
L'Orient, French-language newspaper, moderate Maronite/Christian with centrist and pro-Western tendencies, archives, *L'Orient Le Jour,* Beirut.
La Revue Phoenicienne, monthly review, archives, St Joseph's University, Kaslik.

Certain non-Lebanese publications were consulted for key dates, etc
Asie Française, archives, St Joseph's University, Kaslik.
The Observer, archives, Senate House, London University.
Oriente Moderno, archives, St Joseph's University, Kaslik.
The Times, Institute of Historical Research, London University.
New York Times, archives, AUB Library.

Other Printed Primary Sources

Official
Cabinet Papers 1926–1948, ed. Yussuf Kozma Khouri, Muassassat al-Dirasat al-Lubnaniyyah, Beirut, 1986.
Institut international de recherche et de formation en vue du développement integral et harmonisé, besoins et possibilités de développement du Liban, *Etude Préliminare, vol. I: 'Situation économique et sociale', vol. II: 'Problematique et orientation Beirut, 1964'.*
The Lebanese Constitution (1926 text with all further amendments, including the Ta'if Agreement), Beirut, 1991.
Lebanon: Official Gazette (weekly Lebanese government), consulted especially for the dates of 5 October 1932 and 21 September 1990.
Minutes of the Lebanese Chamber of Deputies, 1922–1958.
Parliamentary Debates, 1942–1943, vol. 387.
Receuil des statistiques de la Syrie et du Liban 1945–46–47, vols 1–3, Beirut, 1947.

Documents diplomatiques français, vol. I, 1 Jan–30 June 1957, Commission de publication des documents diplomatiques français, Paris.

Documents on US Foreign Relations, ed. Paul Zinner, Harper & Bros, New York, 1955–8.

Foreign Relations of the United States 1955–1957, vol. XIII, Near East: Jordan and Yemen, Department of State Publication, no. 9665, Washington DC, 1988.

Foreign Relations of the United States 1958–1960, vol. XI, Near East: Lebanon and Jordan, Department of State Publication, no. 9665, Washington DC, 1992.

Unofficial

Yussuf al-Sawda, 'Al-khiyana al-uzma' (The Biggest Betrayal), pamphlet, Beirut, 1957, archives, AUB Library.

Ismail Moussa al-Yussuf, 'Thawrat al-'ahrar fi lubnan' (The Revolt of the Free in Lebanon), Manshurat al-Zayn, Beirut, n.d. (but evidence dates it to 1958), archives, AUB Library, copy from the collection of this author.

'Bayan jamiyat ittihad al-Shabiba al-islamiyyah' (The Petition of the Muslim Youth Society), presented to the minister of the interior, Lebanon, 19 June 1946, archives, AUB Library.

'Bayan al-lajna al-tahdiriyyah lil mutamar al-daim lil-hay'at al-Islamiyyah fi lubnan', (Statement by the Preparatory Committee of the Muslim Conference), 6 March 1953, archives, AUB Library.

'Bayan min al-Lajna al-tanfidhiyyah lil mutamar al-islami' (A Statement From the Executive Committee of the Islamic Congress), 5 August 1943, archives, AUB Library.

'Hizb al-najjadah: a qanun al-assassi' (Bylaws of the al-Najjadah Party), printed by Minet Press, Beirut, 1 July 1958, archives, AUB Library.

'Istaikizu ayuha al-muslimun al-niyam' (Awake, Sleeping Muslims), pamphlet, n.d., acquired by the archives, AUB Library, on February 28, 1951.

Letters, Patriarch Agnatius Moubarak, 1947, published by the Maronite Patriarchate, Bkirki, 1947, archives, Maronite Patriarchate, Bkirki, includes an undated Open Letter (after the 1947 elections) from Ignatius Moubarak to Bishara al-Khoury, (a copy of which has been placed in the collection of this author) and an Open Letter of 24 August 1947 from Ignatius Moubarak to the 'Lebanese People' (copy also placed in the collection of this author).

'Moslem Lebanon Today', pamphlet, Moslem Organisations in Beirut, Beirut, 1953, archives, AUB Library.

'Mudhakkarat al-Kutla al-islamiyyah ila rais al-jumhuriyyah al-lubnaniyyah' (Memorandum of the Muslim Bloc to His Excellency the President of the Lebanese Republic), archives, AUB Library.

'Mudhakkarat mutamar al-tawaif al-islamiyyah' (The Resolutions of the Congress of the Muslim Sects), 21 June 1943, archives, AUB Library.

'Mudhakkarat al-lajna al-tanfidhiyyah lil-mutamar al-islami ila m. halleu safir faransa' (The Petition of the Executive Committee of the Muslim Congress to His Excellency M. Helleu, the Ambassador of France), archives, AUB Library.

'Revendication du Liban: mémoire de la délégation libanaise à la Conférence de la Paix', Patriarch Elias Howayek, Paris, 25 October 1919, from *Documents of the Maronite Patriarch*, published by the Maronite Patriarchate, Bkirki, 23 February 1936.

'The Crime of 25 May 1947', pamphlet, Bloc National party, Beirut, 1947, archives, Bloc National party, contemporary copy in the collection of this author.

Books Published to 1960

Bad al-khutub wal mudhakkarat li sahib al-mufti al-kbar al-shaykh muhammad taufiq khalid (Some Speeches and Petitions by the Grand Mufti Shaykh Muhammad Tufiq Khalid), Dar al-Fatwa Fi al-Jumhuriyyah al-Lubnaniyyah, Beirut: al-Kashshaf Press, n.d.

Michel Chebli, *Fakhr al-dine ii ma'n, prince du Liban, 1572–1635*, Librairie Orientale, Beirut, 1946.

Michel Chebli, *Une histoire du Liban à l'époque des amirs*, Librarie Orientale, second ed., Beirut, 1955.

Charles H. Churchill, *The Druze and the Maronites Under Turkish Rule from 1840 to 1960*, Bernard Quaritch, London, 1862, reprinted, Garnet Publications, London, 1994.

Charles H. Churchill, *Mount Lebanon: A Ten Years' Residence from 1842–1852*, Saunders & Otley, London, 1853.

Edward Creasey, *History of the Ottoman Turks from the Beginning of Their Empire to the Present Time*, London, 1880, reprinted, Khayat, Beirut, 1961.

Yussuf Debs, *Les maronites du Liban*, Lecoffre, Paris, 1875.

M. Jouplain (Boulos Noujaim), *La question du Liban: étude d'histoire diplomatique et de droit international*, first published, Beirut, 1908, reprinted, Fouad Bilan et cie, Jounieh, Lebanon, 1961.

Henri Lammens, *Inventoire des richesses archéologiques du Liban*, al-Machriq, Beirut, 1898.

Henri Lammens, *La syrie: prècis historique*, first published, Beirut, 1914, reprinted, Dar Lahd Khater, Beirut, 1994.

Bessie Parkes-Belloc, *Peoples of the World*, Cassell, Petter & Gilpin, London, 1867.

Desmond Stewart, *Turmoil in Beirut: A Personal Account*, Allan Wingate, London, 1958.

Nicola Ziadeh, *Syria and Lebanon*, Ernest Benn, London, 1957.

Oral Interviews (Tapes of these interviews are in the possession of the author.)

Dory Chamoun, son of Camille Chamoun currently leader of the National Liberal Party, London, 30 March 1992.

Raymond Eddé, son of Emile Eddé, Minister of the Interior in 1958, leader of the Bloc National party, Paris, 20 March 1991 and 19 July 1994.

Joseph Freiha, lawyer, state prosecutor in 1958, currently a leading judge, Beirut, 4 January 1993.

Amine Gemayel, son of Pierre Gemayel, the Kata'ib Party leader, Paris, 27 March 1992.

Geneviève Gemayel, wife of Pierre Gemayel, Paris, 19 March 1996.

Dr Albert Moukheiber, Minister of Health in 1958, designated delegate to the United Nations Observation Group in Lebanon in 1958, pro-Chamoun figure, Bayt Meiri, 15 April 1995.

Salim Nassar, leading journalist with the pro-Egyptian *as-Sayyad* in 1958, currently working for *al-Hayat*, London, 20 May 1995.

Sofia Saadeh, daughter of Antun Saadeh, the PPS leader, Beirut, 2 January 1993.

Saeb Salam, Sunni politician, opposition leader in 1958, subsequently Prime Minister of Lebanon, Geneva, 4 January 1991.

Ghassan Tueni, journalist and politician, influential editorialist in 1958, current owner of *an-Nahar*, involved with the Third Force in 1958, Beirut, 30 July 1992.

Bibliography

Secondary Sources

Books

Selim Abou, *Le bilinguisme arabe-français au Liban: essai d'anthropologie culturelle*, Puf, Paris, 1962.

Selim Abou, *L'identité culturelle*, Edition Anthropos, Paris, 1981.

Abdul Rahim Abu Hussein, *Provincial Leaderships in Syria, 1575–1615*, American University of Beirut, Beirut, 1985.

Fouad Ajami, *The Arab Predicament*, Cambridge University Press, Cambridge, 1981.

Engin Akarli, *The Long Peace: Ottoman Lebanon 1861–1920*, University of California Press, Berkeley, 1993.

Yussuf al-Hakim, *Beyrut wa lubnan fi ahd al-uthman* (Beirut and Lebanon During the Ottoman Period), Dar an-Nahar, Beirut, 1969.

Naji-Karim al-Hulu, *Hukkam lubnan 1920–1980* (The Heads of the State and Chief Ministers of Lebanon, 1920–1980), Muassasah Khalifa Lil-tibaah, Beirut, 1980.

Bassem al-Jisr, *Mithaq 1943, limadha kan wa limadha saqat* (The National Pact, 1943, with Reasons for its Existence and Failure), Dar an-Nahar Lil Nashr, Beirut, 1978.

Farid al-Khazin and Paul Salem, *Al-intikhabat al-'Ula fi lubnan fi ona ba'd al-hrb* (The First Election After the War), Dar an-Nahar Wa Markaz al-Lubnani Lil Dirasat, Beirut, 1993.

Bishara al-Khoury, *Haqa'iq lbnaniyyah* (Facts About Lebanon), Maktabit Basil, Harissa, 1960 and 1961.

Yussuf al-Sawda, *Fi sabil al-istiqlal* (Towards Independence), Dar al-Rihani, Beirut, 1967.

Yussuf al-Sawda, *Histoire culturelle du Liban*, Dar al-Rihani, Beirut, 1972.

Sami al-Solh, *Mudhakkarat sami bey al-solh* (Memoirs of Sami Bey al-Solh), Maktabat al-Fikr al-Arabi, Beirut, 1960.

Gabriel Almond and James S. Coleman, *The Politics of Developing Areas*, Princeton University Press, Princeton, 1960.

Gabriel Almond and James Powell, *Comparative Politics: A Developmental Approach*, Little, Brown & Co., Boston, 1966.

Nura Alamuddin and Paul D Starr, *Crucial Bonds: Marriage Among the Druze*, Caravan Books, New York, 1980.

George Antonius, *The Arab Awakening*, Hamish Hamilton, London, 1938.

M. S. Anderson, *The Eastern Question, 1774–1923: A Study in International Relations*, Macmillan, London, 1966.

W. Awwad, *Ashabal al-fakhama ru'asa lubnan* (Their Excellencies, The Presidents of Lebanon), Dar al-Ahliyyah, Beirut, 1977.

E. Azar, *The Emergence of a New Lebanon*, Praeger, London, 1984.

Abdo Baaklini, *Legislative and Political Development: Lebanon 1842–1972*, Duke University Press, Durham, 1976.

Halim Barakat, *Lebanon in Strife: Student Preludes to the Civil War*, University of Texas Press, Austin, 1977.

Karl Barbir, *Ottoman Rule in Damascus 1708–1758*, Princeton University Press, Princeton, 1980.

Victor Barnouw, *An Introduction to Anthropology*, Dorsey Press, Homewood, Illinois, 1971.

M. Baton (ed.), *Complex Societies: The Social Anthropology of Complex Societies*, Tavistock Press, London, 1966.

Muhammad Jamil Bayhum, *Al-naz'at al-siyassiyyah fi lubnan 'an al-intidab aa al-ihtilal* (Political Attitudes in Lebanon in the Mandate Period), Beirut, 1977.

Louis de Beaudicour, *La France au Liban*, Paris, 1879.

R. B. Bells, *Christians in the Arab East*, Athens, 1973.

Robert Brenton Betts, *Christians in the Arab East: A Political Study*, Lycabettus Press, Athens, 1975.

Robert Brenton Betts, *The Druze*, Yale University Press, 1988.

Salwa Mardam Bey, *Awraq jamil mardam bey: istiklal suria, 1939–1945*, Shirkat al-Matboua't Lil Tawzi' Wal Nashr, Beirut, 1994.

Ahmad Beydoun, *Identité Confessionelle et Temps Social chez les Historiens Libanais Contemporains*, Publications de l'Université Libanaise, Beirut, 1977.

Leonard Binder (ed.), *Politics in Lebanon*, John Wiley & Co, New York, 1966.

Peter Blau, *Approaches to the Study of Social Structure*, Free Press, New York, 1975.

Barry Blechman and Stephen Kaplan (eds), *Force Without War*, the Brooking Institution, Washington, DC, 1978.

Mary Borden, *A Journey Down a Blind Alley*, Harper & Bros, New York, 1946.

Jawad Boulos, *Tarikh Lubnan* (History of Lebanon), Dar an-Nahar Lil Nashr, Beirut, 1972.

Fouad Bustani, *Introduction à l'histoire politique du Liban (du 17e Siècle à 1943)*, FMA, Beirut, 1993.

Marwan Buheiry, *The Formation and Perception of the Modern Arab World*, Darwin Press, Princeton, 1988.

Odd Bull, *War and Peace in the Middle East: The Experience and Views of a UN Observer*, Westview Press, Bristol, 1973–1976.

E. H. Carr, *What is History?*, Penguin Books, Handsworth, 1964.

Georges Catroux, *Dans la Bataille de Méditerranée (1940–44)*, René Julliard, Paris, 1949.

Georges Catroux, *Deux missions en Moyen-Orient 1919–1922,* Librairie Plan, Paris, 1958.

Camille Chamoun, *Crise au Moyen-Orient*, Gallimand, Paris, 1963.

Camille Chamoun, *Mudhakkarati* (Memoirs), Beirut, 1969.

Maurice Shihab, *Le rôle du Liban dans l'Histoire de la Soie*, University of Lebanon Press, Beirut, 1968.

Dominique Chevallier (ed.), *La Société du Mont-Liban à l'Epoque de la Révolution Industrielle en Europe*, Librairie Orientaliste Paul Geuthner, Paris, 1971.

Michel Chiha, *Le Liban d'Aujourd'hui*, Edition du Trident, Beirut, 1942, second edition, 1961.

Michel Chiha, *Politique Intérieure Beyrouth*, Editions du Trident, Paris, 1964.

Helena Cobban, *The Making of Modern Lebanon*, 1985

Charles Codey, *Social Organization*, Harper & Row, New York, 1962.

J. Coleman and R. Nisbet (eds), *Community, Disorganisation and Conflict*, Harcourt, New York, 1971.

Laurence Conrand (ed.), *the Formation and Perception of the Modern Arab World*, Darwin Press, Inc, Princeton, 1989.

Miles Copeland, *The Games of Nations*, Weidenfeld & Nicolson, London, 1969.

Charles Corm, *La montagne inspirée*, Editions de la Revue Phénicienne, Beirut, 1964.

Georges Corm, *Géopolitique du conflit libanais*, Edition La Decouverte, Paris, 1986.

Massoud Daher, *The Origins of the Confessionalist Question in Lebanon 1797–1861*, Mahad al-Inma al-Arabi, Beirut, 1984.

Norman Daniel, *The Arabs and Medieval Europe*, Longman, London, 1979.

Ernst Dawn, *From Ottomanism to Arabism: Essays on the Origins of Arab Nationalism*, University of Illinois Press, Chicago, 1973.

Roderick H Davison, *Reform in the Ottoman Empire, 1856–1876*, Princeton University Press, Princeton, 1963.

N. J. Demereth III and R Peterson, *System, Change and Conflict*, The Tree Press, New York, 1970.

William Doyle, *The Old European Order, 1600–1800*, Oxford University Press, Oxford, 1992.

Claude Dubar and Selim Nasr, *Les Classes Sociales au Liban*, Presse de la Fondation Nationale des Sciences Politiques, Paris, 1976.

Raymond Eddé (ed.), *Raymond Eddé et Raymond Helmick, Corréspondance: La question libanaise selon Raymond Eddé expliqée aux Americains par Raymond G Helmick*, Libanica II, Cariscript, Paris, 1992.

Dwight D. Eisenhower, *Waging Peace: 1956–61*, Doubleday, New York, 1965.

Georges Enczowski (ed.), *Political Elites in the Middle East*, American Enterprise Institute for Public Policy Research, Washington, DC, 1975.

John Entelis, *Pluralism and Party Transformation in Lebanon: al-Kata'ib, 1936–1970*, Brill, Leiden, 1974.

J. Esman and I. Rabinovitch (eds), *Ethnicity, Pluralism and the State in the Middle East*, Cornell University Press, Ithaca, 1988.

Rahiba Abou Fadel and Antun Saadeh, *Al-naqed wal adib al-mahjeri* (The Critics and the Writers of Emigré Literature), Maktab al-Dirasat al-Qimat, al-Matn, Lebanon, 1992.

Nazir Fansa, *Ayam husni al-Zaim* (The Days of Husni Al-zaim), Dar al-Afak, Beirut, 1982.

Hani Fares, *Al-niz'aat al-ta'ifiyyah fi tharikh lubnan al-hadith* (On Sectarian Struggles in Modern Lebanese History), Al-ahliyyah Lil Nashr Wa al-Tawzi, Beirut, 1980.

Walid Fares, *Al-Ta'adudiyyahh fi Lubnan*, (On Pluralism in Lebanese and World History), Beirut.

N. A. Faris and M. T. Hussein, *The Crescent in Crisis*, University of Kansas Press, Lawrence, 1955.

Antoine Fattal, *Le statut légal des non-musulmans en pays d'islam*, Imprimerie Catholique, Beirut, 1958.

Leila Fawaz, *An Occasion for War*, I B Tauris, London, 1994.

Leila Fawaz, *State and Society in Lebanon*, Tufts University & the Centre for Lebanese Studies, Oxford, 1991.

David Fromkin, *A Peace to End All Peace*, Penguin Books, London, 1989.

Charles De Gaulle, *War Memoirs: The Call to Honour, 1940–45 Documents*, London, 1955.

A. B. Gauson, *The Anglo-French Clash in Lebanon and Syria, 1940–45*, Macmillan, London, 1987.

E. Gellner, *Nations and Nationalism*, Basil Blackwell, Oxford, 1983.

E. Gellner and J Waterbury (eds), *Patrons and Clients*, London, 1977.

Amine Gemayel, *Peace and Unity*, Colin Smythe, Gerrards Cross, 1984.

Amine Gemayel, *Rebuilding Lebanon*, University Press of America, Boston, 1992.

Maurice Gemayel, *Le pari Libanais*, An Nahar, Beirut, 1970.

Nasser Gemayel, *Les échanges culturels entre les maronites et L'Europe du collège maronite de Rome (1584) au collège d'Ayn Warqa (1789)*, Beirut, 1984.

John Bagot Glubb, *Britain and the Arabs*, 1959

David Gordon, *Lebanon: The Fragmented Nation*, Croom Helm, Beckenham, 1980.

David Gordon, *The Republic of Lebanon: Nation in Jeopardy*, Croom Helm, Beckenham, 1983.

Wade R. Goria, *Sovereignty and Leadership in Lebanon, 1943–1976*, Ithaca Press, London, 1985.

Philippe Gouraud, *Le général Henri Gouraud au Liban en Syrie, 1919–1923*, L'Harmattan, Paris, 1993.

J. A. S. Greenville, *A World History of the Twentieth Century: Western Dominance 1900-45*, vol. I, Fontana Press, London, 1987.

John Gulick, *Social Structure and Cultural Change in a Lebanese Village*, Wenner-Gren Foundation for Anthropological Research, New York, 1955.

Robert Haddad, *Syrian Christians in Muslim Society: An Interpretation*, Greenwood Press, Westport, 1970.

E. Haley and S. Lewis (eds), *Lebanon in Crisis: Participants and Issues*, Syracuse University Press, Syracuse, 1973.

Theodor Hanf, *Coexistence in Wartime Lebanon*, Centre for Lebanese Studies and I B Tauris, London, 1993.

Ilya Harik, *Lebanon: Anatomy of Conflict*, American Universities Field Staff Reports 49.

Ilya Harik, *Politics and Change in a Traditional Society: Lebanon 1711–1845*, Princeton University Press, Princeton, 1968.

Jean Hayek, *Al-tarikh al-'Ilmi, al-Jiz' al-Awwal* (Scientific History), Maktabit Habib, Beirut, 1994.

Muhammad Hasanein Haykal, *Sanawat al-galayan* (The Years of Turmoil), Al-Ahram, Cairo, 1988.

M. Herper and R. Israeli (eds), *Islam and Politics in the Modern Middle East.*

Phillippe Hitti, *Lebanon in History: From the Earliest Times to the Present*, Macmillan, London, 1962.

Eric Hobsbawm, *Nations and Nationalism Since 1870*, Cambridge University Press, Cambridge, 1990.

Antoine Hokayem and Marie Claude Bitar, *L'empire ottomane: Les arabes et les grands puissances, 1914–1920*, Les Editions Universitaires du Liban, Beirut, 1981.

Albert Hourani, *Arabic Thought in the Liberal Age, 1798–1939*, Cambridge University Press, Cambridge, (Revised Edition), 1983.

Albert Hourani, *A History of the Arab Peoples*, Faber & Faber, London, 1991.

Albert Hourani, *Maronites in the Arab World*, Royal Institute for International Affairs, London, 1947.

Albert Hourani, *Syria and Lebanon: A Political Essay*, Oxford University Press, London, 1946.

Albert Hourani, Philip S Khoury and Mary Wilson (eds), *The Modern Middle East*, I B Tauris, London, 1993.

Albert Hourani and Nadim Shehadi (eds), *The Lebanese in the World: A Century of Emigration*, I B Tauris, London, 1992.

Michael Hudson, *Arab Politics*, Yale University Press, 1979.

Michael Hudson, *The Precarious Republic: Political Modernization in Lebanon*, Random House, New York, 1968.

Adel Ismail, *Documents diplomatiques et consulaires relatifs à l'histoire du Liban et des pays du Proche-Orient du XVIIe siècle à nos jours*, Editions des Œuvres Politiques et Historiques, Paris, 1975.

Adel Ismail, *Histoire du Liban du 17eme Siècle à nos jours: le Liban au temps de fakhr al-din II (1590–1633)*, vol. I, Maisonneuve, Paris, 1959.

Adel Ismail, *Lebanon: History of a People*, Dar al-Makchuf, Beirut, 1972.

Joseph Abou Jaoude, *Les partis politiques au Liban*, Publications de L'université St Esprit, Kaslik, 1985.

Michael Johnson, *Class and Client in Beirut: The Sunni Muslim Community and the Lebanese State, 1940–1985*, Ithaca Press, London, 1986.

Kamal Jumblat, *I Speak for Lebanon*, Zad Press, London, 1982.

Kamal Jumblat, *Haqiqat al-thawra al-lubnaniyyah* (The Truth About the Lebanese Revolution), Dar An-Nashr al-Arabiyyah, Beirut, 1959.

Elie Kedourie, *Nationalism*, Praeger, London, 1960.

Maurice Keen, *Medieval Europe*, Penguin Books, London, 1968.

Malcolm Kerr, *Lebanon in the Last Years of Feudalism 1840–1868: A Contemporary Account by Antun Dahir al-Aqiqi and Other Documents*, American University of Beirut, Beirut, 1959.

Antoine Khair, *La moutassarrifat du Mont-Liban*, Publications de l'université Libanaise, Beirut, 1973.

Samir Khalaf, *Lebanon's Predicament*, Columbia University Press, New York, 1987.

Samir Khalaf, *Persistence and Change in Nineteenth-Century Lebanon*, American University of Beirut, Beirut, 1979.

Rachid Khalidi, Lisa Anderson, Muhammad Muslih, Reeva Simon (eds), *The Origins of Arab Nationalism*, Columbia Press, New York, 1991.

Walid Khalidi, *Conflict and Violence in Lebanon: Confrontation in the Middle East*, Harvard Center for International Affairs, Cambridge Mass., 1979.

Chehdan Khalife, *Les relations entre la France et le Liban (1958–1978)*, Presse Universitaire de France, Paris, 1983.

Hilal Khashan, *Inside the Lebanese Confessional Mind*, Universities of America Press, Boston, 1992.

Lahk Khatir, *Ahd al-mutassarifiin fi lubnan, 1861–1918* (The Mutassarifiyyah Era in Lebanon), Publications de l'université Libanaise, Beirut, 1967.

Boutros Khawand, *Al-quwat al-nizamiat al-kata'ibiat* (Publication of the Kata'ib Party), Habib Eid Publishing, Beirut, 1986.

Enver Khoury, *The Crisis in the Lebanese System: Confessionalism and Chaos*, American Enterprise Institute for Public Policy Research, Washington, DC, 1976.

Gerard Khoury, *La France et l'Orient Arabe*, Armand Colin, Paris, 1993.

Philip S. Khoury, *Syria Under the French Mandate: The Politics of Arab Nationalism, 1920–1945*, Princeton University Press, Princeton, 1987.

Philip S. Khoury, *Urban Notables and Arab Nationalism: the Politics of Damascus 1860–1920*, Cambridge University Press, Cambridge, 1983.

Stephen Koss, *The Rise and Fall of the Political Press in Britain, vols 1–2*, Hamilton, London, 1984.

Boulos Labaki, *Introduction à l'histoire économique du Liban, soie et commerce extérieure en fin de periode Ottomane*, Publication de l'université Libanaise, Beirut, 1984.

Georges Labaki (ed.), *Chekri Ganem: écrits politiques*, Dar An-Nahar, Beirut, 1994.

Kenneth P Laughton, *Political Socialisation*, Oxford University Press, London, 1969.

Henri Laurens, *Le royaume impossible*, Armand Colin, Paris, 1990.

Bernard Lewis, *The Middle East and the West*, Tinling & Co Ltd, London, 1964.

Bernard Lewis, *The Arabs in History*, Harper & Row, New York, 1960.

Bernard Lewis and Peter Holt (eds), *Historians of the Middle East*, Oxford University Press, London, 1962.

Margot Light and A. J. R. Groom (eds), *International Relations: A Handbook of Current Theory*, Pinter, London, 1985.

Stephen Longrigg, *Syria and Lebanon Under French Mandate*, Oxford University Press, London, 1958.

David Mcdowall, *Lebanon: A Conflict of Minorities*, Report No. 61, Minority Rights Group, London, 1983.

J. E. Mcgratto, *Social and Psychological Factors in Stress*, Holt, Rinehart & Winston, New York, 1970.

J. A. R. Marriot, *The Eastern Question*, Oxford University Press, London, 1951.

Leila Meo, *Lebanon, Improbable Nation: A Study in Political Development*, Greenwood Press, Westport (reprint) 1976.

R. Merton and R. Nisbet (eds), *Contemporary Social Problems*, Harcourt, New York, 1971.

Antoine Nasri Messara, *Théorie generale du systeme politique libanaise*, Cariscript, Paris, 1994.

Colin Mooers, *The Making of Bourgeois Europe*, Verso, London, 1991.

Elizabeth Monroe, *Britain's Moment in the Middle East, 1914–71*, Chatto & Windus, London, 1981.

Elizabeth Monroe, *The Mediterranean in Politics*, Chatto & Windus, London, 1993.

Matti Moosa, *The Maronites in History*, Syracuse University Press, Syracuse.

Anis Moussallem, *La presse libanaise*, Librarie Generale de Droit et de Jurisprudence, Paris, 1977.

Said Murad, *Al-haraka al-wahdqwya fi lubnan bayn al-harbayn al-alamiyatayn 1914–1964* (The Unionist Movement in Lebanon Between 1914 and 1964), Maahad al-Inma al-Arabi, Beirut, 1968.

G. P. Murdock, *Social Structure*, Macmillan, London, 1949.

Robert Murphy, *Diplomat Among Warriors*, Collins, London, 1964.

Sami Makarem Nasib, *the Druze Faith*, Caravan Books, New York, 1974.

David Nicholas, *The Evolution of the Medieval World: Society, Government and Thought in Europe, 1312–1500*, Longman, London, 1992.

C. A. O. Van Niewenhuijze (ed.), *Commoners, Climbers and Notables*, Brill, Leiden, 1977.

R. Owen (ed.) *Essays on the Crisis in Lebanon*, Ithaca Press, London, 1976.

Bernard Porter, *The Lion's Share: A Short History of British Imperialism, 1850–1983*, Longman, London, 1984.

J. R. S. Philips, *The Medieval Expansion of Europe*, Oxford University Press, Oxford, 1988.

Gabriel Puaux, *Deux Années au Levant*, Hachette, Paris, 1952.

F. Qubain, *Crisis in Lebanon*, The Middle East Institute, Washington, DC, 1961.

Edmond Rabbath, *La formation historique du Liban politique et constitutionelle. Essai de synthése*, Publications de l'Université Libanaise, Beirut, 1973.

Edmond Rabbath, *Unité Syrienne et Devenir Arabe*, Librairie Marcel, Paris, 1937.

Jonathan Riley-Smith, *The Crusades*, Athlone Press, London, 1987.

Karam Rizk, *Le Mont Liban au XIXe siècle de l'amirat au Mutasarrifiyyah*, Publications de L'Université St Esprit, Kaslik, 1994.

Pierre Rondot, *Les Chrétiens d'Orient*, Peyronnet, Paris, n.d.

Pierre Rondot, *Les Institutions Politiques du Liban*, Institut d'Etudes de L'Orient Contemporain, Paris, 1947.

Riyadh Najib al-Rayyis, *al-Masihiyun wa al-Urubah*, Riyadh al-Rayess 1988.

Inmea Sader (ed.), *Syro-Lebanese Relations 1934–1985*, vols 1–2, Cedre, Bayt al-Moustahkbal, Beirut, 1986.

Sofia Saadeh, *T he Social Structure of Lebanon: Democracy or Servitude?*, An-Nahar, Beirut, 1993.

Edward Said, *Culture and Imperialism*, Chatto & Windus, London, 1993.

Saeb Salam, *Massirat al-Salam* (The March of Peace), Markaz Saeb Salam, Beirut, n.d.

K. S. Salibi, *A House of Many Mansions: The History of Lebanon Reconsidered*, I B Tauris, London, 1988.

K. S. Salibi, *Maronite Historians of Mediaeval Lebanon*, American University of Beirut, Beirut, 1959.

K. S. Salibi, *The Modern History of Lebanon*, Caravan Books, New York, 1965.

K. S. Salibi, *Crossroads to Civil War: Lebanon 1958–1976*, Caravan Books, New York, 1976.

William Sands (ed.) *Middle East Report 1959: Nationalism, Neutralism, Communism, the Struggle for Power* (A Series of Addresses Presented At the 13th Annual Conference on Middle Eastern Affairs, Sponsored by the Middle East Institute, March 20–21, 1959), Middle East Institute, Washington, DC, 1959.

Yussif Sayeg, *Entrepreneurs of Lebanon: The Role of the Business Leader in a Developing Economy*, Harvard University Press, Cambridge Mass., 1962.

Yves Schmeil, *Sociologie du Système Politique Libanais*, Université d Grenoble II, Grenoble, 1976.

S. Seikaly, R. Baalbaki, P. Dodd (eds), *Quest for Understanding: Arabic and Islamic Studies in Memory of Malcolm H Kerr*, American University of Beirut, Beirut, 1991.

Michel Seurat, *L'Etat de Barbarie*, Editions du Seuil, Paris, 1977.

Hisham Sharabi, *Governments and Politics of the Middle East in the Twentieth Century*, Princeton University Press, Princeton, 1962.

Nadim Shehadi and Dana Haffar Mills (eds), *Lebanon: A History of Conflict and Consensus*, I B Tauris, London, 1988.

William I Shorrock, *French Imperialism in the Middle East: The Failure of Policy in Syria and Lebanon. 1900–1914*, University of Wisconsin Press, 1976.

F Sluglett and P Sluglett, *Aspects of the Changing Nature of Lebanese Confessional Politics*, Peuples Meditérraneains, 1982.

Anthony Smith, *The Ethnic Revival in the Modern World*, Cambridge University Press, Cambridge, 1981.

John Spagnolo, *France and Ottoman Lebanon: 1861–1914*, Ithaca Press, London, 1977.

Michael Suleiman, *Political Parties in Lebanon: the Challenge of a Fragmented Political Culture*, Cornell University Press, Ithaca, 1967.

Alan R. Taylor, *The Islamic Question in Middle East Politics*, 1988.

Kathryn Tidrick, *Empire and the English Character*, I B Tauris, London, 1990.

F Tonnies, *Community and Association (Gemeinschaft Und Gesellschaft)*, Routledge & Kegan Paul, London, 1955.

John Tosh, *The Pursuit of History: Aims, Methods and New Directions in the Study of Modern History, second edition*, Longman, London, 1991.

Toufic Touma, *Paysans et Institutions Féodales chez les Druzes et les Maronites du Liban du 18ème Siècle à 1914*, Publications de l'Université Libanaise, Beirut, 1971.

Judith Tucker, *Women in 19th Century Egypt,* Cambridge University Press, Cambridge, 1985.

B. Turner, *Weber and Islam, A Critical Study*, Routledge, London, 1974.

Jan Vansina, *Oral Tradition As History*, James Currey, London, 1985.

P. J. Vatikiotis, *Conflict in the Middle East*, George Allen & Unwin, London, 1971.

David Vincent, *Literacy and Popular Culture*, Cambridge University Press, Cambridge, 1989.

Bernard Voyenne, *La presse dans la société contemporaine*, Armand Colin, Paris.

Max Weber, *The Sociology of Religion*, Methuen, London, 1965.

Max Weber, *The Theory of Social and Economic Organization*, The Free Press, New York, 1969.

Malcolm Yapp, *The Making of the Modern Middle East, 1792–1923*, Longman, London, 1987.

Malcolm Yapp, *The Near East Since the First World War*, Longman, London, 1991.

Meir Zamir, *The Formation of Modern Lebanon*, Croom Helm, Beckenham, 1985.

Ali Zayn, *Lil Bahth an Tarikhina fi Lubnan* (Researches into Lebanese History), Beirut, 1973.

Zeine N. Zeine, *The Emergence of Arab Nationalism*, Caravan Books, New York, 1973.

Zeine N. Zeine, *The Struggle for Arab Independence*, Khayats, Beirut, 1960.

Articles

Abdul Rahim Abu Hussein, 'The Feudal System of Lebanon'.

Abdul Rahim Abu Hussein, 'The Korkmaz Question: A Maronite Historian's Plea for Ma'nid Legitimacy', *al-Abhath*, XXXIV, 1986.

Abdul Rahim Abu Hussein, 'The Ottoman Invasion of the Shuf in 1585: A Reconsideration', *al-Abhath*, XXXIII, 1985.

Abdul Rahim Abu Hussein, 'Problems in Ottoman Administration During the 16th and 17th Centuries: The Case of the Sanjak of Sidon-Beirut', *International Journal of Middle East Studies*, 24, 1992.

A. Abu Khalil, 'Druze, Sunni and Shi'ite Political Leadership in Present Day Lebanon', *Arab Studies Quarterly*, 7.4, 1985.

Muhammad Shafi Agwani, 'The Lebanese Crisis of 1958 in Retrospect', *International Studies*, 4 (4) April 1963.

J. P. Alem, 'Troubles insurrectionnels au Liban', *Orient* 2 (6), 1958.

H. Barakat, 'Social and Political Integration in Lebanon: A Case of Social Mosaic', *Middle East Journal*, 27 (3), Summer 1973.

V. Birieuzov, 'L'insurrection populaire au Liban', *Temps Nouveaux*,16 (21), May.

Jawad Boulos, 'L'influence des données géographiques et historiques sur la personalité Liban', *Action Proche Orient* (Beirut), June 1963.

G. Britt, 'Lebanon's Popular Revolution', *Middle East Journal*, 7 (1), Winter 1953.

J. C. Cairns, 'De Gaulle Confronts the British: The Legacy of the 1940s', *International Journal*, XXIII, 2, 1968.

Dominique Chevallier, 'Politique et réligion dans le Proche-Orient: une iconographie des maronites du Liban', *Revue d'Histoire Moderne et Contemporaine*, X, 1963.

R. E. Crow, '*Al-dustur, al-mithak, al-musharak*', (La Constitution, Le Pacte, La Participation), supplément annuel du quotidien *An-Nahar*, 1974–1975.

Ralph Crow, 'Religious Sectarian in the Lebanese Political System', *Journal of Politics*, August, 1963.

R. H. Dekmejian, 'Consociational Democracy in Crisis: the Case of Lebanon', *Comparative Politics*, 10.2, 1978.

R. J. Dubuy, 'Aggression indirecte et intervention solicitée dans l'affaire Libanaise', *Annuaire Français de Droit International*, 5, 1959.

A. Faris, 'The Summer of 1958', *Middle East Forum*, 38 (1), 1962.

E. Frankel, 'The Maronite Patriarch: A Historical View of a Religious Zaim in the 1958 Lebanese Crisis', *The Muslim World*, 66 (3 & 4), June 1976, October 1976.

Eric Hobsbawm, 'From Social History to the History of Society', *Daedalus*, Winter, 1971.

A. Hottinger, 'Zu'ama and Parties in the Lebanese Crisis of 1958', *Middle East Journal*, 15 (2), Spring 1961.

Michael C Hudson, 'A Case of Political Underdevelopment', *Journal of Politics*, 29 (4), November 1967.

J. C. Hurewitz, 'Lebanese Democracy in its International Setting', *Middle East Journal* 17 (3), Autumn, 1963.

P. Keating, 'De Gaulle and Britain, 1940–46', *International Relations*, April, 1965.

Malcolm Kerr, 'Hafez Assad and the Changing Patterns of Syrian Politics', *International Journal*, XXVII, 4, Autumn, 1973.

Malcolm Kerr, 'Lebanese Views on the 1958 Crisis', *Middle East Journal*, Spring, 1961.

Walter Laqueur, 'The Appeal of Communism in the Middle East', *Middle East Journal*, 9 (1), Winter 1955.

George Lenczowski, 'Evolution of Soviet Policy Towards the Middle East', *Journal of Politics*, 20 (1), February, 1958.

A. Lijphart, 'Typologies of Democratic Systems', *Comparative Political Studies*, II 1969.

Stephen Longrigg, 'New Groupings Among the Arab States', *International Affairs*, 34 (3), July 1958.

Charles Malik, 'Call to Action in the Near East', *Foreign Affairs*, 34 (4), July 1956.

Charles Malik, 'Near East: the Search for Truth', *Foreign Affairs*, 30 (9), January 1952.

Charles Malik, 'Outlook in the Near East', *Vital Speeches*, 19, August 1 1953.

Elizabeth Monroe, 'Nasserism', *Middle East Forum* (Numéro Spécial), 34 (4), April 1959.

Elizabeth Monroe, 'Nationalism in the Middle East', *Current History* (Numéro Spécial), 36 (210), February 1959.

Pierre Rondot, 'La crise du Liban', *Afrique et Asie*, 13, 3eme Trim. 1958.

K. S. Salibi, 'The Lebanese Identity', *Journal of Contemporary History*, 6 (1), 1971.

K. S. Salibi, 'Thawrat 1958'(La révolution de 1958), supplement annuelle du quotidien *An-Nahar*, 1972–1973.

G. S. Stevens, 'Arab Neutralism and Bandung', *Middle East Journal*, 11 (2), Spring 1957.

André-Pierre Vienot, 'The Levant Dispute: The French Case', *London Quarterly of World Affairs*, XI, October 1945.

D. N. Wilber, 'Prospects for Federation in the Northern Tier', *Middle East Journal*, 12, (4), Autumn, 1958.

E. Wright, 'Defense and the Baghdad Pact', *Political Quarterly*, 28 (2), April-June 1957.

Q. Wright, 'United States Intervention in the Lebanon', *American Journal of International Law*, 53 (1), January, 1959.

Meir Zamir, 'Emile Eddé and the Territorial Integrity of Lebanon', *Middle Eastern Studies*, May, 1978.

Unpublished Material

Theses

Huda M. Abdel Baki, 'The Study of the Foreign Policy of Lebanon Towards the United Arab Republic and Iraq From January 1958 to September 1961', unpublished MA dissertation, American University of Beirut, 1967.

Raghid al-Solh, 'Lebanon and Arab Nationalism, 1936–1945', unpublished PhD thesis, St Anthony's College, Oxford University, 1986.

Najla Attiyah, 'Attitude of the Lebanese Sunni Towards the State of Lebanon', unpublished PhD thesis, University of London, 1973.

Nasser Kalawoun, 'The Role of the Sunni Leadership and Community Towards the State of Lebanon in the 1950s', unpublished MA dissertation, University of London.

B. Oudet, 'Le rôle du comité central syrien dans la politique syrienne de la France, 16 June 1917–24 July 1920', unpublished MA dissertation, Sorbonne, Paris, 1986.

Raymond Salame, 'The Eisenhower Doctrine: A Study in Alliance Politics', unpublished PhD thesis, Georgetown University.

Linda Schatkowski, 'The Islamic *Maqassed* of Beirut: A Case Study of Modernization in Lebanon', unpublished MA dissertation, American University of Beirut, 1969.

Papers

Abbas Abou-Salih, 'Lebanon and the Middle East Defence Strategy of the West (1946–1956)', Unpublished Conference Paper, Austin, Texas, 13 September 1992.

Farid al-Khazin, 'The Communal Pact of National Identities', papers on Lebanon, Centre for Lebanese Studies, Oxford, October 1991.

Caroline Attie, 'President Chamoun and the Crisis of 1958: Referring to Foreign Service Despatch No. 487, American Embassy, Beirut to Department of State, 18 April 1957', unpublished conference Paper, Austin, Texas, 13 September 1992.

Sam Falle, 'The Middle East in the 1950s', unpublished conference paper, Austin, Texas, 13 September 1992.

Carolyn L Gates, 'Choice, Content and Performance of a "Service-orientated Open Economy" Strategy: The Case of Lebanon 1948–1958', unpublished conference paper, Austin, Texas, 13 September 1992.

Catherine Hall, 'Rethinking Imperial Histories', unpublished conference plenary paper, Women's History Network Conference, 16 September 1995.

K. S. Salibi, 'Recollections of the 1940s and 1950s', unpublished conference paper, Austin, Texas, 13 September 1992.

Index

Note: *Page numbers for illustrations are indicated by italics.*